Iranian
HOSTAGE

A Personal
Diary

OF 444 DAYS IN CAPTIVITY...

by Rocky Sickmann

Iranian

HOSTAGE

A Personal
Diary

OF 444 DAYS IN CAPTIVITY...

by Rocky Sickmann

With a Prologue by the Editor,
Erin Leslie Antrim

Introduction by Mike Printz

CRAWFORD PRESS

A division of The American Companies, Inc.
Topeka, Kansas 1982

Library of Congress Catalog Card Number: 82-71537
I.S.B.N. 0-88103-000-7

Published by Crawford Press
A division of The American Companies, Inc.

Printed in the United States of America
First Edition

Dedication

To my family
     Mr. & Mrs. Virgil Sickmann,
     Gene, Judy, Debbie, and Kurt

And to my wife
     Jill Renee

"The love and loyalty you instill
Fills my heart my darling Jill
The memories we shared together
Mine to cherish forever and ever
If I should survive this strife
Would you consent to be my wife..."

from a poem written in captivity

Introduction

by Mike Printz, Librarian
Topeka West High School

Not one of us will ever forget the emotions that we felt on the cold, clear January Sunday in 1981 as we watched fifty-two hostages return from Iran. Not one of us will forget the reunions that we witnessed on the air field near West Point. Not one of us will forget the poignant Associated Press photograph of Jill Ditch's face as she saw her fiance, *Marine Sergeant Rocky Sickmann* free for the first time in 444 days. None of us will ever forget the feelings as we somehow wished we could shake one of the hostage's hands and express our gratitude, our pride and our love.

The next day, Monday, two juniors at Topeka West High School, Ivan Marchello and Todd Standeford, met me to discuss an audio-visual presentation concerning the Iranian situation. They planned to chronicle a brief history of Iran, the Shah, the events that led to the take-over of the American embassy and finally to delve into the hostage situation and to speculate about its impact. Since they were working with 35mm slides and planned an accompanying tape, we felt it would be most effective if they could have a taped interview with one of the former hostages.

A check of newspaper articles and a map showed that *Rocky Sickmann* was from Krakow, Missouri. The students immediately tried to locate *Rocky* at his parents' home. The telephone had been disconnected. Our letter was one of thousands delivered to the Sickmann home. With the great optimism of youth, Ivan and Todd persisted. One newspaper article stated that *Rocky* had played football for the Washington, Missouri, high school football team. A call to the football coach gave the students the name of Bill Kimme, a lawyer from Washington. Mr. Kimme was handling all of *Rocky's* calls and appointments. Through his cooperation, Ivan and Todd were granted an interview in Washington, Missouri, in early May. With assistance from Connie Skinner, Principal, and Charles Myers, head of the school's Social Studies department, the boys raised the necessary funds to finance the trip to Missouri. With faculty member Bill Pryor, the students went to Washington to conduct two days of interviews with *Rocky and his fiancee, Jill Ditch*. When they returned to school several days later, I sensed that somehow their lives had been changed from the interview and that a committment to *Rocky* and his story was paramount.

After listening to the tapes, I agreed whole heartedly that *Rocky's* story needed to be told to as many people as could be reached. From the speaker of the tape recorder, I heard a story of courage, dignity, desperation, and faith. But most of all I heard a story of survival of the human spirit through all sorts of adversities. In this heroless age, I knew that young adults need to hear what Rocky had to say. I knew that a person with his kind of charisma could get through with a message of the survival of that spirit. Now, along with Ivan and Todd, I was committed.

The school term ended, and our project was not quite finished. I taught a course at Emporia State University's Graduate School of Library Science during the summer, and I wanted my students there to have some type of audio-visual production experience. These graduate students put the finishing touches to the *Rocky* story. They invited him to the "premiere" performance, and he accepted. Governor John Carlin's plane brought our hero to Emporia. Ivan and Todd joined Rocky in a 1920's convertible and led a parade down main street. The day was one we will never forget. *Rocky* answered questions, and his immediate genuineness with all age groups made me realize that he must be invited to Topeka West in the fall to speak to our students.

As the fall semester of school began, a third student, Brian Walton, joined our efforts in bringing *Rocky* to Topeka West High School. The day was set in early November. Students in our school saw the slide-tape production before *Rocky's* visit so that they could prepare questions. Ivan, Brian, and Todd planned the day with meticulous care. A group of approximately fifty students welcomed him at the airport and formed a caravan to the Governor's office where Kansas Governor John Carlin proclaimed the day *"Rocky Sickmann Day."* *Rocky* spoke to students twice during the afternoon. During the first talk there were no empty seats or floor spaces. After the first question and answer session, students were standing on their chairs and cheering. The second question and answer session was to follow immediately, but none of the first group left. Students were literally hanging out the door and windows of our library to get the chance to hear him. At the end of the second session, I could not believe the reaction ... cheers, chanting ... *"Rocky .. Rocky".* The day was truly a peak experience for all those involved. His message had come through. One can survive any experience if the spirit is strong. When *Rocky* was presented to the crowd at the half time of the football game that evening, hundreds of yellow balloons and overwhelming cheering greeted him.

After the game *Rocky* started talking about the diary he had kept when in Iran. He told how the Iranian students had come to him on the night before his release and said that they knew he had a diary and that he should put it with his luggage and they would let him take it home. He remembers thinking it strange that they made such a point of taking the diary home. Past experiences told him not to trust their promise, so he taped the diary to his leg. He never saw his luggage.

I had the privilege of reading the entire diary early in 1982. The same messages of faith, strength and survival are there on a day-by-day basis. It is an important document for three reasons. First, it is the only known diary to be brought out of the hostage experience. It was not written in retrospect; it documents the entire ordeal on a daily basis. Second, it records a period of history that is important for every library to have on its shelves. Third, it is an insight into an experience that we can share vicariously. Through *Rocky's* diary we cannot (and should not) forget that experience. Some readers may be disappointed that the diary is not always thrilling or exciting, and is perhaps a little boring. Being a hostage for 444 days was not thrilling; it was not exciting; and it was boring. We need to experience that also. I dare say anyone who reads this diary will come away from the encounter with a deep faith and respect for the human spirit to survive.

Prologue

Rocky Sickmann was born July 26, 1957, in Overland, Missouri, a suburb of St. Louis. When he was four years old, he moved with his family to Krakow, a small Missouri hamlet 50 miles southwest of St. Louis. The countryside around Krakow is serenely beautiful—wooded, steeply rolling hills, narrow winding roads, and a kind of brooding, misty clarity that reminds one constantly of the dependence people have upon the land, and the fragile, sometimes cruel nature of their co-existence with it.

Because Krakow has no high school, when Rocky finished his grade school years of fishing, hunting and playing baseball, he became a student at Washington High School in the nearby town of Washington, which serves as a metropolis for many farming communities in the area. It was there that Rocky became distinguished as an "all around good guy," captain of his football team, well-known and liked by many. As Rocky's high school years neared an end, his football coach sought a football scholarship for Rocky at a small, four-year college. Rocky says he will never forget the look on his coach's face when he told him he'd enlisted in the Marines instead.

It was also at Washington High that Rocky first met the girl he would marry. Jill Ditch lived in the neighboring rural community of Augusta. She was four years younger than Rocky, though, and during his high school years Rocky had more interest in his friendship with her older brother than he had in Jill herself. It wasn't until a visit home on military leave that he and Jill met again, dated and fell in love.

Rocky entered the U.S. Marine Corps on August 26, 1976. He was assigned to the infantry, and for the next two and a half years was deployed with the navy on Pacific and Mediterranean tours. He reenlisted in May, 1979, concurrently signing up for training as a Marine Security Guard.

His first assignment as a Security Guard was to the American Embassy in Tehran, Iran. The U.S. State Department was gradually, if belatedly, becoming aware of the deterioration of diplomatic relations with that country, and of the severity of the anti-American feeling that was developing there. It saw a clear need to strengthen security personnel at the embassy.

So Rocky arrived in Tehran October 7, 1979. By this time, at the urging of his top aides, Jimmy Carter was just twelve days away from a decision to admit the deposed Shah of Iran, Mohammed Reza Pahlavi, to the U.S. for medical treatment. The decision had already been months in the making. The Shah had fled Iran January 16, 1979, already an ill man, taking with him a sack of his nation's soil. When he arrived in the U.S. on October 22 for cancer treatment, Rocky had been on duty for just fifteen days. In thirteen more days, on November 4, 1979, Rocky Sickmann and sixty-five other Americans would be taken hostage as a part of a planned protest demonstration by a group of Tehran Polytechnical College students, members of the Society of Islamic Students, fervent, militant supporters of Ayatolla Khomeini's fledgling regime.

Within three weeks of the takeover, thirteen Americans—blacks and females—were released. Two hundred and fifty days after the takeover, Richard Queen, foreign service vice-counsul, was released due to an illness later identified as multiple sclerosis. Rocky Sickmann is one of fifty-two Amricans who remained hostage in Iran more than fourteen months of their lives—four hundred and forty-four days.

We are very fortunate to have Rocky's personal diary, written throughout his long ordeal. It is more than just an account of what happened to him. In many ways, it was his sanity for more than a year. Many of the other hostages kept notes, diaries, poems and personal thoughts during their months in captivity, but Rocky's is one of very few such documents to leave Iran. When the hostages were released, they were told to pack all of their personal belongings in bags that would be sent with them to the States on the plane. Rocky taped his diary to his leg, inside his trousers. The hostages' bags were confiscated—and never left the country.

Rocky's diary is about survival. It is about faith; it is about America. It is about despair. It is about tedium, boredom and confinement. It is about the longing for home and family. It is about human rights, and the gaps between two cultures' understanding of that concept. It is about Rocky Sickmann and Krakow, Missouri.

When Rocky returned home, he married his lady Jill. All the forces that tend to delay marriage and commitment in today's world the quest for education, the desire to express one's self as an individual, the need for economic security—lose their deterrent value when confronted with the realization of how quickly that freedom to choose can be snatched away. For Rocky and Jill, there remained the echoing question, "What did I really want from it all?" The answer, for them, was someone to love.

The young Mr. and Mrs. Sickmann live today close to the city of St. Louis, amid the bustle of urban life. Their jobs are there; Rocky is an account executive for FM/KMOX, a CBS-affiliated radio station, and is still a frequently-requested speaker for area schools and organizations. Jill works as a sales assistant at a radio representative firm, and spends a large share of her spare time as a dance instructor at a local ballet studio. But for both of them, home is still in the country. They still spend every available weekend visiting friends and family there.

I was invited to visit them one such typical weekend in late March, 1982. As we crossed the miles from St. Louis to Augusta that Saturday evening, already late for dinner at the home of Jill's parents, Vernon and Joanne Ditch, Jill and Rocky joked away the tensions of the work week. Rocky is a highly personable young man. There is nothing in his friendly, open conversation to suggest that his past is in any way unusual. The months of mental torture and physical deprivation he experienced not so very long ago have left no trace of bitterness or self-pity.

Jill's mother is a lot like Jill; bubbly, cheerful, vivacious. The relaxed mood of the evening shifted slightly, however, when the two women reacted unilaterally to Rocky's concentrated attention to a T.V. documentary on violence in El Salvador. "Turn it off. We don't want to watch that," they said in turn. The memories—and the fears—were too close to home. "But Mom, Jill, we've got to know about this," defended Rocky, backed up by his father-in-law. "It's happening all over again."

A heated political discussion followed, in which the women were inclined to let the rest of the world handle their own problems, and the men responded vehemently that by the time such problems reached our own doorstep it would be too late. It was the classic dichotomy between isolationism and intervention in foreign policy. A chill descended when Jill voiced her final fear, with the certainty of a question in statement form: "You'd go again, wouldn't you? You'd go fight someone else's war."

"I would if I had to," Rocky responded. "You just don't understand what's happening. I've got to think of the children we'll have someday." Jill's heartfelt reply: "I couldn't go through it again." There was no consensus, just kisses and bedtime. For Rocky and Jill, tomorrow would be another day.

After Sunday morning mass, I was privileged to meet many members of Rocky's family; his parents, Virgil and Toni Sickmann, brothers Gene and Kurt, sister Debbie, and six small nieces and nephews. I was unable to meet Rocky's sister Judy, who was travelling in Europe at the time. These are the people whose pictures, letters, and love meant so much to Rocky during his long days of captivity.

There is no mistaking which house belongs to the Sickmann's as you turn up their drive in Krakow, Missouri. It's the one with the oversize flagpole and American flag that flies high over the center of the front lawn.

All the things Rocky says about his family in the diary are true—they are warm, outgoing and generous. But traces of the strain caused by long months of now knowing are still evident in Mrs. Sickmann's face. "Yes, it was hard," she says of the ordeal. "We were criticized for responding to the constant attentions of the media; newspaper reporters, television interviewers, journalists and photographers were always at our door or on the other end of the telephone line. But what people don't seem to understand is how much it hurt. This wasn't fun we were having. More times than I can count, the press provided something I needed desperately—someone to talk to. You just can't keep all those feelings inside you.

"Another thing the press provided was information. That's something we could never get enough of. I don't know how many times I learned what was going on from the media people before I heard it from the State Department."

The emotional roller-coaster ride is ended now, but it has taken its toll. "I would never want to live through it again," said Mrs. Sickmann, poignantly echoing the words of Rocky's wife, Jill, spoken only the night before.

Virgil Sickmann is rugged and individualistic, with an ever-ready sense of humor and an obvious aura of pride. If he reflects strength and solidarity, it is no surprise to his son, Rocky, who tells him teasingly, "You should have known I'd be all right. After all, I'm a Sickmann."

Still, from November 4, 1979, to January 20, 1981, was a very long time for Rocky and all the hostages. Rocky said repeatedly towards the end of his diary that he just couldn't imagine being free again. One has to suspect that youth and resiliency played a part in his relatively easy assimilation of normal life after his release. Another part of the credit must go to Rocky himself, for his maturity, his faith, and his

X

equanimity of spirit that helped him through the lonely days. And finally, but of utmost importance to all the hostages, credit must be given to the love, appreciation and support shown by family, friends, communities and nations upon the release of these fifty men and two women, who had countless opportunities to suspect that the world had truly forgotten them.

Rocky remembers two incidents that occurred during his adjustment period of the first few weeks at home. One took place very shortly after his return, in a restaurant where Rocky, Jill and other family members had gone to eat. Rocky selected something from the menu, not knowing for sure what he had ordered. When the waitress put the plate in front of him, he saw that it was a rice dish. Rocky panicked, saying repeatedly, "I can't eat that; I can't eat it." Jill asked the waitress to take it away and bring him something else. Rocky describes the feeling as one of utter confusion. "It's not that I don't like rice; I do. But to me, that was Iranian food. I'd seen so much of it for so long that it made me panic just to see it sitting on the table in front of me."

The other incident occurred one night a few weeks later, after Rocky had bought the house in St. Louis where he and Jill now live. The two of them were not yet married, but were busy making wedding plans and were together almost constantly. On this particular evening, though, Jill had some work to do at home. Instead of spending the evening together as usual, she went home early and told Rocky she'd see him tomorrow. "It was the first time I had ever really spent any time alone," Rocky said. "Always before I'd had people around. Life had been very busy since I'd gotten back, and all of a sudden there was no one with me at all. The phone didn't ring. No one knocked on the door. It was the first time I had been *by myself* since I'd been taken hostage."

Once again, the panic. "I couldn't stand it. I got irrationally upset; called Jill up and told her she had to come over right away. She did, and then it was all right." The feeling of disorientation took Rocky by surprise. But for him, the recognition of the problem was the beginning of its solution. "I took it slow after that," he recalls. "For a while, I planned carefully for periods alone, keeping them short. But I never had that feeling again."

It is one of Rocky's deep concerns and wishes that none of those who survived captivity with him be offended by the publication of this diary. Tensions and frustrations mounted steadily during the seemingly endless days of imprisonment, and these tensions were occasionally translated into quarrels and misunderstandings among those who shared enforced living quarters. The reflection of this appears in the diary, and it is important that it remain so, as it was a real and true consequence of the strain under which these men were placed.

Rocky most sincerely wishes it known that he feels nothing but deep respect and friendship for those with whom he shared his life, and his hardship, for four hundred and forty-four days. Looking back, he knows that everyone acted in accordance with his own principles and always did the best he could. It is a tribute to all of them that their devotion to their country and to each other's needs never failed during their prolonged time of harsh uncertainty.

I've enjoyed tremendously my association with Rocky and Jill through the publication of this diary. The social, historical and documentary value of this book will be appreciated for years to come. I join with millions of Americans, whose hearts were filled with undefinable emotion as they watched the hostages return home in January, 1981, in saying thank you, Rocky, for allowing a part of your life to become a part of ours.

Erin Leslie Antrim
May, 1982

Editor's Note: Rocky Sickmann's diary is unabridged. It has been edited for clarity only, and has otherwise not been rearranged or altered from its original form. I would like to express my thanks to *Marge Bakalar* for technical assistance in preparing this book for publication.
--E.L.A.

The "Take-Over"

The embassy take-over occurred the morning of November 4, 1979. We were expecting nothing, although we had expected something in the way of trouble the day before, November 3. We had received word of a large demonstration to take place outside the embassy that day, at which Imam Khomeini was going to be speaker. Anti-American sentiment was building to a fever pitch since the Shah's arrival in the U.S., and in anticipation of an unruly crowd all military personnel were on duty to guard the embassy on November 3. All non-military Americans (State Department people, etc.) had been removed to a safe location.

Although the demonstration was large and loud, as expected, there was no trouble. Iranian police were even on hand to control the crowd. Later that day, things returned to normal. Non-military personnel returned to the embassy, tennis and volleyball games sprung up around the embassy grounds, and the sun was shining. I called Jill that night. Told her things were getting a little rough, but not to worry. It was the last time I would speak to her for nearly 15 months.

The next morning, Sunday, November 4, it was raining. I had gotten a "piss call" at 7:00 a.m., which means I was called from post one, manned 24 hours a day by Marine Security Guards. The Marine Corps Ball was planned for the next week-end, so we needed all our uniforms cleaned for that occasion. I was called to pick up the Marines' laundry and take it out to the laundromat. I showered and got dressed, wearing a pair of blue slacks, blue shirt and tie, and my London Fog overcoat. I didn't even eat breakfast that morning, because I wanted to hurry so I'd have time off later in the day. I remember I left my room in pretty much of a shambles. Everything was thrown around and my bed wasn't made, but I was expecting to come back that night. I never did return at all.

1

I headed for the embassy compound at about 8:00 a.m. The Iranian guards were outside the building, as usual. They were supposed to be providing us with protection. At times they would be pretty crazy themselves, and point their pistols at us while we were walking across the road from Bishan Apartment to the embassy compound. We had informed the Iranian police about it, but nothing ever came of it. Some of them just acted like they hated Americans so much that they didn't care if they shot us or not.

I entered the embassy through the remote control doors manned by Security Guards at post one. Corp. Williams and Sgt. Gallegos were on duty that morning. I went straight to the Marine office behind post one, and joined Sgt. Hermening, Sgt. Persinger, Staff Sgt. Moeller and Sgt. Walker in getting things ready for the Marine Corps Ball. I prepared a list of people who had uniforms that needed laundering, and also collected movies for return shipment to Germany, so that we could receive new ones.

After I'd gathered all the film together, I headed for the Chargé d'Affairs house to pick up the movie they had shown there the night before. I left through the front entrance to walk around the embassy, and as I was walking I heard chanting and cheers from a demonstration which was probably two or three blocks away. I was carrying a radio, and relayed the information back to post one, telling them I just wanted to keep them informed. Demonstrations happened so often that they were really nothing out of the ordinary. By this time, it was probably about 9:30. At the Chargé's house, I spent a few minutes talking to the cook about the menu for the Marine Corps Ball, and then headed back to the embassy with the tape. The demonstration was getting closer, but I thought nothing of it at the time.

I finished packing up the tapes, did a couple of other errands, and prepared to leave the embassy grounds. As I was leaving through the front gates at post one, I told Bill Gallegos I'd be back later to meet him for lunch. Out in front of the embassy once again, I could see that the crowd of demonstrators had arrived at the compound. I didn't pay much attention; I was busy chatting with a cleaning lady who was also leaving the grounds. All of a sudden I received a "recall" over my radio, which means *all Marines report back to the embassy*. Immediately I turned around and started running back to the embassy compound. I didn't know what was happening, but I could hear that the crowd had gotten a lot louder. I saw that the steel doors were starting to close in front of me, so I ran as fast as I could to get inside.

Inside the Chancery building, with the doors locked behind me, I looked up at one of the cameras to the outside and saw that the demonstrators were swarming all over the walls. We went immediately to

2

put on our gear; helmet, flack jacket with a Smith and Wesson 38, and a P850 shotgun. We were also supposed to have a camouflage uniform for things like this, but I had worn mine for the big demonstration the day before and it hadn't been returned yet, so I had to put my gear over my shirt, and tie on my gas mask. I was already shaking from all the excitement.

We were assigned to posts. I was assigned to a small room right next to the front door. It looks out to the front, and I could see the crowd out there chanting and yelling. They were loading shotguns and pistols, and I didn't know what to expect. They were also holding up a sign that said the only thing they wanted was a sit-in — no one would be hurt.

About fifteen minutes later we got a call over the radio informing us that they were breaking in through a basement window in the back of the Chancery. We were told to proceed to the basement stairs to prevent the demonstrators from coming up into the first floor of the building. Someone had accidentally popped a gas grenade, so gas was in the air and we had to put our masks on. Things were getting really hectic. The students kept pouring through the basement window, and we kept standing there waiting for the Iranian police to come and give us some help. To avoid any deaths, we just stood there and waited for orders. When they came, we were told not to throw any gas or fire any shots. To this day, I still believe that we would never have made it out of there if we had fired. It looked to me like they all had weapons under their coats, but didn't want to show them at the time.

The gas was getting pretty bad. It had started to affect Corporal Williams, who was situated at post one. I could see him rubbing his eyes, and he motioned me to come over to his post. When I got there, Mr. Golacinski had just finished talking to Mr. Laingen on the phone, telling him he was going to go out to talk to the students to see if he could get them to release the hostages they'd already taken. He was on his way out, leaving his pistol and his flack jacket behind and walking out with just his radio. I took over the post for Corporal Williams while he went to wash his face and get a gas mask.

The radios were going wild. People were calling to let us know what was going on so we could relay the information to Mr. Laingen, the Chargé d'Affairs. Some of the people at the Bishan Apartment were also being swarmed with students. I remember a call from Dr. Hohman, who was on a patio ledge trying to hide from them. He wanted to know what to do, and I told him not to do anything crazy like jump off, but to try to make it to a different embassy or just give himself up if there was no other choice.

3

Mr. Laingen called to ask if the Iranian police had arrived yet out side the gates. I told him there were revolutionary guards out there and people with riot gear, but no one was coming into the compound itself. Then I got a call about Mr. Golacinski. His radio had been taken from him; he had been taken hostage. The students took him over to the motor pool gate and told him to call the Chargé d'Affairs so the students could talk to him. I relayed the message to Mr. Laingen, who then went to find a telephone number so the students could call him. But the students got upset with the delay, and hung up the phone. Kevin Hermening held the phone number up to the window, but either the students couldn't see it or didn't want to see it. They came forward suddenly and started charging the door with a long post. They also started pouring through the basement window in droves.

At that point, we were told to abandon the first floor and retreat to the second. That meant we would have to leave post one, so we gathered up all the gas grenades and weapons, and destroyed the mobile phone units as much as possible before we left. We then proceeded to the second floor, closed the two-inch thick steel door and barricaded it with a refrigerator, couch and whatever else we could find to put behind it. I turned around and saw some Iranian employees and State Department secretaries sitting in the corner. Some were crying. All were really scared. We tried to soothe and comfort them as much as possible—told them not to worry; everything would be all right. Of course we were lying. Everything was not all right.

At that time there were a few people in the Chargé d'Affairs' office on the phone to Washington D.C. They were also talking with Mr. Laingen, who was supposedly over at the Foreign Ministry building.

Before long, we started to smell smoke coming from underneath the door. It kept getting worse, and we thought they were trying to burn the building or the door down so they could get to us. It really kind of scared us. We grabbed fire extinguishers, not knowing what else we could do. What they were actually doing, I realized later, was setting small fires to burn the gas out of the air. The gas was still pretty thick out there.

A while later, we heard Mr. Golacinski's voice outside the door. He told us that the students had hostages throughout the embassy compound and there was really nothing we could do but come out and give ourselves up. He said we would not be hurt.

It was probably two or three hours after that before we actually received orders to walk out and become hostage. During that time, one other person was sent out to try to reason with the students. He was, of course, also taken hostage. A couple of people eventually

4

went up on the roof of the building to see if there was any evidence of help from the Iranian military. When they came back down, they informed the people on the phones to Washington D.C. that there was no help. There were reinforcements outside the Embassy gates, but it looked like help for the students and not for us. Finally, we received orders to open the door.

Corporal Williams was the first one out. They told him to put his hands up, while some more students rushed in, saying, "Get their guns; get their guns!" At that time, there were a few people back in another room destroying all our weapons and ammunition, so we had nothing to give the students. When I walked out, they tied my hands tight and blindfolded me. They pulled me down the stairs, whispering, "Do not be scared; nothing is wrong." The burning paper they held in front of me to protect me from the gas singed my eyebrows and hair.

Outside, it was still misty and drizzling. The blindfold started to get wet, and I could see everyone standing around—girls wearing chadors and people holding plastic-covered pictures of Khomeini. They were all hissing and whispering to us, "Death to America; Death to America."

We stood out there for a few minutes until they were all organized, and then they put us in single file. Some guy grabbed me as we started to walk, and all of a sudden I noticed he was holding a knife to my neck. First they tell us not to worry; then before you know it someone's got a knife to your neck. That's not exactly reassuring. Still, for some reason I wasn't really scared at that time. I don't know why, but I just didn't feel like I was going to die.

They took us over to the Chargé d'Affairs' house. They walked us into the living room and tied us into chairs—our hands to the arms of the chair and our feet to the legs. Then they took the blindfolds off. We'd had a Halloween party in that room the Wednesday before, and all the decorations were still up.

Time just seemed to drag by. They kept bringing people in one by one. They asked us if we needed anything to eat or drink. We honestly didn't know what to think. After a while they got really paranoid about the wisecracks we were making. They seemed to think the Marines were commandos and everyone else was a CIA agent, and if we just looked at each other we were sending a message or code. Eventually they turned us all around facing the wall, so we couldn't see each other.

All this time we kept expecting help to come, but as it started to get dark, we began to get our first glimpse of what was really going on. Night was coming, and there was no sign of help. There was no chance of getting out, because these wild kids were in control.

That night for dinner, they took us into the kitchen three at a time to eat Iranian food. I was really hungry by that time, since I hadn't eaten breakfast or lunch. The kitchen, which had been beautiful earlier that day, was in total disaray. Iranian girls were all over the place, and the place was torn up beyond belief. Guys were walking around eating rice out of pots and pans, and then feeding it to us. They put some kind of spinach/bean topping on it, and I have to say that as my first exposure to Iranian food, it was really upsetting.

We all slept on the floor that night with our hands and feet still tied. They gave us pillows for our heads, but it was an extremely restless night. All night long I kept expecting help to come, but of course it never did.

The next day, they fed us jelly and bread for breakfast. Then I was tied in a chair around a big dining room table, along with about twelve or fifteen other people. We just sat there all day—nothing to do but stare at each other. We were not allowed to speak. "Don't-a speak," they kept repeating. One day they wanted us to stare at a wall, and the next day they wanted us to stare at each other. It just didn't make sense to me. It was not like any hostage situation I'd ever been taught about.

The month of November went by very slowly. The students moved us around several times to different places within the embassy. Gradually, the students separated us into smaller groups. Our hands and feet were kept tied most of the time, and we were given very little to do. The students had several interrogation sessions with us. They wanted to know what our jobs were, what our responsibilities within those jobs were, etc. We would mess around with them a little bit, telling them things that weren't true. They wanted to know who had been in the Viet Nam war—they really hated and despised those people—so the guys that had been in Viet Nam tried to keep it to themselves if the students didn't already know about it.

About a week after we had been taken hostage, there were about twenty of us living in a big room in an underground building we called the mushroom. We asked them if we could watch a movie, because we knew there was a video machine in the room next door. It took them a while to consider the question, because everything with them had to be a group decision. But after a while they all came in and said yes, we could watch a movie. We told them we wanted to see the World Series, so they brought out the 1979 World Series tape. We were sitting there watching the video, when all of a sudden the national anthem came on. I remember it got really silent around the room when that happened. We all just looked at each other, and I

6

started to get tears in my eyes. It was really a touching moment.

After it was over, we all gave a big shout and cheer. The students started running around, wondering what was happening. Finally someone told them that our national anthem had just been played. After that, we never got to watch any more television. The next time we watched video was not until February or March of 1980.

They told us why we were being held, and that we would not be released until the Shah was returned to Iran. I remember telling them that the United States would never send the Shah back. I believe everyone else told them the same thing. They wanted us to help them write statements to the United States people, asking them to join together to get the Shah returned to Iran so he could be executed for his crimes. When they realized I wasn't going to cooperate on that one, they just sent me back to my regular old routine of sitting in the corner, staring. After a while, they did bring us a couple of books. We had to read them with our hands still tied to the chair, but it was better than nothing.

Every time they moved us, they moved us at night. They told us they were doing this to protect us; that the American Government was trying to kill us because we knew so much. Eventually, they started leaving us untied more of the time, but we still had guards that sat with us 24 hours a day. They also began showing us films about the crimes the Shah had committed. The films showed people being shot and people already dead, laying around all bloody with their heads blown off, etc. They were really grotesque. Then they'd tell us how the American government had supported the Shah, and had interfered so that his tyranny could be maintained. After these films, they'd always try again to get us to make statements supporting their position, but we'd get on the tape recorder and say the exact opposite of what they wanted us to say.

We communicated a little bit with each other by reading lips when the guards weren't looking, or passing notes in the books that were exchanged. Sometime around the middle of December, as Christmas was approaching, we started talking to each other. First we started to whisper while the guard was out of the room. Then one day when he came back in, we just continued our whispering. He didn't say anything. Things were getting really loose, and it just seemed like they didn't care any more if we talked or not. Gradually we were able to talk out loud, and then to gather in a circle where we could sit and have conversations.

Christmas was miserable for all of us, although we were some of the lucky ones. We didn't realize it at the time, but there were others still being held in the mushroom with their hands tied. What made us so angry about Christmas was the big propaganda push they turned it into. They wanted us all to go on T.V. to talk to the people of the United States, to let them know we were all right. The only reason we did it was for our families. We knew they'd be worried sick about us, so we really tried to get into the Christmas spirit to let them know we were all right.

They took us down there blindfolded, then took our blindfolds off and fixed us up so we'd look good on camera. Then they shoved us into the room with the lights all set up. When it was over, they blindfolded us again and dragged us back to our room. It was a very humiliating experience.

The students continued to pump us full of the evils of the United States government. They told us of all the different countries the U.S. had interfered with, how it had mistreated blacks, and so on. But gradually they began to leave us more and more alone. Around the first part of February, they started bringing us cards and chess sets to occupy our time. I was allowed to have paper to start writing my diary. Even though all of these things were improvements in our situation, I took them as signs that we were going to be held hostage for a long, long time.

The endless, early days had been very difficult for all of us. Physical discomforts were compounded by a deafening silence from the outside world. We had been so sure, at first, that help was on the way. As the days wore on, that confidence was eroded. It wasn't until near Christmas time that we had any indication that our absence had even been noticed by the rest of the world.

The Diary

Sergeant Rodney (Rocky) V. Sickmann
United States Marine Security Guard
United States Embassy Tehran, Iran
(Sunday, October 7, 1979) Arriving in Iran!
Taken Hostage (Sunday, November 4, 1979,
10:15/14:00, 28 days after arriving here in Tehran)

Sunday February 3, 1980 (22:10)   **Day 92**

Tehran Hilton is the Embassy Building where we are presently be-ing held. The room we're occupying is a white room 15' in length, 10' height, and 11' in width. The room consists of two overhead fluores-cent lights, which we hate to use, and two table lamps, which we use the most instead of fluorescent overhead lights. Sounds strange eh!

Well, it's the truth, and it's not the guards idea either, it's ours. A ventilation system which seems not to work, a 4' by 4' barred window that can't be opened. The only fresh air we accumulate is when the door is opened and a slight breeze comes in from the hallway. One night desk which is used by the guard to do his studies and also used by us to write letters home. One other smaller table we use to store our plates, books, and leftover bread. Two chairs, one gas heater, which we use as a stove sometimes to reheat our bread, a wastebasket, three mattresses and all of our belongings, which don't consist of much.

The other two people I'm held captive with are William Gallegos from Pueblo, Colorado, and Jerry Plotkin from Sherman Oaks, California. Bill's also a Marine Security Guard who was lucky enough to be on duty the morning of the takeover November 4, 1979. I myself was just leaving the Embassy Building from the front entrance head-ing for the motor pool to sign out a driver, to then take me to Diba laundry to have the Marines' laundry done. I never did reach that ob-jective. It seems as though if I had awakened an hour earlier that morning, I might have never been taken hostage. I woke that morn-ing at (08:00). Jerry wasn't in the Embassy more than 20 minutes checking on a return visa and also on how to do better business here in Iran. Jerry's a merchant by trade. The return visa was for Jerry's Korean friend, Mr. Suk, who was also with him at the time, and who was also taken hostage. Jerry heard through the grapevine during the Christmas holidays that Mr. Suk was released, and he was relieved and happy at knowing that, but pissed he wasn't.

Well anyway, here we are just about ready to go on our 93rd day of captivity. Haven't heard from my family since around December 28. It's really hard to believe that they're not writing, there's bound to be an explanation somewhere. I'm hoping and praying that they're doing well.

10

Yesterday we were taken over to the Charge's house to take showers. They (the students) packed all three of us in the back seat of a car with blankets over our heads and took off towards the house like Steve McQueen. Once we reached the house we were taken to the little courtyard area where we're able to walk around, breathe the fresh air and take in some solar energy. While walking around we heard a noise from outside the wall. Just as they (the students watching us so we don't escape) opened the door, a dog flew through. It was good old Hercules, the Embassy compound dog.

I don't know if he smelled us, or saw our Marine camouflage trousers when we got out of the car, but he wanted inside that courtyard with us. He recognized us right off when he flew through that door, and even started to cry. You know how dogs get when they're real excited. They start to moan. I myself describe it as crying, at least that's what it sounds like to me. I don't know why, but I was glad to see that mutt. I got the same exact feeling that I got at Christmas when Reverend Coffin came to give Mass. As we were introducing ourselves he hugged each and every one of us.

As he hugged me, it seemed like something was drawn from his body to mine. Something so good and beautiful I never experienced before. I feel like God has touched me in so many ways since I've been here. For one, I'm still alive to this day. Another one is His talking to us through the Bible. I know it might sound crazy, but to me it sounds as though He's trying to tell us something.

Jerry, who wasn't too much of a believer of God before being taken hostage, has changed his whole attitude towards Him now. We'd be sitting around talking about going home and all, then break off to our own little corners to think or read. Jerry, who is really good at this, would just sit down, pick up his Bible, and open it up without knowing where it would open to. He claims that his eyes would fall upon a paragraph that would say: "Go home to thy friends, and tell them how great things the Lord hath done for thee, and hath had compassion on thee." He just hasn't done it once or twice. I'd be sitting on my mattress watching him, then noticing all of a sudden his eyes bulge out, then he'd read another psalm. We still haven't found anything in the Bible telling us of the day we're to leave though. We're still looking. "Be not afraid, only *BELIEVE!*" (Mark 6:36)

Bill and Jerry are playing chess. They should be finishing up pretty soon, then we'll start on our new game UNO we received for a Christmas present. *End of entry.*

Monday, February 4, 1980 (05:40)   **Day 93**

Just finished working out in the exercising room, which the

11

students call the "sport house". It s right across the hall so we don't have to go far. Jerry and I started our little workout about four mornings ago and plan on going with it as long as we're here, which I hope isn't too much longer. Jerry says he's never been into exercising but wanted to start, and needed someone to show him the different exercises. I told him I'd help for only a small fee, if he gave me his jelly for as long as we are here. He accepted, but I told him I was only kidding and I'd help for nothing.

Jerry and I call the exercising room "the refrigerator", because it's so cold in there, but really it doesn't bother us because then we don't sweat as much. It only consists of a small room with the dimensions of I'd say 8' in width and 10' in length. It's enough to do our exercises and that's about all. They also provided us with a small mat we could use to do our situps on, which was considerate of them.

Jerry's really getting proud of himself with all the weight he's been losing. He has lost a lot since we were taken hostage. I remember him as being pretty heavy, but he has been trimming down, putting muscle where fat used to be.

Just like always we returned from working out, played a couple hands of spades, and now everyone's getting ready for bed. Lately, it's as though we haven't been hitting the mattress till around (05:30) and then sleeping all day, waking only for meals and then staying up at dinner, which is served at (20:00), till the next morning, then continuing the same procedure over. What a mixed up schedule.

One of the guards earlier this morning was saying if the Shah was not to return to Iran, we would then go to court, a revolutionary court, to be trialed to see if we were CIA, or if we had any wrongdoings here in Iran. I really don't know if that's to our advantage or not. He said the person who is going to judge us, Ayatollah (I forgot his name), was the judge who sentenced the Shah's high officials to death.

Hopefully he was just screwing around. I'd really hate to meet him in a courtroom! Either way you look at it now, it doesn't look too good for us.

Bill's saying his rosary now, so I guess I'll close, say my rosary and hit the mattress, too. Still trying to stay optimistic, but it's really hard. Maybe the Good Lord will hear our prayers and free us today. How wonderful that would be. *End of entry.*

Monday, February 4, 1980 (15:00)   Day 93

Well, another day just about gone and still it's not looking too good for us all. Jerry sure takes a lot of shit from Bill and me. I guess it's mainly because we're military and he's civilian and we've had all the training he hasn't! He's never been in the military, and at times he wished he would've gone in maybe making this situation a little easier. I think it's only normal.

Woke twice so far today, once for breakfast which consisted of the usual. Goat cheese, butter, bread and tea. I guess I'm getting used to it, it's really starting to taste good to me. That was around (09:30) or (10:00) when room service brought our breakfast in. Never have to cook a meal around here, or even go to the table to receive it. They always bring it right to you. That's what I call service, the best I ever received from a motel.

The second time I woke was now, (14:00) when we received lunch. Lunch is always the best meal of the day, always something different day after day. Today we had steak, which was fixed great! French fries, lettuce and spinach were also served. They always make sure we get our vegetables to keep us healthy, so maybe eventually if we ever get out of here they want us looking healthy. When though? That's what I would like to know. Hopefully I'll be able to go back to sleep until tonight when dinner is served, and that's at (20:00). Time really flies by with this schedule, but I think I'm getting fat by eating and then going back to sleep.

The guard (we have a guard who sits with us at least 24 hours a day) has his radio on and he claims they're talking about Russia wanting to sell arms to Pakistan, but the United States saying no—that Pakistan is going to buy arms from them. Also something else about Ayatollah Khomaini going to the hospital. We asked the guard for what reasons Khomaini went there, and he replied, "for a check up." We asked him if there was anything about our release mentioned. He said no and just laughed. I didn't think it was that funny, but he probably knows something that I don't. *End of entry.*

Monday, February 4, 1980 (23:30)   Day 93

Students passed around a news clipping earlier tonight that really gave us hostages a lot of hope of getting out of here. *TEHRAN TIMES* (Sunday, February 3, 1980) *"Hostages Only for Shah Say Moslem Students"*. *"The Moslem 'students' holding the American hostages in the U.S. Embassy here reaffirmed yesterday that they would release them only if the deposed Shah is extradited to Iran and his assets returned to the country."* They're not asking for much are they?

They brought mail in tonight, but the only letter they had was for Bill. It was from his girlfriend Dawn. They've been asking us to write home but none of us had. We told them that we weren't writing until we all received a letter from our families written by them within the past month. I'm really worried about my parents and I hope they're doing well.

13

Lately I've been thinking of all the different things I've done in the past, wishing I would've done them differently—especially the way I treated my parents. I feel like I could have treated them so much better. I know they might not think so, but I do! We had our share of arguments but we always seemed to get them straightened out at the end.

I think we've got the closest family in the whole world. We always have a great time when the family gets together, it's great! I miss and love you so much, Mom and Dad, along with the rest of the family. I pray and hope so much that I'm home with you all very soon. *(Stay optimistic Rocky. You can do it old boy.)*

Sitting here thinking about Jill. At times I could really slap myself silly. I shouldn't have built up our relationship to what it was when I left. Although I won't deny the fact that I did fall in love with her those last three days we spent together in Virginia and Washington, D.C. I guess it really started to take form halfway during my 30 days leave that I had before going to MSG* school. Anyway, I asked her to come down for my graduation with my parents and aunt and uncle, and she accepted. Those three days and nights that we spent together, were pure *HEAVEN*!! They were great times I'll never forget!!! I'll never forget some of the things she said those last three days we were together. How she didn't want me to leave because something was going to happen, and I was never going to return.

Well Jill, you were right about something going to happen. I hope you weren't right about me never returning. I hope and pray that she's still there waiting if we're ever released, but if she's not, well, I really can't blame her. There's a little story behind our relationship that I might tell a little later on, but Jill tells it the best. Maybe I'll just wait for if we ever get out of here and let her tell it. I really do love and miss her—hopefully she's doing all right. *End of entry.*

Tuesday, February 5, 1980 (21:00)   Day 94

Nothing much happened today. Jerry and I did our workout again this morning like always. Came back into the room, played some cards together till about (05:00) and then sacked out. Woke twice again today, once for breakfast (09:30) which was the same as always, goat cheese, butter, bread, and tea. Tea always comes when we're finished eating, which is really a drag. You need something to wash that cheese and bread down with besides water. I should really stop my complaining. They don't really have to feed us all these good things, but still they do.

Lunch was the other time I woke (14:00). Today we had rice with some sort of sauce on top, which wasn't too bad. At least it's always

*Marine Security Guard   14

different. I just finished my delicious dinner of "soup" which really wasn't worth waking for. We do have to eat to stay healthy, right? It seems like there really isn't much to write about except for all the meals we have. Nothing ever happens down here in this room, always doing the same thing over and over. *End of entry.*

Wednesday, February 6, 1980 (04:55) Day 95

What a shock we had this morning around (03:00), especially after I wrote in my diary last night that nothing ever happens down here. Jerry and I had just finished working out, and we were sitting down with Bill playing UNO when all of a sudden the door opened and some students, masked and armed, came charging in, masking us then taking us down the hallway.

The first thing that popped into my head was U.S. troops coming to try to evacuate us out, and the students knew it, so they were getting ready to waste us all. The students told us several days earlier that if there was an attempt of U.S. troops coming here to free us we would all be shot before they reached us. That was my first thought; Death was on its way!

They took us down the hall in a hurry it seemed, and stopped pretty close to the room we were at before. Although Bill and I were blindfolded, we still knew where we were from working here before being taken hostage. Jerry wasn't so lucky.

They faced us against the wall in the hallway and seemed to leave us there for so long. My whole body started to shake when I recognized the sound of bolts being forced home on a couple of rifles. It only seemed to be us three against the wall; at least Bill, Jerry and myself were the only ones I heard breathing hard. I started to say my rosary when I was grabbed by the arm and taken into a room where I was told to face the wall and strip. Right then I thought I was a goner for sure and my body started to shake even more so than the first time. I started to remember all the movies the students showed us earlier of all those dead people that were naked, lying in puddles of blood. I then started to think of myself just like one of them.

I got all the way to my underpants, which I don't usually wear, but I'm sure glad I had them on then. Then they told me to stop and put my hands up against the wall. I noticed on the side of me, where I dropped my clothes, that two masked students were going through them like they were looking for something. I wasn't really thinking of them anyway. I was thinking of what it was going to be like to be shot

15

und die. Things of the past just started flying through my head and I was shaking like mad. I remember asking the Good Lord why it had to end now, and like this, then feeling a student hitting me on the shoulder, telling me to put my clothes back on. My mind was blank, I didn't know what to think.

I started to dress, still shaking like a leaf on a tree on a windy day. I've always been a slow dresser and I remember them once, when I was half finished, telling me to hurry. That's all it took, just that one word, "hurry", before I started to put my clothes on any way they'd fit. I remembered I had to turn my socks inside out and turn my tee shirt around the right way when we returned back to the room here. I wanted to get the heck out of that room.

Then they blindfolded me once again and took me out to where I started from. They told me to put my hands up against the wall and then went over and grabbed Bill, who was right next to me. They were doing one of us at a time, each the same way.

Meanwhile, they kept playing with the bolts of the rifles, opening, then closing them. I couldn't figure out what was going on. It seemed like eternity before they escorted us back to our room. Our rooms were in shambles when we returned. It was like they were looking for something. It's really strange, after being here 96 days they want to search us again, but to find what? Maybe one of the guards lost a .45 or .38 and probably thought we had it.

They did take some of our things. From Bill they took a belt, and nail-clippers, from Jerry they took $280.00 he had in cash, also a silver dollar his wife gave him for good luck, which seemed not to work. He really hated to see that go though. From me they got a belt and nail-clippers. Why they took those items I'll never know. Maybe they thought we were going to use them as weapons to escape with, nail-clippers as knives, belts to choke someone with, and Jerry's money to bribe someone with.

That experience we encountered tonight I'll never forget for the rest of my life. Like the saying goes, another day, another dollar!! What a hard earned dollar I'm making. Anyway, I'm here for the people of the United States of America and most of all, for my family! *End of entry.*

Wednesday, February 6, 1980 (05:30)   Day 95

Brown Jacket, who we call Guard Chief, just came in to see if anything happened this morning, like if he didn't already know. We told him he just missed it. We weren't going to mention anything to anyone about it to see what they were going to say, but I guess he was getting kind of uptight. We weren't saying anything about it, so he

16

brought it up. We asked him where he was during all the action, and he replied that he'd just gotten there, putting it in his own words, "Late for work." He told us that was their special force made up of students. We told him it was very impressive, especially when they had all the weapons in the first place and had all of us under guard. *(How much easier could you have gotten it!!)* I do have to say though, they did scare the living shit out of me. *End of entry.*

Thursday, February 7, 1980 (04:20)   Day 96

Another day gone by, and yet, no news! Just finished working out with Jerry, and let me tell you. That guy's determined to lose that fat and go home a new man. I hope the workout we're doing isn't hurting him in any way. I'd hate to have him fall over with a heart attack or something while we're working out. Tonight I had him jog around in circles with me, in that little room. He was really surprised to see that he could do it, and especially for so long, 13 minutes. He's really proud of himself, and I hope we're able to go home so he's able to show his wife what he's accomplished. He says he's never been this thin in ten years.

Nothing really happened yesterday the 6th, except for that show the students' special forces put on for us. Also we found out that our cook was sick, so we started back on Iranian food. For the morning we had the usual cheese, bread, butter, and tea. Lunch was green rice with something mixed in it. I guess it takes awhile for my stomach to get used to it. Anyway, I hope our cook isn't sick too much longer.

Bill's found a way to stop Jerry from snoring without saying a word. Jerry's really a light sleeper, so any little noise and he awakes. The only thing Bill does is hit a pen against a glass and Jerry stops just like that. It seems like ever since we've started working out; his snoring has cut down a little, really strange.

Well, I'm going to hit the sack. There's really not much more to say. We're still praying and hoping that each next day will bring us news of our freedom!! That word "Freedom" sounds so good. *End of entry.*

Friday, February 8, 1980 (04:42)   Day 97

Hello again! Yes, we're still here, waiting it out, waiting for something to happen. This morning around (02:00) while we were playing UNO, Green Jacket, the man we call "mailman", came running in the room with a picture of Jill and me that we had taken together when I was home on leave before going to MSG. He handed it to me and then ran right back out before I could ask him if there was a letter enclosed with it.

17

She had on a sun dress, and I had on my dress blues. I do have to say, we sure did look good, especially her! She was beautiful! It really made my heart sink when I saw it. Boy, I miss her, along with the rest of my family. She's a perfect model, perfect face, and a beautiful body. In fact, she was modeling at Saks in St. Louis, where she was working part-time. I went to watch her once, wanted to bring my camera but she said *no!* Anyway, I thought she did pretty good; really impressed me.

I wrote her earlier, asking her to send one of those pictures, so I guess she received my letter. Haven't heard anything from her since being taken hostage. I called her two days before we were taken hostage; that's the last I heard of her. My parents and family keep mentioning her in all their letters, saying she's doing well and really misses me. I wonder why I haven't received one from her? Now I have a family portrait, which I received in December, and a picture of Jill, which will keep me company every night. They're the greatest, and *I love 'em all!!*

We're supposed to have company today, so that means they'll be taking us to shower and then wanting us to clean our room up. Put on a show once again! They want us looking and smelling good.

We found out from one of the guards that the cook had a toothache and was sent to the dentist. It must be a long journey by camel to get there. He's been gone for two days now. I hope he hurries back, I don't know how much longer my belly can hold out eating this Iranian food. Yesterday for breakfast we had the usual cheese, bread, butter, and tea. For lunch we had soup which is really a change in the menu. For dinner, we had the Iranian favorite, (which is starting to be mine too) rice with a bean sauce on top. I guess they were starting to get the hint that we were getting tired of soup every night, so they thought they'd switch it around a little. Have soup during lunch and the special, which I call it, at night. Pretty tricky. I wonder what we're going to have today, since company's coming? Maybe barbecued ribs and apple pie!

I told Jerry that we were going to take the morning off from working out, but he didn't like that. He's determined to lose that fat, so I told him I'd work him twice as hard tomorrow morning. He didn't care as long as he lost it. Guess I'll close for now, going to lie back and take a long look at Jill's and my family's portrait. Boy, how I wish I was with them now! I love them all so much! God Bless and protect them! *End of entry.*

Saturday, February 9, 1980 (17:20) **Day 98**

Well, I just got up about two hours ago, recovering from all the excitement and company we had yesterday. Didn't get much sleep yesterday morning. After I finished writing my entry and what have you, I got about an hour's sleep before they came in to get us for showers. The students were in a hurry. They took us over, showered, and brought us right back. Didn't even get to walk around in the courtyard.

After we returned, they brought us in a vacuum cleaner to clean our room with. The students were even cleaning the hallway, which had to be the first time since the takeover of the Embassy. The students sure wanted to impress whoever was coming.

Right before Monseigneur Nolan and Archbishop Pucci arrived, the students passed out mail, which must have been hand carried from the States. Anyway, it was the first time in about a month and a half that I heard anything from my parents and family. I was expecting one from Jill, but no luck! It was great to hear that everyone is doing good, just waiting for all of us to return. They even mentioned Jill in their letters, saying she was doing great, kept real busy, but really missed me.

The visitors we had were Monseigneur Nolan, Archbishop Pucci and Imam Khomaini's son, whose name I forgot. Once again, the feeling Monseigneur Nolan and Archbishop Pucci brought us was very heart warming. They both emphasized that the hard times have passed and the easy ones are yet to come. We've all been sitting here thinking about what they said and can't make but good things out of it. Even the letters I received emphasized that freedom was near. Boy how I hope they're right.

I sent out a Valentine's card and letter to my parents and Jill. Hopefully they'll get it. I believe Monsiegneur Nolan is supposed to hand carry them back with him.

Once again, I dreamt about being home in my sleep this morning and when I woke all of a sudden I found myself here. Why did it have to be a sad ending?

Imam Khomaini's son was here also, like I said before. He wanted to know how we've been, if we had any sicknesses or if there was anything he could do to make our stay any more pleasurable. We told him we were all fine, just waiting to go home. I wonder what the occasion was for everyone coming to see us? It was kind of nice seeing different faces, especially American! Oh Yeah! Jerry got his first letter from his wife today and was he ever happy. His first letter since November 4, 1979. I'm sure glad he got it, he sure needed one. He says he feels 100 percent better, which I believe. Going to continue our workout tomorrow morning, get back into our old routine. That's about all that happened yesterday and today. Maybe tomorrow we'll go home! *End of entry.*

Monday, February 11, 1980 (05:30)   Day 100

Another day gone by and another to start. Bill and I are lying on our mattresses listening to Super Bowl 14, Pittsburgh Steelers vs Los Angeles Rams. Jerry was, but he crashed out on us. What a party pooper he turned out to be.

Alex Paine recorded it for us. I was told he was also in charge of the Christmas cards that were delivered to us during the holidays. If and when I ever get out of here, I'd like to give him a personal "thank you" for all the things he's done.

We waited to hear the National Anthem at the beginning of the tape, but it never played. We heard through mail it was dedicated for all of us over here, so we were looking forward to hearing it. Just heard the game announcer tell the listeners that the game would be recorded and then heard by the 50 hostages in Iran. It's really a great feeling knowing we're not being forgotten over here.

Nothing really happened yesterday. Ate once, and that was breakfast, bread, jelly, butter and tea. The other two meals weren't worth getting up for so we just continued to sleep. When we woke last night we continued our same routine, chess, cards, and read. Been slacking off on our workout lately. The morale hasn't been the best around here. We've really been disgusted and at times you catch yourself jumping all over somebody (Jerry or Bill) for unnecessary things. We all do it, but we understand what's happening, so we just let it fly by. Being in this cramped room doesn't help out any either.

Well, the Steelers won the Super Bowl once again, 31-19. Really a good game right down to the end. Sure wish I could have seen it. Maybe I'll be able to whenever we get out of here. *End of entry.*

Tuesday, February 12, 1980 (06:05)   Day 101

Still here. The morale is really going down in this room. One hundred and one days and we're still here. We know the American Government isn't going to give back the Shah while we're still over here, but still these people are determined they will. I wish I could feel that confident. How many more days, weeks, months, and the last one I hate to say, years, is it going to take them to realize this? Whenever we ask them if we'll ever go home, they say eventually you will, but when! Only President Carter and God know that answer. Myself, the only person I think who knows is the Good Lord. But at times I really have my doubts if He even knows. Hopefully one of these days "Freedom" will arise.

Brown Jacket was in to see us as usual. He was saying that the cook was still sick and we told him we could see that from the kind of food we've been receiving. We gave him a suggestion to take up in front of the committee, or whatever, to see if the three of us could cook in place of our regular cook until he returns in good health. Every day we see leftover food in the wastebasket that the hostages didn't eat. I know it's a sin to throw away food, but my stomach just isn't fit to eat the food they're used to eating. Brown Jacket said he'd see what he could do.

Yesterday's meals weren't too bad. Breakfast was the usual; lunch and dinner they switched around on us again. Lunch was soup, which we usually have for dinner. But for dinner we had rice with a topping of lamb meat and potatoes mixed into a sauce. It was excellent with a little dab of catsup. I don't know what I would have done without it.

Jerry got his hair cut yesterday. He said it had been bothering him for quite some time, so he just decided to get it cut. We've been finding little knots on our heads lately, I guess from not washing our hair regularly. I really do miss taking my two showers a day. Now it's one every five or six days. They've been having some problems finding hot water, but they said hopefully soon they'll have the problem solved. When we shower is the only time we use hot water. Other times I get my hot water from the students, who boil it for me. I use it to soak my face. That seems to do a pretty good job of clearing the acne up.

Been having stomach problems again. Don't really know what it is. Maybe the food or even our nerves. The Doc says it's our nerves, which I'm hoping is right. They have a student doctor that comes around checking on us. Whenever they're not sure of something they call in a registered doctor who gives the final analysis. Not too long ago, I thought I'd picked up some kind of skin disease, so I called for the student doctor. He wasn't sure of it. He told me he was going to try to get in touch with a skin specialist to see if he could come and look at it.

Sure enough, about four days later some students came in and woke me from my sleep and told me that they were going to take me to the doctor. I got dressed. They blindfolded me and then walked me outside to a car where I was then taken to the old Marine house where Doc Hohman, the Embassy Doctor, had his doctor's office. They took me in a room where I sat for about a minute, and then the door opened and in walked the student doctor and the doctor who was going to examine me. The doctor greeted me with a handshake and asked how I was. It really surprised me when he greeted me in such a kind way. I took it as all the Iranians hating the hostages. Not this

21

doctor! He was very kind, considerate and spoke good English. To make a story short, I didn't have any kind of disease, at least that's what he said. Anyway, it showed me that the students really do care about our health, and are willing to do anything to help us except help us escape.

The students have really been getting slack with the guards lately. They hardly ever have anyone in the room with us anymore. They all sit out in the hallway. In a hospital you ring a bell and a nurse comes running. Here you knock on the door and an Iranian opens it. Not a nurse, either. We've been wondering if the cut on guards means a slight hint towards going home soon. I wish we had a date to shoot for. At least then we'd have a goal to try to accomplish. The way it stands now we could be here for years.

This is the third day we've had the tape recorder. We've heard the Super Bowl twice and there's one tape that Bill keeps running down the batteries with. The name of it is "The Good, The Bad and The Ugly." I bet he played that thing more than one hundred times yesterday, and believe it or not he's still playing it. The music's really dragging on now; the batteries are ready to go dead any minute.

Last night we tried recharging them with the lamp cord from the lamp. We disconnected the wires from the lamp and taped the wires to the positive end of the battery, each wire to one battery with another battery behind the first with the positive touching the negative. It seemed to work a little, but we didn't want to risk getting electrocuted so we stopped. Finally one of the students came in and asked why we weren't playing the music. I guess he was listening earlier from out in the hallway and was wondering why we weren't playing it. Told him we needed some batteries and an hour later they came in with some. It would be a lot easier if they would find the extension cord, then we wouldn't use up so many batteries. Really lucky to have this, I hope we keep it! I sure wish we had our freedom. *End of entry.*

Wednesday, February 13, 1980 (06:40) Day 102

Hello there again! Well, yesterday the students showed us that we'd be here a little while longer. Right after breakfast yesterday morning some students came in collecting our shoes, putting our names on them first, then throwing them in a box. Just for someone taking a pair of shoes away, it sure gave me a sad feeling inside. A little while after they left, they returned bringing plastic cups and taking our glass ones away. I wonder what the reason was for that? If that doesn't show that we're going to be here a long time, I don't know what does. We were thinking that maybe one of the hostages tried to

22

escape, so they probably thought they would prevent us from doing the same thing by taking all those items. They exchanged our shoes with some sandals that were brand new. They said we could keep them whenever we leave, but no doubt they'll be worn out by the time we get out of here.

We slept like always yesterday, except for Jerry. Our cook's not back yet, so we're still getting Iranian food. We brought the subject up again about letting some of the hostages cook, and they said once again they'd see what they could do. Back in the States the guys in prison make license plates to pass the time. Here the only thing we do is read books, play cards, work out a little and whatever else we can find to do. One good thing, I'm catching up on all the reading I didn't do in school.

Mailman came in this morning and passed some news. He had two pictures from an Iranian newspaper. One of them he claimed had been taken in the United States (New York) of demonstrators demonstrating about the draft. From the paper he read, he stated the United States started the draft back up. In the picture, the demonstrators were holding up a poster that said "Draft the Shah". We really got a laugh out of that one. The other picture was of a committee that was supposedly sent from the States. I really don't believe they came here to discuss our release though.

Students took the recorder last night and said that they were going to give it over to some of the other hostages to listen to. I guess my guess was wrong the other night when I thought that all the hostages had one. Share and share alike!

I was just thinking about my stereo sitting back home in its boxes, in my room waiting to be played. If I don't ever get out of here, which I'm praying and hoping I do ... anyway, if I don't, my little brother's going to have a nice stereo.

They said they got some mail in, just for Bill and me, nothing for Jerry. I'm hoping to see one from Jill Renee. It gets me so homesick looking at our picture. I guess I'll have to stop looking at it if it continues. I pray to God that she and my family are all doing fine.

We made up a little chess competition among us three and yesterday we had one of the students playing with us. This guy could really play, but of course he's been playing since he was five years old. The students have really been good to us, except for the fact they still hold us hostage. They're still continuing to make our stay as pleasant as possible. At times we get a couple of political prisoners coming in talking to us about the times they were in the Shah's prison. They really tell some gruesome stories of some of the torturing they used to go through along with some of their friends. We really have to be grateful to the students for how they've been treating us. But then again, times can always change within a snap of the fingers. Hopefully they'll continue to stay like this.

From what I see, looking out this basement window of the Embassy, it looks as though it's going to be another beautiful day. We can hear loud chanting going on—I guess they're all out front. Wonder what the occasion is today? Maybe they heard that the Shah was returning on his own. Boy, how I wish this would end today. God Bless America!!! *End of entry.*

Thursday, February 14, 1980 (03:20)   Day 103

Once again, another entry! Received three letters tonight, but nothing from my parents, family or Jill. I hope they're all doing well. Jerry and I worked out again this morning in what the students call the sport house. This time I had him run around in circles with me for twenty minutes. It looked as though he could've done more too. He's really improving on his exercises.

We got our cook back yesterday for lunch, our best meal of the day. We had turkey, cranberry sauce, potatoes and gravy. Was it ever good! For dinner we continued with our usual soup. If we continue to get fed one good meal a day like the one we had yesterday, we wouldn't need the other two. Still, it does help if we get fed three times a day, gives us something to do besides just sitting around all day.

Did our same routine yesterday as we do other days. Slept, card playing, reading books and whatever else we could find to do. Otherwise, nothing else happened. We're really getting bored and want to get out of here awfully badly! *End of entry.*

Friday, February 15, 1980 (05:30)   Day 104

Last year on this night I met Jill Renee at her brother's and wife's apartment in Washington, Missouri. It was the first time I'd seen her since I graduated from high school. When she opened the door of the apartment that night of February 15, 1979, an amazing feeling caught me inside. I guess it was telling me that something good was going to happen of this first meeting from so many years past. She was so beautiful standing there in the doorway, more beautiful than I expected; not that she wasn't beautiful before, it was just that I hadn't seen her for so many years. She had changed so much. We really had a nice time together that night, her brother and his wife (Judy and Jerry) whom I both graduated with, and Jill.

A queer incident happened earlier that night when I had to drive my parents and brother's wife Laurie down to St. Louis to pick up my brother Gene at the hospital where he had been taken to the emergency room after having an accident at work. To make a long story short, I drove my brother's truck back from St. Louis with my Dad following me in the rear with my Mom, Gene and his wife Laurie. We got to the parking lot in Washington where we had met earlier before going down to pick them up. My parents had their car there; Gene and Laurie had their family car and I had mine, too. Now the thing we had to figure out was how Gene was going to get his truck from point A to point B. I told him I'd solve it when I took Jill home from our date. Everyone agreed, so we departed. That night I asked Jill if she'd do me a favor and follow me to my brother's house with my car so we could drop off my brother's truck. She agreed, not mentioning the fact that she didn't have a driver's license. I guess I should've taken the hint when I always had to slow down for her to catch up. The reason she told me she drove so slow was because she didn't want to wreck the car. Jill never told me about not having any driver's license until after we started to go out with each other more frequently. She told me she would've been embarrassed to tell me she hadn't gotten her driver's license yet, so she just played along like she had it. That's *my* crazy Jill Renee!

Anyway, one year ago tonight I met that beautiful girl, and how I'm glad I did!!! Yesterday was Valentine's Day and no flowers were sent to either my Mom or Jill. I bet I'm in the dog house now! The students did give us some Valentine cards to send home. I sent one to the family and one to Jill, plus wrote a letter to everyone in the family to let them know how I was doing.

A lot happened yesterday afternoon. Fifty Americans from all walks of life came to talk to two of the hostages. Bill and Paul Lewis were chosen to talk to them. Some of the questions they asked were our feelings of the situation, our mental and physical state of being. They told them they could only answer for themselves and the people they were with. The others they didn't know. After the interview the fifty Americans gave the students flowers, candy and cake to hand out to all the hostages for Valentines. The students said they were over here in behalf of the American people to find out the truth of the Shah and all his wrong doings. Now since they know we're being treated okay, the only thing we can do now is sit back and enjoy the goodies they brought for us and wait to see if any word changes in behalf of our release. Once again this morning the students emphasized that in several weeks from now something will be happening on behalf of the freedom of the hostages. I don't know if they're just saying that to keep our morale up or what; if they are, it's working! I'm just hoping they're right.

Last night, Mailman came in with a song that was written about this situation. He wouldn't tell us who produced it or where they made it. It sounded like a black group singing, but I could be wrong. Anyway, they sounded pretty good. Some of the students brought a white rabbit, which they called Mr. C., meaning Mr. Carter, into our room to show off. I wonder when we're going to have that for dinner?

Mailman brought us some bar bells at last. We told him a long time ago the only thing they had to do was go down in the basement of our apartment and pick up the weights we had and bring them over here to let us use. So finally today they brought some bar bells. Now we'll be able to strengthen our arms up. Jerry and I just finished working out again. It looks as though the fat's disappearing and maybe turning into muscle. He's really getting to be proud of himself. We're to receive mail some time today, so hopefully there's one from Jill and my family. Cross my fingers on that one! The food's really been good lately since our cook's back. Thank the Lord for that. Things are looking brighter towards freedom! *End of entry.*

Saturday, February 16, 1980 (04:55)   Day 105

Not too much happened yesterday. Received three more letters. One from my aunt, one from my cousin and one from a girl in Ireland. It's really good to hear from people saying everyone is praying for our release and not to worry, that we'll be home soon. Nothing from my parents, family and Jill. Jerry didn't get anything, which he wasn't too happy about. I wouldn't blame him though; I'd be pissed too. Bill got a couple of letters from people he knew, and then some from people he didn't know. The letters raised our morale a little, except for Jerry!

Instead of soup last night for dinner we had spaghetti and jello, which was great! Anything besides soup nowadays is excellent. The food's adequate and we're making it. Been working out with the weights we got the other day quite a bit now. It looks as though my arms are starting to form back into place like they used to be. I'm sure glad our muscles are starting to form, because I know our release sure isn't. *End of entry.*

Sunday, February 17, 1980 (05:00)   Day 106

Answered some cards and letters for the first time yesterday morning after I wrote in my diary. I would have started earlier, but I had my doubts. I felt kind of bad anyway, all those people taking time out to write me and here I sit with all the time in the world and still don't write. Jerry decided to do the same. At least it gives us something to do to pass the time away.

We wrote till around breakfast which was served around (09:00) or (09:30). It was my turn to do dishes, and when I returned to the room everyone was crashed out already. I don't know if I mentioned it earlier, but we've got our own little system for doing dishes. I do the morning, Jerry lunch, and Bill dinner. The students used to do them, but I guess they finally caught on and decided we could do our own.

Believe it or not I stayed in my mattress from yesterday morning around (10:00) till this morning, only waking for meals and once to go to the toilet. I sure hope I'm not coming down with some kind of sleeping sickness. Jerry couldn't believe I did it. He really envies Bill and me for sleeping all we do. Last night we had a dessert of blueberry pie and boy, how I wished I had a whole one. It was really good! I was just sitting here thinking about how I was only on this program (MSG) twenty-seven days, and here I am held hostage for one hundred and six days already. *End of entry.*

Monday, February 18, 1980 (09:30)   Day 107

Wrote a couple more replies to cards and letters yesterday morning, staying up till lunch and then crashing out till this morning around (01:00). Bill and I've been sleeping pretty much, but Jerry not quite as much. It seems as though we're having a hard time reading lately. Always daydreaming about going home, but still the pages of your book keep flickering in front of you. Not knowing what you were reading, you then try to go back to where you first started and start all over. It's really been hard trying to keep our minds off home during this situation. What an experience it's been.

Jerry and I worked out in the sport house once again this morning. The students have cut our time down for using the workout room to fifteen minutes now. I wonder what the reason was for that? I know there aren't that many hostages that like working out at (04:00) in the morning. So I know it wasn't because we were hogging the room. Really hate to exercise in this room. It gets so stuffy, and starts to stink at times since the windows don't open. Jerry's wife is really going to be proud of him if we ever get out of here to show her what he's accomplished.

The weather's really ugly today, snow and rain mixed together. Can't wait till summer, maybe we'll be out of here by then. If not, it'll be a hot one! It looks as though they aren't going to have too much traffic at the airport, so it looks like we aren't going to be freed today.

We just had breakfast and now Jerry and Bill are crashed till lunch. I've got dish duty once again, so when I'm finished writing here I'll

27

call one of the students, first putting a towel over my head, and have him walk me down to our kitchen—the toilet—where the manual dishwasher—my hands—will do the dishes. It's really not bad, at least we get a little walk down to the toilet and plus it gives us something to do.

Really been having a hard time not thinking about home, family, Jill and my past. Thinking about my past isn't bad, it's just thinking about if we'll ever get out of here, and wondering if everyone is doing well. I really try not to worry but I guess it's just natural. Jerry and Bill both do the same. How many more days, weeks, etc., is it going to take? If only we had something to keep us busy. Here we sit, nothing we can do except pray, sit around, and hope for the best!! *End of entry.*

Tuesday, February 19, 1980 (10:30) Day 108

Absolutely nothing happened yesterday! No one came to see us, so we slept all day till this morning, around (01:00). Came from washing dishes this morning and found Bill with our little rabbit friend. One of the students said they showed it to John McKeel (one of the Marines) and he told them to get rid of it before he ate it. Sounds like something John would say. John's one of five Marines, besides myself, that was picked to come over here after we graduated. Around Christmas time when John, Paul Lewis, Jerry, Bill and myself were living together in the Charge's house, we gave John a nickname of "Stick", because he was getting so skinny. Haven't seen him or Lewis since; hopefully they're doing all right.

Jerry's been really wishing he could sleep like Bill and me. He says he gets so bored sitting there waiting for us to wake, he doesn't know what to do with himself. I wish he could sleep like us, too. The days seem to be flying by so fast, sleeping like this.

Really surprised that Brown Jacket (guard chief) and Green Jacket (mailman) haven't come to visit us lately. Maybe something's up. Hopefully something good, like our release! Starting to hear gunfire at nights again. They must really have some trigger-happy guards out there guarding us. Wrote a couple more replies yesterday morning. Probably do the same this morning when I'm finished here, too. I've got eight pages to my diary so far. Would've liked to have seen how many I would've written on those first couple days—wow! So much I could've written, but then again, it would've been kind of hard to write with my hands tied up. Sure wish we had some word of encouragement of when we're to go home. God Please Help Us!!! *End of entry.*

Well, they brought and then took the tape player from us yesterday. It really didn't bother any of us until last night when we were sitting around eating our dinner in the normal usual quiet manner we always do. It seemed like we didn't have anything better to say, so we started an argument over a piece of paper they brought in earlier that day regarding news from the States. The argument got carried away at one point and dishes started flying, leaving them broken on the floor. It kind of startled the guards, so they came in wondering what happened to the broken bowls. We told them we accidentally knocked them off the table and assured them that everything was okay!

We've been really having a hard time keeping our tempers down lately. It's really foolish though, having these arguments over such small matters. I guess it's just a sign showing us that this place is finally getting to us. No way though! I ain't giving up this easy. I'm fighting till the last straw is pulled, and I know Jerry and Bill feel the same. It's not that we hold any grudge; it's just at times we get so wound up inside we have to let it unravel before we do something foolish. We're trying to keep our marbles together as best as possible.

Jill would really love the music we've been listening to. To tell you the truth, I'm really getting to like those Western songs. There's nothing like Charlie Daniels, all smooth and mellow music, nothing hard. They don't let us listen to any rock music, they say it's bad for the head! I wonder what they think keeping us hostage is doing to our heads?? We recently heard a tape that was recorded off a station in Colorado, and in between each song they had a Christmas wish to each and every one of us here. Although it was late, it was still heartwarming.

They say we're to receive mail today, but I won't believe it until I see it. Worked a couple math problems today to see if my mind was still functioning correctly. Maybe if we ever get out of here I'll go back to school. *(With God's Will.)* We just got finished with lunch and now everyone's crashed out, even Jerry! Pretty good lunch we had today. Hamburgers, french fries, and carrots.

Not too much more to say. We're pretty much staying to our own routine of sleeping, reading, playing cards, working out and most of all, waiting desperately for a word of encouragement. *End of entry.*

Thursday, February 21, 1980 (11:05)   Day 110

Last night Mailman brought in some news of a black New York action committee that gave a statement on the United States' crisis in

Iran. Just some propaganda about how our Government had wrong doings over here and so on. It seems like there's so many people arguing why the Shah's kept in the States, but still here we sit. We sure wish we knew what the news was back in the States.

They asked us last night to write home and ask why the Shah's still retained in the States and why we're still here. It is hard to believe the Shah's in the States living it up and here we are serving his time in hell (being held hostage is my definition of hell). Just heard some news of five men coming from the United Nations to start a United Nations committee over here to see what they could find to accuse the Shah of so he could be extradited back to Iran. At least that's why the students say they're over here. That's about the best news we've heard for a long time. Now hopefully something will happen for the release of the hostages, not just some of us, all of us!

They said we're to receive mail today, but that's what they said yesterday and still we haven't received any. Really looking forward to a letter from Jill and my family. I sure hope they're not suffering through this ordeal.

We heard from the students last night that the reason the U.S. brought the draft back was to get a special force together and come over here to kill the hostages and then blame it on the Iranians. Of course that's the students' idea of the draft being brought back in. We told them it wasn't true, because if they (the U.S.) wanted to get a special force together and come over here to kill us, they wouldn't need the draft. We have enough who are capable to come over to do that sort of thing without the draft. This situation is so unique, at times I can't believe it's happening!

The only thing we do now is sit back and wait and see what happens with the five men from the United Nations. What happens if the men from the United Nations don't find any wrong doings? We keep praying day and night that freedom is soon! *End of entry.*

Friday, February 22, 1980 (07:55)   Day 111

Forgot to write that Wednesday the 20th was Ash Wednesday, but to us here it was just another day, just as it was on Christmas. We slept the whole day yesterday, waking this morning around (04:00) and starting our same old routine we usually do. Card playing, chess, exercising, and a little bit of getting on each other's nerves. Nothing more to write about, just trying to stay busy to keep our marbles intact. Will there ever be a solution to this problem? *End of entry.*

30

Wrote some replies to some more letters yesterday. Hopefully soon I'll have answered everyone. Writing really makes the time fly by, but what really disappoints me is I keep repeating myself in each letter I write. What can I say? There's really nothing more to talk about.

Mailman came in with some word yesterday that kind of excited us at first, but ended kind of discouraging. He said that the papers back home had stated that we were supposedly to have been released last week, but as our families and loved ones can see, someone told the mass media a lie! Got everyone worked up for nothing. My heart dropped to the floor when he told us we were that close to going home, but still here we sit. Really a discouraging moment! I hope our families are doing well, especially after hearing that we were to be released and then finding out it wasn't true. So close, but still so far away! Mailman's still assuring us that something's going to be done within the next several weeks regarding our release. I think they're just saying that to keep us off their asses. Every time they come in here we ask them when we're going home. So I guess they figure that's the best phrase to use. Then at other times, when other students come in and we ask them when we'll go home, they come up with the real facts. When Shah comes back, you go home! Those no doubt are the real facts, and if they continue to hold to those thoughts, we're going to be here a long time!! What a political scandal we've gotten ourselves into. Today it's been one hundred and twelve days we've been held. How many more await us?

Received mail last night, nothing from Jill, but I did receive one from my parents telling me that Jill is doing good, got another job so she's really kept busy. She must be working her rear end off. My parents also told me that Mrs. Ditch has really been upset over this ordeal. Sounds like Mrs. Ditch! I wish I knew who was holding Jill's mail back from me. But then again, there's so many things I wish I knew, but I don't! I'd love to hear from her though. My parents assured me that they were doing great, not to worry, just to take care of myself. That's parents for ya! They wouldn't tell you if anything was going wrong anyway. Just the same, I hope they're doing good! Jerry received nothing! That's a question he really wants answered, why he hasn't received any letters from his wife? He knows she's been writing, but still no letters. Excuse me! He has received one from her, ONE since Nov. 4th, 1979. Awful strange! Bill received one from his girlfriend, but nothing from his family. What's weird is Bill gets letters from his girlfriend but none from his family. It's the opposite for me. I receive them from my parents but none from Jill.

Been six days now since we've taken our last shower, and boy do I ever miss my two showers a day. Now in between every sixth day we just clean ourselves as best as possible by using the sink in the head to wash up. We really don't get dirty except when we're working out, and then we're only able to take a bird bath to clean ourselves. You don't get every part of your body, although we do try, the parts we miss just have to wait till shower day. Can't wait till that day comes where I'm able to put back on my old clean clothes and I'm able to take a shower whenever I want to. I wonder if such a day will ever appear?

From looking outside our barred window, I can tell it isn't as pretty as it was yesterday. Raining this morning, but yesterday the sun was shining with enormous light. The sky was as blue, as Jill would say, as my eyes. I remember her always telling me how she loved my eyes. To tell you the truth, that's probably the only reason she went out with me. I'm only kidding, but she did always talk about my blue eyes. Thinking of all those things really makes me homesick for her. I really do love that girl!!

Really amazing how things can change so fast. One day it's ugly, the next it's beautiful. Just as one minute we're free, the next we're taken hostage!

Green Jacket came in last night and told, I guess Bill and me, that the students are getting kind of disturbed about how we've been acting. We like to mess around when the days are really blue, but then again, what do you expect keeping two Marines locked up together in a little room? We have been getting a little belligerent with the students, but what else is there to do? They never taught us how to sit on our asses for one hundred and twelve days! These are some of the hardest days of my life so far. I know that relates to all the other hostages' feelings, too. If it doesn't, something's gotta be wrong with them.

He asked us if we could keep our voices down a little, and we told him we'd try but it would be hard. He mentioned something about peeking out the door, but I didn't catch all of it. I think it was just a warning that he didn't want to catch us doing it. Why would we do that anyway? The only problem we have with the door is that we sit there at times knocking for what seems like an eternity before someone comes to answer it. Then other times we get some students who sit right outside the door and listen to our conversation. I just take it they're trying to learn English, but they're too scared to come in to ask us to teach them so they just sit outside the door and listen to us. We've been calling them guards lately, but they insist that we call them students. They don't like the term guard, they say it sounds too cruel.

They don't want us to feel that we're in a prison; they want us to feel that we are their guests for a stay here in Tehran. The bad thing about the stay is they won't let us go anywhere.

I received two souvenirs yesterday; I guess I'll be able to call them souvenirs if we ever get out of here. Anyway, they were two small items carved out of wood, a face, and a pistol (of all things) with a broken barrel. Some of these guys are really good people, but then you get your bad ones, too. It's the same everywhere, you have good ones and bad ones.

We can hear the roach coach coming so they must be bringing breakfast. Room service hasn't been too bad lately! *End of entry.*

Sunday, February 24, 1980 (07:15)   Day 113

Another day passed and once again no news! The most exciting thing that happened yesterday was lunch. That's about the most exciting thing that ever happens anyway. We always look forward to it. We've got a guessing game every morning to guess what we're having. Usually I'm the best at that. Really had a good one yesterday, steak, baked potatoes, green beans, and bread. Really filled us up, but then again, it doesn't take much nowadays to do that. We're pretty well adapted to everything now, so food's no problem.

Switched doing dishes with Jerry this morning. He usually stays up in the morning after breakfast and at lunch time he usually crashes out when it's his turn to do them. Being a good guy like I am, I traded him breakfast dishes for his lunch dishes. Anything to change the monotonous routine.

Once again this morning Guard Chief and Mailman both emphasized that something in the following days ahead is going to happen. Sure! Something's going to happen in the following days, but the following days might be next week, month, or even following years. They don't give us any day, I wonder why? Probably because they don't even know. We have a strong feeling something's going to happen in March, hopefully it is! If not, I guess we'll have to shoot for another month.

Mailman just told us about a woman from California, Nancy Esther Thomas, U.S. citizen, who wrote a letter to George Hansen giving her opinion of the crisis over here in Iran. The title of the letter read, "U.S. Citizen Reveals Hansen Duplicity". Really an interesting letter! What a unique situation we're in. Will we ever be free again?

Looking outside our hazed window, it looks like another cloudy day. Doesn't really matter to us, we'll be in here all day. Thought for sure I heard the Marine Corps Hymn yesterday when I was in the

33

head doing the dishes. If I did hear it, it no doubt came from the head right next door. The walls are pretty thin, so you can hear just about everything that goes on in there.

The only other hostage I've seen since we left the Charge's house the morning of the 28th or 29th of December was Jim Lopez. Jim's one of the other Marine guards I graduated with and was assigned over here with. Accidentally saw him a couple weeks ago when we were over taking showers at the Charge's house. He didn't look too bad, getting a little skinny; his hair was getting long, too. I wonder what the Marine Corps says about our hair now? How great it would be to be FREE once again. *End of entry.*

Monday, February 25, 1980 (19:30)   Day 114

It seems as each day goes on we're starting to get back into our normal routine of sleeping at night and staying awake during the day. Yesterday after lunch I did the dishes, came back and read awhile before crashing out. Hopefully we'll get back into our normal lifestyle one of these days, meaning being FREE.

When I woke this morning I found four letters lying along side my mattress. Before I had a chance to open and read them, they came in and told us we were to take showers. They were in the day before, but we told them to come back this morning. I guess they figured it was time for us to have one. So here we were, off at seven o'clock in the morning, blankets over our heads, sandals on, marching out through the slush to the vehicle which was waiting to take us to the Mushroom. I should've never worn my socks. When we returned back to the room they were soaking wet, Jerry's and mine both. Bill was lucky. The students gave his shoes back when he went to that interview with those fifty Americans. They never asked for the shoes again so he's just kept them. The snow started around (03:00) this morning, ruining our walk in the courtyard. No fresh air this week. The Mushroom was closer so I guess they figured they'd take us there to shower. The place was definitely a lot cleaner from when we were living down there in December. Maybe they (the students) have some of the hostages held down there yet. If they do, we didn't hear or see anyone. There were a lot of students still down there; maybe they made it a home for themselves. Anyway the shower felt good, so good we didn't want to leave. One of the things I want to do whenever I get out of here is hit a nice hot tub of water. How relaxing that's going to feel.

Came back to our rooms right after and started where I had left off opening my mail. None of us got any letters from our families. Once again just different cards and letters from people throughout the world. It's really strange how we receive them from all those people, but hardly anything from our families or friends.

Some of the students wouldn't let Jerry and me work out together in the sport house, so we had to go in at separate times. I guess some students have different rules than others. The only thing we can do is go along with the program. I was the first one to go in and work out and as I walked through the door I could hear people yelling, chanting. We could hear a little from our room but not as much as I could hear in the sport house; it was loud! I was curious to know what was going on so I asked the guard what they were so happy about. First thing I asked him was if the Shah returned? He said no! Laughed and walked out. Been wondering why every time we ask them if the Shah's back or if he's coming they always laugh. I myself don't really think it's a laughing matter.

It sounded like a big crowd; some people were beating drums, too. Sounded like a big festival or something. After I walked in, Guard Chief followed me into the room and explained to us that the Iranian people were having a parade for their new President, also displaying the show of arms that Imam declared as everyone being part of the Military. Everyone that's able to carry a weapon, meaning children, too. I wonder if they're planning on going to war with someone? Hopefully not, especially while we're over here. We're in a big enough mess as it is, we don't need a war to help it out any.

We told the students tonight that we are getting tired of soup being served all the time and that we weren't going to have it anymore if it continued to be served every night. Since they're so protective about keeping us healthy, maybe we'll start to have something else besides soup every night. Cross my fingers on that one though. I don't know if I mentioned it earlier in my diary or not, but every morning one of the students comes around handing out vitamins. It's amazing how they want to keep us healthy. They're so determined that the Shah's going to return.

We asked them once what they would do if he never did return, shoot us or what? They said they would never shoot the ones who never did any harm, because it wasn't the Moslem way. They did say the ones that were accused of being CIA agents would be sent to court and then executed. They probably won't execute us; they'll just leave us over here for the rest of our lives. I know I'm talking over my head, but what else can they do if the Shah doesn't come back? Once again today they emphasized that in several weeks something would be happening regarding our release. I'm really looking forward to seeing what's going to happen. Someone's going to be called a liar if something doesn't.

Guard Chief keeps coming in wanting Bill to teach him karate, but Bill keeps telling him to come back the next day. Next day comes around Guard Chief never shows. All these guards want Bill to teach them karate. They really like karate, but then again, not like soccer. I take it that soccer's their main sport. Well, still no Shah, no freedom!! *End of entry.*

Tuesday, February 26, 1980 (23:00)   Day 115

Last night I felt the best I ever have; it was a spark to my life! I received my first letter from Jill last night. Such a beautiful and encouraging letter it was. I miss that girl so much; it's like she's already a member of the family. If I have it my way when I get back she'll be a member of the family real fast! She must've been writing from her new place of employment. The stationery she was using no doubt was advertising her new place of employment, "Anixter". She asked me in her letter if I've received any of her letters yet? So that tells me she hasn't received any of mine yet. Anyway it was so good to hear from her, such a morale booster it was!! This letter's going to go through hell until the next one comes, which I'm hoping is soon!!

It snowed all last night and I think we've gotten back to our normal routine of sleeping. We went to bed for the first time at the normal hour last night. I didn't fall to sleep right away. I laid in my mattress watching the snow fall and at the same time thought about how nice it would be, being with Jill walking along the road at their house in the country. Such a beautiful picture it was in my head, now if only it could come true!! I describe a treasure chest as being all the memories of home and all the dreams I dream of yet to come. All those things I'll hold close to me for the rest of my life! It's really a sad moment when you have to come back down to earth and face the reality of being here never knowing when we'll leave.

I really can't believe this is all happening just over one man. A man accused of murder, stealing and many other things but still our government keeps him under protection. Like I've said before, I'm not a person to judge if the Shah is innocent or guilty but what I do know is that there were a lot of people killed/misled and the person responsible should pay! I guess I'll never learn the truth about all this until I return home and see our point of view, too! The students are so determined that the Shah's going to return. We wish we were as determined, but we're not! Still each day and night we sit and pray, hoping that each next day will bring good news. There's still that sad feeling inside me hinting to be prepared for a long stay. How I hope that feeling is wrong!

The talk we had with some of the students last night regarding having soup every night must've worked out. Tonight for dinner we had spaghetti and fruit cocktail. At times it seems like they really take into consideration the things we say. They really try to make this stay as pleasant as possible, I'll give them that much credit! Things could be a lot worse but they're not. Their reason is, they believe in human rights. Taking over the Embassy isn't too good an example of practicing human rights, I wouldn't think. Their explanation for that was, to get everyone's attention worldwide! They sure succeeded. Such a unique situation we're in; I know I've said it before but I'll continue to say it for the rest of my life!!! No one can deny that, that's for sure!!!

Jerry and I worked out today, together this time. It must be the guard's decision, whoever's on at the time, to decide whether or not to let us go together. This student seemed pretty nice so he let us work out together. He even stayed in for awhile to work out with us. He knew a couple of exercises, so we did his and he did ours. They've got a pedal bike in there now, maybe I'll be able to get my legs back in normal shape with that. Jerry kind of likes it!

When we got back to the room Guard Chief was asking Bill once again when he was going to teach him karate. He wants to learn it so bad. He asked us if we would teach some of the students English and we told him we wouldn't have to teach them; they'd learn perfectly well for as long as we're going to be here just by listening through the door. From the sound of things, it sounds like we're going to be here a long time. For how long though? Hopefully my family/Jill are all doing well. *End of entry.*

Wednesday, February 27, 1980 (NO ENTRY!!!)   Day 116

Thursday, February 28, 1980 (13:05)   Day 117

One hundred and seventeen days today; how many more will there be? It's pretty cloudy today, just like it was yesterday. Bill went over to the Mushroom yesterday with Mailman to pick up some text books. If this ever gets over, I'll probably be getting out of the Marine Corps and maybe go back to school part time. Starting to do a little study to prepare myself—couldn't hurt.

Rearranged the room a little today, but really not much. The reason it probably looks so different is because I also cleaned it out, good! I guess I was getting tired of looking at the same thing every day so I decided to change the scenery around. It looks a little more like someone is living in it now. They brought the tape box back to us yesterday morning, and believe it or not, we're listening to the same tape we had in yesterday morning over and over. James Taylor's Greatest Hits. There's no problem with getting tired of it, we don't

37

hear music too often. Not too many tapes we like when they bring them. The ones we do find which we all like we constantly play over and over, not just for one hour but for twenty-four hours. The thing gets no rest around here.

Doc (the student doctor) was in to see us last night. Came to see how we were all doing. Wonder what the occasion was? I felt like I was getting hemorrhoids so I asked him if I could get some Preparation H? He said he'd see what he could find, but before leaving he talked to us a little more. It was about twenty or twenty-five days since we saw him last, so we just sat around and talked. Pretty good guy Doc is! I keep teasing him about how I want a ring like his. He says whenever we're released he'll bring me one. Whenever the students say encouraging things like that it really makes us wonder when we are going to be released?

A couple of hours after Doc left, some other students came in handing out goodies. Gum, Life Savers, pretzels, chocolate-covered cherries, nuts, and a Daffy Duck puzzle. They asked us how long we thought all that would last and we asked, "Why, how long are we going to be here?" They just laughed. Either they must have received all that through the mail or else they went out themselves and bought it for us, but WHY? First the Doc comes, then they bring us goodies. It sure seems like something's up. Maybe someone's coming to see us.

It's really good being back on the normal routine of sleeping during the night and staying awake during the day. I guess the nightlife just wasn't for me!! I wrote my parents yesterday telling them I had a sad feeling that we were going to be here a while, but not to worry because I was going good and holding out strong. Myself, I think we're talking about months maybe even years. It seems like it's going to take the Iranian people that long to understand that they're not getting the Shah back. I sure hope I'm wrong though. I don't know if I can hold out that long being kept in a room. I guess if it really came down to it, being held in a room that long, I guess I could do it. Just thinking about it makes me sick. They told the students at the beginning that they weren't going to get him back, and we're still telling them now. When will they learn???? What's really strange, whoever heard of a Government to hold hostages???? That's what we can't figure out. Once again, *when . . . when . . .* will these people ever learn that the Shah's never coming back???? *End of entry.*

Friday, February 29, 1980 (23:00)   Day 118

The students moved us to a new room last night right after dinner. They were saying lately that the room we were in was a little small for three people anyway, which we all agreed. I was kind of disappointed leaving right when the vent was giving off some good noises. It had just started that day, too.

Anyway our new room is much bigger than the other. Two barred windows, 4 ft. by 4 ft., which we are even able to open. Otherwise the dimensions of our new room are about 12 ft. by 16 ft., a lot roomier and a little better furnished. It's on the first floor of the Embassy, the side facing the beautiful snow-capped mountains which we would've been exploring this winter skiing if we weren't taken hostage. I don't know if the students brought the chairs in or if they were already in here, but they're really comfortable. Nicely leathered, swivel type. One huge desk we use to write letters and whatever else on, with one smaller one we use to play cards and eat on. We even have our own filing cabinet, but nothing to put in it. We've got our own air conditioning unit also, so I guess they're getting us ready for the summer months. It seems like the only thing we'll have to worry about are the mosquitoes. Been seeing a lot of them lately.

It shows by all the things the students have been doing that they're trying their best to make us comfortable as can be. They keep reminding us not to worry about going home, that we will eventually go. Sure wish we knew when. This morning about noon a professor from the university, who teaches engineering, at least that's what the students said, came to see us. He was by himself, no cameras, just the students following. He asked us a couple questions, how we're treated, fed, and so on. We told him we were being treated and fed good, but that we were waiting to go home. He said that we shoudn't worry about that, but that it was good to take four months off work and take a rest. We all got a kick out of that one. I had just gotten to Iran to work; I wasn't planning on a vacation so early. Wonder what his reason was for coming to see us?

Being in our new room for the first day we got fed awful good. Breakfast we had our normal cheese, butter, bread and tea. Lunch was a biggy; it always is when we get rice. Along with the rice we had chicken with a topping (sauce). Really filling! Dinner's what really topped it off. We had six hot dogs, potato salad, jello, and bread. We couldn't believe our eyes when they brought us six hot dogs each. We were wondering if they released some more hostages since we were getting fed more. What new adventures will happen tomorrow? Haven't heard from my parents for a while, hopefully they're well! *End of entry.*

Saturday, March 1, 1980 (NO ENTRY!!!)   **Day 119**

Sunday, March 2, 1980 (13:50)   **Day 120**

Well today is exactly four months from when we were taken

Hostage, 120 days! Jerry and I worked out in our new sport house which was made out of the RSO's office. Didn't really recognize the old office with all the furniture gone. Got a lot more room in there than we did downstairs, plus they brought up a few weights. It's not as cool as it was downstairs, so we had one of the guards open a window to let a little fresh air in. It looks as though the students use the room to sleep in, there's blankets, a couple pillows, and an alarm clock lying around. Posters of Imam and a couple revolutionary ones hanging up, too.

The students have really been good to us and they continue to say that any day freedom might arise. At times it seems as though they know when we're leaving, and then other times it seems they don't. They brought Bill some magic tricks that were sent from the States. They (the students) know that Bill likes magic, so they bring him all the stuff and occasionally come in for a performance. It seems as though they all get a kick out of it.

The meals have really been delicious lately, and really filling. They're even starting to bring seconds around making sure we have enough. They're still continuing to make our so-called visit as pleasant as possible, but still no day is mentioned of when we're to go HOME!! Never know, maybe our lucky day's tomorrow? *End of entry.*

Monday, March 3, 1980 (22:10)   Day 121

Just finished another book; this one was "Brian Piccolo". I can't believe all the books I've read since being here. Most of them I read I can't even remember anymore. Reading is absolutely a perfect way to pass the time, but at times we get to a point where we really get tired of reading and have to search for something else to do.

Didn't work out today; didn't really feel like it. Jerry really gets pissed at times when I tell him I'm not working out. He's really dedicated to his workout, really determined to go home with a new figure! I really shoudn't turn him down like I'm doing. I know exercising is great for passing the time and especially good from the physical point of view. Woke around the normal time this morning (09:30 or 10:00), ate breakfast and then played cards till lunch time. After lunch we were taken for showers and fresh air. Hercules was waiting for us in the courtyard once again. Still the playful dog he always was. The fresh air was great like always; too bad we couldn't stay out there all day!

It seems like they don't want us taking showers at the Charge's house anymore. They didn't say why, they just told us to put our blindfolds back on and we would be taken to take a shower. They dropped Jerry off at the DCM's house to take his and then took Bill and me over to the Mushroom to take ours. That was the first time they ever did that, and I know Jerry was wondering what was going on, him getting out and Bill and me staying in the car. They said the reason they did it like that was because one of us always had to wait when the other two were taking a shower. So by doing it like this we could all three take our showers at once. Anyway the hot water felt great and like always I didn't want to get out of it, neither did Bill. The hot water really seems to be helping my acne. Too bad we can't get hot water like this everyday. I've never had a problem with acne like I do now; wonder what's really causing it? At times I hate to look at myself through the mirror.

Washing our clothes has really been a problem, that's if we give them to one of the students to do. If we do them ourselves, we don't get them as clean as the wash machine, but at least we get them back. Recently we gave one of the students some clothes to wash for us. Two days later we asked the same student where our clothes were; he replied he'd have them back the next day. The next day came and here the student came with half our clothes. Really a screwy system they have for washing clothes. The famous one who does this is Jacob. Remind me to tell you a story about this guy. Other times when they bring the laundry they give us other hostage's clothes. We usually take them, figuring they'd take ours. It's really crazy sometimes.

They just recently brought mail to us, and like always Bill received a bundle. Jerry received one and I received three. None of us received any from our families once again. Bill's got one helluva fan club by all the letters he's receiving. Jerry isn't too happy when he doesn't receive one from his wife, but still he holds out great. Really all of us do! Something that really got to me tonight is that while handing out mail, Mailman was dropping and throwing our mail around the room. Of course he wasn't doing it to Jerry, which I was glad of; he was just doing it to Bill and me. Luckily he told us later that he meant nothing by it, that he was just messing around. It's really hard not to take them seriously, when here they are holding us hostage. Some of the things they do and say I try not to let bother me, but it really gets to be hard at times. I know I don't want to do anything foolish, so I just have to keep my cool. When will we ever leave here to return to our families and loved ones? *End of entry.*

Tuesday, March 4, 1980 (NO ENTRY!!!)   **Day 122**

Wednesday, March 5, 1980 (18:30)   **Day 123**

Green Jacket brought in a typewriter today which we can practice on. I think they're trying to get Jerry to start working on a book. At times Green Jacket (Mailman) would come in and emphasize to Jerry that he should start on a book. It's really strange though; they never say anything to Bill and me about writing one. I don't even think the students know about my diary entries.

Been practicing a little and got it down pretty good. I had a little typing in High School, but not as much as I did before coming on this program. Before coming on this program, Marine Security Guard, I was being broken in to become our Company's Training and Education NCOIC. The guy who was breaking me in (John Garrabrant) was supposed to be getting out of the Marine Corps in a couple of months, and meanwhile was assigned to break me into the new job. By the way, John was a homey of mine, St. Louis, Mo. As the days proceeded we started talking about Marine Security Guard duty, and at the same time I started to learn more and more about my new job as Training and Education NCOIC.

To make a long story short, John decided to reenlist for the MSG program, and we'd talked so much about it that it even interested me, so I went over and reenlisted with him. Since we were both going to reenlist and go to MSG school, the company had to find another person for the job I was supposed to take over, but now wasn't. Our Company Commander wasn't too mad, for I was reenlisting and he loved it. Well John and I went to MSG school together, graduating at the same time. He was assigned to go to South Yemen and I was assigned here. How lucky I was! No doubt John's laughing his ass off. I think yet to this day if I hadn't ever met him I might not be in this mess I'm in now. I'm only kidding, John was really a good guy that helped me out in a lot of ways. I know I'll have a lot to tell him if or when we ever get out of here.

I'm thinking about typing my diary out to give me something to do to pass the time. We're still being fed soup, but not as much as we were at the beginning. We're really being adequately fed and if you don't do any kind of exercises you will definitely get fat. The last time the student doctor was in, we asked him if we could get some vitamin A, E and wheat germ. Well today he brought them in for us. It's really ly amazing the things we ask for and if they can get them we'll have them. I know I've said that before, but this is what really gets me! Still they don't know when they're going to release us!

Occasionally we can still hear gunshots at night, and if we're still up the students will come in and make a joke about it. "Well, we just killed another hostage." We know they're only kidding, but still what are all the gunshots for? The shots don't really bother us as they used to. Now it's just one of the everyday noises we hear, no big deal! I

42

know they won't shoot us; at least that's how I feel now. Now if you would've asked me the first couple weeks, I would've said, yes, they'll shoot us, but to tell you the truth if we did try something like that, we'd never make it out. The only thing we can do is sit and wait.

I still have feelings, with all the things happening, that we'll be going home soon. I pray to God I'm right. Then other times just by the way the students say or do things I feel like we aren't going home until the Shah returns. If that's true, we're going to have a long wait. Like I said before, the only thing we can do is sit and wait and try to stay optimistic.

Now since we're in our new room we're able to have our window open all the time. It's really nice; we can smell spring coming on and at times feel a nice breeze blowing in. Whenever we want the window closed, we have to call one of the guards. They warned us not to ever look, or else! Both windows have parapets, so the only way we can look out, besides looking into the sky all the time, is looking over the parapet. That's one of our no-no's we can't do.

Green Jacket came in yesterday and hung pictures of Imam and a couple others of Carter kissing a little Mexican girl and right on the side of it was a picture of a little girl, who seemed to be in a camp of some kind. I guess they were trying to emphasize the kind of people the President associates with. The girl he was kissing was nice and clean where the girl on the other picture was crying, dirty, and unhealthy. Now why would they want to hang those pictures up in our room?

The other day they brought us candy and the doctor came in to check on us, and a day or two later the professor came to see us from the university. I told Bill and Jerry that I have a feeling someone's going to come see us. I guess we'll just have to wait and see.

Mailman just brought in a message that was supposedly written by the Iranian people addressed to the American People. I got the impression he wanted us to send them with our next letters. The letter mainly talks about the accused crimes the Shah supposedly committed, plus how our Government was interfering over here. I figure if the United States people don't know all these things now, they aren't ever going to know them. It looks as though the students are determined that the United States people are going to send back the Shah, not the government, the United States people! It's really hard to believe that something like this could happen without any action taken from our Government. Not unless the students here think there'd be a revolution in the States. How crazy are they, to think that something like that would ever happen in the United States? They're so sure that once all the people in the States hear these things about

Shah and the interference our Government has done, they'll send him back in no time. It seems like they're using the Viet Nam war as an example. The United States people protested about that and finally it was stopped, so now it looks as though they're hoping for the same thing to happen. He (Mailman) said that the Iranian people are thinking that the five men sent from the United Nations are just stalling around to make it look like they're interested in what they've found, but really they're not. They said they weren't too sure of them in the first place, because President Carter approved their coming here. What do you think when you hear things like this??

Read an article in the Washington Star where Betty Cuniberti was saying that the Olympics weren't doing too good. She summed it all up saying: "What an incredible hassle this has been for everybody. Recapping the events, it seems like a Mel Brooks movie!!" Such a turmoil the United States seems to be in; hopefully everything will turn out for the best, for our sake, too! God Bless America!! *End of entry.*

Thursday, March 6, 1980 (NO ENTRY!!!)   Day 124

Friday, March 7, 1980 (NO ENTRY!!!)   Day 125

Saturday, March 8, 1980 (14:25)   Day 126

This entry will include the last two days and a little of today, too. The sixth wasn't much different than any other day except we did get mail. None of us received anything from our families, but we did receive some encouraging letters from our fellow citizens. It's a great feeling to know that they're all back there praying and waiting for our return. Nothing striking catches my mind that happened the sixth. I remember it took them till (21:00 or 21:30) to bring our broth. Then again all meals have been served late, lately. Wonder what all the fuss is? I shouldn't really criticize our cooks; as far as I know they might be forced to stay to cook for us. Guard Chief was telling us a little while back that that wasn't true. He said the students were paying them $500.00 a month for cooking for us. If that's true, I guess I do have a right to bitch.

From some of the notes I took yesterday I had down that things were getting pretty bad, and that we were getting pretty tired of looking at each other. The things we bitch about, it could be a lot worse if we were put in solitary. Have to stop bitching (although I tried not to do it outloud). Have to face it that we do have it pretty good.

Meals are still filling as always. Last night instead of six hot dogs we received three. We made a little joke about that one. We thought maybe they went out and took some more people hostage so that's why we didn't receive as many as the last time. Music was brought in for us to hear last night. Two hours and it was gone, I guess to the other hostages. Sure wish we could have had it more, but then we have to think about the other hostages, too.

This morning was really bizarre in the room. It started off with Santa coming in with a questionnaire for us to fill out. It was asking three different questions. How have the students been treating us? How was the food, was it enough? And the last one, how were the sanitation facilities? I put that the students are treating us like human beings these last couple months, food is great and well filling. For the sanitation question I put that we've been limited on hot water, and then mentioned a little about my acne. After those were finished and collected we went about our daily routine.

Right after breakfast I was sitting on my mattress soaking my face with hot water when a student came in and wanted some pictures of us. I wasn't too happy about the thing, but like always Bill didn't mind, so after a little discussion/argument I finally gave in and he took some pictures, even some of me soaking my face.

After he left, a little while later Guard Chief and another student (one of the guys that wants Bill to teach him karate) came in and wanted Bill to go down and do some karate moves in the sport house. Bill told him he wasn't going to go down unless I went with him. I wasn't too much for the idea, but they were really wanting us to go down. They said they wanted to get a couple pictures for the students' sake and no one else's. We finally gave in and they took us down the hall to the sport house. We'd just stepped into the room when a T.V. camera and it's crew came in right after us. That really pissed me off when I saw that. They said it was only for the students' sake and here they bring in the T.V. camera and all. We did a couple exercises and then lifted a couple weights. I guess the T.V. crew had enough so they spoke to us for awhile and then left, and we returned to our room.

We were back in our room playing cards when a commotion stirred outside our room, stopped for a second, and the door opened. In walked a man (a doctor) with a stethoscope around his neck and the instrument to take your blood pressure with in his hand. In the other hand he had a notebook and pen. Right behind him once again were our good friends from the T.V. crew, along with the students of course. We had to write our names on an empty piece of paper so when he checked each of us he could put the results down. The doctor said they were for our families, so they'd know we were all right. Why don't they just let us go; then they wouldn't have to worry about all this? The cameras were rolling again, making sure they got the doctor

45

touching all of us. They even got Bill's little act he put on. They'll really like that back in the States.

I got to talk to the guy that was shooting the film, asking him how the Olympics were doing and so on. Right as he was leaving, being pushed out the door, I told him I wished I could be home to watch the Summer Olympics this summer. He turned around while being pushed, winked his eye and said that I would!! I would be home this summer to see the Olympics on television. He kept saying not to worry, and at the same time he and one of his crew members kept winking whenever something was mentioned about going home. I'll never forget those encouraging words he said and I just pray to God he was right!!! He really seemed sure of himself, too. It seemed like he wanted to tell us more, but couldn't.

Forgot to mention that last night when Mailman came in to pick up the tape recorder he mentioned that next week he'd give us some news (good news!). Boy how I wish next week was already here. Maybe our time has come! Oh how I pray to the Good Lord that it's true. He was mentioning something about a girl he met lately and was thinking about getting married. Now if he was shooting the shit or telling us the truth, that I guess we'll never know. Here they are telling us about how they are thinking about getting married and here we sit, thinking and worrying about what our families are thinking and how they are making it. Still the kidding goes on like nothing is really happening. What a joke!

(21:00) Nine o'clock at night and we're still waiting for dinner. We just got finished playing UNO. I guess we were playing for about two and a half hours and didn't even know that much time had passed. Boy how time passes when you're having fun. Also Guard Chief was just in to talk to us. He gave us some encouraging words/thoughts if that's what you can call them. He thought we'd be out of here in five months. That was his own feeling. Hopefully he was wrong, hopefully it's earlier. I can't see myself staying here another five months, but if it calls for it I guess I could do it.

Jerry's been a little discouraged about what the doctor had to tell him today. The doctor thought Jerry was a lot older than he is when he listened to his heart. I told Doc that we had been working him out a little lately, and he replied that we shouldn't overdo it. I guess we'll have to cut the workout down a little. He's been keeping himself pretty busy with those puzzles of his. Everyday you see him working on them, but he seems never to run out of them. During the days I usually catch him trying to lay on his rack and crash out, but I catch him and tell him not to rest now or else he won't sleep tonight. He says he's been having a hard time sleeping, but from my ears I can't tell any

46

problems. He still snores. The only thing I can tell is that he wakes early in the morning, but of course he's used to that, just like my Dad waking at (05:00) in the morning, every morning.

Tonight one of the students came in and asked why this room is so noisy? I guess they've been getting pissed off about us yelling all the time. We always do this when we've got things on our mind we want to get off. What else can we do when we're frustrated? In my whole life I've never been in bed longer than 48 hours, and here we are being kept in a room for 126 days! What a change of life. I guess whatever you set your mind to do, you'll do.

Bill just said he'd seen Sgt. Moueller walking down the hall with his blindfold on. They must've been taking him to the head at the west end of the Embassy. Wonder who else they've got down here? The students were saying that the U.S. Government doesn't even know how many hostages the students have. After 126 days they still don't know; how strange. I think there's about 50, but the students say there's more. They should know, they're holding us!

Bill just had some spectators in for his magic show. One of them was Juggler. He seems to be a pretty good guy, always giving new ideas about things to do. Whenever he comes in we're always competing against him in different things. He really seems to be a good athlete and especially a good chess player. It's amazing how we have to give all the students names such as Juggler, Mailman, Guard Chief, Santa Claus, etc. They don't wish to give us their real ones, so we just make them up.

About two minutes ago they brought in three oranges and that was it. I sure hope they're not planning on just feeding us that; if they are, there's going to be hell in the hot town tonight! *End of entry.*

Sunday, March 9, 1980 (15:20)   Day 127

Once again this morning we had the movie cameras, and a girl (might have been Mary the Kidnapper) came in to do an interview on the same questions that were on the questionnaire we filled out yesterday. I kind of thought something was up last night when one of the students came in and wanted to talk to Bill. Bill was sleeping, so I asked them if there was anything I could do for them. He asked if we would want to do an interview for the students. I asked him for what; he replied on the same questions that were on the questionnaire. I told him we already filled out a questionnaire, why do you want it again? He said it was for the students once again, and then left. That's what the same guy said this morning when he wanted some pictures of Bill and me. Here they came with T.V. cameras and everything else. I guess the guy finally got the message that we (Jerry and I) really didn't care for the situation, and finally left.

Later this morning, the same guy came in again and asked Bill if he wanted to do it. Bill figured there wasn't any harm in doing it, so he agreed. We thought they were going to shoot it somewhere else, but they all started to come in and set everything up. That was getting me pissed off so I asked them what they were doing. Like I figured, I guess since they asked Bill and he approved, they assumed that Jerry and I would do the same thing. Well I told them Mr. Plotkin and I weren't doing it, we never gave our okay, and we were getting sick and tired of being used as propaganda.

They assured me that it wasn't going to be put on television, it was just for the use of the students. Santa finally came in and assured me that it wasn't going on television; it was just for the students. Well after a long while of arguing I finally decided to do it. I was really pissed though. Why would they be using all these pictures? I think I heard someone say it was for their school yearbook, what a joke! Really been getting pissed lately with all these pictures they've been taking. It just looks like going home is that much further away. Hope not though.

(17:25) Political Prisoner was just in, along with six or seven other students to get some pictures. At first he came in and just asked if he could get some pictures for his scrapbook. It seemed strange, but we agreed. Right as we sat down, the door opened and in came the students. After the students were behind us and Political Prisoner was taking pictures, he finally told us that they were going to be sent home to our parents so that they know that we are among friends, friends that won't let us have our freedom! Now I know what the animals in the zoos feel like. Make it look like we're having a great time, then we'll be able to stay here longer. How much more of this can we take? *End of entry.*

Monday, March 10, 1980 (18:00)   Day 128

One hundred twenty-eight days today and still no one knows when we're leaving. The only answer they give us is when the Shah returns we go home. I guess it's as simple as that.

Just finished reading two books within the period of last night and now. Can't believe how my vocabulary and speed in reading books has increased while being here. At least I can see one good thing coming from this situation. I've never been the type to just grab a book and start reading it, that is until now. I was never a scholar in grammar/High School, just did what was required, a little extra and that's all. At times I can slap myself in the face for things I wish I would have done better, most of all paying attention more. I was too much

48

involved in sports, which I enjoyed dearly.

To this day I still get pictures in my head of all the sports I participated in. Those were the good old days! In fact, I've been having a lot of dreams lately of my days in high school. They're so clear it's like I was really there, replaying it all over again. I can still remember Coach Scanlan's face that night at St. Francis Borgia's basketball game when I told him I enlisted into the Marine Corps. At that time he was working on getting me a scholarship to a small school for football. I guess you can say I had a chance back then, but I messed it up! At that time I really couldn't see myself going to college and now look at me. If that's true about the draft coming back, it looks as though I would've been coming in anyway. My number would have popped up sometime or other. I would've been graduating this year. I could've came in as an officer. I wonder how many of my friends are going to have to come in??

Mailman came in last night acting dumpy about the incident that happened earlier that day regarding all the pictures that were taken. So we had to fill him in on all the incidents. We told him we didn't really care for all that shit, and if anyone ever wanted to take any more pictures, he (Mailman) had to come in and tell us what it was for. Surprisingly enough he apologized and said it would never happen again.

By all the sounds coming from outside it sounds as though the students are playing soccer or volleyball out in our softball/football field. It started a couple of days ago and has been going on ever since. Yelling and screaming having a good old time. I told Mailman to let us get a team together, hostages against the students on a game of American football, but he said nothing. I know I'm talking a little crazy, but it would be a great way to get revenge on the takeover of the Embassy. Myself, I think the Marines could kick their ass!!!

The demonstrating seems to be going on every day with people giving speeches over the loudspeakers. What they're talking about we never know. I guess it's better like that. It sure shows me that these people are really dedicated to this cause. Shooting has still continued, for reasons unknown to us. Really as long as they keep their aim away from the Embassy, they can shoot as much as they want. I've really been wondering how many people have been killed by misuses of weapons over here. I don't think we've been through a night that there hasn't been a shot. Trigger happy people! Well Easter's right around the corner and it seems as though we'll be spending that holiday over here, too. How lucky we are.

(22:10) Mailman was just in to drop off some music, grape powder and some encouraging news. Before he started, he told us that what-

49

ever he said we shouldn't pass on to the other students, because the other students don't think we ought to know what's going on. I think the only reason he said that was because he knew we're still pissed off about all the pictures being taken, so he thought he'd cheer us up by telling us a little news.

Anyway, he said that in a couple of days the U.N. committee would be ending their investigation of the Shah's accused crimes. Mailman said that an attorney the Iranian people hired had a ton of documents of crimes the Shah had committed. How could they go wrong with that many documents? I hope this attorney the Iranian people have hired is something like Perry Mason who always wins his cases. If the U.N. committee doesn't find him guilty, no one will.

Maybe my movie camera friend was right about being home to watch the Summer Olympics. Mailman brought in a picture of Bill that was taken at his first interview. He was saying the Iranian people have a group of pictures that they had bracketed, and Bill was among the top ones. Anyway Bill was bracketed number 94. He even said I had a picture, but forgot what I was bracketed. Jerry too, I believe. Big celebrities we are over here!

Listening to a little James Taylor now while I'm writing my diary. Gives me something to do, plus whenever we get out of here someone might want to read it, so I've decided to start typing it all out from the beginning. Jerry's sitting here next to the lamp reading his book. Bill's getting ready to crash out, and he really gets disturbed about the light being on. So not to start any fuss, we turn it off and we all go to bed. That's what I call sticking together! Hoping and praying that everything is well back in Missouri. Think of my family/Jill so much. Pray to God they're WELL! With God's will, we will be home soon! *End of entry.*

Tuesday, March 11, 1980 (21:25)   Day 129

Just finished another dinner of soup and now Jerry and I are sitting around waiting for our evening tea. Today was kind of busy for us, considering the only thing we usually do is sit in our rooms every day. To start if off they took us over to the courtyard to get some fresh air and to play with Hercules for a while. It was really beautiful, around 75 or 80 degrees. After we gathered our solar energy, we were put back into the car and taken to the Mushroom to shower. This time we all went together, not to the "clean shower", but to the other one on the other side. This thing was a mess, but at least it did have hot water. We made the mistake of taking a shower first, when Guard Chief had asked us if we'd clean it out. I guess we were so anxious to get into the shower we didn't really care. So after we were finished taking our hot shower we did a little clean up. By the time we were finished we were just about the same as when we first got down there. We washed our feet off a little, and then talked to a couple students before Guard Chief came and got us.

I forgot to mention the little encounter I had with an Uzi* when we entered the head to shower. One of the students was there on the pot; he must have been on duty or something because he had his Uzi sitting on a chair. The student that took us in there must never have seen it as he passed. I was the last one in and as I was waiting by the chair I happened to look down and see an Uzi. So easily I could've reached down and picked it up—and done what? That's what kept flashing through my head, what would I do if I did pick it up? I figured one Uzi couldn't take on the whole city of Tehran, plus I would've been taking the risk of all the other hostages lives, too. So many things started flying through my head, pick it up, don't pick it up!

Just then one of the students came up behind me and grabbed it, as the student that owned it came out of the shitter. We both looked at each other, and the one grabbing the Uzi smiled. I'll never forget that chance I had to grab it, but didn't. I hope the decision I made, I won't be sorry for later!

When we returned to the room the window was opened all the way. I guess they wanted to give the room a little airing out before we came back to stink it up again. A beautiful breeze was flowing in; really felt great. Right after we returned they brought in lunch consisting of roast beef, potatoes, spinach, bread—tasted great! Last night we had a dinner consisting of chili, but there wasn't enough. We kept waiting for them to bring more back, but they didn't. That was a bitch, no seconds!

We're two doors down from the head, but still they make us put a towel over our heads to go there, with a student to guide us. This thing's really starting to be a big joke. I think they're really paranoid about us trying to escape. Mosquitoes are really getting to be bad around here lately; hopefully they're not carrying any kind of diseases like malaria or yellow fever. Being in this situation is bad enough; we don't need any diseases to help it out any. Mailman came in tonight to take the tape player. We've been listening to that James Taylor tape over and over every time we get to listen to music. I'll give it a couple more weeks before we have to throw it away from being worn out. When, when will we ever be free. *End of entry.*

51

*An Israeli 9 mm submachine gun

Wednesday, March 12, 1980 (22:20)

To tell you the truth, not jack shit happened today. Jerry and I worked out once again doing our usual sit-ups and push-ups. Trying to keep our bones and joints in a good working order. Maybe one of these days we'll get out of here.

Mailman came in today bringing some orange powder (Kool-aid), but then took two other grape bags. He also left us some Nestle hot cocoa mix which Bill and I already drank. We left Jerry's though. He also brought us some coconut. I could've eaten a whole bag of that tonight for dinner instead of the soup we had. Here the soup's only juice; it's nothing like the stuff Mom made at home with all the goodies in it. Otherwise, besides the soup, all the other food is pretty good, really filling!

Still remembering what the doctor said about not working Jerry out too hard. He can usually do 40 sit-ups but I've only been having him do 25, which really gets him pissed off. I told him the only thing we can do is play it safe, at least until he gets out of here and gets a physical. Here I am sitting at the desk looking at the chess set. You can really tell no one has played for a while, there's dust all over it. We've been mostly sticking to ourselves, reading books, playing a little cards, and for myself, working a little on my diary. Jerry really gets bored at times when Bill and I are reading and nothing is said between us, but Jerry just continues on reading, staying as strong as ever. How much more of this can we take? God Please Help Us and Take Us Home! *End of entry.*

Thursday, March 13, 1980 (23:00)

We've got Jerry reading his watch in military time now. I guess Bill's and my military is rubbing off on him. He's starting to turn military all the way. Typing my diary has really been keeping me busy, and I'm gaining experience, too. This afternoon Mailman came in and asked if we would like to go out and get some fresh air. We usually don't go out for fresh air until we take showers, so it seemed like something was up. We had just taken a shower two days ago, and weren't expecting to take another one till next week. We all agreed of course! Whenever there's a chance to go out and get fresh air, we'll always grab it.

Once again the blankets were put over our heads and we were led to the car that was waiting for us down at the basement west exit to take us to the courtyard. Flash Gordon, the guy I gave a hard time the other day when he wanted to take some pictures, was over there to take some more. Once again he said it was for the students only, but then they kept making it look like it was just for the students' use. Wanted pictures with Hercules, and then some of Bill swinging on the clothesline pole. I think he finally said they were going to be sent to our families so they can see how we're doing.

The weather was really nice, pretty clear to see the mountains too. They still have pretty much snow on them, really looks nice. Yelling and screaming was heard once again today from outside. They must have been playing soccer or volleyball. Sure wish we could've been out there! Not much talking over the loudspeakers today; wonder what happened there? One hundred and thirty-one days today we've been held hostage. Maybe the United States did forget about us! Maybe I ought to ask for some citizen papers for Iran since I'll never be leaving here. It seems like no one wants these fifty lost sheep.

Mailman brought us some dominoes today. I've never played the game before, but I know I'll learn real fast here. He also dropped off a Mad magazine for us to read. It seems like he's getting these things somewhere, maybe through the mail? If he is getting them through the mail, maybe we'll have some from our families. We haven't heard from any of our families for a long time. No mail, No freedom, No nothing.

The only nice thing that happened today was I heard a bird early this morning chirping outside our window. I had my head under the covers at the time and I was trying to imagine I was at home, but when I lifted the covers I found myself here. What a terrible way to start a day. *End of entry.*

Saturday, March 15, 1980 (11:50)   Day 133

Didn't have time to write last night; Bill, Jerry and I had a long discussion after dinner (21:00) that ran into the late hours of midnight. The discussion consisted of a little bit of everything, but most of all it was a time of throwing everything that was bothering us off our chests. Everyone had a few things to say to each other, bad and good, but not once did the discussion get carried away. At times voices got a little high, but they gradually went back down to normal. Hopefully the discussion made a little impression on each of us on how to make our stay here with each other a little more helpful and pleasant. It was the first time we've had a discussion like that, and I know there were a lot of things on each of our minds that we had to tell each other.

The exercise room had been closed down for some odd reason yesterday, so Jerry and I had to do our excercises in the room. Wonder why they closed it? Played dominoes for the first time last night which

53

started with a little argument on how to play with three people. San-ta must have been in his office next door and heard us discussing dominoes, so decided to come over and see what was happening. We told him what the problem was and instead of finding us a three handed game, he taught us a two handed game. Once he saw that everything was under control, he left. At times it's really hard to believe that we're really hostages when Santa's around. He's always got something funny to say to brighten up a day. Great sense of humor!

Mailman came in this morning right after we finished up our discussion, and told us some very discouraging news. He said the committee (U.N.) had left three days ago. He said that before they left, the Iranian people had made a deal with them. If they publicize the Shah's crimes nationwide the Iranian people would allow the committee to come see the Hostages. Then if everything went well and the Shah was released from the United States, we would then be released. He said that the committee had just left Iran without saying anything about us. That was sure nice of them. After telling us that, he left and came back a little while later with mail for all of us. Jerry received one letter from his mother and two from his wife. He even received some pictures, which really topped it off. The guy was on cloud nine! Like always Bill received quite a few, but nothing from his family or girlfriend. I received one card from some people in St. Louis. Nothing from my family though. Hopefully they're all doing well. The letter Jerry received from his mother (Feb. 4) was saying that they were expecting us to be freed any day now according to the news on T.V. I sure hope they're not still sitting in front of the television waiting. No good news. No nothing.

Somehow we got on the subject of punishment, so Mailman was telling us about Lopez being punished for cursing at a guard. They said they put him in solitary, but didn't say how long. Lopez is pretty strong, in the head that is, and as long as he can have books to read nothing can bother him. Hopefully he's got books! I can't believe this is all happening to me! *End of entry.*

Sunday, March 16, 1980 (12:30)   Day 134

They brought music in yesterday for us to listen to and this time they brought some John Denver, which really made us think about home, especially Bill. We had it in the morning, and then around noon they passed it on to the other hostages. The only exciting thing that really happened yesterday was that we got tapioca served for dessert with our soup. Not too often do we get dessert, and when we do it's a real treat. This morning we were awakened by thunder and lightning which startled all of us, especially Jerry. Now that I think of it, that was the first time I've ever heard it do that in Tehran. Encountering new adventures every day it seems like.

Going on our 134th day today and still no encouraging word of freedom. No maybes, No mights, No nothing! Sure hope my family/Jill are all doing well. Really do miss hearing from them.

Mailman brought in a treat of gum this morning but not too many words were passed between us. How much longer will the students keep our freedom from us? *End of entry.*

Monday, March 17, 1980 (10:55)   Day 135

Happy St. Patrick's day! Starting out another boring day here at the Tehran Hilton and let me tell ya, what a bore it is! We've been getting to the point where we hardly say anything to each other except when we ask Jerry what time it is. When it gets to be around an hour before eating, we usually break from whatever we're doing and play a little cards until they come with the food. Trying to find new and exciting things to do as each day continues. The old things are getting boring.

They had us fooled yesterday for lunch thinking the cook had left us. Instead of coming with the daily special, they came in with rice/spinach topping. I put the topping to the side and just ate the rice with a little ketchup they brought in. Bill did the same as I, but didn't finish his rice so I finished it for him. Jerry found it all pretty appetizing and ate it all. When they brought in the tea I guess they noticed we didn't eat most of the topping so they asked us if we would like some spaghetti? Bill said sure, I was full, but Jerry said he'd have a little. A little while later the student came back with a spaghetti out of a C-Rat box. Jerry had never had a C-Rat before so to kill his curiosity Bill gave him a little which he fixed by putting over the small heater we had here in the room. He really found it to be delicious.

Dinner is when they fooled us by bringing in steak, mashed potatoes, carrots and bread. I guess they thought they'd change the monotony a little and switch the meals around; anything's helpful! Mailman just brought in some powdered milk, which we've been asking for. I believe the last time we had milk was around the end of November or the first part of December. We were still living in the Mushroom at the time.

I remember how my mother would always buy powdered milk, but none of us kids would drink it because it tasted awful. Here we can't be choosey so I'm going to learn to like it real fast. My Mom always said that the day would come that I wouldn't have the real stuff and

I'd have to do with powdered; well, she was right the day has come. How much longer are we going to have to hold out here? I praise the Lord for giving me the strength he has for holding out this long. How much longer will it be though, before I get up some morning and take a swing at one of these students? So many times lately I've had that thought, but I desperately hold myself back. I ask myself what situation would it put me in (or even my fellow comrades) if I did? Probably just in a worse situation then what I am.

It seems like the students know when we're in these moods so they come in and try to cheer us up, or ask if there is anything reasonable they can get for us. I admire the students that do this, but on the other hand I wonder why they don't just release us and that would solve the problem of pleasing us. They got the Shah out of the country and their new Islamic government is starting into effect soon so why do they want to do this? I'm still saying my rosary every night hoping and praying that the good Lord hears my prayers and takes us to freedom. *End of entry.*

Tuesday, March 18, 1980 (11:20)   Day 136

We broke the monotony yesterday afternoon by reading our books till about (16:00) and then played cards till about (20:30) when dinner came. Cards are really getting boring to play with only three people. We asked Mailman a couple of days earlier if we could get another person in our room. He asked for some suggestions on who we'd want. We said "Lopez" or "Odie". He said he had to take it up with the Committee. Last night he came back and said that Mr. Odie didn't want to leave his room because he had the sun shining in his room and we don't. I could understand why he wouldn't want to move in with us. It'd be pretty crowded for him and plus we'd probably drive him crazy.

Mailman said that the Committee wouldn't allow three marines together, so that's why they didn't move Lopez in with us. We'd really have a great time if they brought him here. We'd probably switch the situation around on them and take them hostage. Oh yes! Yesterday was St. Patrick's Day and I'm surprised they didn't feed us green rice.

Mailman gave us some news last night, which like always we don't know if it's true or not. But anyway he said the Iranian people were planning on doing something about our release, and then he brought up the month of June. But he said that if the Shah is returned earlier, then we would be set free. So now it looks as though June's our month to shoot for. Even if we don't know if he was lying or not, it's still a little encouraging.

The Iranian New Year is in three days (21 March) and they asked us what we would like to do for it. We replied, "We'd like to go home." They asked us if we would want to have a celebration and we told them whatever they want they could have. They are holding us hostage; we aren't holding them. It's pretty kind of them to invite us to their New Year celebration. But no doubt they want us there so they can make up some more propaganda on T.V. and etc. I guess we'll have to wait and see what the outcome is Friday.

Mailman just came in and told us that we would be seeing a movie tonight on videotape. Of what? That's a question to be answered once they start showing it. Hopefully American.

We had a visitor in our room last night while playing cards, a mouse. Don't know where he came from, but he escaped underneath the door that connects the room next door. Jerry and Bill saw him first. I had my back turned, but they said he was running back and forth behind my mattress. I wonder how long he's had that turnpike behind my mattress. I've never been bit, so he must be a friendly one. I don't know if I wrote it earlier, but when we were down in the basement at nights you could hear something in the ceiling. Something big running around. It sounded like a cat, but I doubt if there are any cats in the ceiling, probably rats! The holes we found in the walls don't seem big enough for rats to get through. We're just hoping we're right. But still keeping our eyes open for those little mice. I'd hate to wake some morning and find one in my pants.

Some students told us last night that the people they accused of being CIA have been kept in a room by themselves and had no one to talk to. They tell us how lucky we are being kept in a room with three people and they are by themselves, which is true! I pray to God that if we ever leave here, that we all leave and we all leave together. *End of entry.*

Wednesday, March 19, 1980 (11:25)   Day 137

One hundred and thirty-seven days of being captive and yet no positive news of when we'll be released. It's a beautiful day today, not like yesterday raining and all. We're supposed to be taking a shower today so that means fresh air, too. Hercules will be over there like always so we'll be able to play with him. Something different besides playing cards and reading every day.

The weather's getting warmer as the days pass; you're able to hear more motorcycles from outside our window running up and down the back of the Embassy. If I ever get out of here, I'd like to get myself a bike. I always wanted one, and I know I'll have enough money saved up to get one. That's if we ever get out of here.

Never went to see what we were supposed to see last night, and also Mailman said we were supposed to go over to the library yesterday to pick up some books. Why he never came to get us for either I'll never know. We were here in our rooms all day like always. I guess it just goes to show whatever they say you can't believe. Just like they think something will happen between now and June for our release. I think they were just saying that, too.

Mailman told us some news that was in an Iranian newspaper of how the United States is interfering in Iran again. He said that the United States sent a city in Iran (Treprez) three billion dollars to help fight Imam's followers. I wonder where the newspapers received all their information? I think it's a lie, but then I don't know what's going on outside in the world. Not even with my family! I hope they're all well. Not too much going on around here, except for the fact that we're waiting to get the fuck out of this situation! *End of entry.*

Thursday, March 20, 1980 (13:00)   Day 138

Just returned from taking a shower which we were supposed to take yesterday but never got around to it. It was another beautiful day with the sun shining bright, which made it really warm. Hercules was there once again so we had our usual play session which we all enjoyed a great deal.

Today at (14:00) the Iranians start their celebration of their Christmas and New Year. I think they decided on not having us participate in their ceremony knowing that none of the hostages really gave a damn. The only thing we want is to go home.

Mailman came in this morning early and told us that we would be moving again, upstairs. The reasons he gave us were because there were too many people down here using one head and that we were able to see the mountains a lot better. Hell, we can see the mountains right from this room but if they want to move us, they're the captors!

He brought up the subject about phone calls again. He said the Committee decided on Bill to call home because his family seemed the poorest. He said that Jerry and I could write out some messages for our own family and Bill could read them to his parents, then send it on to our families. I'd like to know why the Committee keeps picking Bill for these things. Another thing, how do they know Bill has a poor family? Sometimes I get so fucking sick of some of the bull shit they feed us. I think they're holding my mail back from me. I've received one letter this month so far and nothing from my family since last month, but the letter I got was written about January 14 which was late news of their health. I wonder who's playing games with my mail?

Yesterday afternoon we didn't do much of anything except for the usual, read and play cards. The meals have been adequate. Last night with our hot dogs and potato salad we had some fruit cocktail, which was great. Mailman came in yesterday and told us that they'd try to show us a movie sometime this week. Then this morning he came in and said they'd show us one tonight. He said he went out himself and bought a movie for us which cost $50.00. How true that is only God knows.

Had a little argument with one of the guards last night. He wanted me to close the door after I walked out of the room to go to the head. He was a new guy. I guess he was supposed to be a hard ass or something. Here we are going to the head blindfolded and he wants me to close the door after I come out of the room. All the other guards usually understand our situation and they close it for us. Then you get some real assholes who close the door right in your face and then we walk right into it blindfolded. There aren't too many guards like that though, more good than bad. *End of entry.*

Friday, March 21, 1980 (15:20)   Day 139

Well we got moved once again last night, to the top floor of the Embassy, just above the last room we occupied. You can see the mountains a lot better from up here, but the room itself is about the same size or maybe a little bit smaller than the other one. We got a feeling that they moved us because Bill wrote his and my name down in the head, on a clover leaf they had hanging. Right before we left from down there I went to the head and discovered a typed message stating: "Hostages, please do not write on the walls!" We figured that was the reason we were moved.

Slept pretty good in our new room. Got a little cold, but I sleep better when it's cold. Awful cloudy out today. Looks like rain. Not hot though. I've found out that the weather has a lot to do with the way we act, so I hope the sun shines tomorrow. Mailman just brought us a plant awhile ago and asked us if we'd like to care for it. We said sure, it gives us something to do.

They took us downstairs about an hour ago and showed us two German teams playing soccer on television. I liked it for two reasons and I believe Jerry and Bill did too. For one, we all like sports, and the other, it's a change of schedule. The last time I watched any television was December of last year when the students showed us some picture of their revolution. Anyway, we all enjoyed the soccer game, or what we saw of it.

We all three had a great workout this morning in the room here.

We had something different, a jump rope! We all built up a pretty good sweat jump-roping and lifting weights. Really good workout. We even played handball with one of the tennis balls, right here in the room. The guards kept coming in checking to see what all the commotion was about, but we had a good time playing it. Like the old saying goes "Do with what you got", and that we're doing!

Once again this morning Jerry had another religious experience. We had just finished working out and I was in the head cleaning up. Jerry had just walked from the table to the window and was looking up in the sky asking the good Lord to make this be over soon. He then turned around and started to walk back across the room to the table, when all of a sudden he heard a sound coming from the window. He turned around facing the window, and right there, on the outside of the window sitting on a bar, was a gray and white dove looking right at him. He said he motioned to Bill. Bill looked up, seeing it too. The bird then turned and flew off. They said they were both stunned. When I returned from the head they told me about it. Some of the things we've experienced here we'll never forget as long as we live. How wonderful the Lord works. *End of entry.*

Saturday, March 22, 1980 (13:50)   Day 140

Students brought in some goodies last night to help celebrate their New Year's—coconut, gum, chocolate covered cherries, nuts, cookies, brownies and soda pop. Believe me, those cookies and brownies were tremendously enjoyed, although I only had two cookies and one brownie. They were great.

Bill went down to call last night but never got through. Jerry and I both had messages written for Bill, so he could pass them to his parents and then pass them on to my parents and Jerry's wife. So much for that. Mailman even brought music for us last night. John Denver, James Taylor and an empty Linda Ronstadt cassette container. I would have loved to hear her. John Denver and James Taylor are all right though. It's really hard to believe we still have the recorder. Usually they only let us have it for two hours. I sure ain't going to complain to anyone about it though.

Didn't eat breakfast this morning. Neither did Bill. I was pretty tired from that workout we had yesterday morning. I think it was the jump rope and handball. My calf muscles are really sore, which I'm glad of. At least now I know they're getting a workout. They were getting awful small on me. Have to continue that jump rope and handball. Good for reflexes.

Just finished writing two cards, one to my parents, the other to Jill.

There's really not much to say to them. To tell you the truth I keep repeating myself in each letter I write. I hope they're all well. Time's been spent lately just remembering the past. All the good things and all the bad. Boy how I wish I was back in high school. Best times I've ever had were within those four years. If I didn't have my memory, I don't know how I would have survived this thing so far.

Santa Claus and the Juggler just stepped in to say hello and just walked back out. Santa Claus was carrying a big bag that looked like mail. We asked him if we had any. He said no. So much for mail. *End of entry.*

Sunday, March 23, 1980 (15:00)   Day 141

I hung all my pictures last night, and the more I look at them the more I want to go home. Our room's so bare you can hear an echo sometimes when you talk. Wish we had some more pictures to hang. The only thing we have in here now are three mattresses, three chairs, two small card tables, one desk, one coat rack, one small heater, one small flower Mailman brought us the other day, a few books, our eating utensils and personal things which I said before isn't much. We have all the adequate things to live on. Toothbrush, soap and etc. Last night they brought us each a new tee shirt and new dress shirts. A little while ago they came by with a cart that had different items. Glasses (plastic), water pitchers and napkins. We already had all those items except for napkins so we grabbed a package of those. Every time they bring any of those items around, it makes it seem like we're going to be here a lot longer.

Bill just returned from making a call to his parents. They were really overwhelmed to hear from him. Bill said his Mom was so excited she started speaking in Spanish. She was cut short on that when the guys that were listening in with Bill couldn't understand, so they told Bill to tell her to speak in English. He said our parents have met on different occasions and are doing fine. Just waiting for us to return. Bill said that Mailman was saying that I might get to call home for Easter, which I'd love. I'd even like it better if I was home with them. Bill's Mom even said that the families have been writing all the time, but still we haven't received anything. His parents just told him to stay strong and that we'd be home soon! I pray to God they're right.

Last night they came and got the tape recorder. We hadn't listened to it all day. The electricity went out in the sockets so we just had it to look at.

Jerry received two letters from his wife today. One of them that was written the 19th of Feb. sounded as though we were to be released any day, and then the 2nd was sent the 23 of Feb, and told Jerry just to stay patient and to stay strong. Well, we're doing the best we can.

Jerry and I played handball again this morning. There's not really that much room, but we manage to get some fun out of it. Anything to pass the time with. We've got two students in the room right now. Bill's trying to teach them some tricks. It seems like whenever they come to our room they leave laughing. We even entertain sometimes. Anything to pass the time.

(19:15) Just returned from watching a little Charlie Chaplin on T.V. Once again it was great to change the daily schedule especially to get to watch T.V. It was really an old movie. But still we got a couple of laughs out of it. They also brought in some napkins that were sent from Johnnie's Foodmaster Supermarkets Inc. I take it they were supposed to be for St. Pat's Day. They've got clover leaves all over them. One of them has a leprechaun holding a mug of beer, which I wish I had instead of him. It was pretty thoughtful of them sending them to us.

Is this really happening to me? That's a question I keep asking myself. Not have I ever thought or dreamed that anything like this would happen to me, never! A simple little Missouri boy like me. How great it's going to be when we get home, being with my family and loved ones once again. Boy, how I crave for that day. *(Oh dear Lord, please make it come true.) End of entry.*

Monday, March 24, 1980 (12:50)   Day 142

Just woke from a long and restless night's sleep. I think I finally crashed out around (02:30) this morning after saying my rosary around three times and after the mosquitoes had their midnight snack. Mosquitoes have really been bad lately. I guess we're going to have to close the windows and run the air conditioner pretty soon.

I guess the reason I was awake all night was because I was thinking of all the mail I received. I heard from my parents, which was really a relief. The only other person from the family I heard from was Debbie, my sister. She's expecting any month now. That would be great if I make it home around the same time she's due. Received a letter from Rev. John E. Jakle, who is really a close member of the family (a great person).

Also received a card from my high school's varsity and junior varsity basketball team, which to me was very touching. Something else that was even more touching was I heard they had an assembly at the high school for me and the other 49 hostages where they lit 114 blue and white candles and kept two for me for remembrance when I get home. Senator Eagleton was even there and even gave a speech for eleven minutes. Everyone says it was a very touching moment and I believe it was. Just sitting here thinking about it gives me goose bumps. I've been having a lot of dreams about my four years at high school, and all of a sudden I hear they have an assembly in honor of the hostages. What an honor! It's still hard to believe that this is happening to me.

Just finished eating lunch. Steak, french fries, and spinach, and once again they brought in the dirty pans that held the steak and spinach so we can clean them. It started the other night when Bill asked them if they had seconds. They brought in a pot that still held a little food so we took it, and Bill had to open his big mouth and tell them we'd clean the pan out too. Right when he said that I knew we were asking for trouble. Those guards must have passed it on to others saying Room 212 does the dirty dishes if you have any food left over. Today, they first brought in the steak pan which had one steak remaining. We didn't even eat the whole thing, just half. Then a little while later, they brought in the dirty spinach pot and said we could clean that one too. These pots aren't small either. I don't know how many people are on this floor, but it seems like they bring up enough food just for this floor and the other two floors have their own. I don't know if that's true or not; it's just my own feeling.

Jerry received four or five letters from his wife yesterday. He received more yesterday than he has the whole time we've been here. Bill received one from Dawn, but none from his family. We all had a hard time sleeping last night. It seemed like everyone was so sure we'd be going home soon. My Mom said she was sending a tape to Germany so I'd be able to hear it. I believe it had something about the assembly at the high school. Jerry's wife mentioned Germany in her letter. It seems like everyone back home knows where we'll be going after we leave here, and they probably know how long we'll be there too. But still, no one knows when we'll leave here.

From all the letters I received it sounds as though my parents are kept busy, which is great. Didn't hear anything from Jill, but my Mom, sister and even Father Jakle mentioned her name a couple times. My Mom said she called the house the day before she wrote which was (28 Feb.) and said she was still waiting for my letter. I'm really curious to know how many letters she's received from me? Jerry's sitting down trying to answer all those letters he received from his wife. He already threw away one piece of paper. I wonder how many are going to be thrown away before he gets the right words out. Very intelligent man, who knows how to use his words. To me, he'd be a good writer. Bill trimmed my bangs today. Jerry was really amazed by the fact his wife was honored with the privilege of dropping the ball New Year's Eve at Times Square. Also my parents told me that Pat Boone wrote a song (really pretty my Mom said) about the hostages, and even wrote my parents a letter.

All the things I keep hearing of the happenings in the States are really hard to believe sometimes. How 50 hostages can raise so much stink to all the American people. It just goes to show that we're all one, fighting for what is right. America, the land of beauty and love. *End of entry.*

Tuesday, March 25, 1980 (12:15)   Day 143

Yesterday flew by pretty fast. The only thing I did was write in my diary and write two letters. Otherwise nothing happened. I woke this morning about (11:30). They've got some big demonstration out in front of the Embassy again, so they're all out there yelling and screaming. Right now there's someone speaking, so they're all listening. I sure wish I knew what they were saying. Then we might know what's going on around us.

Washed my hair in the sink this morning. It's been five days now since we had our last shower. Your hair and body gets really dirty working out, playing handball and just lying around. I wish we were down in the Mushroom where we could take a shower every day. It doesn't really matter. We're here and making it just the same.

Jerry's working on his puzzles once again. He really gets down into them. Bill's just lying on his mattress staring out the window. I think he's trying to figure out what they're demonstrating about and what the speaker's saying. I hope they're not talking about us. They're all cheering awful loud for something really happy!

(20:30) We went to see Charlie Chaplin once again tonight. It was the same exact one we saw the other night on T.V. We watched a little sports news. They were interviewing a soccer team here from Iran. They showed a couple shots of when they played Singapore, beating them 11-0 (Iran winning). The announcer was speaking in Farsi, so the students who were sitting with us that spoke a little English acted as an interpreter. They were saying something about how they want to go to the Olympics but they couldn't.

From that room we went down to the Pay Office room (blindfolded of course). Anyway, Mailman wanted us to help him move some desk and safes from one large room to a small one to store them in. He said the room we were cleaning out was going to be used as a movie room. All these things they're saying they're doing for us. Making a library and making a movie room sounds as though we're going to be here a little while longer. Thank you Lord for giving me the strength to hold on this long, now just so I can continue.

After we were finished moving all that stuff, we grabbed the wall pictures that were hanging on the wall and carried them up to our room. Now this room looks as though someone's living in it. We've got two huge Pan Am pictures. One of them is a picture of two people watching a sunset, and on the bottom in real big letters the word Guam is spelled. The other Pan Am picture is taken in Hawaii overlooking a beach off a cliff. The two other ones are smaller. One of the small ones is advertising a German cruise with a boat cruising through the water. The last small one is a shot overlooking a river in a thick forest with mountains surrounding it. They're not much, but at least they give off some color and like I said before, it makes it look like someone is living here.

After we dropped off the pictures we went to another room down the hall and watched T.V. off the videotape machine. That was the first time we had seen anything that was American since around the end of Nov. last year, when they showed us the first part of the World Series. The program we saw was "WKRP Cincinnati". I believe it's a series on television. It was the first time I've ever seen it. Really good.

What really surprised me was they brought three other hostages in to watch it with us. Bruce Jerman, Bob Ode and Mr. Blucker I believe their names were. We spoke for a few seconds when they came in. They were amazed by the hair we Marines had. Mr. Blucker remembered Jerry from the little meeting they had that morning of Nov. 4, 1979, right before the takeover. Anyway we were cut short, so we continued to watch the show. After it was over we said our good-byes and then were escorted back to our rooms. It was great getting to see all of them. It kinda makes you feel you're not the only one held hostage. Boy, how great it's going to be to be free once again. How much longer are they going to hold us. Years, months, weeks, days. Oh God! Please take us home. *End of entry.*

Wednesday, March 26, 1980 (12:20)   **Day 144**

Just returned from watching a little television. It was a videotape done by "TV Eye", produced between the time of Black Friday up to the time Shah was thrown out of Iran. Very interesting tape regarding the Revolution. Mailman said they had some western movies but they were going to show them later. I guess I'll do some more typing on my diary today. Getting tired of writing letters. I keep repeating myself in every letter I write. Maybe I'll try tomorrow. *End of entry.*
65

Received more mail last night which raised our morale. Jerry received a St. Pat's card from someone he didn't know. Bill received two, one from Dawn and the other from his uncle. I myself received five which I all knew. Father Kincel wrote once again saying he's keeping in touch with Bill's and my family. Says they're all doing great, just waiting for all of us to return. Also received one from Marianne Riordan, the girl that wrote me when I was stationed in Okinawa, Japan. After I returned I went out with her a couple times. Had a really good time. She happens to be a neighbor of my sister (Judy) in St. Louis and sometimes babysits for her little ones, Missy and Ben. She was saying my little nieces and nephews were really getting big, especially little Ben. She said he was looking like a two ton truck midget size. I believe it too. He was getting like that right before I left. It was really good hearing from her. The other letters I received were from my neighbors back home. They all assured me my family is doing fine and not to worry. Lori Brinker sent me an envelope, stamp and clean piece of paper to write her back on, so I guess that's a letter I'll have to write today. Twenty-one days it took for all those letters to get over here, which I thought was pretty fast. Sure hoping more comes.

Santa Claus brought in the tape recorder last night while we were all lying in our mattresses getting ready to crash out. He said he'd bring it back to us in the morning if we liked but we said "no" we'd listen to it. So what I did till the wee hours in the morning was listen to John Denver over and over. The mosquitoes must have hated it. They hardly bothered me. It's (16:00) and still we have it, but we're not complaining. We're only supposed to have it for two hours, but this time and a couple times before we've had it a little longer.

One of the students brought in a poster this morning showing a large picture of President Carter with his mouth open real wide with the Shah hanging out of it holding two suitcases with money signs on it $. The poster said: "The American Government must return the Shah to the Iranian people so he can be tried." I do have to say it is a good drawing.

Santa Claus brought in some Off and Libby's Tomato Juice before lunch. We told him the other night the mosquitoes were getting bad, so he said he'd bring some Off. Then he asked us if we liked tomato juice. We said yes so he said he'd bring that too. He kept his promise and brought it all just like he said. They used to have a jump rope floating around somewhere but it seems to have disappeared. I told him the other night I'd have my parents send me one and he said no, that he'd go out in town and buy one. They are trying to make our

66

stay as pleasant as possible. Showing movies, listen to tapes. I've never heard of a better hostage situation than the one I'm in now. The only thing they need to top it off is to let us all go. Boy how great that would be.

One of the students brought in a picture of me shaking Archbishop Capucci's hand when he was here with Monsignor Nolan. He said it was taken out of Time Magazine. It's really hard to believe I, Rocky Sickmann, made Time Magazine. What a trip. *End of entry.*

Friday, March 28, 1980 (21:30)   Day 146

Just got finished eating dinner which was pretty good. Cold roast beef sandwiches and potato salad. Seriously it was good. Went and saw another revolutionary videotape this morning that was produced by ABC cameramen. We were supposed to see some different movies like "Chips", "Hawaii Five O" and etc. but we never saw them. Mailman came in tonight and said that we might see some tomorrow.

They finally came in this morning and snatched the tape recorder from us. We really hated to see it go, but we know we're not the only hostages. Didn't do too much else today. We ate lunch in with our three other companions while watching the movie. They've been letting us fraternize a little with them, but not much. It's really good seeing different American people again.

I wrote Jill's parents today to congratulate them on their new member of family and Jerry wrote his wife. Bill didn't do much of anything. Read and sleep. I've really been keeping myself busy lately and it seems like the time really flies by, which I love. Not much more to talk about. Just staying busy typing to make the time fly by.

Political Prisoner came in to ask what we wished to have for Easter, April 6, and we replied just a priest to serve communion. He asked if there was anything else and I said yea, we want to go home. I hope they don't make a big thing out of it like they did Christmas. I hope it's just the priest and us, but I really doubt it. *End of entry.*

Sunday, March 30, 1980 (15:50)   Day 148

Nothing exciting or interesting happened around here yesterday. This morning they finally came and got us for a walk around the small courtyard and then to take our showers. Boy I was really needing one too. After my half-hour shower they took us into a room they made into a library in the Mushroom. All the books were lying in rows, alphabetically arranged. Bill and I were the only ones there besides our guard. Jerry was left over at the Charge's house to take his shower. So we collected some books for him and then drove back to the Embassy "Tehran Hilton".

After we were back in our room, after an hour had passed Santa Claus brought in mail. I received two beautiful letters from Jill that were so encouraging. Every time I hear from her it just makes me want to be with her so much more. She told me her little nephew's name is Jeremiah Daniel Ditch and he can't wait to see his "Uncle Rocky". Oh how I can't wait to have her in my arms again!!! Received a card from Jim and Karen Lawless and family. They're my true and lovable cousins. We all have a great time when we're together. I also received some other various letters from people of my hometown. It was great hearing from all of them, especially my love "Jill". I know what's in store for me if I ever get out of here.

Today's Palm Sunday, the Sunday before Easter. The three of us decided to fast the whole week till Easter Sunday. Eating one meal a day, lunch. We could think of nothing else to do for the Holy Week, so we decided on that. We're hoping for a priest Easter to give mass and serve communion. Most of all we're hoping for our freedom.

The weather today is really lousy looking. Cloudy and it looks as if it's going to rain. I guess if it wasn't for those letters today we'd probably be in a terrible mood. From all my letters it sounds as though everyone's sure of our freedom being soon. Oh how I pray they're all right. Everyone assures me that my family is well and doing great under these situations.

Santa Claus just came in and saw all my notes, asked me if I was writing a book? I said no, just keeping a diary. If we ever make it out of here I hope they don't take all these and destroy them. These are all factual happenings and actual thoughts and feelings coming from me. *End of entry.*

Monday, March 31, 1980 (15:20)   Day 149

Just finished my usual everyday thing, doing the lunch dishes. Boy how I miss working! Like I wrote in my diary yesterday, we started fasting for Holy Week. Jerry and I started yesterday and Bill started today. I wasn't really that hungry today from not eating since yesterday at (14:00). Believe it or not, I even gave up tea this week. I might even continue to give it up since my teeth haven't been hurting as much since I've stopped. I believe it was all the sugar I was using. I guess I've got a couple of cavities. There ain't no use drinking tea if I can't use sugar; otherwise it tastes rotten.

Jerry even held out well from not eating since yesterday, too. We had a little workout last night before we went to bed and this afternoon right before lunch came we had another hard workout. Hopefully we'll be able to continue it all week under our fast and then even continue it thereafter.

Last night Mailman came in and asked if we wanted to watch a movie. Of course we said yes. Everytime he says "movies" I think of the two hour episodes but he's only meaning different series like "Chips", "Hawaii Five O" and so on. Mr. Ode and his roommate, I forgot his name, anyway they were there also watching it with us. They're letting us talk to them a little more, but of course, nothing of our situation and anything dealing with it. They're both looking well!

Santa Claus brought Bill a harmonica last night which he's been asking for. I asked him where my jump rope was. He said he was going to be going out in the next two days to buy one. He also brought us some "Pet Evaporated Milk" this morning which I've been asking for. The doctor was in the night before. I think I forgot to mention it; anyway, he brought us some more vitamins and also some medication for my acne and also some librium for Jerry.

The students have really been kind, but then like I wrote earlier in my diary you get a couple of those hard asses. Anything we've asked for and if it's possible to get it, they'll pick it up for us. The only thing they won't give us is our freedom. They say we are their guest and that we should be comfortable and patient. How much longer is it going to be? How much longer are we going to be kept in from the outside world? *End of entry.*

Tuesday, April 1, 1980 (14:55)   Day 150

"April Fools Day". Just finished our only meal of the day. Like yesterday they brought us seconds. They also brought us one C-Rat meal, just the meat. We all scarfed that down along with our meal of egg plant, cheese and meat. They make it like lasagna but instead of putting noodles they put egg plant. Really good.

Jerry and I played ping pong this morning for the first time. They had it set up in the room we cleared out the other week. First they told us they were going to put the movie projector down there and instead they put the ping pong table there. Mailman said they were going to be moving the library from the Mushroom to one of the rooms over here then we could go down anytime and pick books up. All these things they're doing just makes it sound like we're going to be here a little while longer.

Mailman brought in the tape recorder last night for us. He also brought in some comics from an Iranian newspaper that showed President Carter crying about something. But he wouldn't explain it to us. Something he did say was that President Carter was contradicting himself. A helicopter just flew over the Embassy dropping pieces of

69

paper. I wonder what that was all about?

I'm surprised that John Denver tape we're listening to once again isn't worn out. Everytime we get it we play it continuously. I really don't get tired of it either. The weather's really nice today from looking out the window. Sure wish I was out there! *End of entry.*

Wednesday, April 2, 1980 (17:55)   Day 151

Just returned from watching Fantasy Island on videotape. Last night we saw another part of the series "Chips", so it looks as though we're going to be watching more television as the days proceed.

This morning we went downstairs to help Mailman clean out a room and put shelves up for our new library. Mailman let us pick up a calculator, electric typewriter and some other little small odds and ends. They just took the electric typewriter away. No one could find a ribbon for it, so they brought the manual back instead. What a bummer. I was looking forward to typing on the electric.

Last night while we were in watching "Chips" Mailman said that they got a priest to Tehran; supposedly he speaks English. Still going strong on our fasting. Today for lunch we had stew and boy did they fill our plates. I guess our stomachs are shrinking on us. I'm hoping I lose some weight. The meal really filled us up, and to tell you the truth I didn't even eat all mine.

One of the students told us an interesting story on why they can't eat our meat. It has to do with how we kill it and the prayers we don't say before killing it. Really impressed me. Learn something new every day!

The weather's been really ugly today, which I hope clears up before Easter. We hear them over in the field once again today. They've gotta be playing soccer or volleyball, one of those two. I sure wish I was out there playing.

When is it we're going to be free once again. How I worship that beautiful word "freedom". Still all the people in the United States think we're going to be home soon. I know they don't know that, but still they're saying that to try and make us feel good. How I wish they were right though!

(21:00) Just got finished reading an article in "The Sporting News", April 5, 1980, where President Carter told a group of Olympic athletes that they would not be participating in the Summer Olympics held in Moscow. Still the Olympic Committee is going ahead with plans for sending American athletes in hopes that changes might occur by May 25, the deadline for responding to the formal invitation by Moscow. Also just read about the 29 Americans who were on their way to Poland for a boxing competition and were killed in a plane crash. What other tragic incidents are going to happen to the American people? *End of entry.*

Thursday, April 3, 1980 (19:15)   Day 152

This day's gone by pretty fast with all the exciting happenings. This morning when we woke up Jerry and I went down and played ping pong for about an hour and a half. After we returned, Bill had our big lunch of spaghetti waiting for us. Once again the students piled our plates with food, which I was lucky to get down. It really doesn't take that much to fill us up anymore since we've been fasting. Since I also gave up tea for this week, last night I had a cup of coffee which really cleaned my system out this morning. That stuff really does the job. This morning I had another cup and I've been running to the head all day. I think the guards are really getting tired of running me back and forth.

Santa Claus and Four Eyes (Four Eyes is another student who's been bringing us things we've been asking for, I guess he's Santa's Helper!) came in last night and asked once again what we'd like to have for Easter. Once again we told them we'd like to go home but if that couldn't be arranged, we'd settle with a priest coming and serving Mass. This morning Mailman said that Archbishop Capucci might be coming, but two American and two Iranian Catholic priests were coming for sure. Hopefully Archbishop Capucci will give us some more encouraging words along with the two American priests.

Went to the television room this afternoon and saw a part of the series "Lucan" on videotape. Once again Mr. Ode and his roommate were there with us watching. Again it was a break from our everyday schedule. It's good to do different things besides sitting in this room all day.

Had a heck of a storm last night which continued all during the day today and is still going now. I'm not for sure but I believe Spring is their worst season for bad weather.

Jerry received some more pictures from home today. Once again he was thrilled to death and supposedly tonight Santa Claus is to bring some more mail for all of us. Boy how I love that phrase "mail call". Although we're fasting, they brought in peach pie to us tonight which we're saving till tomorrow at lunch. Boy, it was so tempting to take a bite out of it tonight while putting it away for storage till tomorrow. Hopefully it's still good tomorrow.

(Santa Claus = Ahmad) (Mailman = Hamid) *End of entry.*

71

Just finished reading my mail we received a little while ago. I received one card from a person in Arizona. Bill received six letters, one from his parents also. Jerry received two letters and one of them was from one of his good friends he hadn't seen in ten years. I guess you can say this situation has been helpful to let all your old friends know what you've been up to and where they can get in touch with us. In the letters Bill received they all mentioned that they had seen us on television the times when they came in and got us to workout in the workout room and when the doctor was in to examine us.

What really gets me disturbed is the fact the students said they would not be putting it on television, that it was only for their use. But of course their motive in the first place was to put in on television. Why didn't they just come out and say they were going to have it on television in the States, instead of lying to us? I told them I hated to be used as propaganda and that I didn't want my picture taken anymore.

This morning we helped pile books in boxes down in the Mushroom and then they were taken over here in the Embassy where we had fixed up a room as a library for all of us. We tried to get all the good books we could find, leaving a lot down in the Mushroom. There really wasn't much room in the new library to store books, not unless they get more bookcases to put in there. Once again, it was something to do and it made the morning fly by.

Last night one of the students came in and asked us if we'd like to go down and watch a movie—The Ten Commandments or Moses & The Ark was the name of it. Didn't catch the beginning so it was either of those two. It was an American movie but translated in Farsi. The only thing we could do was watch the picture. Burt Lancaster starred in it, playing Moses. Once again, it made the time pass away pretty fast, so we enjoyed it.

That peach pie we saved from last night really tasted good today. I probably could have eaten a whole one by myself. Can't wait to get home to some of my Mom's and Jill's home cooking. Boy how I can't wait!

(18:30) Just returned from playing ping pong with Jerry. It seems as though we've been having competitions against the students lately. I've played five different students and the only one I seem not able to beat is Mailman. All the other four players put up a good fight, but I beat them. *End of entry.*

Saturday, April 5, 1980 (13:55)   Day 154

Just returned from watching "Chips" on videotape so that was a change in the morning schedule. Mr. Ode and his roommate were also there with us but neither of us said anything to anyone. I guess you can say we're down in the dumps for being here for Easter.

This morning Santa Claus came in and asked if we would want to go in and decorate the room where Mass is going to be said tomorrow. We thanked him but said no! There aren't really that many decorations you could use for Easter. A Mass would be fine. I told him last night I didn't want to go if there was going to be television cameras and so on. I asked him why they had to have all that, and he said that the American people would want to see their 50 hostages having Easter, but I said sure! They'd rather see us home though, not here still being held hostage.

I know if they have goodies lying around tables like they did Christmas, I'm not going to be stupid like I was then and leave them sit. I'm going to fill my pockets up. I wonder when they're going to come get us for showers. They're going to want us to look our best for tomorrow.

Today's our last day of fasting, so tomorrow morning we can eat our three meals a day. Myself, I think I might continue on one meal a day. It hasn't really been hurting me, and plus I won't gain that many pounds. I just might stick to my lunch and maybe whenever we have a good dinner I might eat it too.

Woke up this morning and found the lamp on our desk we've been asking for. Like Santa Claus says: We ask for too much! That might be true, but you never know when they might change their minds and decide to shoot us. Ask for it now while there's still a chance on getting it. That's my motto! *End of entry.*

Sunday, April 6, 1980 (12:25)   Day 155

Happy Easter! I was sure wishing we'd be home by now but I guess the time wasn't right. Just returned from taking a bird bath in the head. Washed my hair too, really smells good once again. Jerry just went now to take his.

Mailman took us down to our new library last night to let us have a look at it. They did finally get some more bookcases to store more books, and the new library really looks good. They're thinking about putting a hostage down there to run it, and even to run the videotape and movie camera machines also. They said it would give us a job to do instead of having to sit in the room all day.

We asked him if there was any way we could get more fresh air. He said they'd see what they could do. We also asked him if there was a way to put a hostage in charge of the laundry instead of one of the students. It seems to take them such a long time to have clothes

73

washed, and then sometimes we might not ever see them again. If they let one of the hostages do the wash it'd give us jobs to do, plus we'd get the clothes back to everybody.

Santa Claus (Ahmad) brought us some Hershey bars and nuts last night, I guess to celebrate Easter. This morning Bill and I ate Hershey bars with peanut butter, which tasted great. For the first time this morning they served us peanut butter for breakfast. Last night was our last meal we had to fast so this morning Jerry ate breakfast and Bill ate a little bread. I told them I wasn't eating breakfast unless they brought cheese, and sure enough they brought me cheese. I didn't want to get out of my mattress so I decided I'd save it for lunch.

I finally got out when Mailman came in and asked me if I'd like to call home and of course I said yes. So we went down to the telephone room, but they couldn't get through. It was busy! One of the students took me back upstairs, but Mailman said they'd try again later on this afternoon. How I'd love to talk to my family now.

It's already (14:30) and still lunch is not served. Service is really getting bad. Really expecting some good meals today since they (the students) know it's a special day for all of us. A couple students came in this morning and wished us a happy Easter. We told them it could be a lot happier if we were home.

We'll try to go down to the play room today and play some more ping pong. Jerry and I broke the ping pong ball so they went to find another one. They brought back two brand new paddles but no ball. They said they had to go out and buy new balls yesterday, and they'd have them by today. *End of entry.*

Monday, April 7, 1980 (17:35)   Day 156

Our Easter service was held in the new library with the two priests and one reverend from the United States. Their names were Father Podiper, Father Bernard and Reverend Thompson. Anyway they did a great job of bringing the Easter joy into our hearts, and it was so good to see Americans once again. What really surprised me was the students let us talk to them about anything except, of course, the security, which we don't even know about. Once again they assured us that we have the support of all the United States people and not to give up, that we'd be going home. When? They had no answer for that so here we sit once again. Sitting back waiting for something to happen.

They had all the goodies sitting out in front of us just like at Christmas. This time Bill and I wore our camouflage utilities with the big pockets to stuff as much as possible. Let me tell you, that's just what we did, filled our pockets with eggs, nuts, oranges, apples, jelly beans and candy bars. We also had cake which we kept till we got back to our room. The priest and reverend even helped us stash goodies away in our pockets. We told them we wore those trousers for this special occasion. Christmas time the students had the same set up, but with more food, and we hardly got anything. We sure made up for it this time.

Before the ceremony the students passed out mail, but none of us received any from our parents or families. I'd say we spent about an hour down there in the library for our ceremony. It was really good. Brought all of our spirits up sky high. They took our phone numbers so once they got back in the States, they'd call all our families and give them our messages.

We came back to our room and started to munch down on all the goodies but I didn't get too far when my teeth started hurting. I guess I've got a couple cavities; those babies have sure been hurting me when I brush them. I've been trying to cut down on all sweets, but when I saw those goodies yesterday, I told myself just a little. Just that little was all it took before they started hurting again. Can't wait to get out of here so I can get them worked on. That's if we ever get out of here.

Nothing much was happening in our room, like always, so we decided to go down to the workout room and workout and play ping pong. While we were down there Archbishop Capucci came down to visit us. He said he was sent from the Vatican City with the Pope's regards and not to worry, keep staying strong and keep your faith with the Lord. A very encouraging man! He also brought messages from our families which were delivered this morning. The message wished us a happy Easter, and also told me my sister was due in another two weeks and that Jill was writing every day. It was signed by everyone in the family.

I just got finished calling home around (15:30), and talked to my Mom, Dad, little brother Kurt, sister Judy and her family. It was so good to hear from them. They were saying that Jill was over yesterday (Easter), and they all went to the show together. They said she loves me so much and misses me dearly. They didn't know they could call over here so I gave them the phone number and now hopefully I'll be able to hear something from Jill. It was really so good to hear from my family and good to know they're all doing well. They all sounded good.

Jerry just returned from making a phone call to his wife. He said his wife had just gotten off the phone with my sister Judy. He said she was sitting around hoping and praying that Jerry would get to call

too, and sure enough he did. This situation looks as if there's no end to
it. How much longer will we have to stay here, be away from our
families and loved ones. To us here it looks to be a long ... time. *End
of entry.*

Tuesday, April 8, 1980 (14:35) Day 157

I was awakened this morning by Santa Claus with some questions
he wanted to ask me. In his hand he had pieces of my diary I had
thrown away after I had retyped it onto another piece of paper. The
question he asked me was if it was my handwriting. I said yes, it was
part of my diary I had thrown away. Right then I knew something
was wrong. He said they found it on one of the hostages, and figured
we were sending messages to each other. I don't know what hostage
found it. The only thing I can figure out is that when the guards emptied out our trash can, they emptied it out in the head, and one of the
hostages found a couple pieces of my diary. I don't know if whoever it
was that found it could make anything out of it. Like I said, I had it
torn in little pieces, but maybe they were trying to make a puzzle out
of it.

It's not my fault the guard empties the wastebasket out in the head
where all the other hostages go too. Anyway, I guess they figured I
was passing notes, but I explained to them what it was and I guess
they believed me. They better have. It was the truth I was telling
them. Now whenever I get finished retyping a page and I'm going to
throw it away, I've got to give it to the guard so they can destroy it.
Probably read it too!

After that little interrogation, they came in and took us over to the
Charge's house for a walk around the courtyard, and then into the
house for a shower. I wonder why the change up from taking a
shower in the Charge's house instead of the Mushroom. Hercules was
in the courtyard already, I guess waiting for us. He must've not been
feeling well. He came over to greet us but after that he went back over
to where he was lying down and never got up again. I think he's been
doing too much running around at night. We're always hearing him
barking. I don't think he likes the students that much and I don't
believe they like him.

Santa Claus-Ahmad brought in an electric typewriter for us last
night. Now maybe I'll be able to get my diary typed! Jerry's been
learning. He wants to type his poems he's made up recently. To my
knowledge, which ain't much, I think they sound great. He's got
a-hell-of-a head on his shoulders. He's thinking about writing a book
when we get out of here, and I think he can do it. The only thing
we're waiting for is to get out of here!!

A lot of time's been passed down in the workout room lately. Most the time's passed playing ping pong. Jerry and I are always taking on the students, and most of the time beating them. At times when we're down there you'd never think we were hostages. Whoever heard of hostages playing ping pong with their captors?

Four Eyes just brought us music to listen to. Both tapes he brought are orchestra, but at least it's something to listen to. Found out the other day Four Eyes is in charge of laundry too. Now I know why we never got our laundry back the last time. They didn't know what to do with it. We gave Four Eyes our bed sheets which haven't been washed for I don't know how many months. The only reason we gave them to him is that he said he'd for sure have them back. That is one of his many jobs here, laundry, mail, etc. Now at least we'll have clean sheets once again. *End of entry.*

Wednesday, April 9, 1980 (15:00)   Day 158

Mailman brought in our library numbers last night so now whenever we drop off books we have to leave our number, mine is 8998. Can't really believe we've got our own library numbers. I wonder what else they're going to come up with?

Mailman got kind of perturbed yesterday when he left us in the television room by ourselves and told us never to touch any of the videotape machinery. He left us in there and told us to call the guard when we were finished. Well, we did exactly that after watching "Kaz". We called the guard and he left, bringing back the Juggler. The Juggler asked us what we wanted and we told him we just got finished watching T.V. and were ready to go back. He asked us if we wanted to watch another one and we said sure. He told us he didn't know how to work the machine but that we could go ahead and put another one on. We told him Mailman told us not to ever touch but if he was there to take responsibility, I'd put another one on. So I put on "Starsky and Hutch". Once again after that one we called the guard, and he then took us back to our rooms.

About an hour later Mailman came storming through the door staring directly at me and asked me who said we could watch another movie. We gave him the description of Juggler; we didn't know his name. I guess if they find him and he denies what we said, I'll be in trouble. Yesterday just wasn't my day. First I get accused of passing notes to other hostages and then secondly I get interrogated on why I showed a second movie. I guess they must have gotten it all straightened out. Nothing's been said since. Maybe they just decided not to show us any more movies. We'll just have to wait and see.

I couldn't believe my eyes this morning when Santa Claus brought me three letters from Jill and one from my parents. It was so good to hear from them again especially Jill. I never got to talk to her when I called home the other day. My parents said they saw me on television with Bill and that we really looked good. They said they've all been kept busy, which really makes the time fly by. Now I can't wait to see my Jill Renee once again. She says she's waiting patiently for me to come home and how she loves and misses me so much.

I received my first letter from some good friends back home, Michelle and Jim Wesselschmidt and family. Michelle was my grade school sweetheart, but as we grew up I found out we were too good of friends to be going out with each other. Anyway, she's married now to a really great guy. They just sent me a notice stating they had a little baby boy. They've got a little girl already. Takes after her mother. They're really happy about their new little son, and hoping I'll be coming home soon. Great people and I'm so happy for them. All the letters I received keep emphasizing not to give up, but to keep staying strong.

Just came up from playing a little ping pong and working out a little. We weren't down there more than 45 minutes. Jerry and I will probably go down there later tonight to work out a little more.

Santa Claus came in today and weighed us. Before taken hostage Bill weighed 180, and now he weighs 159. Jerry weighed 205, and now he weighs 165, and for myself, I weighed around 170 or 175 and now I weigh 180, the same amount I weighed my senior year and when I got out of boot camp. I didn't put on weight, I put on muscle. I'm probably the only hostage that's gained weight since I've been here.

(20:30) Just returned from watching "Salvage One" so I guess they aren't going to punish us from yesterday for watching that extra show. *End of entry.*

Thursday, April 10, 1980 (18:15) Day 159

Jerry and I just returned from working out and playing ping pong in the play room. Bill didn't want to come. He decided to work on his magic tricks from the magic book he received last night. More he practices at it the better he gets. We'll probably start having audiences of students in here one of these nights, so Bill will be able to perform for them. They really seem to get a kick out of watching it. I guess you could say that Jerry and I were down in the sport house about a half hour before they came and got us to go back to our room. I guess it's a maximum of 30 minutes you can stay in there, and then some more hostages come. I think the students play in it more than we do!

We can hear the students from outside our window. They must be over in the field playing soccer or volleyball. It's really a nice day today. Sure wish we could be out there. From looking outside the window of the play room, you look up and out to see the trees, with their blossom of spring. So many colors I can distinguish. It's really beautiful!

My hair was getting a little dirty from the workout so I decided to give it a wash in the toilet! We're not due for another shower till next week. Try to stay clean as best as possible. Received some of our laundry back last night. Like always something was missing. This time it was our towels. Hopefully I'll be able to get another one before we take a shower next. The one I have now is really looking filthy.

Jerry's over at the desk going over the poems he's made up in the past week and they truly sound good. Bill's lying on his mattress. I guess he's trying to crash out till dinner. I decided last night that I was going to cut down on eating, especially dinner. I decided if they had something else besides soup I'd eat it, but soup I'd skip. I figured if I really had gained weight, I should lose a little on this diet.

Just heard Hercules outside. He must be chasing the cars right out back of the Embassy here. I bet he really misses us Marines. *End of entry.*

Friday, April 11, 1980 (14:30)   Day 160

Didn't get to sleep till early this morning. Jerry and I stayed up talking about the situation we're in and the things we're going to do when we get out of here. They've been speaking over the P.A. system since early this morning. Doesn't sound too good for us. Every time he finishes a line, you can hear people chanting and yelling. So whatever he's saying, he's saying in behalf of the people not in behalf of our release.

Jerry and I went down and played ping pong last night. Once again, we only stayed for a half hour. They said some other hostages wanted to use the room, so we left. I guess we're not the only hostages that are night owls.

(19:30)   Just returned from watching "Police Woman" on videotape and playing a little ping pong in the play room. Bill's been practicing long on his magic tricks, and last night for the first time we had a small audience in our room for him to perform to. It seems like we've all got our little things to keep us going. Bill's got his magic tricks, Jerry's got his poems and workout, and for myself, I've got my diary and small workout I do with Jerry. Can't forget about ping pong. That takes up a good portion of time too! *End of entry.*

79

Just finished eating dinner which consisted of spaghetti, bread and an orange. Every other night we have soup, but the other nights we have something different. It's a lot better now than it was at the beginning, when every night used to be soup. Showed us another part of the "Salvage One" series right before dinner. It really made the time fly by.

Santa Claus came in today and had me read an article from Bill's hometown newspaper of when he called home. Wouldn't let Bill keep the article. Must have been something on the back of good interest. They said we got mail, but we won't receive it till tomorrow. We're all looking forward to receiving letters from our families. Cross our fingers on that one. For going home also!

Some of the students that walk in at times ask me what all these papers I'm writing are for? I tell them it's a diary for when I get back to write my book. They all ask me if I would send them a copy when I'm finished and I reply, I will if you ever let us go so I could go back and start on it. No answer from them after that. From the little things they say, like, will you send me a book and stuff like that, it sounds as though we'll be going home, *but when*?? Then other times we get students that come in and tell us (at least I hope they are kidding) about staying here for one, two, three more years. The only thing we can do is go along with their jokes and pray to God they're only kidding. There's always this one person, Santa Claus (Ahmad) who can come in our room when the morale is really low and leave us with the spirit he raised. He'd be a great comedian. Really good guy, even though he's our captor.

Noticed a girl sitting outside in the hallway tonight with her chador* on. There must be women right across the hall from us, or somewhere around here. Mr. Ode's roommate Bruce German—he was the Budget Officer for the Embassy—anyway, he hasn't been feeling well and has called for the doctor all day but still none has shown. Hopefully he's feeling well tomorrow. Like I've said before, just being here is bad enough. I know we don't need any sicknesses to help it out any.

Political Prisoner just brought in mail for us all. Jerry received one from his wife, but Bill and I received letters only from people we knew at home and other ones from people we didn't know. None from our families/Jill. Receiving quite a few letters from people saying they would have written earlier, but they figured it would've been over and we would've been home by the time their letters got to us. *End of entry.*

---

*Combination head-covering veil and shawl worn by Moslem women   80

Just returned from having our weekly walk around the courtyard and shower. Last week when we were in the courtyard the vines that hang off the wall were barely blooming but today they were in full blossom. Really pretty. Green as can be. Parrots were all over the place today. There was a storm coming up so I guess they were going around to find shelter until it blows over. No sun today, but just the smell of spring was rewarding enough to go out and smell.

Josef (our cook) came out and talked to us, bringing with him three orange sodas which he gave to each of us. Just by looking into his eyes it looked as though he was really happy to see and talk to us. He said he's been kept really busy cooking and he hoped that we've been enjoying his food. We thanked him and assured him that the food was good. But I forgot to ask him if we could get some pancakes some morning. It was really good talking to him. The last time we saw him was Christmas. It seemed as though he lost a little weight. I wonder if he's able to leave the Embassy grounds?

Guard Chief took us over to the Charge's house today. It was a while since we had seen him last so we asked him how the situation looked for our release? It seemed as though he had a strong feeling for May, or maybe I just made that feeling up. Anyway, we made a deal. If we're not out of here by May 13 he owes me a kilo of nuts. He wasn't too sure of it, but we shook on it anyway.

The last month I shot for was March and something did just about happen regarding our release. Now the month I'm shooting for is June, but Jerry and Bill are shooting for May. I don't know if I said it earlier in my diary, but Santa Claus gave us some words of encouragement of something happening around May or June. The only thing we're doing now is praying and hoping that something is done regarding our release. If not, I guess we'll just have to pick out another possible month and shoot for it, continuing on with our everyday schedule.

This morning around (09:30) Jerry and I had just returned from playing ping pong when Mailman and three other students came into our room, asking if we had just looked out the window, meaning one of us. We told him no, that we had returned from playing ping pong just before they walked in. I guess he didn't believe my first answer of "no", so he asked again. I told him a second time that we had just returned from playing ping pong. He then left with the three students following.

The rest of the night I heard bolts of rifles being opened and then closed outside below our window. Even in the hallway at times, too! I'm not saying it's been the first time they've been playing with the

rifles like that, but this morning it seemed as though they did it an extra amount. I guess to tell us they better not catch us peeking out the
window, or else!

Really been hard trying to get to sleep at nights. Usually don't crash
out till early morning and then wake around (14:00). I sure hope I
don't start that schedule of sleeping during the day and staying awake
at nights. Usually Jerry can't sleep either, so we talk about our future
plans if we ever get out of here. I'm seeing such a change coming into
my life. Such a great day that's going to be, the day of freedom!! *End
of entry.*

Monday, April 14, 1980 (17:15)   Day 163

Mailman just came in awhile ago and said the Red Cross was coming in to see us. Well, the two gentlemen just left but they didn't look
like they came from the Red Cross. I'll take that back; one gentleman
had a suit on and the other was dressed in the robes of their high
priest. The gentleman in the robes asked all the questions, while the
one in the suit just watched. He asked our names and jobs, what we
were doing, and if we knew who was responsible for the situation
we're in? He wished us that this situation would be resolved very soon
and that we'd be able to go home, but no encouraging words of when
our release will be. I guess our only hope is if the Shah returns.

Jerry and I hit the ping pong table once again last night around
(21:30) and didn't return till this morning around (00:30). I guess the
reason they let us stay down there with them so long was I was teaching them how to lift weights and Jerry was giving a couple of the other
students a good fight in ping pong.

Still not able to sleep like I want to; visions of home keep flashing
through my head. Maybe someone's trying to tell me something,
something like we'll be going home soon! *End of entry.*

Tuesday, April 15, 1980 (12:55)   Day 164

Another day, another thought! Just returned from watching "Kaz"
on videotape. Once again it was good to take our minds off our situation and kill time. Mr. Ode and Bruce, his roommate, were there.
Bruce said he was feeling better from the other day, when he wasn't
feeling good.

I guess Jerry and I'll be on television for playing ping pong. Yesterday around (16:30) we went down to the play room figuring that all
the company had left for the day, meaning the high priest and the
other gentleman in the suit, who we found out this morning from
Mailman was a representative from Red Cross here in Iran. Anyway,

we were down playing ping pong and in walked a movie camera crew, and following them were two Swedish Red Cross representatives and three Iranian doctors with some students.

We all introduced one another and then one of the students told the Red Cross representatives that we'd be checked in our rooms. They looked around the room, greeted us again, telling us they'd see us up in our rooms and left. The movie crew continued to film Jerry and me playing ping pong for about another minute, then left themselves.

We came back up to our rooms about (19:15) expecting to see the Red Cross representatives but they still hadn't come. It wasn't till after we had our dinner of roast beef and potato salad that they came. No movie cameras, just cameras. They took our names, address and phone numbers, so once they left and returned to Switzerland, I believe they said they were going to call and speak to our families. They also gave us a Red Cross telegram to write a message to our family, and when our families received it and wrote their message, he would then hand deliver them back to the students, who would then deliver them to us. He asked us if we received the first messages that were written? We told him no! He said not to worry, that these messages would definitely reach us.

Santa Claus just brought in some music to listen to (Nat King Cole and Ray Conniff and Love Story and Jean). Music really lightens our days. It's so much better listening to that instead of listening to them playing out in the field or all the chanting and yelling. Music really makes me happy and brings back so many good memories. Santa Claus said we would be listening to a lot more music. Maybe Red Cross gave him some recorders and tapes for all of us.

There's supposed to be another skin specialist come to look at the acne on my face and give me a treatment for it. At least that's what the Red Cross doctor told one of the Iranian doctors he wanted done. Now I wonder if he'll come and when?

This morning Mailman came in with a tape recorder and Spanish tape that he wants Bill to translate into English. Couldn't make out anything on the tape so it was useless to translate it.

Haven't been able to sleep at nights, thinking too much about home! Having the Red Cross coming to see us yesterday made it seem like we're going to be here another long while. We told them this, but he assured us that their visit meant nothing of our release. He said we might be released tomorrow or the next day, but their job was just to check on our health, and also to have a message sent to our families to assure them we're alive waiting to go home, no matter how long we are here. Nothing was said about our release though! I wrote my message to my parents telling them how great it would've been to walk out of here with those Red Cross representatives and to be free once again! How great that would've been!! *End of entry.*

Wednesday, April 16, 1980 (14:30)   Day 165

Bill received the first box of goodies last night from a family living in Texas. The only reason we got it was because they were all canned goods that haven't ever been opened. Political Prisoner, who brought it in, said those are the only type of goodies we can receive, no homemade stuff, just stuff that's directly from the factory.

Anyway, he received two 12 oz. cans of Planter's peanut candy and one 35 oz. can of Kool-Aid mix. One peanut candy can is gone and the Kool-Aid tasted great with our stew we had for lunch today. It seems like it took quite a while to get here, too. Mailed Feb. 12 and arrived I guess yesterday, April 15. Approximately 64 days it took to get to us. At least it got to us! I know my family's been sending goody boxes, but not one have I received yet.

Mailman brought in another sports magazine, "The Sporting News". It's dated April 19, 1980, but today's only April 16, 1980. I wonder what goes there? Read about the baseball players being on strike and that no exhibition games are being played until reckoning day of May 22, when they find out if they continue to strike or play baseball. Also read some more information regarding the Olympics. The boycott is still on and Russia has delayed the deadline for answering invitations from May 25, I believe it was, till June 1. It sounded as though there were a lot of unhappy people who don't agree with President Carter's decision to boycott.

Sounds like something big is happening in Afghanistan! No wonder we're not out of here. There's so many things happening back in the States, baseball strike, boycotting the Olympics, they're probably forgetting about us, except for our families and friends. As every day goes on, it seems more obvious that if the Shah doesn't return, we won't go home. Just as simple as that. I never thought my life would end living in another country, especially like this! I guess that's just one of the prices we have to pay for being one of the world's finest, "a United States citizen!" How proud I am to be one, too.

After saying my two rosaries this moring before going to bed, I asked the Lord to give me a sign to let me know he was with us here, said a couple more prayers and crawled over to my mattress. I guess I was over there about two minutes staring at the ceiling when all of a sudden the door vibrated. When I looked over at it through the darkness it stopped. One of the students came to the door, opened it, looked in and asked us what we wanted. We told him nothing. He then turned on the light and asked us again. I guess he figured we were playing games with him but we weren't! That door vibrated by itself.

I told Bill about asking the good Lord to give me a sign and he told me he had done the same, but asked Him to give a sign if we were ever going to get out of here. Just sitting here thinking about what happened gives me the chills. I really do believe that was a sign intended for us. I'll always believe it until the day I die.

(19:30) Just came from watching "Executive Action", a videotape movie that had to do with the assassination of President Kennedy. Bill hasn't been feeling good, so he slept while Jerry and I went and watched it. Santa Claus and a student (student doctor) came in just now to check on Bill. Bill said he's feeling a little better. He's been taking some medication he received from one of the students this afternoon. The student doctor just told him to relax. He said his stomach muscles were too tight.

Do they expect us to relax when we keep thinking that we might not ever see our families and loved ones once again? I wish it was as easily done as said, but it's not! The only thing we got going for us now is the good faith of our Lord. *End of entry.*

Thursday, April 17, 1980 (20:45)   Day 166

Received mail early this morning. Received a letter from my parents but nothing either from the rest of my family or Jill. Parents said they're all doing well. Always kept busy. Received a couple other letters from people I didn't know, some friends and my cousin. Jerry didn't get anything from his family, just from other people. Bill got a letter from Dawn, but nothing else from his family. He also got letters from people throughout the world, but no one he really knew.

It's really something when they come in to distribute the mail. We all get up in a sitting position, like fierce dogs getting ready to attack a prowler. It's the second main event we look forward to every day. The first is going home, but as you can tell, that hasn't happened yet. Anyway, we sit here and watch whoever it might be handing out the mail, hoping we hear from our families and loved ones. It's really a disappointing moment when he says that's all and you have three or four cards in your hand and you don't even know who they're from. Don't get me wrong; it's really nice hearing from different people. It's just that we look forward to hearing from our families so much, that it's really a big let down.

Bill's been feeling a little better, but then with all the sleep he's been doing, he should feel pretty good. Last night about (23:30) one of the students came in and asked if we wanted to go down and play ping pong. It was really strange. Usually we have to ask them if we can go down and when we do ask, it usually takes them another ten minutes before they come back to get us to go down. Last night they came and asked us. Maybe the students wanted a little competition to play against.

They were saying they're getting another table and some more weights to make another "sport house", as the students call it, up here on this floor. That would be a lot nearer. Right now they've got us staying in there for thirty minutes. They say they have it scheduled so that each hostage has about the same amount of time in it. What's fair for one is fair for all!

Bill doesn't like ping pong, but I don't know why he doesn't come down and work out. Anyway, Jerry and I played for a half hour before dinner, so we're hoping they let us go back down tonight to work out. Hate to mess up our schedule.

Ate breakfast for the first time in a long time this morning. Jerry did, too. I skipped dinner tonight (except for a piece of bread) so I could stay on my two meals a day. Wrote home today telling them since we're going to be over here so long, that they might as well try and send us some more goodies. Told them to make sure they were all canned goods that have never been opened. Those are the only goods the students said we could have.

Today I came down with another feeling that we weren't ever going to leave here. I keep telling myself I've got to stay optimistic but it's so hard. You look at the calendar and it says one hundred and sixty-six days and still yet, no word of freedom. It really hurts deep down inside when I start thinking of this situation and what Jill and my family are going through. I love them all so much! Please Lord, give me another chance. Don't take me from the ones I hold so dear to me!!

Jerry's really been producing some good poems lately. Like the old saying goes: Practice makes perfect. I think it works the opposite for me though. The more I seem to write, the worse it seems to get. Jerry doesn't think so. He says it's been sounding pretty good. I think he's just saying it to make me feel good. Either way, good or bad, I'm continuing. I kind of enjoy it, and it really makes the time fly by.

One of the big things that really keeps us going are the dreams we have of if we're ever released. So many things I want to do and hope to do. But they'll never come true if we're never released from here. *End of entry.*

Thursday, April 18, 1980 (21:05)   Day 167

What a boring day it was today. I woke late this afternoon, around

(13:00). I guess the workout Jerry and I did last night before crashing got to me. Really slept great compared to the other nights. Jerry and Bill weren't that lucky. Jerry said he woke off and on all night, and Bill's still not feeling good. Santa Claus came in this morning and asked him if he wanted a doctor, but Bill said no! Tomorrow if he's still feeling ill I'm calling one for him.

After lunch I spent a couple hours reading out of the biology book we've got. I read about the liver and its different functions. Very interesting and important part of the body. Jerry and I went down and played our half an hour's worth of ping pong. Bill stayed in his mattress like always. Came back to our room and found a *Sports Illustrated* dated January 7, 1980. They (the students) know I like sports so whenever they get a sports magazine they bring it to me. Can't believe how I've gotten to enjoy reading while I've been here. Before this situation there were very few times when you'd catch me sitting down reading. If I wasn't sleeping, I'd be up and around doing something. Now look at me! I hate it!

Not too much more to scribble down. Waiting for our tea to come. Once we're finished with that, we'll try and see if we can go down to work out. Exciting eh? Really seemed to be quiet around here today since it was Friday, their prayer day. Other Fridays seem to have chanting and yelling people, but not this one.

Some Iranian girl students must have a room right next door to us. They're over there right now and they sound like a bunch of women at a Tupperware party. They're all yakking away. I don't know how they can understand each other. *End of entry.*

Friday, April 19, 1980 (23:00)   Day 168

A lot to write tonight. Last night around this time (23:00) Mailman came in and got Bill and Jerry and took them to the T.V. room. I was in the head doing the dishes our food was served on. At first I just went in to go to the toilet, and as I was washing my hands I noticed the note the students put up on the wall regarding the washing of the dishes the food's served on to all the hostages on this floor. The note says: A volunteer hostage is needed to do the hostages' general dishes. "Start" if you are a volunteer! I volunteered and did the dishes.

When I returned to the room everyone was gone so they took me to the T.V. room. Mr Ode and his roommate Bruce also joined us. We watched two series. One was "Lou Grant" and the other was "How the West Was Won". They lasted till about (01:00) this morning.

We then came back to our room where Jerry was met with a message from Alex Paine and a letter from, I believe, his niece. The message from Alex stated he was here in Iran and he's making sure we received more mail from home. We were really curious today wondering why Alex is here? Jerry wrote Alex a message with regards from Bill and me to pass on to our families. Right after he wrote it, Santa Claus came in and asked Jerry if he had a message to give to Alex. I just mentioned to Jerry and Bill that I bet Santa Claus went to see him (Alex). Santa Claus hasn't been here all afternoon.

Jerry and I went down to try out the new weight room/ping pong room this evening. Mailman just left, giving us our new hours. We're to use it in the morning (10:00-11:00), in the evening (17:00-18:00), and late hours from (22:00-10:00) in the morning we can use anytime. The new room is really nice. Nice ping pong table and a nice set of weights. They even have a bench for presses. All these new furnishings, I hope they're not thinking about keeping us here long!

This afternoon Jerry and I (Bill was down in the library) had a good conversation with one of the students I call Nose. Really a good guy! Anyway, he gave us some encouraging words and figures. He was saying that in June something is going to be done about releasing the hostages through the Senators of their new government and the Islamic Republic. We asked him if they were making negotiations with the United States. He said no! The only negotiation that "might" be made will be between the government and the Islamic Republic of Tehran. He put in a lot of "mights" but still it's something to shoot for. I still have my strong feelings that something "might" happen also in June. Santa Claus told us a couple weeks ago that he thought that something was going to happen, too. What? That, I guess we'll have to wait and see. I pray to God it's freedom!!

June, that's the month of Jill's birthday. Maybe I'll even be home for mine, too, in July. How great that would be!

Bill's feeling a little better. Tonight one of the student doctors came in and examined Bill and me. My chest was breaking out with some kind of rash and my left eye looked as though it was forming a sty, so I had him check it out. At the same time he checked Bill out, too. He said I didn't have anything to worry about, but Bill he wanted to do more tests on. He gave me some eye drops and said that he'd get some medication for my acne, too. The skin specialist still hasn't come since when they said they'd get one. That was when Red Cross was here. I'm not really in need of him. If he comes, he comes. If he doesn't, he doesn't. I hope it's nothing serious though. Things are looking up toward freedom. Just hope they stay that way. *End of entry.*

Saturday, April 20, 1980 (21:25)   Day 169

Had our shower and walk in the courtyard this morning. Really a beautiful day with the sun shining bright. We really hated to leave. The sun was feeling great! Hercules wasn't there to meet us. We were wondering where he was. We made it back right on time to receive our lunch. Steak, french fries and brussel sprouts, tasted great!

Bill asked Four Eyes if it was possible to get some coins for some tricks he had planned. He said he'd see what he could do and left. Fifteen minutes later he came back with ten coins (Iranian). He said he collected them from some of the students, which I thought was really considerate. It really gets me; anything we wish to have they do their damnedest to get. I wish they were like that about our freedom!!

Once again today I asked for my glasses, but everyone says I've got to talk to Santa Claus about that. They probably want Santa Claus to tell me that I'll never be able to get them back because they've thrown everything away. I wonder what they did with all of our stuff? Wonder if we'll get everything back if we ever get to go home? I shouldn't say "if". Got to stay optimistic! When will we leave here?

Right now we're listening to Charlie Rich and John Denver on the tape recorder that Four Eyes just brought in awhile ago. Charlie Rich's first song brought back memories of every time I'd go over and pick up Jill for a date. I'd walk through the door of their house and the first thing I'd hear is the country western station they had playing in the kitchen. I know I've said it once, but I'll say it again, I've really gotten to like the country western music. Jill's really going to like that.

All three of us went down to the workout room this afternoon, downstairs. They added more weights to the set they had down there, so now they've got two nice sets in each sport room. I wonder why they're just coming out with all these good things now? We spent our hour down there and when it was up they brought us back up here. As we were going up the steps they pulled us off to the side and had us stop. I could hear voices of women (Iranian) but then I heard some little comments from what sounded like American women. As I walked through our door I turned back and saw they had the door across the hall open and the girl that usually stays out there was gone. It was probably their turn for the play room, so they were taking them down as we were going up. When, if ever, will we ever be released? *End of entry.*

Sunday, April 21, 1980 (21:25)   Day 170

Just finished our dinner that consisted of chili and bread, but no seconds. Never any seconds when chili's served; just when soup's served there's seconds. Didn't need that second bowl anyhow. It's just that it's so appetizing when we eat the first we wish we had another. All the weight lifting we've been doing I guess really puts an appetite on us.

They've been keeping pretty closely to their schedule of the hours we're to be in the sport house. Must be having everyone going down to at least play a little ping pong or lift a little weights. Maybe they're trying to get us looking good for when we go home, if it's true what we heard the other day.

Jerry and I were on our way last night around (23:00) to go down and play some ping pong. Bill was practicing his magic tricks. Anyway, Mailman cut us off right when we were getting ready to descend the stairs and asked us if we would instead like to watch videotapes. We said definitely videotapes. Mr. Ode and Bruce his roommate followed us in. Mailman went back to our room and got Bill. We watched one of Mr. Ode's specialties "Lucan". Really it's one of the ones he really hates. He keeps asking for M*A*S*H but Mailman never shows it. We really do get a kick out of listening to him, Mr. Ode that is.

Also saw a second series of "How the West Was Won", which really surprised me. They even let us in the room together by ourselves. I guess they've finally realized that there ain't much we can do anyway, so they let us sit alone. Frequently a guard will come in to check on us. But I think they just come in to see an American movie. Oh yes! They even let Bill or me work the videotape machinery now, too. All these changes. I wonder if they mean anything?

We returned back to our rooms about (01:30) this morning. Turned the tape recorder on, said my prayers and fell asleep listening to the good music wishing I was home. Woke late this morning, finding Jerry up as usual. Today he said he's going to start to cut down on smoking and might even quit. He usually smokes seven a day and so far, he's only smoked four and said those are all he's smoking today. I think he can stop smoking. When he first started working out, he could barely do ten sit-ups and now he's doing sixty. That shows me if he can put his mind to something he wants to do, he can do it. I know he can stop smoking.

Santa Claus was just in talking to us, and to me everything he said to us sounded very encouraging. What really caught my ear was how he talked about "how they tried to get the Shah back, but failed." How we shouldn't be worried about going home, but to think about what we're going to do to help ourselves and so on, when we do get home. I told him I'd worry about that once I get there; now I'm worried about getting out of here. I know I've written about "if" we'll ever get out of here earlier in my diary. I know these people won't keep us over here forever. Whoever heard of a country where their government held hostages. It's just the thoughts about things that might happen when we are released. I'm not going to feel safe until I'm back home in good ole' Krakow, Missouri, once again. How great that's going to be!

Freedom is looking closer every day even if it isn't till June. Being hostage for six months, June will just seem like next week to me. One month isn't shit, that's if it is June. I'm praying and hoping every night that it's soon. *End of entry.*

Monday, April 22, 1980 (18:30)   Day 171

Another amazing thing just happened. We had just gotten back from working out and playing ping pong in the sport house. I was reading a *Sports Illustrated*; Jerry was reading a book and Bill was lying on his mattress looking out the window. Bill told me to look around to the window. Sitting on the window was a dove. We weren't really sure if it was gray or blue. It was just sitting there staring at us.

The first thing that popped in my mind was the priest who was here at Easter telling us maybe the next time we'd be seeing a dove, it would be a symbol from God that freedom was on its way. Jerry had told him about the earlier visit we had from the white dove. Now we get a second one. Was it really a sign? Oh Lord, please take us home!

Jerry and I had a long stay down in the sport house last night. A very emotional night I had last night, doing some things I wish I hadn't. I said three rosaries asking the good Lord to forgive me, so maybe that dove was a sign that he had. So many things I've experienced since I've been here. Now just so I'm able to go home and start all over. Enjoying the rest of my life with my family and dearest Jill. Oh God, please make her be there when I get back.

This morning for the first time we had scrambled eggs, can you believe it? I sure couldn't! I remember mentioning a while ago, if they ever start serving eggs to us, you'd know something was up. Maybe it's just another sign that freedom's near. Like always, I guess we'll just have to sit and wait it out.

One of the students that we played ping pong with today (Jamsid) asked if we would invite him to the United States. We said of course we'd invite him, but he said, no, I wouldn't want to come because we would take him hostage. That's the first time he ever said anything about going home. I think they all know something we don't. *End of entry.*

Tuesday, April 23, 1980 (21:00)   Day 172

Received mail this morning. One from Jill which was once again very encouraging, but nothing from my family. The letter from Jill was a lot different from any of her other ones. This one was video-copied and sent through a different address from all her other ones. She was still asking me if I've ever received any of her letters yet so I take it she hasn't gotten any of mine. The reason she said she's sending this copy was she was trying to send it through two different address-es, hoping it would get through. I think she's doing that so she can prove if I ever get out of here that she was writing. Anyway, it was really good hearing from her and great to know she's still back there waiting.

Jerry got some letters from his father-in-law and other members of his family but nothing from his wife. He believes they were brought with Alex Paine because they were all dated around the same time. Alex was over to visit Jerry's wife February sometime. They were old letters but he didn't mind.

Bill didn't get anything from either his family or Dawn, just differ-ent ones from people that were hoping he received their previous let-ters. One out of the five letters he has heard from, but the others were the first. There's bound to be more mail somewhere. Sure wish we had it.

Last night they came in and got us to show us a movie, as they call it. It was just a part of the "Spencer's Pilot" series. I believe it lasted about a half hour and we were back in the room. Wasn't bad. I think we did more talking to Mr. Ode and Bruce instead. They told us they received eggs two mornings ago, so I guess that concludes our theory about serving different foods on each floor each day. Mostly talked about how we couldn't believe how long we've been here so far.

Went down and played a little ping pong after the movies, didn't stay long though. I was really tired, I guess from all the working out we've been doing. We came back within a forty-five minute period, said my prayers and crashed out.

Lately we've been getting in good workouts. Every day we go down to the sport house. Jerry's been going strong on his sit-ups, 21's, and his bike pedaling. Don't let him lift too many weights. He said his back's been bothering him. Don't want to take any chances!

By the time Bill and I get finished with our workout and Jerry with his, students usually start coming in wanting to play us in ping pong. United States vs. Tehran, Iran! Usually get some good games, draw-ing some large crowds. They also love to watch us lift weights. But really, they'd rather play ping pong than do that. Sometimes you get a couple who ask you to show them how to lift. Even Jerry gives lessons.

Not much more to talk about, hanging on as best as possible. Days are usually spent reading and waiting to go home. When's that day going to come?

A couple of student doctors were just in to see us. Asked us if there was anything we need? I told them I was supposed to see a skin specialist for my acne, but no one has ever come. He said one would be here in a couple days. The best one he can find, he will send. Wonder what all the check-ups are for? They brought Jerry some Geritol; maybe they want him looking young when he steps off that plane when we're freed. *End of entry.*

Wednesday, April 24, 1980 (22:10)   Day 173

My eyes have really been hazy lately, really straining so I'm able to read. I guess the only thing I can do is ask for my glasses again and hope maybe this time they can get them. Went and saw another part of the series "Spencer's Pilot" this afternoon after lunch. We don't really care for "Spencer's Pilot" too much, but still it gets us out of this room and anything that can do that can't be all that bad.

Jerry and I had our normal ping pong tournament last night downstairs with some of the students. It's starting to be an every night thing. Bill's been working on his magic tricks pretty frequently. Occasionally we get a couple students that he performs for. Not too many students come in anymore like they used to.

Had a speaker on the P.A. system most of the day; otherwise the last two days before this one everything seemed pretty quiet. Tomorrow's prayer day. Wonder what they'll say about us?

Four Eyes and another student brought candy in this morning. Gum, Charms, Half-sweet/Half-sour pops and then left. Wonder what the occasion was? Maybe someone's coming to see us. Last night the student doctor checked up on us and then this morning candy was given out.

Stayed in my mattress till lunch this morning. I hope I don't go back to the old routine of sleeping during the day. The workouts we've been having have really been strenuous, putting us right to sleep at nights.

(23:00) Jerry and I just returned from our ping pong tournament with some of the students. We just finished our usual night sit-ups. Bill's already crashed out and Jerry's reading his book until I get finished here writing. Prayers are being said over the loud speakers outside, no doubt throughout the whole town. One hundred and seventy-three days today. How many more await us? *End of entry.*

Well, here we sit in our new house. Where it's located is a mystery to us three and the other hostage that came with us. The other hostage who was with us for that ten hour miserable ride, we never got to speak to. We did hear him say a couple words when they were situating us in the van, an elderly man about the same age as Jerry. As far as we know, us three and six others we saw last night walking through the hallways blindfolded are the only ones here. But why?

Yesterday started out just about like any other normal day at the Tehran Hilton. Woke early eating breakfast with Jerry. After we had finished, Jerry crashed back out saying he had a bad night sleeping. He never succeeded in stopping smoking, so he's back to his seven a day cigarettes. I guess all this moving isn't helping him out any. It's really had him nervous.

After breakfast yesterday morning Four Eyes brought the tape box in for us to listen to music. For the first time we had Frank Sinatra (Greatest Hits) and then our two other favorites, Charlie Rich/John Denver. Read and listened to music till about (16:55) when things started happening.

We went down to the sport house at our usual time, (17:00). We weren't down there more than half an hour when one of the students came in and said we had to go back up to our rooms. We asked him for what reasons. He said it wasn't important. We were just to "hurry up", put our sandals on and go back to the room. Right as we walked into our rooms he told us to start packing all of our personal items.

Right then I had such a good feeling that we were going to be released. Everyone was quiet while packing our things. I guess they were all feeling the same. Mailman and Santa Claus kept coming in telling us to change our luggage. First they said to take everything, then a little while later they would come in and tell us just to take our personal things, one blanket and "just a couple of books". All the things I had packed at first, I wish I would've brought.

What really caught my ear was the comment about the books. They told us only to bring enough books for a couple of days. Why just a couple days? They bring us to a new place, put us in a room that doesn't have anything and they only tell us to bring a couple books. Why move us from the Embassy where they just got both sport houses fixed up, a schedule to watch videotapes and most of all, move us from our new library we just finished working on? Why move us from a place that had all the accessories to keep us healthy and occupied to a place that doesn't have much of anything except for a toilet. I asked Santa Claus today if we'd be going back to the Embassy. He answered, no! Why all this movement?

94

I said about ten rosaries last night while waiting for them to come get us to take us away. I was praying it would be to an airport, but they said we were to be in a vehicle for ten hours. I knew the airport in Tehran wasn't that far of a drive away.

They finally came and got us right after we finished eating our chili and I mean right after. They really seemed to be in a hurry. They asked if we wished to go to the head and reminded us that we'd be in a vehicle for about ten hours. Really it was only nine. They (the students) blindfolded us and then took us down back of the Embassy where we had heard them earlier moving vehicles and messing with weapons. On the way down a couple students said the Shah came back. I had to ask him if he was kidding. He didn't give any reply, but as I can see now, he was.

They loaded us in one of the vans, handcuffing Bill's hand to Jerry's and Jerry's other hand to mine. The other hostage was right in front of us. We rode in that van for nine hours, blindfolded, handcuffed, not able to talk to anyone. Right before we left, Mailman came down to assure us that we were safe and not to worry. I asked him where we were going and he said not to worry, that I'd understand later. I wonder what he meant by understanding later?

Whatever direction we came from (today we decided that we went west or southwest), it was one helluva bumpy ride for us all. I could only make out four other students in the van with us. Four students, four hostages. Jerry just reminded me of something I said when we were getting situated in the van. I gave him a bump in the ribs when they were handcuffing us, telling him this would be one helluva chapter for a book!

When we first started off it sounded as though we had a motorcycle escort, but as we stopped the four times we did I never heard that sound again. One time we stopped, I thought for sure I heard them eating outside the van. They always made sure to leave a student inside each time they got out. That was the longest nine hours I've ever spent in a vehicle. Restless, too. Jerry asked for a cigarette once. They told him to be quiet and he never got one until we got here this morning around (06:00).

Something I forgot to mention that happened on the way. Right before we left our room, I filled my pockets with the bread we had left over from dinner. Anyway, I guess we were half way here, more or less, when I started eating some of the bread. Of course I whispered to Jerry and asked him if he wanted any. He said no, neither did Bill. While I was eating, one of the students grabbed my hand and put a hunk of cheese in it. At first I didn't know what it was. I thought
95

maybe he was playing a joke on me until I smelled it and found out what it was.

It occurred to me that I was having a difficult time keeping my blindfold on while chewing. One time I was trying to get someone's attention, but couldn't, so I just spoke up. A couple seconds later I got one of the student's hands tapping my mouth telling me not to speak. I really got pissed off at that. The only reason I did it was so he could retie my blindfold because it was just about to fall from chewing. I finally got through to him what I wanted. I wished I wouldn't have told him. He retied it really tight that second time. It became loose a couple other times while I was chewing my gum, but I kept it to myself, bending down to pull it up with my hands. It kind of worried me though. I thought maybe the guy behind us that was working the radio would get on to what I was doing, but he didn't.

We finally reached our destination around (06:00) after a long, rough ride. We didn't get that much sleep with all of us being cuffed together, but we did manage a little. The first thing I heard when they turned off the motor was birds singing. After we turned our engine off, I could hear two other engines being turned off. They then told us to get out, all of us still handcuffed together. The birds were louder then, and a dog started barking. The first impression of where they had brought us was a cave. I guess it was because of the birds chirping and some of the students' voices echoing that it sounded so much like a cave. I didn't realize until later, as I walked through it and into a doorway, that it must have just been a porch patio with a lot of birds nesting up in the concrete foundation. Those birds were really loud though, but it sounded great. Have heard nothing like that in a long time.

The house we're in now the students say used to be owned by "Savak" but now is owned by the revolutionary guards. We're really moving up in life. First we were held hostage by the students in the Embassy and now we're being guarded by the revolutionary guards in the "Savak's" old house. We don't know if this is supposed to mean being closer to home or meaning longer being here.

I wonder if our moving has anything to do with what my sister was trying to ask me April 7th when I talked to her. I remember her asking if I knew anything about our moving, and then we were cut off by Mailman telling us not to say anything about that. I didn't know what she meant anyway.

Like I said before, there was nothing in our room when we first got here, but after our personal items arrived and were put in place it started to look like something. At first we thought it might be a waiting entrance from outside, but now we think it might be the breakfast room. Of course, there's no table, just the radiator heaters standing. The room has a lot of windows on each end. One end leads to the outside, and the other to a larger room. Three wooden lockers, one not opening. Wondering what's behind it. Two door passageways, one we use. Once again the other unexplored.

The design of the room is really nice; I kind of like it. It has built-in shelves that we store our items on and three light cords hanging from the ceiling, one working. Get this one! We even have our own servant button that Bill tested this morning and found it to work, bringing one of the guards wanting to know what we wanted. We just told him we wanted to see if it worked, and sure enough it does. The glass that trims the doors that lead outside and downstairs is mostly green. Looking through the glass doors into the other large room, you can see a long stained glass window reaching I'd say about 20 ft. Really beautiful! Otherwise the room's bare just as this one before we got here.

This morning we looked out the patio windows seeing a lot of vegetation, night lamps on poles, and a tennis court to the left. Really couldn't say for sure. It was quite a way off and mostly camouflaged by trees and all. It also looked like a circle drive but I couldn't be too sure of that either.

I know they've been driving back and forth back here most of the day. Plus a lot of guys were walking around earlier this morning. Every one of them had a weapon of some sort. I guess it was a show of force or whatever. I don't think President Carter has this much protection.

After waking this afternoon before lunch I looked to the patio door that leads outside to find it taped up from the outside with a white sheet. This morning earlier the sun was shining in with a good ray of heat, but this afternoon it wasn't, because of the sheet. It sure does stay cool during the day in here, really amazing. It seems as though we'll be taking a lot of cold showers in our new house, unless they plan on fixing the hot water system. Probably take time out tomorrow and clean one of those heads up. It seems as though it's been a while since that's been done.

We played cards for the first time in a long time before lunch this afternoon. It really got boring so we quit early. They surprised us with ham and spinach (cold) this afternoon for lunch. Tonight the real surprise hit us when they brought in hamburger sandwiches which they had to buy somewhere. Store bought sandwiches, two each as a matter of fact. That gets to add up if they're buying them for all of us who are here. It doesn't make sense! Take us from the Embassy where we had a cook, food and everything else to feed the hostages to a new place nine hours driving distance away and where they have to go to town to buy us food.

We know there's at least a town nearby. We heard news coming from a loud speaker system and also people chanting/yelling earlier tonight. We also know there's an airport nearby which we heard planes taking off from today. Where we're at is a mystery to us.

After lunch this afternoon they came in and got us to get fresh air. They took us to a little remote section of the grounds where we weren't able to see the house because of trees, etc. Once again for only us three, I think they had seven guards guarding us, some were revolutionary guards and some were students. They were well armed, ready I guess for anything to happen. The only things we observed were a little water tower, a newly plowed garden (which just caught my mind that they might want us to make, I wouldn't mind it!), a lot of trees and vegetation. Seems like they got us out in the sticks somewhere, but where? The fresh air lasted about 30-45 minutes which was great. Hopefully it will continue.

Something else that just caught my mind. I remember the Red Cross representatives saying they were going to see what they could do about more fresh air. I wonder if this has anything to do with it? We're also just wondering if we'll get those messages back from our families that the Red Cross is supposed to have? Hopefully we'll be home by then. Cross my fingers on that one though!

Santa Claus and some other students came in to talk to us tonight. We tried asking them why we were taken from the Embassy and where we were, but nothing could be answered. One thing Santa Claus did say; he's still keeping his word about something happening in June. What's going to happen is something I guess we'll have to wait and see. He also said that the United States people are doing things nowadays in trying to get us free. What they're doing, he didn't say. They said the same thing about American people doing things regarding our release about two and a half months ago. Look at us. Here we still sit.

Four Eyes and a couple other students brought in some mattresses, pillows and white sheets just awhile ago. The students' attitude towards us is still friendly and kind just as always. We can't figure out why they took us from the Embassy and brought us here. It doesn't seem like they brought everyone, just a few of us. But why? That's a question that bothers all of us three. Is this just another step towards freedom?? *End of entry.*

Sunday, April 27, 1980 (13:30)   **Day 176**

Just woke from a pleasant night sleep, waking once for breakfast that consisted of the usual bread and butter with I'm not sure if it was blueberry or cranberry jelly. Oh yes, and our tea. I forgot to mention last night that they brought us new plates, bowls, spoons and tin cups. So this morning we had tea in the new tin cups. I really don't care for them that much. They hold a lot less than the plastic cups. After I ate my breakfast I started to read a book but crashed back out. Jerry said he thought of about 78 different drama parts for a series this morning. Now the only thing that stands in our path is the question, when are we going home? All our plans and dreams stand before us. Will we ever be able to accomplish them?

Santa Claus and Four Eyes both at different times came in this morning asking if we knew how to cook. We told them of course! They said they're planning on letting us cook. They didn't say for who, or when we were going to start if they decided, but just the thought that they did decide on something like this is great. Give us something to do to pass the time. I guess they found out last night by going out and buying us those sandwiches that they'd have to find another way to feed us or else stay at the old way of buying food and then going broke. I really hope they decide on letting us cook.

It's another beautiful day just as it was yesterday. Birds are all chirping, sun shining bright and guards walking back and forth by the patio door leading outside. Last night when we went to bed they had the same security out there and then even another guard walking in the large room that connects this one. Either our lives are really in danger or they think we're going to escape. No way where we can escape. Where would we go anyway?

I really wish they'd take that sheet off the door outside and let some of those sun rays flow in. Even better, I hope they let us go out and walk around once again today. Even better yet, I hope they let us go home soon! How great that would be. They still blindfold us when taken to the head. Why that is I'll never know. Well it's just about time for lunch and now since we ain't got our normal cook it's really going to be exciting to see what they're going to have for us. Probably some more cold cuts.

At times, sitting or lying down I think of this situation I'm in and can't get it in my mind that this is really happening to me. It seems so much like a movie, at times I come to ask myself if this movie will never have a happy ending? *End of entry.*

Monday, April 28, 1980 (5:30)　　　　　　　　　　Day 177

Just finished taking one helluva cold shower. When the guard took me to the head I asked him if we could take a shower, hoping he would say yes. He kind of hesitated, I guess because the water was so cold. It was eight days since we took our last one and I know I couldn't bear another night smelling myself under the blankets, so I insisted I needed one.

I guess the guard thought I was crazy or something for taking a cold shower, so he must've told Four Eyes what I was doing and then he came and talked to me. He started out saying something about the water being on every fourth day. That's why it was cold now. Then he started talking about once we got to our new place we would have hot water every day and then I added, yes, and we would be cooking our own meals, too. He nodded his head approving what I said, and one of the students behind him said, maybe!

This must be one helluva place they're taking us to. Nine hour drive from Tehran, hot water every day and maybe even a place where we cook our own meals. At first when they started mentioning all those things it sounded something like "home". The only thing though, was would they take us on a nine hour drive to turn us back over to the United States?

From the way Four Eyes was talking, it seemed like he wanted me to wait to take that shower, maybe until we got to the new place. It seems like we'll be leaving here pretty soon. But it doesn't look like we'll be going home. Last night Santa Claus brought us mail in while Bill and I were kneeling saying our prayers. He told us to add a couple prayers for him, too. Anyway he also brought up the subject about leaving here in a couple days, moving to a place where we'll be able to cook ourselves. How strange this is all starting to be, not knowing where we're going, only that the students say we're northwest of Iran.

I got an interesting letter from my sister last night saying something about the students turning us over to the revolutionary council. She wrote the letter 3/7/80 saying she heard that on the news the night before writing the letter. She said they weren't getting their hopes up because all the other times they did, nothing happened. From the way it sounded, if we are turned over to the council, something regarding our freedom is going to happen. That letter was written a good month and a half ago, but we've been wondering if that's what they're doing now. Turning us over to the council. The only thing that's weird though is that nine hour drive! Why take us so far away?

That's probably what my sister Judy was asking over the phone, when she asked if I know anything about our movement to another place. Can we consider this another step closer to home? That's what we've been asking each other, while running all the past events and things we've been hearing through our heads. We can't make anything out of it; I guess it's really better we don't know what's going on. We're really looking forward to seeing what our new place looks like, though; shouldn't be too much longer!

Bill heard through a letter last night from a lady, that Carter said all the hostages were brainwashed. He's really got the nerve to say that!

All the food we've been eating looks as though they bought out the nearby town. Yesterday for lunch we had barbecued chicken, bread. Last night for dinner we had hamburgers just like the night before. This morning for breakfast we had our usual bread, jelly, butter, and for lunch today we had hot dog sandwiches instead of hamburgers. Same bread and all. It's just that instead of hamburger we had hot dogs. There must not be too many of us here if they're going out buying us each meal like this.

I was really surprised to see that we got mail last night and really surprised to see that they were all written to me after Easter, except for the one from my sister. My parents wrote one, but listing a different address, saying they were really glad to hear from me April 7th. They reminded me that Jill is doing well, waiting patiently for me to return. The other two letters I received were from people I didn't know. Still it was good hearing from them.

Jerry received nothing from his wife, but he did get a couple letters dated from February from some of the members of his family. Bill received nothing from his family (a couple months it's been) and nothing from Dawn either. Just eleven other letters from people that have been writing before and a couple he didn't know. It's really strange though they're still wanting to drive nine hours back to Tehran to pick up mail for us. I wouldn't be surprised if we're not still in Tehran! Maybe one of these days I'll understand this whole situation a lot better.

(18:20) We just came from our 45 minute walk outside. Really nice once again today. Sun's shining bright as ever with that continuous breeze that seems never to quit. Once again we had our heavy protection/guards, along with one guy dressed in green fatigues just like the other one that was out there the other day, if I'm not mistaken. I think one of the students said he was a revolutionary guard. They were very well armed and had their eyes on us at all times.

This time Bill brought out a tennis ball which we played pitch and catch with. Had to be careful where we threw it. Didn't want anyone thinking we were trying to escape going after a tennis ball. They finally came up to us and told us we had to go, that our other friends still had to come out yet. Sure wish I knew who our friends were. Anyway they blindfolded us once again and led us back here to our room, where we sit now waiting for the next exciting thing to happen. That, no doubt, will probably be dinner. Really anxious to see what

101

we're going to have to eat.

(20:45) Santa Claus just left our room, not before telling us a few interesting things. The first thing that interested us was the thing about why they moved us. They said our lives were in danger, so they wanted to move us to a new place, where no one knows where to find us, maybe better security, and one of the other things he said, to have better facilities. He said at the new place we'll be able to cook our own meals, take a shower every day and maybe have our own tape box to listen to music. *End of entry.*

Tuesday, April 29, 1980 (22:00)   Day 178

Well, we just recovered from our long journey we had once again last night. They weren't sure if they were going to take us last night or wait till today and take us. Anyway I returned from the head last night right before I was going to retire, and Jerry and Bill were packing their things. They (Jerry and Bill) said the students came in and said we were going to move to our new house, so we were to get our things together and get ready to move. I thought the Marine Corps was bad with the ole' sea bag drag, but here we were again wrapping all our things up in our brown (supposedly white) sheets for another "hurry up and wait hostage brown sheet drag."

A lot of new students came greeting us, telling us we'll really like our new house. It sounded so good, I asked them if we were going home? The reply was no, that our new place would be our home for the time being. If we weren't going to be released, I was really curious to see this new place where we'd be able to take hot showers/baths and cook our own meals. Four Eyes (Hamid) and Santa Claus (Ahmad) said they wouldn't be going with us but would be by to see us frequently. It's surprising, Santa Claus is still with us, but no word from Four Eyes. Word must've gotten changed somewhere along the line.

Some of the students finally came and got us after we were sitting in our rooms for about a half hour waiting. Once again the blindfolds went on, with my eyes adjusted to the darkness, and this morning when the students took them off it really took a while to get adjusted to the sunlight. After the blindfolds, our last walk was taken through the house which we know nothing more of except for the fact it used to be a Savak's house. At least that's what the students said. Oh yes! We also knew it was about an eight or nine hour drive from the Embassy and another six or seven hour drive from our new home here, which I wouldn't be surprised if it is Tehran, Iran.

The three days we were there weren't so bad. Little boring at times, but the fresh air was great. I don't think this new place is going to offer the fresh air we received at the last house.

It seemed like they put us right back in the same van we came there in. Same back seat and everything. This time I traded places with Jerry in the middle so he wouldn't be stuck with both hands cuffed. This morning when we arrived I told him I knew what he meant about having your hands cuffed to two other people, eyes blindfolded for a six to seven hour bumpy ride. That's what I call torturing, not severely, pretty close though! The students tried not to put them on tight, but shoot, you drive seven hours handcuffed to another person when he's trying to sleep and you're trying a different way. It starts to get to the one wrist, if you know what I mean. One helluva bumpy ride and once again, stopping every so often.

We did stop twice for gas, I remember. They always seemed to have a hard time putting the gas nozzle into the gas tank. We had a follow-up car which we learned this afternoon was driven by Guard Chief. I remember hearing Guard Chief talking to our driver (Crazy Man). It seemed like every time we stopped, which had to be around seven times, including stops for gas, our chubby driver (Crazy Man) would always go to the back of the van, open the door and play around with some plastic bags. I sure wish I knew what was in those bags. No doubt it was food. He looks like he's a chow hound anyway. Really nice guy though, considering he's holding us hostage. Didn't have too much trouble with my blindfold, like I did the first time. One of the students had to check it once when they noticed I was able to see over the top. Really couldn't do much with both hands cuffed.

Boy, were we ever glad to get here though. The sun was shining pretty bright, so you could imagine how hot it was getting with nine people in a van that's been on the road for six to seven hours. It was getting hot. I forgot to mention earlier that we had two other hostages along with us, elderly men. Our guess is that we're the only five hostages here.

It was kind of funny tonight before dinner. Santa Claus said that I could cook dinner tonight for the first time, but I was to make enough food for five people, us three and two other students who were sick. That's the excuse he gave me for the other two hostages who were to eat, too. I don't know why he just doesn't come out and say the other two hostages. We've got a room right next door to them and can hear them knocking. What's the use in covering it up?

The room we're in now is just big enough to fit three beds—yes, I said beds! Kind of forgot what they looked like, but they still feel comfortable as ever. Anyway, it's really not that big a deal, because we're supposed to be moving to another room tomorrow. Here in the same building, wherever this building is, whatever it used to be. The rooms remind me of hotel or motel rooms. Nicely furnished.

Santa Claus came in tonight and asked us where we thought we were at. I told him I thought we were back in Tehran. Bill and Jerry said they didn't really know. Before leaving, he stated we were back in Tehran. Now if he was joking, I guess we'll just have to wait and see. One of these days maybe we'll find out what's going on and where we are! It seems like Americans used to live here.

Like I said earlier, Santa Claus let me fix dinner tonight. The only thing it was, was spaghetti in a can, and the only thing I had to do was heat it up. Today earlier he came in and asked us what we wished to fix for lunch tomorrow. The first thing that popped in my mind was chicken, and tonight while I was fixing dinner he showed me the two chickens he went out and bought earlier, along with some potatoes, grease, and tomato sauce. We've got a lot of canned goods so that should last us for a while.

He said we wouldn't be having to cook for those other two so-called students for much longer. They're probably planning to move them somewhere, and then for us to have this one place for ourselves. This situation is starting to look stranger as each day goes by. Some days I really ask myself, am I really a hostage or what? They treat us so good, but still they won't release us.

All these things that are happening, is it a sign that freedom is near or is it a sign showing us we'll be here a while longer? It's been kind of hard lately. Nothing much to do except read and try to figure out what's happening. We're doing our best to wait patiently, and I'm thinking only good thoughts of all the things happening. Hopefully I'm right!! *End of entry.*

Wednesday, April 30, 1980 (22:30)   Day 179

The last day of one of the most exciting months we've had since being here. Some of the most exciting days are yet to come and oh how I can't wait for that beautiful day.

Well, here we sit in our new room, a different room from the one we were in this morning, but it's still in the same building. The windows are all barred especially made for us, I guess from the students. I was wondering what all the noise was yesterday, but I should've figured they were doing something like that when they told us our rooms weren't ready to be moved into.

Last night they moved our two neighbors. It was kind of late when they moved and they made enough noise to wake everyone, except for Jerry. He used to be a real light sleeper, waking whenever there was any little noise, but not now! He can sleep through anything now. It seems like they took them from the building. They had a couple vehicles running when they left their room. A little while later, the vehicles drove off. We didn't have to cook for those other two sick students either; I wonder why?

Jerry and I did a good cleaning of the head this morning. Scrubbing down everything, walls, ceilings, bathtub, everything. We could really tell a difference when we were finished. I plan on taking a nice hot bath tonight after our little workout. We've slacked off on the workouts the last couple nights. Too many things been happening. It seems like we'll be here a while so we might as well make ourselves at home.

The new room we're in now is about the same dimension as the one we were in this morning, "small". We've still got our three mattresses. It seems like they follow us everywhere. They asked us if we wished to have the legs from the beds we used this morning, but then they said we'd have more room if we just stuck to our mattress. It really doesn't bother us, so we're just using the mattress.

Otherwise there isn't much more room to do anything, but then again, what more can we do? We have a little space right in the center to play cards and chess, and also a desk which I'm using right now with a lamp placed on top. I know we don't have to worry about not having enough light. We've also got a light fixture on the ceiling and two on the walls. I sure wish I could say the same about getting some sun in here. I guess we'll have to wait till morning and see if it will shine in.

Cleaning out the head gave us something to do. Really made the time fly by. I wish they'd let us do the same in the kitchen, but for some odd reason whenever we're in there cooking our meals, they're always behind us, telling us to hurry. They won't let all three of us go in at the same time, so Jerry had to wait in the room tonight while Bill and I went in to fry chicken and fry potatoes. I thought we did pretty good, considering I had to gut the chicken/cut its head off and then cut it up. One of these days I'll learn how to cut a chicken the correct way instead of tearing it all up. Otherwise I thought we did pretty good in preparing our first homecooked meal. I guess I really shouldn't say that now. Maybe tomorrow after all the food's been digested, I'll say it was pretty good. Keep my fingers crossed now.

The students have really been treating us well. This afternoon I gave Santa Claus a list of things we need to cook with, and tonight when they took us to that kitchen, he showed me some of the things I asked for and said he could try to get the others later. Also tonight when they brought us here they also brought with them three roses, one white, one red and one pink. They were really beautiful, especially the white one which I never in my life had seen before until tonight.

Well, I wonder what kind of things are being said back in the States regarding our release. It sure doesn't look as though there's much being said over here. Will this thing ever come to an end? Oh God, please help us!

There's a lot of movement outside our window. Sounds as though they're carrying something heavy. You can hear their feet shuffling and then at times some grunting. Like always we hear the weapons, bolts being closed and then at times the tapping of the magazine. I guess it's a sign they're trying to use in telling us not to do something, or else.

Really been seeing some different faces since we've been moving around so much. I guess those are the main guards outside. All the students that come answer the door are all the same ones we had at the Embassy. It's surprising how close they have us stored next to a busy street. During the day there's constant movement, honking and whatever else it takes to make it sound like a main street. Really surprised there hasn't been any demonstrating out front yet. But then again, they probably got us here without any one else knowing. *End of entry.*

Thursday, May 1, 1980 (23:45)   Day 180

The first day of a new month. Wonder what's in store for us? It was our first morning in our new room, and like always breakfast was served once again by Santa Claus. Haven't seen him the rest of the day; must've had a date or something.

Crashed out right after breakfast, that is, right after I finished drinking my milk, which they've been giving us every morning and then listening to the demonstrators out front for a while, crashing out once again. Last night I think I put in my diary I was surprised there wasn't any demonstrating being done, and this morning I awake to chanting/yelling people with one loud one over a loudspeaker system. It reminded me of back at the Embassy. I guess the students were just letting us know that they were still with us. How nice it was of them.

Surprisingly enough, I happened to crash back out until waking from the call of lunch Bill had sounded. We just had breakfast at (10:00)! Here he is at (13:15) with lunch. If this keeps up I will leave here fat. He had Sloppy Joe's with beans mixed together, producing a pretty good lunch. But then again not as good as my chicken last night and my hamburgers tonight.

Tonight they let all three of us in the kitchen to fix dinner. Jerry and Bill peeled the potatoes, and I fried them along with the hamburgers, which was well observed by Bill, like always. Really came out well. They want us to eat in the kitchen, but we said no we'd rather go back to our room where we had the hot sauce stashed which we stole from the other room, and we had the salt and pepper in there besides. We told them tomorrow we'd eat in there, so they agreed. They kept coming in and out, looking out the kitchen window when we were in there. It seemed like they were waiting for someone to fall out of the sky or something.

While I was in the head later tonight, Jerry and Bill heard them receive a strange call over the telephone. The phone's close to the room so they could hear a little. They said they overheard Guard Chief (Ahmad) speaking in English ask the person who was calling where he got the number and then telling the caller that the hostages were well. After that they didn't hear too much more. One of the students came in to talk to Jerry and Bill. When I returned they told me about it. Such strange things have been happening lately. What's going to happen next?

Guard Chief said there is a swimming pool nearby which we might get to use this summer. Sounds like they're expecting us to be here a while. They took us to another head all this morning and afternoon. I guess they like the way Jerry and I had cleaned the other out. They wanted this one the same. They never asked us to clean it or anything like that, but since we're going to be using it and since we don't have nothing else to do, I told them we'd clean it tomorrow, and boy, does it need a cleaning! The hot water wasn't working today, but they said they were working on it and we'd have some soon. Might as well make the best of it while we're here.

Whoever used to live here really had a nice place. Sure wish we knew where we were at. Once again they gave us a clue, at least that's what I take them as. Anyway he said we were in "The City of Roses". I've heard that said once before, but can't place where it was. From that phone call we had tonight it looks as though someone knows where we are. What happens now??

Days are mostly spent to ourselves, reading books and mostly daydreaming. I guess we should really get back into our old routines of playing cards, chess, etc. Haven't even been doing our exercises. I just haven't been able to do much lately. Think a lot about home, the family and especially Jill. What they're all going through and their feelings of our release. What are they thinking? I miss and love them all so much. Why am I being kept from them? Jill's birthday's next month, June 22, and here I'll probably still sit. The only thing I

107

thought I could send as a present would be a nice letter with a poem attached. *End of entry.*

Friday, May 2, 1980 (03:10)   Day 181

Guard Chief just left from having a light discussion in ideology/politics. He told us to believe that we are helping poor people by being here and not to worry, that God is on our side. He said God wants everyone equal, and that's what they are trying to accomplish. I can't see what they're gaining by holding us. To me it's just putting a bad image on the Moslem religion and the country of Iran.

Found out why there was so much honking on Thursday night. Their Thursday nights are like our Saturdays in the States for having weddings. After they are married, they drive around honking their horn to symbolize their marriage. Sounds familiar!

Guard Chief described a little about their religion and their mosque (like our church) where they pray. Most of the time was spent telling us not to worry about going home, just to think about how we are helping the poor people. I guess they see us as being rich people or something. Everything I got in my life I had to work for. I can't see why everyone else couldn't do the same. Guard Chief plans on having these discussions every night. I know I've got things to say, but at times I doubt if I should say them.

It seems like everyone's got their different opinions on why we were moved. Guard Chief says he'll tell us this later, but now's not the right time. I guess it's just like the skin specialist that was supposed to come to check my acne, but never did. Red Cross probably dropped our family messages off, but we never received those either.

Since yesterday I've been asking for some cleaning gear to clean out our new dirty head. I guess I was right in the first place when I said we already cleaned out the other one, so they moved us out of that one to a dirty one. Plus the new one doesn't even have hot water for showering.

I've got a feeling that Santa Claus doesn't care for me too much anymore. I guess I've been asking for too much and he's getting tired of running around. They could easily let us go and not ever worry about us anymore. But no, they want to play their games. Jerry's been asking for Librium, but still hasn't received any.

Demonstrations have still been going on pretty frequently. They never give up it looks like! They were doing some work in back of our window all this afternoon so we had to keep our drapes shut. I just don't understand these guys. I think they're really scared we're going to split on them. We're in a city that we don't even know and still they blindfold us to go to the toilet, which is about fifteen feet away. What a joke!

We let Bill cook lunch and dinner today. Give him something to do. Even the students have been wondering if anything's wrong with him.

(22:30) Santa Claus was just in to tell us some very interesting news about a Special Force group that tried to come in to evacuate the hostages. He said that eight military personnel were killed in the attempt, but didn't say anything about how many were involved in the attack. I knew that something like this would happen, meaning the first couple months we were here that they would try to get us out. I'm really surprised we're not dead this very moment.

The students said they warned our government about such an attack and if they tried to come in they would kill the hostages, but instead of the students killing us, they moved us here. It explains the quick movement we had all of a sudden. We were really shocked by the news. I still can't believe it. He said he would bring in the *Time* magazine and show us the pictures of the military men who were killed sometime tomorrow. It's really strange!

It's the second night we've had a discussion group. It's like they're trying to find out what we're going to say if and whenever we're released. Some good and encouraging words he did say last night was that we should be sure we wouldn't be here over eight months. Our eighth month is June, so I'm crossing my fingers on it. So close we came to death, but still the students treat us good.

I hope my family and Jill are all doing well after hearing about this evacuation failure and the eight men being killed. I bet they're worried shitless. *End of entry.*

Saturday, May 3, 1980 (13:00)   Day 182

Woke early this morning to have breakfast with Jerry. Bill never eats it. About half an hour later, Santa Claus came in to show us the pictures of the eight military men who were supposedly killed. I didn't see anything saying it though, but did see their pictures along with a couple of other pictures of some hostages. Why would they show those pictures of the hostages after showing the pictures of the eight men killed? Like always he wouldn't let us read it, but said he might come back later to read it to us. I'm really interested to see what it says. On the front of the cover President Carter stated he took full responsibility of the occurrence. Santa Claus also said that Vance resigned. That must have been one helluva upset in the United States. What next is in store for us.

I got my typewriter this morning and believe it or not, it was electric. Got a lot of typing to catch up on so it should keep me busy for a while. They must have gotten a washer and dryer, for this morning they asked for all our dirty laundry to wash. They said we could use the head on the other side once again this morning. Bill went over to take a shower and came back to say the water wasn't too warm, meaning it was a little cold. I guess they never got it fixed yet.

I forgot to mention that we received mail yesterday. I was the only one that heard from my family (Debbie and Jill). Also a letter from a far cousin I never knew I had, living in California. Once this is over I'll probably be meeting so many cousins I never knew I had. What a way to get relatives together once again.

I'm so proud of how Jill's been holding out, and especially proud/happy of those beautiful letters she sends. If I ever get out of here, which I know I will, I know she'll be the one! Such a brave and patient little soldier she is. I love you, Jill Renee! Always will, too!

Bill didn't hear anything from his family or girlfriend. Hasn't for a while now. Of course we all (except Jerry) got letters from people all over the place. It's so good to know they're still thinking of us. How I can't wait to get out of here. So great it's going to be. Still wondering what my sister had, boy or girl? They're thinking of letting us make a phone call to our families to assure them of our health and safety, which I think is a great idea. Like I said before, I know they're worried to death about us.

Yesterday Guard Chief came in and asked if we would want to watch some Iranian football (soccer). We said sure. A little while later they came in carrying the television set. They also asked if we like cartoons, if we did, they would bring it in whenever they came on. I've never heard of a hostage situation this good. What a trip!

Sun's out once again today, but with the tablecloth they've got hanging over the patio door, none of the sun comes in. At least we get some nice fresh air that comes in, along with the sound of birds chirping. It's not that bad. Like I've always said, we could have it worse. Thank the good Lord we've got it this good, especially after the evacuation the U.S. attempted. The students could have easily shot us, but they didn't. It shows they believe in human rights, which I'm glad of! Never have I ever known a hostage situation so unique. *End of entry.*

Sunday, May 4, 1980 (00:10)   Day 183

Santa Claus was in tonight with another discussion. We talked a little about the situation we're in, and then he told me about my family supporting President Carter's military actions, which kind of shocked me. I forgot what he said about Jerry's wife, but he said Bill's parents were undecided in the middle. Like we all said tonight, everyone is entitled to their own opinion, and I know whatever the reason my parents took that point of view, they had a reason for it.

Santa Claus also showed us some pictures of Mrs. Herrmaning who came to see her son. Underneath the picture it had an article of where President Carter had put a boycott for people entering Iran. A $2,000.00 fine plus four years imprisonment just if some of the families came to see us. That's what I call inhuman! It's really surprising that President Carter is still in office, especially after all the things he's supposedly done.

Once again tonight Santa Claus emphasized that in a month and a half some word of freedom will arise. It's very encouraging to hear these words, especially how he says them. They sound so real and beautiful, "freedom".

Tomorrow we're going to start a class on Farsi to keep us a little busy. Anything to pass this time is great, especially learning a new language. We let Bill do the cooking today, and for both meals once again we had beans. Our poor assholes! I was kept busy all day retyping my diary, so finding something to do isn't hard.

(22:10) Days seem to be flying by lately. Really been keeping myself busy retyping my diary. We let Bill cook the meals to keep him busy; plus today he built an airplane out of three by five cards. The students were really amazed by it. He's been a little more active lately, but at times it's really hard to talk to him. Jerry doesn't have that much to keep busy, but he does a good job at it. He has already read the book Santa Claus brought him last night, but luckily enough Santa Claus picked some more up at the College of Art & Science Center this afternoon. Otherwise Jerry hasn't had too much to do. He still works on his poems, producing about two a day.

I know the toilets are going to be needing cleaning pretty soon. That will be something to do. We still haven't cleaned the one we're using now; maybe tomorrow we will. Jerry and I've been doing our exercises at night recently. Last night was really hard, especially after all the beans Bill's been making for our meals.

Today he changed the schedule a little. For lunch we had tuna fish, and tonight for dinner Jerry and I had Iranian rice with a little of Bill's beans and fried potatoes. I don't really mind the rice; it really fills me up. I made out a list and gave it to Santa Claus this afternoon for things we need (food). Now maybe we'll start having something else besides Bill's beans.

The only thing we have to do is ask for it, and if they can get it, we'll

111

have it. This afternoon they brought in ice cream cones. This morning Bill was just messing around and asked them if we could get some ice cream. A couple hours later one of the students comes in with three ice cream cones, each in a sealed plastic bag. What a treat that was!

Earlier this morning, before noon, they came in and got us for fresh air. Put the towels over our heads and walked us out right in back of our room here. The sun was shining bright, which felt good/great. Nice size swimming pool out there, too. I asked if we could clean it out since we were going to be here for such a long time and he said he'd see what the other students say. I doubt if they'll agree though.

We were only allowed to walk underneath the patio above us and that's all. One guard was on the other side of the pool and two guards were up on the patio above. They all looked to be well armed too. Anyway the sun felt good, while it lasted.

We also had a Farsi class this afternoon. Santa Claus taught us how to say a few things. Good morning, how are you? What are you doing? I am reading a book, I am eating my lunch, I am writing, studying, I want to clean the pool. Nothing wrong with learning a new language. I find it kind of hard though. Just don't have the right tongue for it.

Santa Claus, Guard Chief and Crazy Man (driver) just left our room from having another discussion on religions. Finding the talks are helpful to pass the time. We all feel that way. It really helps to take our minds off this situation. Wonder what the word is back in the States regarding us? Sure wish it was something like freedom, but I think they're all trying to recover from the loss of those eight men. The good Lord has been with us and I hope and pray He continues to do so. *End of entry.*

Monday, May 5, 1980 (22:30)   Day 184

Our hundred and eighty-fourth day today and we're still shooting on going home in June, praying and hoping that is! Santa Claus just left us with some more up-to-date news. An F-14 crashed down at the Persian Gulf, just today. He said the two pilots were killed. Never mentioned how it crashed, but it's really strange. First the other eight men killed in late April or early May, and now today those two pilots of an F-14.

All these men being killed for the protection of only one man. Is he worth the ten Americans' lives that have been sacrificed already? It really seems hard to believe with all these things happening now that the Iranian government is going to justify something towards our release. The only thing we can do like always is just sit here and wait and hope that something does happen. It looks to be the only way to freedom!!

Santa Claus also stated that Capucci was in charge, along with the Red Cross, of delivering all the bodies back to America. It could've not happened if the students and Iranians didn't believe so much in human rights! I pray every night, asking the good Lord to stay with us and so far He's proved that.

A funny thing the students did today. Jerry and I were working on our diaries and poems. Bill was reading his Bible. Guard Chief came in and asked Bill if he would want to come out and take part in a discussion, which we found out later from Bill was about how poor families and different minority groups were going to start demonstrating more to get the things they want. Bill said he also said something about if the Pope came out and told the American people to turn the Shah back to Iran he'd be back in no time. We've thought that ever since the beginning of this ordeal, but it looks like maybe the Pope has different feelings.

Talking about my diary, Jerry started a sequence of special thoughts and events that he could remember from the first 90 days, ending the day I started my diary, and put them in a poem form. They're really sounding good. I also started typing out the poems we had finished, and the more Jerry and I talk about it the more I look at the things we've got to start a book, I think to myself that we can't miss. The only thing that stands in our way is the most important thing, freedom.

Bill finally had a change in the meal schedule this afternoon. For lunch we had hamburgers and fried potatoes, which didn't taste too bad, and tonight once again we had the Iranian rice. Bill fixed himself beans once again, which I ate a little of. The rice has really been good and filling. Jerry thinks the same, too. He's hoping he doesn't get too fat eating it all the time though. This afternoon he started doing some exercises during the day, too, and then also along with me at night.

A weird thing just happened right out front on the street. We can often hear the cars flying by and then some burning rubber as they start off and then some skidding. Sometimes they seem to be screeching around a corner. Whenever I hear one of these cars like this, I always make a crashing noise to imitate a wreck. Well, this time I didn't have to imitate the crashing noise, because it sounded like a car went right through a house next door to us. The noise was so great (the screeching tires and breaking of the glass) it sounded as

113

though it happened in just the other room. It might have been a room connected to this house. I guess we'll never know. Maybe tomorrow the students will tell us about it.

Can't hear the students' voices outside our room like we were hearing before the accident. They probably all went over to see what happened. It's really weird though. All the time I'm making fun of the screeching tires and then an accident, and here I sit hearing the real thing taking place.

Santa Claus also mentioned that we wouldn't be staying too long, but that we would be taken to another house/building where they'd have a beautiful garden we could see. When we would be leaving he didn't say, but he said we would stay in this city. If it is true what he said tonight, we are in Shiraz (the City of Roses). I guess I was wrong about being in Tehran! He said that one of the students would be going to the Embassy the day after tomorrow, so if there was anything we wanted and they could get, they would bring it back for us. Told us if we wanted mail to be sent, we should have it ready by then and they would take it along.

I forgot to mention that I found a wishbone in my chicken and rice tonight. I'm letting it dry now and tomorrow we'll make our wishes and then wait to see whose wishes come true.

We had our Farsi class once again today. Maybe by the time we're released I'll be able to speak fluent Farsi. I really doubt it though! This afternoon one of the students put a lock on the outside of our door. Why they did, I'll never know. I guess they think we're going to make a break out of here or something, so now they're going to lock us in.

A couple students just came in to describe the accident that happened. Seven people were in the car at the time but were thrown out before it was demolished. They said it was the work of the Lord that saved them. I believe it was. We were discussing other things, too. One thing Guard Chief said was that the Iranian Embassy in England was taken over and blown up with about 20 Iranians killed. They believe it was the doings of Carter. He said that the Iranian people wanted to go to England to the Embassy but the Imam wouldn't let them.

All these things happening I'm really surprised the Iranians haven't killed us, but they don't. They say Imam keeps asking how the hostages are doing. They say he knows some of them are innocent people, and even the accused people should all be treated well. So many strange things been happening lately, it's so surprising we're still alive. That's the honest truth. What other discouraging things are we going to hear? Being here without our freedom is bad enough, but still we

114

hear all these things happening.

One of the things we were discussing was cars. They say they pay $10,000.00 for an Iranian car, $25,000.00 for an American automobile. The prices are unreal for vehicles, but gas is only 55 cents a gallon, which is still pretty high. The things I learn everyday, amazing. *End of entry.*

Wednesday, May 7, 1980 (12:45)   Day 186

Just woke up from a good morning sleep. We haven't been hitting the mattress lately till early parts of the morning, sleeping pretty much into the afternoon. Jerry and Bill were already up, just sitting around. Jerry is reading one of the books Santa Claus just recently brought him, and Bill is practicing his card tricks. I started on my diary last night, but stopped when Santa Claus, Guard Chief and Telephone Operator came in to talk a little about theology.

They were saying there are eight hundred million Moslems worldwide, fifty million in Russia, forty-five million in Iran and about ten million in the United States. Those are some hard figures to believe. We also talked a little about nationalizing fuel and then a little about other national crises. They were talking about the terrorist incident that happened in England. Two Iranians that were employed were killed, and the terrorists are being held in England. He said the Iranian people were all upset about the incident, so now they should understand how the American people feel towards our situation.

Bill had a surprise visit by Ayatollah Khalkhali (the revolutionary judge) yesterday when he was in the kitchen fixing our lunch. Ayatollah Khalkhali had been out giving a speech to the demonstrators that were out front. I guess a couple students must have invited him in, and at the same time they found Bill making lunch. Bill said they took a couple pictures and he told him not to worry, that we would be going home, and he hopes it is soon! Those were some encouraging words coming from the Revolutionary Judge. He's a well-known man for his two minute court sessions. They said they didn't want to bring him around to see everyone, because a lot of the hostages might have been scared or something. Bill said he didn't want to see Jerry because Jerry had a bad reputation. I guess it was because Jerry is a merchant. They still hold that against him.

We gave the students our letters and a list of things we need, so when they go back to the Embassy today they can mail our letters and pick up the things we asked for from the Embassy store. They're supposed to leave sometime today, and return who knows when?

Every night the students come in and give us the feeling that freedom's going to pop up anytime now. I'm still hoping and shooting for June, but if it comes before then, I sure won't bitch about it. He said the release of the hostages is determined among the Imam and the people. So it seems that the representatives of the people are at work to see what they can do. I remember "Nose" telling me that some kind of decision like this would be known in June, so that's one of the reasons I think we'll be leaving. It seems like it's our only way out!

Woke this morning and found some nuts on the desk for me. All these treats/talks at night seem to be leading up to something! We're sure hoping it's what we think it is.

(23:50) Santa Claus just left from having a short discussion on how after having a revolution and succeeding like they did, they have to start thinking about cultural things. He said their President had just been on television giving a speech on the subject.

Right before dinner he came in and asked us what we wished to have for a meal tonight. Jerry and I had already agreed on having rice but Bill wanted some beans. We told him from now on we would be having Iranian rice for dinner (all of us) and for lunch we would make up our own meal of whatever we want. We told him we would eat rice for lunch, too. But he said we didn't have to if we didn't want to. Whatever we ask for, if they can get it, we'll have it. I think I can talk for all three of us, we've really gotten to like the food.

Had Farsi class once again today. Bill was sleeping so he didn't participate. He finally woke when Santa was leaving. About an hour later Bill had a crowd of students in the room, showing them his tricks. Like always they all loved it. Jum-Chi came to visit the students, so he was among our guests. All the other ones were just the ones that live with us.

Been eyeing several bugs crawling around the room. No doubt they're all being attracted to the food we drop and are not able to pick up. The students told us we could eat in the kitchen, but we turned them down. It reminds me of camping out!

Some of the students left for the Embassy today and won't be back till Saturday. Hopefully they'll bring mail back for us. Kind of anxious to hear what they all have to say. Santa also mentioned that another F-14 had crashed near the Persian Gulf. That's a total of two so far that crashed. Myself, I don't think they crashed, I believe they've been downed, but by who?

Jerry asked him about his phone call home and he started to say it wasn't important, but then changed his mind and said that all lines had been cut in the States to here. Maybe he was about to say that the phone call wouldn't be necessary, because we would be going home soon. I wish he would've said it! He also mentioned that there were a

116

lot of hostages here and that some of the older ones were moved to a better location with better medical facilities. He was saying a couple of them had bad hearts. I know this situation isn't helping them any.

We had a little dispute tonight on whose turn it was to do the dishes, but after a little reasoning, we finally solved it out. Little disputes like these are the ones that can lead into huge arguments. Have to remember to keep my temper low!

I thought we left all the barking dogs back at the Embassy, but I guess we didn't. I can hear them now, and last night or the night before Bill and I heard a rooster crowing. Closed my eyes and it reminded me of home. Whenever you can't hear the barking and crowing at night, you can usually hear the students in the other room talking; sometimes it seems you can hear your names mentioned, but I can't be sure. No doubt they have their discussions over what they think of each of us, and other times what they think about the situation now, and then sometimes they probably talk about things we discuss in our discussions. You can usually hear them talking.

Each day I wonder how many more days we'll have left, but I hardly discuss it with Jerry and Bill. Try to keep myself as busy as possible along with Jerry. I finally got his poems typed tonight, so tomorrow I'll start typing my diary. I pray and hope I won't have to cross too many more days off my calendar and please God, make it be soon that we are freed. *End of entry.*

Thursday, May 8, 1980 (24:00) Day 187

Just finished another conversation with the students. This one was on discrimination. It first started with thoughts on who is going to be the next descendant from God and what would he be like? These are questions they always bring up. I guess just to see what we say. I believe Guard Chief got a little upset with some of the things we were saying and decided to leave.

Once again they emphasized that a revolution would be needed to gain control, nothing else. In fact, they said that a revolution has already started in the States. To my point of view, it looks as though they want every country to be a revolutionary country, and every person to be a "Moslem", plain and simple. Santa said if everyone stuck to what the Bible says, we would have none of the problems of today's society. Really some interesting conversations we've been having lately.

Woke once again today around noon. I guess all the nightlife we've been having is getting to me. Bill had spaghetti for lunch, and for dinner we had Iranian rice, which once again filled me up. For some strange reason Bill did both the lunch and dinner dishes, really surprised me.

This afternoon Santa came in and instead of having a Farsi class, he had Bill read a short story from the book BROTHERS AND SISTERS, edited by Arnold Adoff. It was short stories that emphasized black experience, discrimination of blacks, etc. Before leaving (I don't know if he was kidding or not), he emphasized that I should read it. I guess he sees me as being a discriminator.

Last night I forgot to write that right after we ate dinner, Santa came in with a special that was being heard from England (on the radio) of Stravinsky, the famous Russian composer. He said whenever they have things on like this, he would bring in the radio and let us hear it. He's really a listener of symphony music!

Otherwise not much more happened. Worked on my diary, and Jerry worked on his; Bill practiced his magic and read the Bible. I guess I'll finish now and do my exercises with Jerry, say my rosary and hit the rack. Had a hard day at the office today! "Please release me, let me go!" God bless America!!!! *End of entry.*

Friday, May 9, 1980 (22:55)   Day 188

Just finished working on my diary and thought that I'd write a little to wrap up today. I guess I'll start by describing the fried chicken I fixed, right when I woke this afternoon for lunch. There aren't too many words I can find to describe it except that it was great. I have to give a little credit for Bill's fried potatoes. They were pretty good. After we scarfed that down and sat around for a while, Jerry and I went in and cleaned the kitchen up. It definitely needed cleaning and when we were finished we sat at the table (kitchen table, no guards around, except occasionally) and talked about our families and future dreams. Really enjoyed sitting and drinking tea around the kitchen table. Like Jerry said, it took our minds off the situation. When we returned to our room about an hour later, Santa came in with ice cream. The last kind we had last was on a cone, but this was in a plastic cup, made from different fruits. It was excellent!

They still continue to treat us, as Jerry would say, like "guestages" (a new word he made up), but nothing is said about our release. They said the people finished electing their new Parliament today, but it wouldn't be effective for another month. It seems as though their new government is our only hope of freedom, so like always we sit back and wait to see what happens. If it is true that the Parliament won't be in total operation for another month, it will be around the same time Santa said that something will happen! I pray to God it's true.

Started to work on my diary this afternoon when they came in and asked if we would want to watch "Charlie Chaplin". Of course we said yes, and they came in (just about all the students with the T.V.) and we sat around till dinner watching it. It had to do with back in the depression days.

Around seven forty-five the movie was interrupted for prayer time. They started off with scenes of Iran, mosque, ocean shots, etc. Then a person was put on to give a reading of the Koran. It gave Jerry and I both thoughts about the movie we would love to do. After that was finished, a speaker was speaking in front of a group of demonstrators. We watched a little, before they came in and told us to turn it off until Charlie Chaplin continued. About a half hour later we checked to see if Charlie had returned, but he hadn't so they took the T.V. back. I guess whatever the speaker was saying the students didn't want us to hear, although he was speaking in Farsi. I guess they figured all the Farsi classes we've been having, they couldn't trust us. What a joke.

After dinner, tea was served to us as usual with Santa coming in with his radio to try to pick up something from England. We picked up the same channel we did the other night, but nothing was on interesting so we decided not to listen to it. After he left, the students started messing with the outside of our door. We think they're tying a string or rope on it, so the door doesn't bounce back and forth all the time. Whenever it's closed the wind blows it, making it sound as though someone's knocking, and the students come and open it up to find no one wanting anything.

Haven't had Farsi class the last two days. I guess they figure we've learned enough. Well, tomorrow the student comes back from Tehran, hopefully with some mail for us. We're all looking forward to it, so I hope we're not disappointed! When will our freedom day arise? God, please help us! *End of entry.*

Sunday, May 11, 1980 (00:30)   Day 190

What a boring day it was yesterday. It started off with being woke by the sound of music that Santa brought in for us to listen to. I stayed under the covers listening to Bill and him talking about it. It was the station from England playing different types of music, Irish, Swedish, etc. About fifteen minutes later, the program ended and the news (worldwide news) started to come on, but he turned it off. They asked him to let them listen, but he said no and left.

After a while of trying to get back to sleep, I decided to get up and take a shower to start the day out right. Bill got a little pissed when I asked if I could take a shower and they said yes. Supposedly he asked earlier and they said no. The water was a little cool. I was hoping it was still hot from the night before, but my luck it wasn't.

Came back to the room and saw they had come to get Bill to make lunch. It was his last turn today to cook (for a week) and his specialty was spaghetti once again! Jerry and I start tomorrow for a week, and I asked Santa for some eggs, so we could have them for breakfast. I believe tonight he said he got some, so tomorrow morning we're going to have fried eggs!

Jerry and I both took days off from working on our diaries and poems today and instead just laid around. I guess it was around (16:00) when Guard Chief came in and asked Bill if he wanted to go outside. Jerry and I were both sleeping, so they didn't want to wake us up. A little while later Jerry happened to wake and saw Guard Chief looking through the window. He then asked Jerry if he would want to come out, and Jerry of course said yes. Any chance we can get to go outside, we grab it. He was going to try to wake me but Guard Chief told him to let me sleep. So I missed out on going outside.

By the time they came in it was time for dinner. No rice tonight; it seemed like it was some kind of bean stew. Pretty good, too! Two helpings. For lunch the spaghetti didn't fill me up, so the students offered me some of their rice, which I've found I really like lately. I feel like I'm putting on a couple pounds with all the rice and spaghetti we've been having.

Santa came in a couple hours ago. He wanted me to tell him about my hometown. We were talking about winter and Jerry mentioned that he hopes we aren't still here by winter. Santa assured us we wouldn't be, but just to make sure that I heard correctly I asked him again. The same answer was repeated. Well, it seems certain we'll be out of here by winter. I guess that's November or December. We all have our hopes up so much for next month. There are really going to be some disgusted/angry people around here if we're still here by June 30. Oh God, please help to deliver us to our families and loved ones once again! All of us, not just some, all.

Jerry and Bill are both crashed out. Excuse me, just Bill. I just woke Jerry. I had to show him what Bill was and still is doing. Bill's always making fun of how Jerry always blows out of his mouth when he's sleeping. Well, tonight Bill's doing the exact same thing. We're really going to jump on him tomorrow about that.

The students must be having a party upstairs or something. They're right above us bounding around and talking really loud. I'm sure glad they're having fun. The students that were supposed to come back from Tehran today never made it. Santa said they're not expected till

Sunday. Better chance we might have mail then. Cross our fingers on that. *End of entry.*

Sunday, May 11, 1980 (23:20)   Day 190

Just finished with a little discussion with Santa. We ended up talk-ing about going home, which he never seems to want to talk about. One interesting thing we found out today is that we'll be flying back to Tehran upon our release, so that cuts that long truck ride. I'm so sure we'll be released in June I'd lay any money on it. It seems like they know when we'll be released and where we'll be going once we leave here. Germany it sounds like for sure! The only thing we need to know now is when?

Today was Mother's Day, I believe, and for breakfast Jerry and I had fried eggs, fried potatoes, Spam and milk/tea. Bill wasn't in-terested so it was just Jerry and I in the kitchen fixing it. What a great way it was to get our minds off this situation.

Santa just stepped in with a radio to let us listen to some country western music played from England. It was considerate of him to bring it in. Otherwise not much happened today. Continued to work on my diary and Jerry on updating his ninety days. Kept us busy most the afternoon. Made the time fly by pretty fast.

Bill's thinking about going on a diet this week, for what reason he didn't say. I know it's not because he's getting fat. He doesn't even eat that much. Can't tell him anything though. I guess we'll just have to let him do what he wants. I still don't see why he has to fast!

Santa said tonight that the students who went to Tehran the other day are returning tomorrow with a lot of mail. Didn't say who for though. We're all looking forward to receiving one from our families. Going to close for now, do my exercises with Jerry and then maybe see if I can get a shower in tonight. It seems as though freedom is ap-proaching, but when? That question we'll just have to wait and see. *End of entry.*

Monday, May 12, 1980 (23:05)   Day 191

Well, a little excitement was brought into our lives today when Santa brought us a tape recorder and an American tape to listen to. The students that were in Tehran had just returned, so they must've brought it with them. It was one of the many things we had put on our list of things to get, and it seems as though that's all they brought. He let us listen to it for about five hours before taking it away. Why would he want to take it away? Maybe to give it to some other hostages.

The tape we listened to (one of the five he said we had) was mostly disco, and then there were a couple like ELO, Fleetwood Mac, etc. Really surprising they're letting us listen to all this. Earlier, and even today, they said the music we listen to is bad for our minds. They feel like this, but still they let us listen to it. Maybe (my own thoughts) they're trying to get us back in the groove of the Western World, which they call it, for when we're released.

I'm still keeping my hopes up for June, but at times I feel like we're going to be let down. Like today we asked Santa if the students that returned from Tehran brought any canned food, etc. He said no, that everything is being trucked down here. Plus he brought up the subject of being moved again. Didn't say when though. Did say it was still in this city. Thank God for that!

I just got finished telling Jerry that might be their excuse in telling us that no food was going to be sent, and maybe freedom is closer than we think. I hate to think that it is true about the food being trucked here. Hearing that just makes it seem like we're going to be here so much longer. I hope and pray it's not!

They didn't bring back mail, but said we still have it sitting back at the Embassy. Santa told us he is leaving for three days, supposedly to go back to Tehran, do some things, pick up the mail and return here. The later he picks up mail the better chance we have to receive a letter from our families. Cross our fingers on that one!

This morning Santa brought in an Arabian magazine that showed the wreakage of one CH-53 and another one right behind it, undamaged it looked like. The wreakage of the one in front showed a charred body with some wreakage on top of it. Really a sickening sight. He also told us that Musky is Secretary of State now. At least we're being told a little about the world news. Too bad we can't hear anything about when we're to be released.

Jerry and I had hamburgers and fried potatoes for lunch. Bill's still fasting his lunch meal only. It's really strange he doesn't eat lunch, but eats dinner. Something to do with Mother's Day and something else he told us. Maybe he doesn't like my cooking.

For the first time in a long time we played two hands of spades this afternoon when they brought the music. After the first hand the enjoyment of the game was gone for me. Can't get into it like I used to. Listening to that music really made me wish I was home with my family and Jill Renee. How much longer can we hold out like this? I get a lot of times when things are really bothering me. I do my best to try to brush them off to the side, but it's really hard at times. I hope the good Lord stays with me, to guide me through.

Not much of anything else happened today. The students are still determined to make our stay as pleasant as possible. They say there is no boss here. Whatever they decide, they decide together. There is no such thing as a boss.

I told Santa that we need meat for tomorrow's lunch. We hadn't had hot dogs for a while, so I told him we need them. He said okay he'd get them by tomorrow's lunch. All these good things they do for us, but still they keep us hostage/guestage. If they are to let us go in June, what's going to be the difference if instead they let us go now? That's if it's true we're to go home in June. Once again, wait and see. Things are getting hard mentally. Hopefully we can stick together, but for how long??? I pray to God my family and Jill are all right. Will there ever be a solution to this problem? How many people will die???? *End of entry.*

Tuesday, May 13, 1980 (23:00) Day 192

Our hundred and ninety-second day today as hostages, but no word of the day we're to be released. I've bet Jerry a case of beer again on June. The whole time I've been held hostage, I've never been so sure of myself as I am now about going home in June.

Tonight I was talking to Santa about my glasses. He was saying one of the hostages had sent home for his, so I told him I was going to send for mine, too. I don't know if he meant to say it or not, but he said not to, that I wouldn't be needing them. Then Bill a little while later asked him if he could write his parents and tell them to send magazines Santa said no, it would take too long. That was twice it seemed like he hinted that we wouldn't be here too much longer. Everyday he seems to do this but still nothing is mentioned of a day.

He's been telling Bill and Jerry what he wished to have from the States. I've already invited him to my wedding, that's if I get married. Anyway he hasn't told me what he wished to have from me. Bill's going to send him all of John Denver's specials. Jerry's going to send him some classical music. Maybe he's thinking of something real good for me. I know that if we're released, whatever he asks for I'll try my damndest to get.

The days (last two) seem to be going by real slow. I guess I've got to stop watching the calendar so much. I know the days won't go by any faster doing that.

Santa brought us the tape recorder and a new tape this morning (by the way, we've still got it, too). This tape's of the Doobie Brothers, Bruce Springstein and The Grateful Dead. The music they've been bringing us really surprised me. They don't allow it in the Moslem religion, but still they let us listen to it. Listening to the music really brings back memories, and also puts dreams in my head of the future to come. How I can't wait to get home! How great that's going to be!!

Not much really happened, just stuck to ourselves in things we always do. It's still my turn to cook today, so I had a pretty filling meal. Spam, potatoes and Spaghetti O's. Wasn't too bad. The weather's really been getting humid lately. We've been teasing the students of when they're going to bring us an air conditioner, also some water so we can fill the pool and swim.

Are our days growing nearer to freedom, or are they just giving us these hints trying to make us feel happy? I pray to God they're not. Please take us home! *End of entry.*

Wednesday, May 14, 1980 (24:00)   Day 193

We've got two of the students in here learning how to speak English. They teach us Farsi and we teach them English. We've had some funny conversations. Passes the time. Well, Santa left for Tehran today. He didn't say why he went. He did say he was going to pick up our mail. We all wrote letters for him to mail to the States for us in Tehran. He's supposed to be gone for four days. Maybe he'll bring some encouraging word for us. Cross my fingers on that one.

Before he left he brought us the tape recorder and a couple tapes, and we've still got it in our room, too. The first tape he brought us we told him we didn't really care for, and a little while later we told him it broke. I guess he thought we broke it. He didn't look too happy. Anyway, a little while later he brought us a couple other ones.

Not much really happened today. Didn't have too much to fix for lunch except for some Spaghetti O's and hamburgers. Santa told me just to fix Spaghetti O's, and he would get some rice, too. Didn't bother me though. I could eat rice every day if I had to. The stuff really fills me up. Bill doesn't care for it too much. He tells the students he does, but usually you see him take a milk carton, open the top of it and put the rice in it. We used to do that in grade school when the teachers stood by the garbage baskets making sure we ate everything, and here I see it again with a Marine that doesn't want to show the students he doesn't like their rice.

While the students were in talking to us, Bill looked as pale as white paper. After the students left I asked him if he was feeling well. He said he hasn't felt well since he's gotten here. I told him he's never looked that pale that I can remember. He wouldn't say anything anyway if he was sick, at least not to Jerry and me.

The weather's really been getting humid lately, but occasionally we get a nice cool breeze flowing in underneath the sheet hanging over the patio door. Sure hope we're not here during any of the hot months this summer.

Forgot to mention earlier that Santa brought Bill and me mail this morning. I received one from my cousin Carol (Embassy address), and Bill received two from some people he's received from before. Doesn't look like we're going to receive any more. Santa told Jerry he had mail back at the Embassy, but they forgot to bring it for him.

Still continuing to work on my diary when I'm not reading. Jerry's just about finished with his up-to-date. When he's finished with that I'll have something else to keep me busy typing it out. It really looks as though the poems and diary are coming around great. The only thing we need now is to get out of here. Pray to God it's soon! *End of entry.*

Thursday, May 15, 1980 (00:05)   Day 194

After the students left early this morning, Jerry and I did our exercises. After that I took a hot shower, which felt great. Came back to the room, said my prayers, let my hair dry and listened to the tape recorder. Not much was playing. Around (11:00) Jerry and I went in and fried some eggs and potatoes. Bill was fasting once again.

Guard Chief came in and teased us about eating like rich men. He describes rich people as people who eat at tables and eat two different courses at one meal. Trying to take all of our American ways from us.

This afternoon the students came in once again for English class. Really get a kick out of trying to teach them English. Now I know how they feel when they teach us Farsi.

One of the students brought us a dessert of mulberries tonight after we had our Iranian rice. I can feel all the pounds I'm gaining from all this rice I'm eating. I've really gotten to like the stuff, and one plate fills me up to the max. Can't wait till we get out of here so we can do some walking around. I know all the laying I've been doing isn't good, but what else is there?

We've still got the tape recorder, but we still haven't heard anything good come out of it. We all three think/hope Santa's going to bring some encouraging word back from Tehran with him. Please make it be true! *End of entry.*

Friday, May 16, 1980 (23:50)   Day 195

Bill just came back from the kitchen after doing the dinner dishes and said that we had gotten some canned food in tonight. Also yesterday Guard Chief said that they were trying to find us a ping pong table. Hopefully all these things they're doing like finding us a ping pong table and having food sent from the Embassy don't mean we're going to be here longer.

Started today off by having a nice lunch of hamburgers and potatoes. When I returned back to the room, after doing lunch dishes, the students had brought in the television and it was showing the wrestling matches that were taking place in Tehran at the "Freedom Stadium". Bulgaria, Russia, Cuba, China and Rumania were some of the countries that were participating. While watching the wrestling matches they brought us some pineapple and some cashews to eat. We were all sitting around having a good old time. Really didn't seem like we were hostages.

After the wrestling matches a cartoon came on, a little news, and then a Japanese movie The Bullet Train. During the movie one of the students brought in Charm Pops. Had a little soap powder on it, but after you washed it off it tasted great. Jerry started to tell me how he couldn't believe all this stuff, watching wrestling, cartoons, movie, meanwhile eating cashews, pineapple, Charm Pops and then in came one of the students with a box of pastries (cookies they said). They were just like a miniature size cake with jam in the middle. We couldn't believe all this was happening all at once. Especially in one day.

Guard Chief just came in and handed Jerry a letter from his brother and sister-in-law and said that I had a letter from a Miss Jill Ditch. He then asked if I knew her. I told him of course I know her, she's my fiancee! They must have known Bill and I were anxious to get mail so they just brought it in. Bill received a kind of discouraging letter from his girlfriend Dawn. The letter I received from Jill was very encouraging, telling me she's waiting dearly for me to return home. From the way she wrote it really looked as though she knew when we're to be released. It would sure be a relief if they at least knew. If and whenever I get out of here I'm going to marry that girl. What a doll she is! She also assured me that the family was all well. I was really surprised when I saw the address (IWG) and especially surprised when I saw it dated April 2nd. It's such a good feeling to know she's still back there waiting!!

Gave "Football Captain" a few lessons in reading tonight. Had him read a few lines in Jill's letter, which I believe he enjoyed. The students have been continuing to treat us great, but still no word of freedom. I asked one of the students this morning why Santa went to Tehran, for a vacation or what. He simply replied not for vacation but for business! We're really curious to know what kind of business. Pray to God it's something about freedom!

Guard Chief brought in a paper with some pictures that were taken about the 1920s of some so-called Americans hanging and burning some people that supposedly had changed their religion to Moslem. A couple of other pictures of two policemen in riot gear with a black man handcuffed, bleeding in the face, and then one other one of a group of blacks, all chained together walking along a street. We asked them why there's always pictures of blacks being abused and never any pictures of them being treated right. He said that people should be taught of things that happened in the past, and then said that they do show pictures of blacks and other minority groups being treated well. To this day yet, I haven't seen any.

Said that fighting in Kurdestan has ceased once again, but fighting is still going on in Afghanistan against the Russians. He was saying that there's around one million in Tehran alone that want to go to Afghanistan and help fight against the Russians. What dedication these people have, and still they continue to believe that by keeping us hostage they are helping many poor people!

I think Santa forgot to tell the students to take the tape player away from us for a while while he's gone, because we've still got it from the day he left. Listen to music whenever we want to. We're hoping so much that Santa comes back with good news. How many more days are we going to be kept from the outside world and from the people we love?? *End of entry.*

Sunday, May 18, 1980 (17:00)   **Day 197**

Well, once again here we sit in our new living areas. Last night right after dinner, which was served kind of late (21:30-22:00), Telephone Operator came in and said we would be moving once again to a new place. He said to get all our things ready to go and then crash out for a while, because they really didn't know when we were leaving. Right after he left Guard Chief came in to talk to us for a while. Like always, he really didn't tell us the truth about why we were moving, just that it was a special place and that the CIA was after us. CIA part I believe he was kidding about, but the part about being a special place I believe now!

Anyway we all got our things together and crashed out till about (04:00), when Guard Chief and Soccer Captain came in to get us. They said the ride was only about five minutes long, and now when I look back it wasn't even that long. Of course the ride was made with blindfolds and blankets over our heads so we wouldn't see where we were going. Like I said, the ride wasn't that long, and when we arrived at the place, we were taken up the stairs to the second floor. The room in which we live has stairs that go up another level; so as far as I know it's a three story building.

127

As soon as we got into the room, Jerry, Bill and I started looking around wondering what this old building used to be. Soccer Captain was with us. Right then a shot was fired right outside our window. Everyone hit the deck, figuring someone was taking potshots at us. I could've sworn I felt debris flying through the air, but I guess it was just the percussion from the blast that made me feel that. This morning I took a look at the window and found no bullet hole. I do have to say it scared Soccer Captain a little, too. He kept assuring us that everything was all right. They really didn't say what had happened, so we just decided that one of the guards was playing with his weapon and it accidentally went off.

After that was all finished, a couple other students, Crazy Man and English Student came in and laid a couple of blankets on the tiled floor. We encountered another student we hadn't seen since we left the Embassy. This one I'm going to call Friendly. He's always checking in to see if we need anything. He and Jerry really get along pretty well. Right after they had turned the lights out and we were lying on the blankets, the door opened and here they came in with mattresses and all our stuff we had wrapped up in our white sheets. Wanted to get a little sleep before I got up in the morning to explore this place, so I just grabbed a white sheet and my pillow, laid on my mattress and crashed out in no time.

When I woke up this morning Jerry had unpacked most of his things, but Bill had done the same as I had done, grabbed a sheet and pillow and crashed out. The room looks different in broad daylight. Noticed a lot of things I didn't see earlier this morning when it was dark out yet. Instead of the corners being square face, they are rounded. The windows are huge, about six feet high and about five feet wide with the old wooden shutters on the outside. Screen doors and storm windows on the inside. The window edge is really huge, covered with tile (I'm writing on one now). The ceiling is about 20 feet high with some weird artwork at the top. In our bedroom we've just got a light fixture hanging from the ceiling, but from looking at a couple other rooms through the windows above the doors, I can see some other rooms have beautiful chandeliers hanging.

At first this morning while I was lying in my mattress, I told Jerry and Bill it looked like an old school house we had back home in Krakow. That was just by looking at our room. Right as I was about to get up, English Student came in with a plateful of dates and two milks. Right then is when I discovered that right next door was a room with a ping pong table. They said they were going to try to find me one and they did.

Forgot to mention that earlier this morning I had to get up and go to the head. Like all the times before whenever I had to go to the head I knocked on the door, but no one came. I finally opened the door and looked out in the hallway, and saw a toilet a few feet away. I just decided to run in real quick instead of pounding on the door anymore. I figured they'd never know I left the room. After I finished I returned to the room, closed the door and went back to sleep. Well, when I found out this morning we had a ping pong table right next door, the students, Ostard and Telephone Operator, proceeded to show me the two bathrooms, one of which I used earlier and the other huge one with the bathtub. They said instead of having them take us to the head all the time, we could go by ourselves from now on. They were saying that the one small head they were going to turn into our kitchen since we could use the other head to bathe, etc. I guess they're going to bring us a little hot plate to cook on, because I know I didn't see a stove in there.

Let me tell you, now that we've got the ping pong room all cleaned out, our living quarters cleaned and rugs laid which they brought this afternoon, our kitchen cleaned and huge bathroom all cleaned, it's so nice to be able to sit back and enjoy them. Go to the toilet whenever you want and give your feet a little exercise. This morning they had a few problems getting the water turned on, but when they finally got it, we had some steaming hot water. Jerry and I cleaned the bathtub out really good, so tonight I'm going to fill it up and sit right in it.

Ostard and Soccer Captain were just in talking to me. Ostard was saying that this building's about 50 years old and it used to be a school house. He said it belongs to the government now, but before the revolution it used to belong to one of the Shah's relatives. This building reminds me so much of that old school house in Krakow. Plaster falling down, cracks in the wall, but to the three of us it's not too bad of a place, especially since we can walk around and go to the toilet whenever we want.

I hope all this movement and all these privileges don't mean a longer stay! So much we're hoping for the new Islamic government to do something regarding our release. But the students keep saying once the Shah is released you will be released. What do you do when you hear things like this? The only thing I guess you can do is hope for the best!

It's slowly starting to get dark now, but still I can hear the heavy traffic of wherever we're at, and also hear some students or guards outside playing basketball. Really sounds as though they're having a good time. Sure wish I was out there doing the same thing. Still these people are believing so strongly that the Shah will return. Will this thing ever come to an end? *End of entry.*

Just heard some shocking news tonight about Martial Law taking place in eight states of the United States. Martial law. Never can we remember it ever happening in the States. Really shocking news that was. A huge demonstration supposedly had taken place in Boston, with one of the hostage's mother and daughter in the lead. One of the statements made at the rally (demonstration) was how our government should apologize to the Iranian people for taking military action and also for supporting the Shah. That was the only place they mentioned a big demonstration taking place (Boston) but no doubt there are more if they've announced Martial Law from (8:00 pm, 20:00) to (06:00 am).

The students always said that that's what the United States needed was a revolution. Also they said a revolution needs blood to grow by, and it sounds like blood they are getting. They were saying that nine or ten people were killed and that there's still more to come.

Santa just left with his radio. We were listening to the world news coming from England. They had Reggie Jackson as a guest speaker. Reggie Jackson was saying that there's a national explosion going on in the United States. From what he was saying it sounded as though the United States is in some bad times. Inflation sounded as though it was hitting hard. A total of 22 people have been killed. The United States is fighting itself, why? Just over one man! Why is this person given these privileges?

Some of the other news Santa told us was that he knew when we were to be released. First he said the fall and then after a little discussion he changed it to summer. Still, they seem to know when we're going home. But they don't want to tell us. I sure wish I knew what all the news was in the States. Hopefully my family are all well.

I took my hot bath last night. Guard Chief was teasing me about being a rich man taking baths. It felt so good though just sitting in that hot water. If only I had a cigar I would've had it made. Jerry and I started our diet today, starting off with breakfast and ending with dinner. Too much of this rice has been getting us fat.

Forgot to mention Santa returned from Tehran early this morning, bringing with him Billy's guitar he asked for. The only thing he had to say really was that he had mail for all of us. He mentioned that once again tonight, and brought Jerry a letter from his brother-in-law. He says now he's received a letter from everyone in the family.

Jerry was telling Santa how he thought everyone back home was starting to understand our situation. Santa replied, looking at me, that he was glad someone was starting to understand. Ever since he

130

read in the magazine about my family agreeing with Carter for taking military action against Iran, he seems to be rubbing it in.

Earlier this morning a couple of students, Crazy Man and Ostard, were working in our kitchen putting a table over the shitter. Later tonight they brought in a gas container, frying pan, and a couple more items to put in there. It looks like we're going to have a gas stove installed instead of an electric one.

Besides fixing up the kitchen, Santa brought us some kind of plastic wallpaper to put up in our room for decoration. It doesn't look that bad either. Ostard and Soccer Captain brought in our desk from the other place, along with Bill's paper plane he made. The plane was pretty well torn up so Bill just threw it away. Do have to say that our new house is really fixed up nice. That doesn't mean I don't want to go home though. I'm just saying that while we're here, we're making the best out of it.

So much I've learned from this situation so far, so much I've still got to learn if and when I ever get out of here. Like I've said before, the students seem to know when we're to leave, but they don't want to tell us. I think they've gotten to like our company so much they don't want to let us go.

One of the revolutionary guards (Pastrian) looked in on us, and about two or three hours later Ostard came in and asked if someone had opened the door and seen us. The students really try their hardest to avoid contact between the guards and hostages. They must have a guard post right above us (on the third floor or roof), and whenever they change guards we've always got to keep the hall door closed to avoid being seen. They probably can't even trust their own guards. Scared they're Savak or something. The only contact we've got with people are with the students who look after us, but it's really security-wise around here. The guards walk around right outside our window.

Bill found the food storage today in the ping pong room. Seems like they've got a lot of goodies in there. We've been sneaking in and out all day ripping off canned goods. What a Marine would do for a can of food!

Guard Chief just left us after having a brief discussion about theology and ideology. So many similar things there are between the Koran and the Bible. But still it seems so much different. He was telling us about their new Parliament, that every 150 thousand people have a representative and any other religion has their own representative. He was telling us a little about marriage, too. He said that girls are able to marry from the age of nine on up, and boys from the

131

age of fifteen. So many surprising things I hear when we have these discussions.

Well, our hopes are still up for June, so if what Santa said is true about not being here for the summer, which starts June 21, our stay shouldn't be too much longer. He said he has no intention of taking back his word on everything he's told us about going home. How I pray/hope that Jill and my family are all well. *End of entry.*

Tuesday, May 20, 1980 (00:10)   Day 199

Santa just left us after having a discussion about all the demonstrating occurring in the States. The students are really believing that it's going to spread throughout the States. Showed us some pictures from an Iranian paper showing demonstrations taking place in Miami. The students were saying that they have been closing schools, and that Andrew Young was sent down there to try to make negotiations between the blacks and the United States government. Santa believes that the reason this has all started is because of inflation.

What's really strange though is all the pictures we've seen have never shown any whites being taken away. If they were demonstrating for inflation, we should've seen more than just black people. It sounds and looks to me like the blacks are demonstrating against discrimination. I do feel like inflation is starting to increase, and something's got to be done to prevent it from getting any worse.

Once again Santa assured us that time is getting short (meaning freedom is nearing) and we will be flying back to Tehran to collect all of our belongings and then be released from there. All these things they know, but still they don't want to tell us the day. Something else that really struck me was that he said our government even knows when we were to be freed. It that's true, then why don't they release us now, and why is there such strong protection for us? So many things I'm so unsure of, but still I've got that strong feeling of freedom next month. What more can we do except sit and wait and pray Santa was telling the truth. I think he was!

Received an Easter card from Aunt Janet and Uncle Les this morning when Santa brought in mail. Enclosed with the card were some pictures they took of Jill, Mom, Dad and myself when they came to my graduation at MSG school. Everyone looks so good in the pictures (even my car!) and I can still remember the good times we all had, just as though they were yesterday. I hope they are well. I love and miss them so. There must be a lot of mail, because Santa said he was going to hand it out every other day. That's not bad; then we'll have something to look forward to.

Still haven't brought the ping pong paddles (what's the service coming to around here!). But Santa said that tomorrow he was going to go out and buy us some. Then we'll have something else to do besides taking hot baths all the time. I took another one in our private bath this morning when I got finished with breakfast. Jerry and I are still continuing our breakfast/dinner meals; maybe we'll lose a little weight. Anyway the bath felt good. Instead of smoking a cigar this morning I read a book. What a life it is being a hostage. Now if only we were sure about going home. Can't have everything, can we?

The students have been continuing to be nice, and once again today Ostard, Santa, and Soccer Captain came in for English class. They didn't stay too long. All of a sudden they all got up and left. Forgot to mention that Santa brought in the tape recorder early this morning and then grabbed it away right after lunch. John Denver/Bruce Springstein/Doobie Brothers. Said tomorrow morning he was going to return it for us to listen to some more.

Been getting a little cautious lately about snatching the food. I think the students are starting to catch on. They still haven't brought the stove. Hopefully soon they'll bring it and then we can start cooking our own meals.

Jerry wrote a quick letter to his wife to be sent with Guard Chief to be mailed in Tehran. I didn't really have too much to say, so I didn't write. Everyone back home should know how I feel by now anyway. I hate to repeat myself. *End of entry.*

Wednesday, May 21, 1980 (13:50)   Day 200

Two hundred days exactly today that we've been held "guestage", and like the word says, "guestage". That's how the students try to treat us, like a guest. The only thing is they won't let us go walking outside whenever we wish, just when they decide on it.

Just finished my daily noon tea and now I'm listening to John Denver and writing. Jerry's lying on his mattress smoking a cigarette and sucking on a Charms Pop. Bill's taking his noon nap. He finished his lunch of beef, potatoes, beans and is now taking it easy.

Jerry and I had butter, cheese, bread, tea and milk for breakfast so that will last us till tonight when we have our dinner. Santa was suggesting that Jerry and I take another one of the exotic foods they served once again today. We told him we knew it was good (everything else is now) but we were on a diet, trying to get back in shape for when we get home. That word home sounds so good; boy, how I can't wait.

A couple of the students came in this morning just to talk and listen to Bill play his guitar. They are always waiting for him to come up

133

with a new song. But none yet.

My ping pong partner came to visit us this morning. I told him we had a ping pong table right next door, but no paddles and ball. He was talking to Santa, and Santa assured us he would go out and buy some. Helps to pass the time a little better if he could get them. The treatment around here has been so good lately.

Remembering back the first couple of weeks and months I never thought this situation would get this far, plus the treatment, too. Still at times it is so hard to believe this is happening to me. We can hear the guards outside our windows playing with their weapons. No doubt they're all bored just as we are. Is freedom really close, or are the students just saying this to keep our spirits up?

Summer's right around the corner and already the weather's getting hot and humid. Sure wish we could go out and get some good fresh air. From looking out through the cracks of the wooden shutters, it looks as though the sun isn't out. Still I can hear the noises of this busy street and the beautiful sound of the birds chirping. So great it's going to be to be free once again.

Finished typing Jerry's update of his first 100 days. Now if I could only do the same for my diary. Take my time, no need to hurry yet.

(23:30) Just finished rereading a couple old letters from my family/ Jill. When things get down that's what I usually do. Anyway, so many good memories I have of all the ones I love, and know it only if they would free us there are many more to come.

The students brought us another exotic Iranian treat right before dinner tonight. This treat was candy. Kind of sugary, but really good. Oh yes. Right before Santa brought in the candy, English Student brought in ice cream in a cup. Snatched some cashews from the storage room (ping pong room) so we had ice cream and cashews. Once again it was a treat which we all enjoyed. The candy was especially good I thought.

We mentioned about going outside today to them and they replied maybe tomorrow. Still haven't gotten the ping pong paddles and balls yet either. I can't believe some of the things happening. Here I am complaining about not having ping pong paddles and balls. But instead they bring us pastries, ice cream and candy. I guess we're getting a litte spoiled the way they've been treating us.

Santa came in around (21:00) tonight and grabbed the tape player/radio, probably to listen to the news coming from England. Usually he comes in and tells us if anything's happened but I guess nothing did. So once again another day gone. Still hoping and praying that each next day will bring news regarding freedom. *End of entry.*

134

These past two nights it's been so hard to get to sleep. Visions of home keep flashing through my mind along with everyone's faces. I keep asking myself, "Is it true that freedom is near?" After about an hour of tossing and turning and saying another rosary besides the one I say before getting in my rack, I'm finally able to crash out. I guess I'm trying to analyze all the things Santa told us about time getting short, not to worry and so forth. Trying to figure out if all those things he said are true or not. I pray to God they are though!

This morning I was awakened by the smell of smoke (burning of leaves) right outside our window. It was really getting hard to breathe. Everywhere I went, under the covers I could still smell that damn smoke. It sounded like they were having a good time doing it though.

Santa didn't want to wake us for breakfast (he thought we were sleeping too well) so we finally woke at lunch when he brought in rice and a spinach topping. The worst one we hate. Jerry wasn't too hungry. He says Bill had turkey with his rice. I ate my rice with a little of the topping. I don't think I'll ever get used to that!

Bill finally got this closet open which he's been tampering with ever since we got here. Found a lot of pottery (made in Japan) and then found a standing clock which seemed to be made of gold. Couldn't spend too much time in it though. The students have been trying to get it opened also but haven't been able to, so I guess we're the only ones that know what's in it.

Santa just brought mail and surprising enough, I got another one from Jill. Her letters have been so encouraging but from the sound of it, it seems as though she's not getting any of my mail. She said that she found out April 7 for the first time that I had finally gotten two of her letters. I know all my previous letters before these I wrote and told her I've received a couple letters, but I guess she never received them.

She seems so worried about me not loving her anymore. Why she thinks that I won't know until I return home. I'm worried she's going to get tired of writing and just say good-bye. Then again from the letters I've been receiving from her, I don't think she has any intention of doing that. Now only if she keeps it in her head I love her more than anything and I mean anything, we'll be all right. I love you, Jill Renee Ditch, so much. Please be there when I return!

Bill received a letter from a guy that had just returned from the U.K. and was now in the brig. He was saying a lot of guys have been turning themselves in because of our situation. They all want to start

135

over and become a Marine like Bill. It's really strange though; you get letters like this and then you hear on the news that there have been unorganized demonstrations in the States. Cities have been under Martial Law and for what? It just can't be over inflation!

Jerry received a letter from his brother-in-law, but once again, nothing from his wife. Bill received nothing from his family again. Santa was mentioning that the other night, that Jerry and I have been getting mail from our families and Bill hasn't.

Weather's really been getting humid/hot. I think that after I finish here I'm going to take a bath, play rich man once again. Ping Pong Player was in a while ago and I believe he went out to buy ping pong paddles and balls.

It's really been getting boring around here. Reading books is about the only thing we've been doing besides sleeping, eating and a little exercising. The only other thing I want to say before I close is I love you, Jill, and I can't wait to get my arms around you once again! *End of entry.*

Friday, May 23, 1980 (00:10)   Day 202

Writing for the end of the 22nd. Ping Pong Player finally brought the paddles and balls to us this afternoon, brand new! The lights had just gone off before he came through the door, so the ping pong room was a little dark, but still Ping Pong Player wanted to try out the new entertainment. In fact, I just got finished playing him a game and beat him too, so now whenever we feel like it we just open the door and go next door and play ping pong. Something else to do to pass the time.

Santa came in to visit once again tonight. We always enjoy his company, always seems to make us laugh and at times brings us encouraging news. All the students (the ones who've been taking care of us) come in occasionally to talk, but one of them, Santa, has got to be the best. Although we don't agree on a lot of things, he doesn't hold that against me. Sometimes he might, but when he does, he does it in a joking way.

Tonight he brought in this Iranian newspaper and showed us pictures of the revolution that is taking place in South Korea. Forgot the name of the town, but he says that the students have taken it over. Then also he showed us a picture of a fire truck which was burning, with a National Guard standing by. This picture he says was taken in Miami. He says that demonstrations are still continuing in the States, but not as much. Thank God for that!

A lot of people must have gotten married here in Shiraz last night, because there's been a lot of honking/yelling going on. Thursday nights are usually their wedding nights anyway. Maybe if I ever get home, something like that might happen to me. Hopefully Jill will still be there waiting. If not, I guess I'll just have to cope with it just like I coped with this situation. *(Don't think pessimistic, Rocky; think optimistic.)*

When I went to take my rich man shower today, I found English Student in the head inspecting the faucets. He was able to tell me in the little English he knows that the water wasn't working, but they were trying to fix it. I told him that was perfectly all right that there was no need to hurry, I wasn't going nowhere. I told him I'd sit right there and read my book until it came on. He's really a happy-go-lucky guy. Everytime I see him just about he always seems to have a smile. I guess I waited reading my book about half an hour, 45 minutes, but no water came. I finally decided to retire back to the room and finish my book on the mattress. That's when Ping Pong Player brought the paddles and all. Anyway, after we were finished checking all the gear, I went back to the head and found that the water was on so once again I took a rich man's bath which felt great.

Santa told us tonight that there were going to be some big demonstrations tomorrow against the United States government on how they treat the black people in the States. He said Imam had enforced it so I guess he just wanted to warn us before we were shaken out of our mattresses tomorrow. Sure wish they'd demonstrate about having the hostages held so long!

He also told us the reason the guards and students were burning the leaves (which they are still doing) was because they want to have a nice place for us to walk around. I think he was saying that maybe tomorrow we might go out and get some solar energy/fresh air. That would be great!

Bill mentioned about not having a girlfriend anymore to Santa, and Santa asked why? Bill told him because she probably found out that we weren't coming home for a while, and then Santa replied that he thought that his girlfriend was going to be sorry for not waiting. It was like Santa was trying to say, like he's been saying, that we really don't have too much more time. But still why won't they tell us the day? They probably think that if we did find out we would start doing some foolish things. I guess it is better off this way. Hopefully it's not too much longer though. I pray to God every night for that. God bless America, the land of beauty and love! *End of entry.*

Jerry and I just finished our last couple games of ping pong before hitting the mattress. Can't believe how much he's improved since the first time playing down in the Embassy. Everything I've taught him he uses right back at me and at times he beats me. I guess I can call myself a good instructor.

Today was tournament day in the ping pong room with the students. Soccer Captain, Crazy Man and Ping Pong Player beat me one right after another. I was so discouraged with myself letting the United States down the way I did—letting these three Iranians beat me like that. Ping Pong Player really rubs it in by parading around like he just won a million dollars or something. Not too often does he get a chance to beat me, but when he does he really knows how to rub it in. Ping pong is really a good pastime game to play. Can't play too much or else you get sick of it, just as we did with chess and dominoes.

Well, they had their demonstration today, just like Santa said last night. I told Santa it wasn't too loud and he said that's because there are more people in Tehran than there are in Shiraz. I guess we can be thankful for that because they were all out there shouting "Death to America." The students keep assuring us that the people don't mean us, just our government.

Besides those two small little things happening nothing else was going on. I changed my diet plan around a little today though. Like always, Jerry and I woke for breakfast, which was served once again by Santa (no cheese this morning). I wasn't going to eat lunch but when I saw they had my favorite (rice and beans/beef) I had to give in and eat. Instead of eating at lunch, Jerry ate dinner and found out he should've had lunch instead. For dinner Jerry and Bill had eggs— hard boiled.

We were just sitting here talking about each of our habits when we sleep. It's really funny the things you see people doing while sleeping. Those things I'll leave out for the time being so no one gets embarrassed.

Days seem to be dragging by now since I've got that stronger feeling about going home. Santa was saying tonight that our government knows nothing of our release, and that when that day ever comes around we won't know until about an hour after they say to release us. Santa doesn't know (at least that's what he says) when we'll be released. I think he does. Anyway I pray to God it's soon.

Tonight was a discussion on what we thought Iran was going to be like before we came here. We all told him our stories and tried to get him to talk about freedom—that he never wants to talk about. I wonder why.

Wrote another letter to Jill tonight. I gave it to Santa and told him what I wrote for a return address, "Hostage/Guestage", so he gave it back to me and said that the Post Office man might not care for that. I guess I'll have to ask for another envelope tomorrow so I can get it sent off. I sent her her birthday poem again, just in case she doesn't get the other letter. I think of her so much, along with the rest of the family. Can't wait to see them once again.

Brought music in for us this morning. ABBA/John Denver. It seems like we never can get tired of John Denver. He just continues to play on. Well I just ran out of my third pen and now I'm using Jerry's two-inch pencil. Tomorrow I'll just have to ask the students for another pen, and also a pencil for Jerry. *End of entry.*

Saturday, May 24, 1980 (22:40) Day 203

There really isn't too much to write about today. We haven't seen Santa all day except for this morning when he brought in our break-fast. I think he's out visiting the other hostages, but none of the students will tell us where he went. We found out tonight from Crazy Man that he's supposed to be back tomorrow sometime. We're kind of looking forward towards Guard Chief's return from Tehran, hoping he brings mail from our families and even some good news.

I finally woke around (13:00) this afternoon—slept pretty good last night/this morning. But before I retired I did my exercises by myself. Jerry's back's been hurting him. Anyway I did my exercises, turned off the lights in the room and went to the head to continue reading my book. I finally decided to come out since a lot of people were com-ing—I guess to use the head, but couldn't since I was in there. I came back to the room, said my rosary and by that time was pretty well tuckered out. Bill and I heard a rooster again; I guess the same one we've been hearing every morning when we crash. Sitting in my mat-tress listening to it brought back memories of the one we used to have at home. "Home", what a beautiful word that is!!

I woke for my breakfast this morning consisting of butter, jelly, bread and tea (no milk), and then crashed out again till lunch when I was awakened by Bill playing his guitar over me. A couple more months of practice and he might become pretty good. They had my favorite once again for lunch, rice and beans which was delicious. That's how adapted I am to this situation—I'm calling rice and beans delicious.

After my lunch tea I snatched my things and went to the head and fixed up the tub to take another rich man's bath. Crazy Man came barging in all of a sudden—I guess to use the toilet. He saw that I was in the tub so as he was walking back out he commented on me being a

139

rich man for taking a bath. They really like to tease us about that.
After I was finished with that Jerry and I played a couple games of
ping pong, which ended with Crazy Man coming in and wanting me
to play him. Yesterday he beat me pretty good, but today I made up
for it. I beat him four out of four and I think he was a little surprised/
disappointed.

I forgot to mention Ping Pong Player's visit at lunch when he came
in to say goodbye before going home. He came in with a mask on his
face that he said was a present for his little brother. Before leaving, he
said he was going to bring back some weights with him so we could
work out. That would be nice. My arms have been getting a little
small anyway.

Like I said, not much of anything happened. Everyone stuck to
themselves, reading, Bill practicing his guitar and occasionally Jerry
and I played ping pong. Trying to keep ourselves busy as possible
waiting patiently for that day of freedom to arise. What more are
they trying to prove by keeping us here longer? *End of entry.*

Monday, May 26, 1980 (00:50)   Day 205

Today supposedly was Memorial Day (Bill says) but I looked it up
in the dictionary and it says it's supposed to be the 30th. How all these
things change without my ears hearing anything about it I'll never
know.

Santa finally came back tonight from having a visit with some of
the hostages. He didn't say who he saw, though, or what cities he
went to. Didn't really expect him to anyway. He told us some news
about the United States helping out Korea with all the demonstrations
they've been having, and also the spokesman for the Secretary of State
resigned. Again, no news regarding the hostage release.

Jerry and I were talking today about what they might be waiting
for. The Iranian government just finished electing their new Parliament and Santa said it wouldn't be in effect till next month, June. So
we were thinking that one of the things the new Parliament would do
was find an answer to the hostage problem. The little discussion I had
with Nose last month seemed to be saying something like that, too.

I've still got that strong feeling of freedom in June, but the days
seem so monotonous and at times we seem to be getting on each
other's nerves. Four more days after today we'll be going on our
eighth month, which is so damned hard to believe at times. I never
thought I could go this long being held in a room like this for eight
months. Amazing what the mind can do.

Activities were just like any other day yesterday. Woke at noon to have my favorite lunch, rice w/sloppy joe on top. Made my mattress nice and tight. Read my book a little until Soccer Captain came in to talk (learn English) and then to play a little ping pong. He said tomorrow we're going to go out in the courtyard to get some fresh air/solar energy, and he was going to bring us some mulberries.

After he left, Ostard brought in some rosewater. I tease him about it all the time, saying it's whiskey and he's a bootlegger for making it. Anyway, it's really good. A little while later they brought us some "pondod", an Iranian dessert. It's really hard to describe, but it's similar to ice cream, and it's delicious. Maybe they're trying to get us fat before we leave. Although it might not be true it's sure nice thinking it.

The dinners have really been small lately, but they've been adequate and filling. Like I've said before our stomachs are used to it! Tonight we had goat cheese, boned chicken in a can, two of them, three small jellies and three pickles. What a meal! Not too much more to say. Really looking forward to going outside tomorrow. *End of entry.*

Monday, May 26, 1980 (23:55)   Day 205

Another boring day just about past and here we still sit! Started this morning off right, drinking sour milk for breakfast and then having the shits the rest of the morning. Santa came in and warned us but I couldn't see too much wrong with it so I drank mine and Jerry's. Santa had got him another one, but it was the same. Anyway my rear end had a busy morning! I didn't eat breakfast or lunch, hoping we'd have rice for dinner and I'd stuff myself with that, but instead we had Iranian spaghetti for the first time—wasn't too bad.

Small demonstration outside today, but didn't really sound too harsh. We never made our trip outside today. I was asking Santa if it was the guards didn't want us outside or what. When he replied, he only seemed to be joking around and said yes, that was the reason. That was all that was said about going out.

The students were busy today visiting different cities (Crazy Man and English Student). Soccer Captain said he had to go to the dentist for a toothache and had to spend two hours and 45 minutes there. He must have gotten it fixed. It didn't look to be hurting him.

Otherwise nothing else was happening. Been sleeping a little during the day—don't really hit the mattress till early morning hours anyway. About the time the rooster crows I crash. Maybe it's just the heat/humidity that's been making me tired.

Ostard came in a couple times to joke around and then tonight San-

141

to come in to rap with us for awhile. We haven't had our ideology discussions like the ones we had at the other place. Lately it's just been anything we can find to talk about. We would like to talk about going home, but it seems as though Santa doesn't care to. We were talking about how when we are released we would be able to see Imam, and something that struck my ear was that Santa said that Imam was in Tehran *now*. Wonder what he's doing there? We were just talking and thinking that maybe they're holding some kind of meeting regarding the hostages. How I pray to God they are—I'm really getting tired of this place and the heat isn't helping it out any.

Earlier tonight Santa brought in another "Sporting News"—at least I've been able to keep up a little on the sports. May 22, four days ago, the baseball players were supposed to decide if they were going on strike or not, and also pretty soon is the deadline for answering invitations to the Summer Olympics (Russia). Wonder if President Carter changed his mind yet.

Also read some interesting news about how the 1984 Olympics were supposedly to be held in "Tehran, Iran", but the Olympic Committee changed their minds at the Winter Olympics in Lake Placid, and switched the 1984 Olympics to Los Angeles. Who would have guessed they were planning to have the Olympics here? I wouldn't have seen it as a bad place if this had never happened.

Still waiting patiently for freedom to come. I'm stating before June 15th we're going to know something, and that something I'm hoping for is to know when we will leave here. Please, God, please free us and return us to our family/loved ones and to the land we cherish so much. *End of entry.*

Wednesday, May 28, 1980 (1:20)   **Day 207**

Santa paid us a little visit this morning. It started off pretty calm, but then I said I was getting tired of being here and if I was still here by the end of June I was going to try to make a break for it. That's when hell let loose.

Of course I was only kidding, which Jerry knew, but Santa took it seriously and then started talking about how the guards outside were just waiting for a peek at us. He said he was going to take us out tomorrow and show us how many there were, meaning we'd never get away. Then he told us how one of the other students had called him from another city where hostages were being held, and said how one of the hostages there wished he could just be allowed to speak several words to someone each day, and how we've had it so good here (which is true, especially for a hostage situation) and on and on. At the time I had my back to him, which must have pissed him off dearly, so occasionally when I turned around he would keep his eyes on Jerry while talking. He was emphasizing how he thought we were children about asking when we would be released and so on.

Santa stood up then to leave, but when Jerry asked something he sat right back down. Santa started telling us how we should analyze all the things taking place and all the things we've heard, and try to put them together instead of acting like little kids asking when we were going home. That pissed me off so I told him, "Don't you think we've already done that ourselves?" He replied, "Well, if you have let me hear it." So we told him what we thought about the new government forming and so on, but told him we really didn't know when everything was going to be put into effect. He then replied, "If you wanted to know that, why didn't you ask?" We told him we have asked, but he hasn't ever given us an answer. So then he said that the government is starting tomorrow (today) and "that it would take another four weeks before they would get settled in."

Settled in for what? They were all elected last month. What have they been doing since then? Anyway he said once they got settled in the hostage situation would be the first thing on the agenda and that it would be no more than two months more. He also said that when we were back at the Embassy, and now look at us! Could it just be a pushover to keep us going until those two months are done and then say it again for another two months? That I guess we won't know until these next two months are over. How I dread to stay here another two months, especially through this heat/humidity.

Today's supposed to be the birthday of the first Imam. Earlier this morning or later last night they were testing the loudspeakers. I guess they're planning to have a lot of noise to celebrate it with. First Imam's birthday and the starting of the new government. It sounds as though Iran's going to be kept awful busy today.

Guard Chief finally came from Tehran this morning bringing with him fresh mail. I received two beautiful letters from Jill telling me she's kept busy and waiting patiently for me to return. What a true little soldier she is—I love her with my full heart—such a sweetheart! Also received one from Debbie before she had her baby. I haven't found out yet what it was. Said that everyone was well and not to worry—really good to hear that. Received two other letters from a couple of kids, really nice! I'm going to have a lot of letters/cards to answer whenever I get out of here.

Jerry finally received a letter from his wife—really happy he was! Bill received a strange letter from his so-called ex-girlfriend Dawn. She was telling him that she had gone on television and was asked if aho thought Bill was brainwashed. She said that he wasn't, and that he was a kind and considerate person who didn't deserve to be over in that mess. I guess she told them! Anyway he didn't get anything from his family once again. Been a long time since he's heard from them. Although my letters were dated April 18 and 25, it was still great getting them. Jill's been such a strong little soldier—I'm so proud of her!

Guard Chief brought two other so-called students in to see us today. One of them I thought I'd seen at the Embassy a while back—wasn't sure though. They seemed pretty friendly but nothing was ever said about why they were here, strange!

Jerry and I cleaned out the heads today. They seemed to be getting a little dirty from the first time we had cleaned them. Anyway we did a great job, so after we were finished I grabbed my gear and went in and took a rich man's bath—taking with me a cigar Santa brought in earlier this morning when he brought the music. I decided I wasn't going to smoke any of the fine Roi-Tan (Perfectos Extra) until the day we are released and I'd share them with four other people—celebration cigars. I sure wish that day would get here.

Also washed my clothes and hung them on the line Bill fixed in the middle of the room. I do have to say the clothes really do dry fast. Guard Chief wanted to trade my cammies for a pair of pajamas (bottoms) but I said no way. Those cammies were mine to keep. Guard Chief said that I would sleep better with the pajamas. I said after four months I've gotten used to them and I didn't want any pajamas.

One meal I had again today—my favorite, rice. Trying to lose a little before we get out of here—that's if we ever get out of here. The way things are looking now, it will be another long wait! *End of entry.*

Wednesday, May 28, 1980 (23:00)   Day 207

What a hard day it was today—mentally that is. Woke for breakfast around (10:00)—jelly, butter, bread, tea and milk. To make the day fly by a little faster I decided to crash back out till lunch. Surprisingly enough Santa wasn't in too bad of a mood this morning after last night's conversation.

After we had our lunch (bean stew is really starting to taste good), Jerry and I were playing ping pong until Jerry knocked one of the balls into a hole in the wall so we had to ask for a different one. I was knocking on the door for a while and I knew someone was out there, but they didn't want to answer. So I went back into the room and knocked, and the first time I did, Crazy Man came to the door. I told him we needed a tennis ball but he said we had to wait until Santa came back. I was wondering why he said that because right before he answered the door I had seen Santa in the hallway walking back and forth past the door I was knocking on. That really pissed me off when he said that. Fifteen minutes passed before Santa came in with a ball.

Then tonight really topped it off when English Student came in beating both Bill and me in football and rubbing it in good. Already our pride and dignity has been taken way from us when they took over the Embassy, and then they have to rub it in about losing to them in football. Not once have I ever rubbed it in to any of the students about beating them in ping pong. Maybe they don't really know they're doing it, but all these small things are starting to add up to big things and it's really getting to me. *End of entry.*

Thursday, May 29, 1980 (01:20)   Day 208

Santa and English Student just left us after we were disturbed by gunfire right outside and artillery fire in the distance. They both left, and then Santa came back and told us to lay on our mattresses and not to stand up. He let us keep the light on so I'm continuing to write my diary here on the floor. English Student just came in and grabbed the tape recorder so now we're sitting in dead silence again.

Like always, we're curious to know what all the excitement is. What are we supposed to think when they tell us that our own people are wanting to kill us—hearing gunfire right outside and artillery fire in the background? It really has us thinking if we'll ever get out of here! I know there isn't much to talk about, so I try my best not to start a conversation about all this. It kind of gets us uptight, so we try to avoid it as best as possible. Not too much more action outside— wonder what all the fuss was?

It was pretty quiet yesterday considering it was the first Imam's birthday. Cousin brought in sugar cookies right before dinner (three each). We had one of my favorites tonight for dinner—coo-coo. It's some sort of vegetable patty, not too bad!

Jerry and I played a few games of ping pong today, but otherwise once again everybody was to themselves reading their books. Like I said earlier, they brought in a small football table which we can play with. All these things, but still they don't give us our freedom!

Yesterday they supposedly started their new government. If that is true, I wonder how long it's going to be before they come to a decision about us. How can other countries continue to go on and do business with a government that holds hostages? Inhuman is what I call it, especially when the only reason we are being held is because we're Americans. Hopefully their new government will find the answer

145

vory soon. Days seem to be getting hotter and harder! Tonight seems like it's going to be a hard night to sleep, worrying about what's going on outside. *End of entry.*

Friday, May 30, 1980 (13:40)   **Day 209**

So lazy I feel this morning especially after such a good night's sleep I had. We hit the mattress around (02:00) this morning, sleeping till breakfast which was around (09:30 or 10:00) and then crashed out till lunch which was served around (13:00). I was still so tired at lunch, I was debating if I should get up and eat or not. When I did get up I had barely enough energy to feed myself.

So here I sit at the desk, drinking my tea and trying to write our exciting occurrences that happened yesterday. Hopefully I'll be able to complete it without having to go to my mattress and lie down. Last night I was just too tired to write, so I said I'd push it off to today. I wish now I would have done it last night instead of now!

Getting back to yesterday's activities—the morning went just like any other morning. Finally waking at lunch, which consisted of rice and spinach. A funny thing happened. We were sitting in the middle of the room Iranian style eating our lunch, when all of a sudden we were hit by a spray of dirt and dust coming from the air conditioning vent. I never thought they had air conditioning in such an old house as this. Telephone Operator was the one working on it, so when he turned it on he came into the room to see how it was working. By the time he got here we had already moved our food from the line of fire and were covering our noses and mouths, avoiding inhaling the dirt. That was about the funniest and most exciting thing that happened yesterday.

I took another rich man's bath yesterday after lunch—sitting in the tub of hot water just taking it easy. After I was finished with that, half the day was finished so I returned back to the room to continue reading my book and playing a few games of ping pong with Jerry.

Heard a few gunshots in the distance. Nothing was really said about yesterday morning's early hour shots (artillery), so we just tried to put it out of our heads and think of it as being nothing, just like all the other shots. I'm not going to start worrying about it until it hits the building I'm living in. No need to worry about the ones in the distance, at least not now.

They had the air conditioner on for part of the day. When they did, we closed the windows, but when they didn't we had to open them because it would get a little stuffy. Dinner consisted of eggs (hard-boiled), potatoes, ketchup they just finally brought in, and also some

146

pickles. After dinner Santa and English Student came in to talk to us about their Friday services they have. (A time to confess their sins.) After a brief discussion on that, we just sat around and shot the shit. English Student was practicing his English by interrogating me— really funny! We always get a laugh when he comes in. In fact, he's here now giving Bill a couple laughs.

Last night was Thursday and like always the honking continued, meaning some more people were married. I don't know if they just like driving by this section of town or what, but there was sure a lot of honking going on. About midnight when Santa and English Student left, Guard Chief came in and practiced karate with Bill. Jerry and I played ping pong while they were rolling around the room here. Guard Chief's really determined to learn karate. After he was finished with Bill, he came in and played me a game of ping pong, and I beat him 21-10 or 11.

Then Jerry and I did our exercises and I said my prayers, asking the good Lord to take us to freedom. By the time I was finished, the rooster was crowing, meaning it was time for my bedtime. So here we still sit. Tomorrow will be the last day of this month and then we'll be going on our eighth month of captivity. My heart's still set for June, but if it doesn't come then we'll just have to continue to fight on, hoping one of these days this situation will be resolved. *End of entry.*

Saturday, May 31, 1980 (01:10)   Day 210

The last day of May today—tomorrow starts the first day of June, the month we are hoping and praying will bring us freedom. The only thing we are waiting for is the government's decision.

Just about all the students were in to see us tonight, talking, playing ping pong and playing table football/soccer. Once again tonight the star attraction was English Student. The guy's still so determined to learn English. Tonight he had with him a piece of paper and pen to take notes, while a couple of the students and Bill and I played table football. I thought Bill and I did a pretty good job of protecting the United States title. Football Captain had to come in one time and tell us to keep the noise down—we were keeping the "guest?" awake. I think they meant the guards awake. They must all sleep downstairs.

They've got the air conditioning running tonight. I asked Santa if they were going to keep it on all night and he said they'll probably turn it off around (06:00) or so. It really feels good. No doubt it will be good sleeping tonight.

I gave Santa a letter to be mailed to Jill tonight. Don't really know when it will be mailed. Hopefully she gets her birthday poem! Jerry finally got his Librium he's been asking for. I thought he was sleeping pretty well without them, but he says he's going to use them to help him sleep more in the mornings while Bill and I are sleeping and he's sitting awake. Whatever makes the day go by faster is really helpful!

Jerry and I just finished our exercising and now he's laying in his mattress, right under the light here, reading his book. Bill's got his covers over his head trying to get to sleep. Forgot to mention Jerry received a pair of pajamas today (bottoms). I know they wish they could get Bill and I to wear pajamas, but I'm really comfortable with my Marine trousers.

Otherwise nothing else really happened since the last time I wrote yesterday, except we had a different kind of coo-coo tonight for dinner. Instead of it being green it was yellow. It tasted about the same as the green coo-coo. The only difference was it was yellow and maybe had a little more eggs, too.

Hopefully the month of June flies by just as fast as May did. Home's constantly on my mind—how can I not think about it? When will all our prayers be answered. Oh God, please help us! *End of entry.*

Sunday, June 1, 1980 (02:00)   Day 211

Jerry and I just finished our usual workout, along with Bill's smart remarks. Anyway today starts a new day of a new month, a month we are all hoping will bring us freedom.

Santa, Telephone Operator, English Student came in to talk to us last night. It really gets me how they come in once in a while. One of the students was carrying a .45 in his back pocket, but no magazine in it. They try to hide it as best as possible by pulling their shirt tail over it. Tonight, Telephone Operator was carrying one. They probably all have their own. But he just happened to have his hanging out tonight.

During the discussion I asked Santa if there was any news from the States, and he replied that the Iranian people thought President Carter had something up his sleeves for re-election of the Presidency. It seemed like he was hinting about a war being started. One good thing Santa did say was that there weren't too many more demonstrations being held in the States. Thank God for that!

It seems as though they're waiting to hear how the primaries come out this month—see if President Carter has a chance or not. We're kind of curious to know too. Anyway, they think he's got some kind of plans for trying to get the hostages out of Iran. Santa says whatever he tries, the Iranian people will be ready!

Like always, he didn't want to talk about our situation. It's not like

148

it was a few weeks ago, when he used to come in with news and pictures of rioting/demonstration. Now he doesn't say anything of these things. Like he said, they're probably not doing it much anymore. Just by listening to him lately, he doesn't seem as sure of himself when we ask him about going home. Now he just comes out and says, "I don't know about these things." If it is true that we're under the care of their new government, I wonder what's taking them so long in deciding about the release or trials? I think we're being told the wrong end of the story somewhere along the line.

It seems like what they really want is for the United States to come over and start a war with them, and then they'll have a reason to put us in prison—prisoners of war! Or else if the United States starts a war they'll kill the hostages and then blame it on the United States for coming over and trying to save us. What a situation I'm in. Anyway, no news of freedom. The only thing we know is that we're starting on our eighth month of captivity. How many more are yet to come?

Santa was a little upset this morning when he found some empty fruit cans, etc., in a closet right across from the head. Bill had put them there figuring no one would find them, and what do you know, Santa comes this morning and asks us what kind of people would do that? I never even knew Bill had them stashed there. Anyway, Santa gave us a little speech about the weird things Americans do, but not once did he mention the weird thing they're doing now by holding us hostage.

I'm really getting tired of all this bullshit about how America does this and that, but not once do we ever hear the nice things the Americans do. From now on whenever I want anything I'm just going to go in the closet and get it without asking for it. I'm getting tired of all this mother-may-I shit! I know it was wrong to put the cans in the closet. I had most of them in the garbage bag in the first place but Bill had to take them out and hide them. I'm really getting tired of all this criticism though. I don't know how much more I'm going to take!

They finally put a gas burner in our head (kitchen) this morning. So far we haven't made any meals on it, but I believe tomorrow they're going to let us start. They even let us fix our own tea! The gas fumes get kind of bad at times. The little window that's in there really isn't big enough for the fumes to escape. Can't really complain though; it's better than nothing!

I took another rich man's bath today just to be doing something. I usually take a book along and just sit in the tub and take it easy, which is about all I have the energy to do lately. Even Bill and Jerry have been complaining about being real weak. Don't really know what it is—the air conditioning or maybe even the heat. I know today once again was just about taken up by sleeping. Didn't even play ping pong today. Crazy Man always comes in and teases me about sleeping too much. Heck, what else is there to do.

Santa brought mail to us this morning and something that really shocked me was I received eight letters. One from Jill Renee, parents, and two couples I'm always excited to hear from. They all said they were well, and I couldn't get over how Jill really seemed "so sure" about all of this coming to an end. All her letters I've received lately seem like that. I wonder what she's been hearing that I haven't?

My parents were saying they went to Chicago to visit Uncle Sam (the State Department), and also to see Dick Stratton. It was really a relief to hear they were all well. One other letter was from one of Jill's girlfriends telling me not to worry, that Jill was well and she is waiting patiently for me. Once I get home I don't know how I'm going to be able to tell Mary Coulter how helpful/encouraging that letter was.

My other five letters were from a Catholic school down in St. Louis. Really nice letters. Jerry received one from his mother-in-law and I believe a couple other ones from people he didn't know. We sure get a lot of those. Bill didn't receive anything from his family, but he did get a picture of his parents which was sent from a woman in Boston. It just gave Bill's parents' name and then the other part was cut off. The picture was taken at Bill's parents' house—they really looked worried/mad. Wonder what it was about?

I sure wish I knew what everyone is doing and feeling back home. I've got a feeling there's some discouraged people back there, just as there are here. I wonder what's in store for us next? God, please help us to be delivered home safely! Amen! *End of entry.*

Monday, June 2, 1980 (00:45)   Day 212

Santa, English Student and Telephone Operator just left. We had just finished listening to a soap opera over the radio, English BBC station. It seemed just like how my parents described to me how they used to listen to stories that were played over the radio when they were little, and tonight it seemed like we were doing the same thing.

Bill, Santa, Jerry and myself were sitting around the radio while English Student and Telephone Operator played football. English Student really loves to display his talent in that game, and no one plays him without feeling the agony of defeat. He continues to come in every night with his paper and pen to receive classes from Jerry. Jerry doesn't mind much; at least it gives him something to do.

Not too much news passed out tonight. Santa did say that their new government was going to make the first move towards our release,

150

which we've been hoping for and waiting for. When's the word going to come then? He said we had more mail also, so tomorrow morning we were supposed to remind him. Really been receiving a lot lately, hopefully some more from Jill and my family.

Santa brought Jerry's and my tea in yesterday morning along with a tea kettle, so I fixed the first kettle of tea, which really didn't turn out that good. I boiled it all too long, giving it a weird color, but otherwise it tasted OK. Jerry made the second kettle tonight. His turned out pretty good. No doubt as the days go on we'll continue to get better.

Bill fixed the first real meal tonight on our new stove—fried hamburgers, creamed corn and tomato/mushroom sauce. It wasn't too bad, although we could have used a little more tomato/mushroom sauce. Couldn't really have supervised him; the room in which we cook isn't big enough for two!

After dinner, Guard Chief came in for his karate class with Bill. Tonight they put two mattresses down in the center of the room and then continued to throw each other around the room, Bill doing a little more throwing than Guard Chief. Bill might have hurt Guard Chief's neck/back but really wasn't sure of the victory.

Didn't get my midday nap in today so I'm ready to hit the sack now. They don't have the air conditioning on tonight so we have to sleep under the nice cool breeze. Forgot to mention, I wrote a letter to my family today, telling them that everything was well here and to keep up the good work back home. I believe Jerry and Bill wrote one too. Santa's supposed to be going to Tehran Friday, so I guess he'll take them with him then.

A lot of honking tonight, wonder what that's all about. Weddings are usually Thursday nights. Not too much more to say except that we have to get the hell out of here! *End of entry.*

Tuesday, June 3, 1980 (00:45)   Day 213

Santa and Telephone Operator came in to talk to us for awhile tonight. Telephone didn't do too much talking; he and I were playing football while Santa, Jerry and Bill sat around and talked. Before that, Jerry, Santa and I played a couple hands of rummy, and Telephone Operator was giving Bill classes in arithmetic.

Then Santa started to tell us about the conference that was being held in Tehran (starting today and ending in four days). The conference included 50 different countries, people who wished to come to Iran to discuss the actions of the American government over here in recent years. Even a person from the United States came (Ramsey

Clark), disregarding Carter's orders that no Americans come to Iran. Santa was saying that Imam decided to do this, to have this conference, after the United States took military action over here. Santa assured us that this conference had nothing to do with the release of the hostages, just to talk about the American Government's doings over here. This reminds me of what they said about the UN Committee coming over and then leaving without saying anything. I wonder what the outcome is going to be this time?

After that discussion was finished, we asked when the new Parliament was going to get around to the hostage situation. First he said one month, then changed to no more than three weeks, putting it around June 21 or 22. Then he was saying that President Carter was doing everything in his power to avoid hostages to go to trial. Why would he be doing this, unless of course he knew that if we did go to court some of us would be found guilty and executed. Why else would he try to avoid it? It seems that June will be bringing some kind of word. I pray to God it's good for all of us.

Once again this morning we received mail and such a big surprise/encouragement it was to get four letters from Jill, one from my aunt Dottie and two other ones from two girls at Our Lady's School in St. Louis. Jill, what a sweetheart, sent me a rose petal (red) from the roses I had my Mom get her. She said she loved them so much. I'm really glad she did, I want so much to make her happy. She's the one and "only." I love you, Jill Renee!

My aunt was telling me that my parents have been fine. They were really surprised to see them on the Christian T.V. station, and to hear my Dad telling Pat Boone, "Well, Pat, it's like this." If I'm not mistaken, Pat Boone was my Mother's favorite singer, and here they are on T.V. with him. I'm *so glad* they are being so well occupied and like always, Jill assured me that they are all well, not to worry, just to take care of myself. That Jill has been such a help; I don't know what I would be doing without her. She's definitely my fuel!

Otherwise, my aunt was saying everyone was doing fine. My cousin Linda had a baby girl, and Rick wants to get married soon, but there have been a lot of layoffs lately and he doesn't know if he'll be able to survive. Really like to be home for their wedding, it's in August, I think!

Jerry received a couple letters from his family, nothing from his wife though. Bill received nothing from his family, but he did hear something about his parents trying to sell their house to come over and see him. He really didn't say much about it so that's all I know. Sounded strange though!

Ping Pong Player was here this morning to visit the students. Jerry was saying he kept coming in and out, checking to see if I was awake or not. They were all in the ping pong room playing and I guess he wanted to play. I finally got up when Santa brought hot dogs and potatoes for us to fix for lunch. So never did get to play ping pong. Matter of fact, Jerry and I never played all day either; slacking off I guess.

Read and sleep is what I usually do every day. Really getting lazy! What can I say; that's what I've been doing for the last eight months! I won't know how to act being able to walk outside like a free man again, if the day ever comes. *End of entry.*

Wednesday, June 4, 1980 (12:00)   Day 214

Santa and English Student were in to see us later last night. English Student was teaching math to Bill while Jerry, Santa and I played rummy. To show our hospitality, we served Santa some tea. Jerry and I make our tea weak, but Santa was saying that he preferred his strong. Anyway, he said he enjoyed the hospitality.

He collected up the last letters we had written ready to be mailed. Tonight he's leaving for Tehran for business. Guard Chief says Santa's going to be married, but Santa says no! Anyway, he's to be gone for four days. The last time he went we were hoping he was going to return with good news. This time I'm not getting my hopes up. Jerry is, though. Wonder what kind of business he's going back to Tehran for?

Yesterday was just about like any other day. I woke around lunch time, decided not to eat but to go in the ping pong room and do a good workout. Matter of fact, that's where I am now writing. Bill and Jerry were trying to go to sleep. Didn't want to bother them so I came in here.

English Student and Football Captain have already come in to see what I'm doing. They all keep telling me once I get back to the States to write my book, everyone's going to read it. I wish!

Anyway, my workout I had yesterday was great. I did mountain climbers, push-ups, sit-ups, jumping jacks, windmills, and at the end took a run around the ping pong table for about 45 minutes. After I worked up a good sweat, which I haven't done for a while, I went and did my laundry and took a nice cold shower.

Jerry probably would have worked out with me, but he'd already had a shower and washed his clothes. My calves are really sore after that run though. Hopefully I'll continue this little workout every second or third day, maybe include Jerry in on some of it, not too much though, still remembering what the doctor said. We have the heat to worry about now too, hate Jerry to have a heat stroke or anything else. Playing it safe is the best way.

Well, Ostard finally came back today. He came in to greet us this afternoon. He said he went to see his family, but didn't say what city he went to. It must be nice to go off for six days and visit the families. Sure wish I could do it. Maybe that's the only reason Santa is going to Tehran—to visit his family, or maybe even to get married. We'll never know why he went.

Crazy Man and Cousin brought in some mulberries and some miniature peaches to us tonight. Tasted pretty good! Talking about peaches, I wonder how our trees are doing at home. My last letter from my parents told how they've been trying to put the garden in but there just hasn't been enough hours in the day to finish it. Can't wait to get back home to some of that good homemade cooking. I even dream about it at nights, wow!

Guard Chief was saying last night that in a couple of days we'll be able to go outside to get some fresh air/solar energy. They said they've been trying to find a place suitable enough to take us without anyone seeing us. They've really been doing a good job of keeping us out of sight, that's for sure.

Really a lot of noise in this part of town this early in the morning. Mostly large trucks I've been hearing, plus the sound of the guards right outside here playing with their weapons or else the sound of water coming from a faucet I guess the guards use to drink out of. Trucks seem to be constantly coming and going—slowing down to cross the speed bump. At first I thought it was a hose of some sort that they had to drive over, but then Santa told us it was a speed bump to keep the speeders from speeding.

It's getting to be pretty early in the morning, so I guess I'll close for now. When will this situation ever come to an end? *End of entry.*

Thursday, June 5, 1980 (01:40)   Day 215

Santa must have left last night because English Student came in by himself, I guess trying to give us a little entertainment. He does a good job of that.

Didn't sleep long yesterday morning. I woke to have breakfast, first taking the rocks out of the bread which were embedded in it. I guess that's how they make their bread, on the rocks. I fell asleep after breakfast but then woke a little while later to eat lunch, my favorite rice and beans.

Everyone stuck to themselves after eating and once in a while one of the students would come in to visit, including Crazy Man who brought in some more miniature peaches. Right before dinner, which consisted of green coo-coo, Cousin came in and challenged me to a quick game, which I won.

Bill's been making popcorn, and occasionally the students will come in and munch down on it. We can sure tell that they have a lot of American ways, playing cards, eating popcorn, etc. I can feel the tiredness sneaking up on me tonight. Need to get some rest. What a joke! Nothing to write about except that we want to go home! *End of entry.*

Friday, June 6, 1980   Day 216

Just finished having breakfast consisting of butter, bread, jelly and tea. Last night while English Student was in entertaining us, I told him to make sure he came in at (09:00) this morning to wake me for breakfast. Sure enough, this morning at (09:00) English Student was here waking me for breakfast. While Jerry and I were making tea in our little kitchen, a student we hadn't seen since the night we left the Embassy (Acne/Marriage Problem) came in to say hello. I gave him a tour of our little suite, asking if he was going to be a guard here now? He said no, that he was only here to visit the other students.

By looking out the wooden shutters, it looks to be another beautiful day which we're not going to be able to go out and see. Guard Chief said that one of these days we'd be going out, but still no one has come to take us. It's been a long time since the last time we went outside. Sure could use some of that solar energy!

Yesterday there really wasn't much happening. When I awoke around noon, Jerry was in the ping pong room taking a little jog, along with Bill in there telling him that he shouldn't do that because he'd have a heart attack. Whenever Jerry's not doing anything (exercising) Bill teases him about slacking off, getting lazy, and then when he is doing something, he tells him that he shouldn't, that he'll have a heart attack.

The other night Jerry and I were working out like always. Jerry was doing his exercises when Bill, like always, interrupted and told me how I didn't have enough sense to stop Jerry from doing so many sit-ups, and how he was going to hurt himself. The next night was different for Bill though; he was in the room teaching Jerry a karate move. I guess in his book you are more likely to hurt yourself by doing sit-ups than by doing karate. Ha! Now since the heat is upon us, Jerry and I both made restrictions on how many exercises we'd do and how often we'd do them. Planning on a nice little workout for today, matter of fact.

155

I'm in the ping pong room writing and at the same time listening to the cars and trucks passing on the streets right outside. Everyone's just going about their everyday chores, acting no different about the Americans being held hostage. Eight months it's been so far and still they continue to let it go on. A couple of the students are still giving us the line about the reason we're here—to think of it as helping the poor people. That I don't think I'll ever understand!

It's really been boring lately since Santa has left. He must've told English Student to come in at nights to talk to us. These last two nights since Santa has left, English Student has been in entertaining us. He really puts on some good shows. Cousin/Mulberry Man came in frequently yesterday. First asking Jerry for a cigarette and then asking Bill or me to play football. Guard Chief, Ostard, Football Captain come in occasionally, but don't stay too long. I haven't seen Crazy Man the last day and a half. Maybe he went with Santa.

Guard Chief brought three letters in yesterday, two for me and one for Jerry, while we were playing ping pong. Jerry's was from his mother, who he's really worrying about. He said her handwriting was really looking bad—looking different from the other letters. I know my handwriting doesn't look too good; I wonder what they think at home?

One of my letters was from a girl from Our Lady's School in St. Louis, telling me everyone is praying for me, and the other was from my sweetheart, Jill. That letter was really mushy. It had my favorite perfume she always wore. I think I sat there for about half an hour, just smelling the letter and thinking of her. How I can't wait to get her in my arms again. It was kind of an old letter. She was telling me she moved back home again, that her grandma and her had a little argument. I've been wondering if it had anything to do with the letter her grandma read over the phone to my cousin Karen. She didn't say what it was about but that's what I guess. Anyway, she was saying that she's got to drive back and forth, to and from work everyday, which I didn't particularly like. The last letters I received from her she was saying that she and Lori McDonald, one of her girl friends, finally got an apartment in St. Louis and were to move into it June 1st. Hopefully, she's doing well. I really do miss that girl!

So often do I dream of her, along with the rest of the family, and then I awake to see myself in this situation, which seems like it's never going to come to an end. It's really a sad feeling, feeling that way, but I keep telling myself, "Be strong, Rocky; one of these days soon it'll come to an end and you'll be home with them all once again." Lately I've been in a mood where I just want to be by myself. I know it might sound strange, but that's just how I've been feeling. Jerry hates those moods and he is always trying to get a game of ping pong or rummy going. I try my best to get into it, but it just doesn't work.

I'm in the room now, and Acne/Marriage Problem and Jerry are in playing ping pong. Jerry asked me earlier this morning if I wanted to play but I was still writing the diary, so a little while ago when Acne/Marriage Problem came and wanted to play ping pong I called Jerry. Bill just woke up, so now the next exciting thing we're waiting for is to see what we're going to have for lunch.

The weather has really been getting hot and humid lately, even more than before. Sure wish they'd turn the air conditioner on. A day never passes that we can't hear the birds singing. Maybe nightingales—Shiraz is supposed to be famous for them. Anyway they're always out there, and it sure sounds pretty at times. Stuck in a fucking room for eight months—how bad can you have it? I know there are people who've had it worse, but this shit's getting ridiculous. *End of entry.*

Saturday, June 7, 1980 (14:25)   Day 217

Here we are, our two hundred and seventeenth day today and still no word of freedom. It really gets to be hard at times trying to analyze our situation, but by the way Santa talks, it seems that he tries to hint to us that their new government within the next several months will come to a decision about the releasing of the hostages. But last night when Guard Chief was in talking to us, he gave us a strange impression that we weren't going home till the Shah returned. We don't really know what to think at times when we keep hearing different sides of the story. Another thing, Santa was telling us that fighting in Kurdistan has ceased, and then last night Guard Chief said that it hasn't. Besides that, the United States is at fault for the fighting. United States is at fault for everything around here by the way these people all talk.

I pray/hope to God that Guard Chief was wrong last night, and that their new government is making some kind of arrangements for our release. I don't know how much more of this sitting and waiting I can take. Things aren't looking any better as the days go by. Each day they keep telling us that we'll be going outside, but as the day ends nothing ever became of it. They always told me Moslems never lie!

Received two more letters this morning, one from a girl at the Our Lady's School in St. Louis and the other from my sister Debbie. My sister was saying that things were pretty well screwed up yet (April 3) but not to give up hope, just give this thing a little more time and that it won't be too much longer. Considering my family, I know that they

157

don't really know when this situation is going to come to an end, but still they say it won't be too much longer. They just say that to make us feel better. Matter of fact, they've all been saying that in every letter I've been getting from them.

I don't think anyone knows when we're to be released, even the Iranian government. But of course I know they've got the power to do so whenever they wish. Why don't they then? I guess that's a question we aren't going to find out the answer to until we're released. Guard Chief is such a strong believer that the Shah's going to return. We ask him why he believes that and he replies, "I know; I read the news; you don't." That's for damn sure. We sure don't get to read the news. Why that is I'll never understand.

We've been here seven and one-half months so far and still the Shah hasn't returned—why do they think keeping us here longer is going to help out any? To me it seems as though it would just piss the United States off. These people aren't afraid if the U.S. starts a war, though. I really think they think they could beat us. Revenge is all they want. June 5th, I forgot to mention, was an anniversary of a day that some thousand Iranians were killed. The cause was because of the United States once again.

Crazy Man just came in to see us. He said he just returned from Hudastan. He said it was very hot there and from the looks of him, it was. He really didn't say why he was there, but my guess was to visit some of his friends that are caring for some hostages. Santa was saying that they've got the hostages spread out all through Iran; wouldn't surprise me. It would make it a lot harder for the U.S. to come over to evacuate us.

Yesterday didn't have much doing. Everyone did their own little workout and then continued on reading books. Jerry and I played a little cards—didn't play too much ping pong. The light fixture went out and no one seems to be able to fix it. Jerry and Bill played a little this morning, the best time to play so the sun shines through the shutters. By late afternoon it gets a little dark in there.

Not too much doing now, either. Jerry's playing around with the cards on his mattress. I think he's trying to hint to me that he wants to play some cards. Bill's in the ping pong room reading. By listening to the voices outside, it seems as all the guards are sitting around shooting the shit. It must be nice to be able to do whatever you want! Supposedly tomorrow Santa's to return from Tehran, hopefully with some good news. Cross my fingers on that. *End of entry.*

Sunday, June 8, 1980 (01:25)   Day 218

Nothing really happened yesterday after I finished writing; just sat around and stayed pretty well to ourselves. Right now we're sitting here listening to Bill's love life—how all the girls were all after his ass. He makes it sound like he was the only one the girls liked. I'm not the type to brag about stuff like that. I had a helluva good time in high school getting dates whenever I wanted, but I don't brag about it like I was a stud. It really gets sickening listening to his love stories over and over.

Ostard brought us the tape player last night and we're still listening to it besides hearing Bill's stories of his high school days. He really had it hard, having the girls chase him and the guys beating the shit out of him. I'm always wondering why the guys were always beating the shit out of him and putting him in trash cans. Earlier tonight we were talking about movies. I hardly ever have much to say, really never saw that many movies, and when I did I never took too much consideration of who was starring and all. I have a bad memory for names anyway.

Guard Chief came in for his karate class tonight, so Bill had his chance to throw him around the room once again. Cousin/Mulberry Man came in and asked Bill if he'd teach him karate, so Bill told him tomorrow he would. Maybe I ought to get the chance to throw a couple of guys around.

This shit's really been getting to me. Nothing ever being said about our release, just that we're to sit back and wait—wait for what though? Santa's supposed to return tomorrow, hopefully with some good news! Maybe I'll be able to get some sleep tonight. The last couple nights and even times before that I've been dreaming a lot about my home. Mostly I'm dreaming of how great it's going to be with J.R. and all the family once again.

Other than everyone talking about getting out of here, we're all doing pretty well. Bill's been getting bit at night from some kind of insect. Back home he's got a problem with all the girls chasing him and here he's got the same thing with those insects. Jerry and I haven't had any of those problems.

Guard Chief was just in to see us. He told us that the Parliament had started to discuss the hostage situation two days ago. Within the next two weeks or a little time after that we might start to hear something. How I hope/pray to God he was telling us the truth! It was really strange to hear what he said, especially after what he said last night about how we weren't going home till the Shah returns. Things are starting to look up for us if what he said is true. Maybe my little movie camera friend was right about being home to watch the Summer Olympics. God, please don't let us down this time when it seems so close to freedom! *End of entry.*

159

The only thing I can say now is that I'm surprised and furious at what's happening. Here we sit once again back home at Tehran, Iran —American Embassy. After a long, rough ride from Shiraz we all made it in one piece, with the help of the Good Man Upstairs.

Right after we had gotten into our new rooms Santa came in to fill us up to date with a little news. His words were, "In two or three days a solution will be found, and you will be moved from this present position to another place." The other place we are to be moved to was never mentioned, but we're hoping that the next place we move to is the United States. It seems hard not to be thinking positively on what Santa said about the solution being found in two or three days. Still it seems so hard to believe that they're going to let us go just like that. Now if you look at the bad side of this mess, we might just be going to court and then sentenced to imprisonment—that also might be the solution they found.

Once again all we have to do is just sit back and wait to see what happens within the next couple days. I pray/hope to God whatever is done is done for the goodness of the hostages (all hostages). Oh God, please help us.

The next parts I'm going to write are going to be entries of the 8th, 9th and 10th, which is today. I'll try to write them as best as I can remember them. I didn't really have much time to write during our journey cross country, as you'll be able to see as I write on.

Guard Chief came in that morning of the 8th at (11:30), waking us, wondering if we would want to go outside. He was telling us we had our choice to go then while it was a little hot or wait until it cooled down. We hadn't been outside for so long we really didn't care how the weather was; we just wanted out. Our plates were put to the side, because English Student was going to bring our lunch out to us. We each carried our own cups and forks and were led down to a little garden—of course with towels over our heads—where they had a little place divided off with sheets, but with no guards around. That's one thing they always seemed to worry about, the guards seeing us.

The air and sun really felt good against our pale bodies. Right away as I got under the sun I started to break a sweat. That just shows me how much water I've got stored up. Underneath some of the shade trees they had a small table with two wooden benches. It seemed like a regular picnic when English Student brought out our plates of rice, bread, ice water and a plastic table cloth to lay over the top of the table. Ostard, Football Captain, and English Student were the only students out there—oh yes, and Cousin/Mulberry Man. They mostly sat around guarding the places they had divided off with sheets, I guess making sure we didn't escape or else making sure the guards didn't come around.

The place we were living in seemed pretty large and well protected. On top of the roof I saw a small parapet which they had made from sand bags, with ladders on the side of the buildings to get up to it. No one was in it at the time though. Surrounding us were a lot of small buildings which seemed to not have been in use for a while. Also around the buildings were a lot of various types of trees—pines, maple wood, spruce, etc. We even had a little guest to share our lunch with, a black cat I had seen a couple days earlier walking through our hallway.

Didn't care for the rice too much, but really loved Bill's popcorn. A lot of birds were flying around above us, fighting against each other. It's really strange, wherever you look nowadays, something or someone is usually fighting. What is it that makes this happen? I'd say we were out there about an hour or an hour and a half before they took us back to the room. I guess the guards wanted to come out of hiding and come back to their own little picnic, so they took us back up.

The air conditioning was running when we returned. Felt a lot better in there than it did outside, but still it was great getting a little fresh air/solar energy. English Student brought the dirty dishes back up for us, and after that we hardly saw any of the students (like always) till dinner, when English Student came back in and asked us what we wanted for dinner. I think we sat there for about fifteen minutes explaining to him that we wanted ravioli, and then explaining what kind of can it was in. Around half an hour later they finally brought it in.

While Bill fixed the whole can, Jerry and I did a little exercise in the ping pong room. Nothing too much, Jerry's back's been hurting him so I've been having him lay off the sit-ups. Boy, does he hate that! I think we ate half the can of that ravioli and gave the other half back to the students and told them we'd have the rest the next day. Little did we know we weren't going to be there the next day, and this morning Santa was saying that the guards were still at the house guarding "nothing"—sneaky people these Iranians are.

I think it was around (20:00) or so when Ostard came into our room and said that we might be moving, but nothing was definite yet. We misunderstood him to say that if we were to move it would only be a two hour ride, but I think what he was trying to say was that we should take an hour or two nap. None of us had any idea we'd be coming back to Tehran.

A little while after Ostard left, Football Captain came in to see

161

what our personal items were going to consist of. Right then I had a feeling we were leaving, but never did it cross my mind that we were coming here. Everyone made their own personal rolls and then we turned the light off to get a couple little snoozes.

It was around (03:00) in the morning when I was awakened by a little nudge from Bill. The lights were still off and Football Captain was standing over by the door. I started to say "what the hell" when I was stopped short by Football Captain putting his finger over his lips indicating me to be quiet. Things really started to get strange then. Still with the lights off (except a reflection from the hallway light) and his voice to a whisper, he told us we were going to be taken down to a truck waiting for us downstairs. We were to stay quiet, taking our shoes off and carrying them. The order in which we would go would be me, Jerry and Bill. After he told us all this he left, but then came back within about a two minute period. He indicated for me to come in the ping pong room, where he had a pair of handcuffs (three pair) waiting to put on me.

Right then I started to get these strange thoughts of how they were going to try to make it look like we were trying to escape and then it would give the guards a good enough reason to shoot us. That thought was washed out, though, when I realized I had the handcuffs on, and why they would want to do that? My next thought was that the United States was sending over another evacuation party and there were people across the way watching the house for any sign of movement of the hostages, so the students had to get us out without anyone knowing about it. Like I said this morning, Santa was saying that the guards are still back there protecting the empty house.

With my hands handcuffed, holding my sandals and Football Captain holding my arm, he led me downstairs, through a room, out a window to the back of a van to sit and wait. Football Captain left me there, eyes still not blindfolded, with a guy walking back and forth behind the van with a .45 underneath a stocking cap.

After we were all three in the van, we were told we would have to wait a couple more minutes before we would start off. We were then blindfolded to sit and wait. Like always when we take a trip like this, the windows were covered over with paper/paint. About fifteen minutes after they had said we would have to wait, a couple guys got in, started the truck, and drove about 100 yards to a garage, it seemed like. Everyone's voice seemed to echo. After about five minutes there we started up once again, and this time I recognized a voice which was Guard Chief. He came in the back of the van and took us up to the seats to sit down. I was expecting a short ride just like this one we took to get to that house. Boy, was I ever wrong.

162

At the time there only seemed to be around six people in the van, three of us and three of them. I'd say we drove for about another five minutes when we stopped to pick up two more hostages—older, about 45-50 years of age it sounded like. By the time we had loaded up new hostages, in all I'd say we had about ten people in that stuffy van. After that the ride was rough and fast. Once in a while a nice cool breeze came in from the front windows.

I couldn't even take a wild guess as to how many times we stopped. The truck was definitely taking a beating and about (14:00) that day it broke down. We seemed to be right in the middle of a desert. Radiator problems I think. We had started out that morning about (04:00) and had been on the road for about nine-ten hours, stopping for gas and other times stopping for I don't know what. The only thing I did know at the time was that truck. (14:00) in the afternoon the desert was as hot as an oven. Water was given to us at this time, still handcuffed and blindfolded, and then English Student passed around little fans so that we could fan ourselves. Then occasionally he would come around himself and fan us all.

I don't really know how long we stayed there. I was too busy keeping the flies away and trying to stay cool. I remember hearing a truck stop, and then a little while later they got us going again, but a lot slower than we had been going before. We then stopped at a place which seemed to be off the road a little ways. I remember we backed down to the place we stopped, and everyone got out except for the guard in the back. The two things I can remember about that place was a generator running loudly and the ice cold water they brought us. Boy, did that ever taste good.

All these stops were getting us pissed off. Whenever that truck was stopped it got hotter than hell, but when we were moving, a nice breeze came in. Well, after they did whatever they did at that place we drove off once again, leaving the sun to the left of us meaning we were driving north—to where though?

We hadn't driven that far once again when we came to a truck stop, it seemed like. A lot of noise. Trucks, cars, people talking, babies crying. Here's where we got our first meal, first feeding us pears and then letting us drink the juice. All this they were doing to all five of us. After the pears they handed us a hot dog sandwich, which we ate by ourselves. The real treat came when they gave us soda to drink, just like a regular picnic out in the desert.

After our little feast at the truck stop we started off once again, stopping a few more places before stopping at Isfaham. I guess they figured it was about time to give us a break after being in that damned truck for 12-13 hours straight. So in Isfaham we stopped at the Shah's
163

brother's house—at least this is what the students said. The house was bare, just like all the other houses we've been living in, but really elegant. Here they took us to a bedroom with two beds, where I got stuck sleeping on the floor two or three of the five hours we were there. I didn't really mind. The beds weren't that comfortable anyway. I laid by a window trying to get a little breeze, which I didn't accomplish too well. I don't know how anyone could live in that house without air conditioning.

Looking out the bathroom window you could see a couple hills in the background. They might have even been mountains, but the heat from the sun really made it hard to see clearly. Four Eyes was there waiting for us, along with a few of the other students we hadn't seen since we left the Embassy. He gave us a few toilet articles and then left. He came in once in a while but really didn't stay around. Guard Chief said we weren't going to be staying there long. I kind of figured his use of long meant hours, because they never brought our bundles in. They just took us in for some sleep and some food. Once when I was sleeping I woke up to eat some watermelon, which tasted great. After I was finished with that I crashed back out until waking for dinner, which consisted of rice and bean stew. Really filled me up. Midway as we were eating, they came in and told us that when we were finished we should use the head and then get ready to move on. That really surprised me. This time was about (21:30-22:00). At least they were smart about driving at night instead of the day.

Blindfolds were put on us in the room and then we were re-escorted out to the van, the same one we had earlier, but this time instead of having Jerry in the middle we had another elderly man. It was kind of funny though; when I first got into the van I thought the person to the left of me was Bill and that he hadn't moved over yet, so when I got into the truck I took the guy's arm and gave him a little punch on the shoulder. The next thing I heard was Bill speaking from the other side of the guy I just hit, saying "Rocky, I'm over here." Right then I knew it wasn't Bill, and it wasn't Jerry because I had left him back in the room. I told the gentleman next to me I was sorry, but the guards stopped us from talking anymore.

The truck was loaded once again, nine or ten people and we were off, stopping every so often like before. The first time we stopped for gas they turned the motor off, and when we were ready to go they couldn't get it started. It seemed like a truck stop we were at. Anyway they pushed the truck backwards, I guess out of everyone's way, and started to work on it. I wonder how many people there knew that there were American hostages in that van they were working on. Outside the truck once again you could hear people talking, babies

164

crying. That brought back memories of my own little nieces and nephews. They finally got it started and we headed off again.

One time I could have sworn we stopped for tea and for water. These stops were really getting to us. The guy next to me would give me a nudge whenever we stopped, and I would reply back to him with a grunt of how we felt about the stops. If we were going somewhere why didn't they just continue to drive until we got there? So many times it seemed like we came so close to having a wreck, but we seemed to avoid it every time. I guess it was because of all the rosaries I was saying.

The closer we got to Tehran the faster we seemed to be going. We reached Tehran about an hour after the sun had risen and then had to drive through the thickest traffic I've been in. Drive 50 yards and then stop, and with the sun coming on strong the van started to turn into an oven again. By the time we reached the Embassy we had been in that van another ten hours, and then we had to wait another ten minutes for someone to come around to the east door and let us in. By the time they did come to take us from the truck we had pretty well had it. We were hungry, thirsty and especially tired.

We were taken to a room, ground level, west end, looking onto the street. I remember this room because I had to bring a working party to this room to hang the curtains that are still hanging. Marines always had to escort working parties throughout the building for different various things, and to this room I escorted the party who hung the curtains. Coincidence, eh?

One mattress was already here. A little while later some students that we hadn't seen since we left the Embassy brought two more for Jerry and Bill. This is about when Santa came in to fill us in on all of the news. Now if he was telling the truth or not, that I guess we'll just have to wait and see. *End of entry.*

Wednesday, June 11, 1980 (19:30)   Day 221

Not much has happened since yesterday except for the fact we're sweating our asses off. Well it's not really that bad, but it's bad enough to where it's very uncomfortable while sleeping. Still can't make too much out of this yet. Especially after Mailman came in to greet/talk to us. He hardly said anything about what Santa said earlier that day about something happening soon.

I've noticed our towels and linen are a lot whiter than what they've been the last couple months. Don't really need any blankets or linen to sleep with anyway—it gets too hot in the room for all that. Last night was kind of rough getting to sleep. Of course it was a lot better than trying to sleep in a van which seemed to be going through a cow pasture at 50 miles an hour. What an experience this has all been so far, all these things I'll be able to tell my grandchildren. That's if we ever get out of here.

The students here haven't been treating us too bad. Once in a while a couple come in we hadn't seen since we left. Second time today they brought us in orange juice. Really tastes good in this hot weather. We've got an air conditioner which kind of startled Jerry tonight by the pop/flash it gave off when he accidentally hit the cord while making his mattress. I don't know why we've got it running. It hardly does any good.

We've got two windows in the room, one with a parapet and the other one without. The one without the parapet is broken, and if you're across the room you can see two bullet holes, one in a side door that leads to another office, and the other one a hole in the concrete wall the size of a softball. The desk I'm writing on is pushed up with my back facing this window through which those rounds came. I guess you could say I'm kind of risking it, but who gives a damn if there's someone out there that wants to get me. I'll give him a chance so he can get it over with. Never know, that's what might happen to me at the end anyway.

Last night when they brought us our dinner of roast beef (meat, wow!) and potatoes and carrots I thought we still had our old cook, but today's food proved me wrong. Today for lunch we had salmon and chicken in a can and then Kraft cheese and blackberry jelly, and tonight for dinner we had the Tehran Hilton Special, "soup." Looking forward to seeing what we have tomorrow.

Not too much more to say now. Jerry and Bill are sitting around getting all uptight about trying to analyze this situation. It's really no use doing it, but it gives them something to do.

The letter Jerry got from his mother, May 15, 1980, mentioned nothing about the military actions President Carter took over here. That was strange. Santa was saying that most Americans despised Carter's actions, but still it's surprising nothing was said about it. Really looking forward to receiving some mail tonight. *End of entry.*

Thursday, June 12, 1980 (23:00)   Day 222

Santa was just in talking about demonstrations the Moslems and the Moslem Marxists had today up by the stadium at the east end of the Embassy grounds, outside the walls of course. Neither Santa nor Mailman said why they were fighting. Santa was saying 100 students had been injured, but with all the rifle shots that were fired, I would've figured there would have been more injuries or even deaths. Santa and Mailman said the students and guards weren't shooting at the people; they were shooting up in the air to keep everyone away from the Embassy. Why would they want to come into the Embassy if the students have told everyone we were innocent? Sometimes I really wonder if the students really told them that. If they did, why do they still want to get us. Mailman was saying once again that most of the blame was on the CIA, who plant people to start things like this.

So here they are with their new government, but still they have people out there trying to kill each other, destroying and shooting up the town. Mailman said they're still trying to situate the new government, kicking the bad people out and replacing them with good representatives. Then Santa was saying that the government is aware of problems between the two groups, but don't really know yet how to solve them. I wonder what the hell their new government is doing if they're not working on the situation of the hostages or the problem between the two groups.

Last night Mailman was saying that we better start praying because half the people were saying that we should be trialed. We don't really understand what the other half wants. They just might want to let us go, but then again I doubt it. It doesn't seem like my plans for getting out of here this month are going to happen.

I'm really starting to wonder if we will ever get out of here, especially after today. It really had us wondering when we started to hear all that shooting, really close too. We told Mailman if they started to come in and get us, that they had better give us a gun to protect ourselves with—at least then I know I would have died fighting. I know the odds wouldn't have been even, but what else is new? Once again today I told Jerry that we really don't need to worry until they start hitting the building near us and then we do everything to protect our ass.

Santa said tonight that it would be another three days before we move again. He said he's been awful busy these past days. I'm wondering, doing what?

Last night we had a little excitement when Mailman brought in a couple other students. Two small ones and one heavy-set guy to arm wrestle with. At first it started off with Bill and the heavy-set guy, who I'll call "Muscle Man", arm wrestling and Muscle Man beating Bill. Then Mailman wanted me to arm wrestle him. I guess he wanted to see how weak we are. Well let me tell you, this guy Muscle Man wasn't too weak and built pretty good; I guess about 70-80 kilos. Well we got down and struggled it out I guess for about five minutes, and not once did he get me close to the ground but everytime I got him down he said I cheated. After a few more times of getting him down and hearing him tell me I was cheating, I quit to let Jerry and a couple other students try. I guess the workouts we'd been doing have done us some good, because even Jerry was winning.

After a little of that I guess Muscle Man was kind of mad for not winning at arm wrestling, so he wanted to try wrestling. I have never been a wrestler, but I did do a little in high school during P.E. Muscle Man looked like a wrestler to me. The only thing I kept telling myself was that I had to be quick, and right then he came at me. At the same time as he grabbed hold of me, I spun both of us around so that he fell and I fell on top of him to put the finishing touch on my pin. I never got that far, though, for when he fell he must've hit a nerve in his elbow and said he couldn't go any further. We really didn't know what had happened to him, but we knew it wasn't broken. They took him to the doctor and then to a specialist today, and they told him it was only a bad bruise and not to worry about it.

Last night he told Mailman, and Mailman translated to me, that I wasn't really wrestling, but fighting or using karate instead. I told him I was sorry for hurting him, and as he left he shook my hand and told me not to worry about it. Today he came in and said that everything is OK, and once he gets well again he would come back and try again. Try and try until you succeed; that's my motto! I've been humiliated too much and I couldn't be last night, too. I don't know where my weak body got all that energy last night, but wherever I did get it I was sure grateful. Have to keep that American spirit.

Mailman just brought in the letters we were supposed to receive last night. I didn't get one from Jill, but got one from my sister Debbie. Finally found out that I have a brand new nephew, Nicholas Robert Filla, baptized May 18, 1980 (12:30). Don't really know when he was born though. I'm glad to hear that everything came out well, and like always Jill was there with a present from both of us. What a sweetheart that girl is—don't know what I'd do without her. Love her so much!

Deb said that everyone is doing well and not to worry, and said that they had received a letter from me. Can't really recall when I wrote it. Anyway it was nice hearing from them. Bill received one from his girlfriend. She said that they're still busy putting ribbons around trees for us. He also received a photocopy of a document that was made from the town he lives in (Pueblo), telling everyone to continue tying yellow ribbons, something that had been started by Mrs. Laingen. So I guess Mr. Laingen, the Charge, did get taken hostage. Anyway, they're still continuing to care for us back home but still nothing's happening over here. What do these people plan to gain from holding us any longer? What's taking their government so long to make their decision? These questions we'd like answered, plus many other ones, but the only thing we have to do is sit around and wait.

Not too much to do in here, it's really too hot to work out. Don't really know when our next shower will be. Otherwise the only thing we have is reading and looking at each other. Occasionally we get a few laughs from the Polack joke book, and Jerry's getting a couple laughs from the book "Stranger in the Mirror." Trying our hardest to keep some sanity, but how much longer can we stay like this? Isn't eight months enough? *End of entry.*

Saturday, June 14, 1980 (13:10) Day 224

Just came back from doing my clothes in the head and thought I'd sit down now to write my entry from yesterday and this morning. There really isn't much to write about yesterday. The only time anyone came in, except for last night when Mailman came in to talk to us, was when they brought breakfast—bread, butter, jelly and tea. Lunch was mixed rice, meat, beans and vegetables, and for dinner we had hamburgers, seconds too. Otherwise we stuck to ourselves again, reading and whatever else we could find to do. I wrote my sister Debbie telling her I finally received her letter about my new little nephew, and said to tell everyone hello. Not really too much more to write.

Last night Mailman came in after dinner and gave four Charm Pops to each of us. Plus he brought in a letter for me that was sent from the First Baptist Church in Union, telling me that yellow ribbons are still being flown in Washington, Krakow and Union for our speedy return home. Besides the Charm Pops and one letter for me, he brought in some comics from the *Newsday*, Long Island's own Sunday newspaper.

I forgot to mention that the night before he brought in a paper that had a picture that was supposedly taken in Florida of President Carter's limousine with Secret Service men chasing after it. It seemed like they had a little trouble with people throwing bottles, etc. Didn't really say why he was down there. Also last night he brought in another paper that had a picture of people demonstrating against nuclear power plants. Something else I caught said something about war with Iran.

They show us pictures of all these things, but nothing about their government working on the hostage situation. He said that they supposedly had started three weeks ago, but it was postponed to clear up matters with the new representatives. He said they might have started again today, and any day a group of us might be released. He keeps telling us to pray that we go on trial, but he claims he doesn't know what the new Parliament is going to do.

The only thing he does say which he sounds sure of is that we won't be here by Christmas, meaning everyone! Six more months till December. I don't know if I can make it that long. The only thing it seems like we're waiting for now is the new Parliament to make their decision. How long is that going to take? They keep saying that they're waiting for the dust that Carter threw in to settle before making another decision, whatever that means. *End of entry.*

Sunday June 15, 1980   **Day 225**

Things have really been boring around here at the Tehran Hilton. Yesterday the big excitement of the day was that we went to the library that we had piled up right before Easter time. The room looked as though no one had used it since. Dust was lying everywhere. They still had a few good books. The other ones they said they've been passing to the other hostages that are spread out through Iran.

Going to see later on today if we can go to the workout/ping pong room. Mailman says we just have to ask the guards and they'll take us. See what happens when we ask them. When we first got here we asked one of the students about it and he said they didn't have it anymore. Everyone's got their different story, I guess.

The food hasn't been bad. I'm already used to rice anyway. Rice for lunch yesterday, soup for dinner last night (every other night), butter, bread, jelly and tea for breakfast (every morning lately), and rice for lunch again today. Hopefully for dinner tonight we'll have some meat.

Well today's the 15th of June, the day I was shooting for, for all of us to be gone. The three days are up for when we were supposed to move, too. The next day I'm shooting for is June 30th. I still have the strong feeling inside telling me that something is going to happen. If it doesn't though, I guess I'll just have to shoot for another date.

The weather has really been hot lately, and without even working out we've been sweating and stinking. I'd hate to see what we'd be like working out without taking a shower. Mailman and Santa haven't come in for the last day and a half. The next time they do, I'm going to ask them when we can have our next shower. My face has been breaking out once again pretty bad. I think I'm going to ask them if I can see that specialist I was supposed to see when the Red Cross was here.

Wonder if their new Parliament has been discussing the hostage situation? *End of entry.*

What an entry I have to write. Here we sit (Dick Morefield and Allan Golancinski, Bill, Jerry and myself) in some kind of prison. At least that's what it looks like to us. We all can't get over how we're all being kept together. For forty-nine days before this they were both living with each other, without seeing anyone else. They said they've also been living in different quarters, but nothing like the places we've been to. They've mostly stayed in Tehran, a couple times in prison.

Ever since we left the Embassy yesterday morning around (03:00-04:00) we've been talking about our past experiences. Talking except for sleeping, and it's so good to hear different Americans speak. We were all surprised to see each other when they put us in this room together. Can't really understand what's going on, but this morning English Student told Bill that we'll be here for another ten days. Now if he was telling us the truth or not I guess we'll just have to wait and see.

It all started yesterday morning when they came in around (03:00-04:00), woke us up, and told us to pack our stuff because we were going to move. I had just gotten to sleep, too. Before that I was listening to the wrecker crew cleaning up the mess of the accident a car and road sweeper had. Anyway it didn't take us that long to get all our things together and then have them take us down to the basement and out the west door to a van that was waiting for us. At the time I didn't know it, but Allan and Dick were already in the van waiting. After we were in, they brought one more hostage in that still we don't know the identity of. The only thing we do know is they're keeping two other hostages across the hall in separate rooms by themselves.

Anyway our ride only lasted five minutes from the Embassy. Still we can't figure out where we're at. We were thinking maybe it's that military base next to the Embassy grounds. When we reached our destination we were led from the van, still blindfolded, from a garage it seemed like, up some stairs, through some hallways, stepping over some barred door entrances, and then to our new room where Allen Golacinski and Dick were just taking their blindfolds and ropes off their hands. The first thing Allan asked Santa before he left to get Jerry and Bill was, "What have you done with my Marines," meaning my hair. Allan's hair doesn't look too bad, considering Mailman cut it.

I don't know where to start on how to describe how happy I was to see them. Jerry and Bill had finally come in. I believe they were kind of surprised/happy, too. After we were all in the room together and

171

before Santa left, Santa told Allan and Dick to ask us three what was up because we have a lot of information. Well, after everything we've told Allan and Dick we still can't come up with a decision about what's going on. Really a strange situation we can't seem to figure out. Like I've said before, ever since we've gotten together, except for sleeping, we haven't stopped talking. We've found playing four handed spades to really be enjoyable. Makes the time fly by.

The students have really been treating us well. Breakfast was normal, but yesterday for lunch we had chicken, potato chips and bread. Last night for dinner we had soup and bread. Menu Man, Jerry's friend, told us that we might get some apple pie. My mouth just waters thinking about it. For lunch today we had steak, spinach, corn on the cob and bread. Really a good meal, especially that steak and corn. Could've eaten a lot more. Wonder what we're going to have tonight.

We can't really figure out why we're here, and especially why they put the five of us together. Santa was telling us the truth, I guess, when he said that we had been to all the best spots in Iran and now they were going to take us to the worst. It seems like they've got everything they need to keep us here for a while. The toilet isn't in very good condition, but at least it's in working order. The showers are right across the hallway, with three shower stalls. No hot water, but then again we don't really need any now with the hot weather.

Last night they brought us a nice 15" fan which really keeps the room comfortable. The room's about 10' by 20', with four nice size windows, but nothing really comes in from them. They're pretty well wired up anyway. I know if we ever wanted to get out of here we wouldn't be going out the window. Otherwise we're pretty comfortable. Last night they brought us skinny mattresses about 4" thick and some white sheets. Everyone said they slept pretty well last night, and after breakfast this morning Bill and I crashed back out till lunch. Jerry, Dick and Allan just sat around and talked. We're always finding something to talk about.

(22:10) Just got finished with dinner which consisted of some kind of Iranian soup (little noodles, beans and some other things) and bread. Al's in the bathroom doing the dishes. It's really something. Whenever we want to go to the head we have to throw a white cloth over the door and then knock.

Supposed to have a doctor come tomorrow to have a look at my acne problem that seems to have really gotten bad. We all think it's not acne but something else. Wonder what the doctor's going to say?

Forgot to mention that Al found about ten other ears of corn today in the trash can. He says he's always been a trash hound, checking for clues of the other hostages. But then we thought maybe the students were eating corn, too.

Al's back now, and we're trying to analyze our situation, trying to figure out the evacuation attempt. Really can't understand that one yet. Today went by pretty fast so hopefully they'll continue. *End of entry*.

Wednesday, June 18, 1980 (16:15)   Day 228

Just returned from the head where I had a little talk with Santa. The first thing I asked him was when I was going to see the doctor and he replied, "he'd see where he was." Then I asked him about the mail, and first he said, "we weren't going to be here long." Then he said the reason for no mail was that they had been busy preparing this place for our stay, and hadn't had time to read it. Maybe the day after tomorrow, he said.

I started to get curious about what he said about not being here long, and asked him about that. He said that I should think and remember what he said earlier, I guess meaning when he said that we'd be out of here by July. Then he said that I shouldn't be in a "hurry". For the last eight months they've been saying that. It's really hard to do, though.

Can't find anything but good out of what Santa said. Just hope he wasn't joking me. Al, Bill, Jerry and Dick are playing spades now. Can't really describe how great it is to have these two other people with us. Ever since we got together I haven't touched a book. We're talking constantly, it seems like.

(17:15) Just returned from the head, where Santa and English Student asked me if I was capable of fixing the shitter. I told them yes, the only thing I needed was a couple bolts, nuts, and rubber washers. They just had the water turned on for the tank sitting on the back of the shitter, so I told them the things I needed and a student went out to fetch them.

Meanwhile English Student and Santa were in there talking to me. English Student told me they already have Bill's and my plane tickets ready, and once the Parliament finally decides the other hostages will have theirs, too. I guess it's true what Al says about the Marines having nothing to worry about. Santa was saying that the Parliament was still working on the new regulations, and that we'd have to understand that it's their first new Parliament. The month I think he was talking about this morning is how long he thinks it's going to take the new Parliament to decide on the regulations. After they decide on the regulations, we (the hostages) are to be the first on the agenda. I

173

thought for sure they told us this had all been taken care of last month, but here they are saying it again. Santa said that we'd be staying here until we leave. It does make a little sense for us to be here. The Parliament is getting ready to make a final decision on the hostages, and here we are well guarded from the people that might not agree.

Santa was asking if he could come in tonight and join in on some of our discussions. He said he had heard some of the one we had earlier this morning (04:00) about Iran's technology and education. I guess he feels as though he wants to come in and give his point of view.

Nothing much of anything else happening. Just waiting for that beautiful day when we are released. I guess I'll get up and watch them play spades. Dinner should be coming pretty soon. I think last night's Iranian soup must have given me the shits. I've been having them all morning. *End of entry.*

Thursday, June 19, 1980 (21:10)   Day 229

It seems like we've all started to run out of things to talk about lately. Right now, just like it's been all day, we're sitting/lying on our mattresses wondering if this thing's ever going to come to an end. We wonder if everything they keep hinting to us is really true or not. Like Dick said a while ago, we're too tired and bored to do anything else, but we're never too tired to think about going home. We didn't even play cards. We all mostly slept the whole day. It was like we were drugged or something.

The students finally got the hot water heater fixed in the bathrooms yesterday, so Jerry, Dick, Al and Bill went to take hot showers while I watched the room. I took a cold shower the day before anyway. While they were gone Menu Man and a couple other students brought in dinner which consisted of my favorite (rice). We had it again tonight, too, along with jello.

We mostly sat around and talked last night. Bill and Al were playing dominoes, but mostly we were waiting for Santa to come in and talk to us. He did finally come in, but he didn't really stay long. He came in a couple of times to tell us to keep our voices down. We were laughing at a few of Bill's jokes. Otherwise Santa never came in to talk to us.

We went to bed pretty early last night, waking this morning to find another little something added onto the breakfast treat, and that was cheese. So we had cheese, strawberry jelly, butter, bread and tea. After I was finished with that, I crashed back out. When I woke up, everyone was lying on their mattresses talking about our situation, trying to find anything at all out of what they've been telling us about things that have been happening regarding our release. We always seem to find ourselves at a dead end, though.

Lunch wasn't too bad today, consisting of roast beef, baked potatoes, butter and bread. The meat was a little fatty and a little raw, but anyway it was just good to have meat. We all sat around our 2' diameter table eating and talking, and then everyone went off to their own little mattress, some of us talking for awhile and the rest crashing out.

The dishes haven't been a problem. We all switch off and on doing them. Right now Al's getting ready to do them when Dick returns from the head. Dick hasn't been feeling too well; neither has Al. Al has a kidney problem which seems to be bothering him frequently. Dick claims to be constipated, so this afternoon I gave him some pills the doctor had given me a while back for the same problem. He just came back and said they still haven't affected him.

As Menu Man just came in to serve tea, we saw a couple of students out in the hall hanging up posters. I sure hope that's not a sign of us being here longer or someone coming to see us. I won't really think much about it until they come in here and start decorating.

A couple of things that Jerry and I talked about a few weeks back regarding Bill are starting to happen. Already, here with Dick and Al, Bill's been saying things trying to make Jerry and me look bad and trying to make himself look like a rose garden. It's just like Jerry and I said about how he's going to try to make us look like he pulled us through this mess. What a joke though! *End of entry.*

Friday, June 20, 1980 (23:35)   Day 230

Today seemed to go by pretty fast considering I spent most of the afternoon in the head fixing the toilet. I asked them if they had finally gotten the parts I asked for earlier, rubber washers, etc. They hadn't gotten the parts, and were trying to fix it themselves, but it never worked. So today myself and another student (Plumber) stole parts from the other toilets and then used plastic and cloth as a seal for all the watertight fits. We finally did get one toilet fixed, so now we don't have to strain to take a shit on the Iranian Shitter. It doesn't really bother me, but Dick was saying the other day that his knees get a little tired squatting down like that. I'm supposed to get some more parts sometime tomorrow so I'll be able to fix another one.

Like I said before, it took me most of the afternoon. Meanwhile Bill, Al, Jerry and Dick played cards. When I walked back into the room everyone was joking about how I smelled like shit. Really I didn't, but they must have asked the students what I was doing since I

175

was gone so long, so they were all joking me. Anyway to please them I went in to take a shower. The water heater has been working pretty well, providing enough hot water. It seemed like they're getting everything ready for a long stay.

The food hasn't been too bad. Today for lunch we had hamburgers, fried potatoes. Tonight we had vegetable soup. The treatment from the students hasn't really changed. It's just the living quarters that have. Do have to say that it's a lot better here than the Embassy. I guess it's because all five of us are all together. Can't figure out why they did that. One thing that's really different is we never hear the noises from outside. Maybe they're trying to keep us from someone!

Well, we're supposed to get mail sometime tonight. Santa said that they were waiting for one of the students to bring it over, I guess from the Embassy. Waiting desperately. Wonder if it was something they just said to make us feel good. Not much being done around here except for talking. A lot of that, card playing, a little reading and sleeping. Waiting for the day of freedom—that's if it ever happens! *End of entry.*

Saturday, June 21, 1980 (23:35)   Day 231

Well here we sit wrapping up the end of the day, talking about home (homecooked food/leaving), our situation, and watching Al paint a picture with water paint. It was a coincidence when Al was talking about how his family was supposed to send him water paints but he never received them, and today Santa brought them in. He started out fine until Jerry walked by with cigarette ashes. The painting was being dried by the fan, so the ashes were accidentally blown on it. A few words were passed. But he's doing pretty good on it.

We never received our mail which we were supposed to get last night, so we all went to bed kind of disgusted. Today at noon, right before lunch, Santa brought mail in to us. I wasn't really expecting it so it kind of surprised me. Everyone was pretty happy except for Jerry and Bill. Neither of them got anything from their families. Dick and Al received some from theirs, and I received three letters from Jill and one from my parents. They were all saying that they were holding out OK, staying busy, which was really good to hear. Jill really seems to be holding out, too, but at times I just feel like writing her and telling her not to wait. It's not that I don't want her to; it's just that I feel she could be having a lot better time not waiting. I hate to see her suffer, but I respect her so much more for the things she has been doing. It's really starting to be hard staying optimistic as each day goes on. Their new Parliament has been in working order for the last month now, but still nothing has been said about the hostages. Wonder what the hold up is?

The food really hasn't been too bad lately. For lunch we had macaroni, cheese, and meat casserole—not too bad. Dinner was soup and peach pie. Peach pie was really delicious. It seems like the students are trying to make our stay as pleasant as possible. Santa came in to take notes of some items he could get for us, and at the same time brought in "The Sporting News". Not too many exciting things in it this time. I noticed that the Cardinals weren't doing too well.

Bill just got finished running his fingers over Al's painting that was leaning against a chair to dry. Al's reply was that he can't trust anyone, that everyone's trying to destroy his work. First it was Jerry and then Bill. Wonder who's next? Going to close for now. Bill and Al are going to try to take Dick and me on in a game of spades. They're really talking big, so I guess Dick and I will have to go separate the men from the boys. How many more days wait ahead of us? *End of entry.*

Sunday, June 22, 1980 (23:00)   Day 232

Happy birthday Jill Renee! She's nineteen today and I hope she has an enjoyable birthday. I sure hope she received my birthday poem I sent last month. Anyway I just hope she has a good time. Once again, happy birthday, Jill!

Another exciting day today. Al's coming along pretty good with the water painting. No one tried sabotaging it today. Really surprised. The morning started out just like any other day. Lights turned on at (09:00 or 09:30) with breakfast being served—butter, bread, jelly and tea. Once again after breakfast I crashed back out till lunch, consisting of turkey three quarters of the way done, potatoes and cherries. If only the turkey was done a little more.

As I went to clean the lunch dishes in the head, I was aware of the fact that our shitter still didn't have a toilet seat so I asked Santa if I could steal one from one of the shitters across the hall in the old bathroom. He said okay, so I went off to work on putting a toilet seat on. Tonight before dinner two of the other hostages (unknown) had a field day cleaning the head, doing a really good job. Anything to find to make the time pass.

After I returned, Al was getting a little tired of painting so he and Bill wanted a rematch of the game Dick and I played them last night. Once again we wiped their asses, even after they tried to cheat. We played with the new set of cards Santa brought us. At the same time I asked him if the doctor was ever going to come for my acne problem,

177

but he said no, that I really didn't need one. It seems like they don't want to bring one. I guess they don't want anyone to know where we are and who they have here. Guess I'll just have to wait till ("if") we ever get out of here. He also brought in a *Time* magazine. "Carter at High Noon" with the flags of Britain, Germany and Japan. Too bad he couldn't have just left that magazine in here with us instead of just showing us the cover (April 26, 1980). They do their damnedest to keep the news from us.

Tonight for dinner we had lima beans, cheese, cucumbers and bread. We were all pretty hungry tonight, so we all took seconds. We told them we'd rather have this than soup anytime, so now maybe they'll drop the soup from the menu. Jerry and Dick are playing dominoes; Bill's lying in his rack reading and Al's concentrating on his masterpiece. I asked Santa today if he could bring some more paints. I wouldn't mind trying it. It looks like it'd be pretty fun, and Al claims it passes the time away great.

We were sitting here tonight discussing how we think we're at the military base right on the other side of the Embassy. Al claims he saw a red light that might've been coming from the huge antenna we had out in the football field. That's just what we were guessing. We were also talking about how we are going to celebrate my birthday and Al's anniversary for being over here one year next month. My birthday is July 26, and Al's cut off date is July 16. We're going to have to see if we can get a cake for the occasion. *End of entry.*

Monday, June 23, 1980 (22:20)   Day 233

Another day just about gone, and still no exciting news from the students regarding our release. This morning Jerry met Phil Ward in the head while taking a shower. Jerry said Phil didn't have too much to say except he was with two Marines and one other guy. Yesterday Bill went to the head to take a shower and saw McKeel and Lewis. Bill was saying they were both looking pretty good. McKeel told Bill to get his hair cut, called him a hippie. Although McKeel and Lewis are together they both came in to the head at different times, telling Bill that they were with Phil Ward and Bert Moore. McKeel told Bill that Bert Moore thought we were here for trials that are supposed to be next month. Too bad we can't be for sure of that, but no doubt that was their feelings of why we were being kept here. We also have feelings of that sometimes too. Once again I guess we'll have to wait and see. Sure wish we knew who else is here!

The morning began just like any others, breakfast and then back to bed till lunch. Macaroni, cheese, and meat was served once again. I

178

didn't mind; it was pretty good. After lunch while Bill and I were beating Jerry and Al in spades, Santa brought in some nuts (pistah) and also said that we would be able to get some fresh air. Didn't mention when, though. Also said that they were trying to get the video-tape machine over here. It sure sounds as though we're going to be here a while, but then they say all these things they do for us don't mean anything about the length of time we're going to be here, so we shouldn't worry, we should just enjoy our stay. Sure wish we had a cut off day for our stay, though!

Dinner wasn't too bad tonight, tuna fish, rice, tomato and a slice of egg. Santa told us yesterday that the lunch was American food and the dinner Iranian food. Just as long as we get fed it doesn't bother me what we have.

Well, summer started two days ago and how I hate the thought of staying here all summer, just as we did for winter and spring. I'm really surprised I've lasted this long. How much longer are we to hold out? Right now we're listening to Bill talk about all the girls he used to have, while Al's working on his painting, Dick is working on cross-word puzzles and Jerry is reading. Listening to Bill talk about all the girls he had is like listening to a soap opera.

Seven more days to this month of June. Then comes July, starting the ninth month of captivity. We were kind of hoping to be home by the Fourth of July but that looks impossible. July might be the month though—cross my fingers on that. *End of entry.*

Wednesday, June 25, 1980 (14:30)   Day 235

Just got finished cleaning our cell. It was really dirty considering it was the first time we'd cleaned it. We even rearranged a few things, and everyone even made their own rack. Santa brought a picture yesterday to hang up on the wall. Could use a couple more to brighten up the area.

Yesterday we were able to go outside (balcony) for about fifteen minutes of fresh air. Weren't able to see the ground level. They had a huge sheet up against the balcony bars. The sun was shining through the top of the sheet and through the bars so that was our only contact with it. Can't believe how pale I've been getting. They even had a little carpet laid down we could walk on with two students on each side of us; I guess so we couldn't escape. Canada Dry soda was even given to us while we were out there. Dick and I were taken out at a different time than Al, Jerry and Bill went. I guess they thought if we all went out together we would've tried to escape.

After Dick and I returned, lunch was being served, consisting of tomatoes, onions and hamburgers. Dick didn't eat lunch. After lunch Jerry and I beat Al and Bill in Spades. Just passing the time. That's about when Santa came in with a "Sporting News" paper (June 28), a Parcheesi game, and that picture to hang up. Talking about pictures, the one Al finished the other day he gave to Santa, and since then a couple students have come in to compliment it and see if Al could do another one for them. I wonder where they've got that painting hanging up anyway?

While Santa and Sunshine (we call him that because he's the one who took us out to get fresh air) were in delivering the items, we were asking them about how much longer it was going to take their new Parliament to get around to our situation. Their reply was that it might be another century before they get all their regulations together. Sure wish we knew why it was taking them so long. Santa said that we were the only hostages who were worrying about when we go home. That I can't believe! It sure sounds strange that we're the only ones thinking about that. Can't even believe what they tell us anymore, but still they tell us that we're all innocent and we'll be going home. Really hard to say if they're telling the truth. We think that the fate of the hostages is more than just waiting for the Parliament to decide.

A little while after they left, Santa came back with a picture for Jerry of his wife and Joe Hall's wife sitting together. At first Jerry didn't even recognize her with her new hairdo. Santa said that we were to get mail tomorrow (today) so we're still waiting, although Santa brought a letter to Al this morning from his fiancee with pictures. It was strange they only brought one for Al, and nothing for anyone else. Al said that Santa told him that we were going to get ours this afternoon. Looking forward to that!

Forgot to mention that last night after having our Iranian soup (looked like stew to me) Santa came into the head where I was doing the dishes and asked me about the quantity and quality of the food. He said he was taking a survey because some of the other hostages were complaining about the food. I told him the quality was good, but the quantity at dinner meals was pretty light. He wrote down my thoughts, and then I asked him about seeing a doctor for my so-called acne. He said he'd get one, but it would take about two days. See if he was lying or not in the next two days!

Santa just brought mail/Red Cross messages in to Dick, Bill and myself. Santa said that Jerry had some, but he didn't know where it was, whatever that meant. Anyway, Bill finally heard from his family. Didn't hear too much though. Sounds like they weren't getting any letters from him.

180

For myself, I received a picture of my new nephew Nick. Brown hair, which I could hardly believe. I found out he was born April 28, 1980, 8:23 am, 7 lbs. 12 oz. Jill was there to greet my sister with gifts from us. What a sweetheart she is! The letter I received from my Mom was saying that Jill was trying to call Iran, I guess to tell me about my little nephew. It seems like she's still back there waiting. I hope she doesn't have to wait much longer, but it looks as though she will.

Besides my three Red Cross messages, I received three other letters, sister Deb's, Mother and Father, and Aunt Jackie. Not much news except that they're being treated well. They talked about the parade they were in down in St. Louis, and said everyone told them they were praying for all of us. Well, I'm just glad my family's getting treated well. For myself, I've started not to even give a damn anymore.

Yesterday we were talking about what we might do for the 4th of July, "raise hell" and fast for a couple days, but we won't decide until sometime around the 4th. Al and Bill just got finished beating Dick and Jerry in Spades and now they're playing pitch and catch with a tennis ball. Anything to pass the time. *End of entry.*

Thursday, June 26, 1980 (23:30)   Day 236

Two hundred thirty-six days of captivity. How many more await us?

Not much happening around here. Finished yesterday up by being taken to another part of the building to take a shower. When Al and I got over there, he noticed that it looked like there were hostages there, too, because there were napkins and food garbage in the trash that was in there. The hot water heater in our head hasn't been working, so they took us there. I was the first one in the shower, using all the hot water, so then Al had to sit and wait for the hot water heater to work.

By the time we got back from showering and washing clothes, dinner (Iranian meatballs) had already been served, along with cucumbers. Forgot to mention that we had spaghetti for lunch— American food for lunch, Iranian food for dinner. After we finished cleaning the dinner dishes, we spent the rest of the night and morning to (04:00) playing different various games, Parcheesi and a new game called Hearts, which Al explained to us. He was kind of wishing he didn't. We kept beating him.

I was too tired to wake for breakfast so I slept till lunch. Bill did the same, but then again he never wakes for breakfast unless we have eggs, and that's not too often. Al and Jerry both woke to eat breakfast
181

and stayed up till lunch, but then made up for it this afternoon, just as I did, by going back to sleep right after lunch till dinner. Now everyone's up. Al, Dick, Jerry and Bill are playing Hearts, and probably won't go to sleep till tomorrow morning late. Too bad I can't sleep like that all the time. Time really seems to fly.

Meals weren't too bad today. For lunch we had chicken, french fries, carrots and barbecued potato chips, not bad at all. For dinner tonight we had rice mixed with potatoes, one hamburger, and a tomato each. I guess the survey Santa took the other night worked, because tonight Sunshine Man came in and asked how the meal was tonight, like they really care! I was talking to Sunshine Man in the head today when doing the dishes and he was saying that he thinks/hopes that we're out of here by the end of July. He says that once the Parliament gets all their regulations solved, the hostage situation will be the first on the agenda. They keep saying this, but who knows if it's true. He was saying that the Iranians are always curious to know what happens. They probably want us all killed.

Last night Santa brought in some militant newspapers with a lot of pictures to show. He wouldn't let us read any articles, although he did say that Carter was meeting with the top seven economic countries. Didn't say what for. Wonder what's being done about the hostage situation?

Well, the two days are up since the last time Santa said that the doctor would come to see me, and still no doctor! Lying and leading us on, that's what these guys do best. *End of entry.*

Saturday, June 28, 1980 (15:15)   Day 238

We just got finished eating the shrimp Jerry and I cleaned yesterday morning right after we got up. Got about 300 shrimp. Would you believe that we only received 6-9 today for lunch. Either they have all the other hostages here, or the students enjoyed eating the rest of the shrimp. Out of all that work yesterday and then having the room smell like shrimp the rest of the day, that's what we get in return.

We do know that they brought three other hostages the 23 of June. Jerry and Bill talked to Ragan in the head before lunch yesterday, which consisted of roast beef and potatoes. Anyway, Ragan, I believe, was taking a shower when Jerry talked to him and told him who he was with, and then Ragan told Jerry he was with Roeder and Metrinko, who supposedly volunteered to go to solitary. That's when Jerry found out that they had just gotten here Monday the 23rd. They didn't really know too much either, though, about whether they are bringing all the hostages here. If they are, that could be either a good sign or a bad sign.

To skip around a little, last night right after dinner Santa came in with a little interesting news about how two months ago (making it right around the time we were moved) President Carter apologized for his actions against Chile and Iran. I believe Imam didn't accept his apology, and now wants something else. That puts us right back where we started with Imam wanting the Shah and nothing else.

I don't see how they really think they're going to get the Shah back, but then again maybe they want something else, like having the U.S. come to Iran's doorstep and beg. That I hope the United States never does. Instead I'd like to see the U.S. drop a bomb over here, even if we are still here. I'm getting tired of being led on! I'm also tired of having my country humiliated. I'm starting to get that feeling of not even giving a fuck anymore. What could be taking their new government so long to decide about us?

Yesterday morning and this morning the students have been listening to the radio, I believe to their President "Banisar" making speeches. Santa was saying last night that the Imam had really gotten disgusted with yesterday's rally. Didn't say why, though. Wonder if they could be talking about the hostages' situation? Shit's really getting thick around here, especially when they say one night that the only thing that they want from the U.S. is the Shah, and then another day you hear that we shouldn't worry because all of us here in this room are innocent, and then that probably we will all go on trial, then that we'll all be home by December, and still other students don't know when we'll leave and say we should just be patient!

Something that really caught Santa off guard last night is when Al told him that the United States couldn't give the Shah back because he wasn't in the United States. That really shocked Santa. Al's got a feeling that these people are going to do something with us in July since there are so many things happening then, like the 4th, Iranian holiday, and the Ramason (fasting time). Although I don't have that feeling, I hope he's right.

Santa switched our Parcheesi for Monopoly game yesterday, so we spent most of all night last night playing. Santa said next week we were going to switch games again, so we wouldn't just get tired of one. Makes sense! He also brought in some more vitamins yesterday, too. To me that looks like a good sign, issuing vitamins and then lately making sure we get enough to eat and giving us games to play and paints to color with. Maybe Al's right after all. But then again it might just be that someone is coming to see us, 'cause this morning they were out in the hallway washing it down. The only other times I remember them cleaning their own areas out were when they expected visitors. I sure hope I'm wrong though, 'cause every time someone comes to see us, it seems to mean that we're going to be here a little longer.

Forgot to mention that we received mail yesterday. I received twelve letters. One from each of my sisters, two from Jill (one of them telling me why she quit work at Saks), and the other ones from people around my hometown. Everyone got mail from their family except Jerry—nothing from his wife. After they gave us all that, they even said that we had more, but didn't say when we would get it. Everyone seems to be doing cool back home, which I'm glad of. I hope it continues to stay like that. *End of entry.*

Sunday, June 29, 1980 (02:30)   Day 239

Two hundred thirty-nine days today. Just thought I'd write a little before I crashed out. Earlier this morning, midnight to be exact, a very touching thing happened while we were playing Monopoly. From one of the cells in the hallway here we could hear a couple of men singing "Happy Birthday" to someone back in the States. It must have been one of the hostage's wife or daughter. It really struck all of us. It's a shame that we're being kept from our families like this, and knowing these people don't understand. The first thing that popped in my head when I heard that is when I used to be a little kid in 4-H, and we used to go around to old folks' homes on different occasions like Christmas, to sing Christmas songs and whatever, but tonight when I heard that birthday song there wasn't any happiness or life in it. Although they were trying, it was really sad. It reminds me a bit of last New Year's Eve when it struck 12 midnight. Bill, Jerry and I got up, shook hands, said "Happy New Year", and then sat back down and wondered what everyone was doing back home.

We just got finished talking about all the things we're going to celebrate once we get back. I feel so sorry for the older guys that have their families back home, sons and daughters. But Dick was telling me tonight that his family is the only thing that is keeping him going, which is probably true for all the hostages, but mostly for the older ones that are married and have children. How much longer can these people continue to keep us from our loved ones?

A lot of sleeping has been taking place lately. Yesterday after I got finished writing, I laid down to read my book and before I knew it I was crashed out till dinner, which was chicken noodle soup and blueberry pie. Menu Man came in after we had eaten, and we complimented him on his pie. He said that he just helped, but that's what he always says. We passed the rest of last night away by playing Monopoly, Jerry finally winning.

Santa brought us some Iranian gum, which wasn't too bad. All these things we've been getting, the vitamins, pie, gum, shrimp, games to play, and all the things happening like the cleaning of the hallway just seems like they're adding up to something. Maybe someone is coming to see us! Not really too much more to say. Tomorrow is the last day of this month, and then starts the ninth one. Really getting tired of this shit. *End of entry.*

Monday, June 30, 1980 (14:00)   Day 240

Nothing much to write except that my hair's getting long and I'm tired of being here. Two hundred forty days, and just four more till the Fourth of July, American's first revolution.

Just finished eating lunch consisting of lasagna, and we're talking about some of the things we were planning for Fourth of July, like fasting for a week showing our concern towards our first revolution. But then we were thinking that if we did try it, what would the students think and do regarding our actions. We figured the worst thing that could happen would be going to solitary, but that I really couldn't see happening. But I could see the students putting Al there, because they figure he's Bill's and my boss and he was the one who started it. Like I said before, though, I really couldn't see the students putting us there just because we were fasting showing our concern towards our revolution.

I really shouldn't say that I can't see the students doing that, because probably they would. They do everything else, just about. Lying is really common to them now. Yesterday when I went over to take a shower in another part of the building I heard other hostages, saw a couple too. When I returned Bill and Al asked to take one too, but English Student said another hostage was taking one. I then asked him, just to see what he would say because I knew there were other hostages over there, if they had other hostages over there too? He came right out and said no, that it was a hostage over here that wanted to take one. Why would he want to lie about something like that? But then it just goes to show that they just might be lying about us going to trial and going home. Everyone is getting really depressed about the whole situation. The days have been getting rough mentally. Yesterday it seemed like everyone woke up in a bad mood, jumping on each other's case. We didn't even play our regular daily Monopoly/card games. Jerry and Al played a couple games of Gin, but otherwise everyone stayed to themselves, reading or sleeping.

I really wouldn't mind if I did get put in solitary, after I told them what I thought about their lying to us, etc. Of course the only thing I

185

would be gaining by saying all that is, like Dick said, my own mental satisfaction and pride. Dick has a feeling that something might happen around the Fourth, but we're still going to think about our fasting if nothing does happen. I'm really getting tired of just sitting around waiting for something to happen. It's been too long.

Everyone's not doing too much now, although we never do much anyway. Jerry and Bill are reading, Dick's walking his four miles back and forth across the room, and Al's sleeping. Wonder what's going on outside in the city today. Not able to hear too much where we are now. We hear the church chimes ring once in a while, a couple of cars honking, and that's about it. The students have started playing with the weapons at night lately. I guess they're getting edgy about us trying to get out of here. Sunshine Man just brought in a *Sports Illustrated* and a coloring book for Bill. I guess you can say that they're getting everything they can to keep us quiet. *End of entry.*

Tuesday, July 1, 1980 (23:25)   Day 241

Another slow day it was today, our 241st day of captivity. Started the day off with breakfast, the usual, and after I returned from the head washing up, a student was waiting to take Al, Jerry and myself outside for fresh air. We were taken to the same place as last time, but this time there was only one student watching us. The sun was really hot, so we took off our shirts to let our bodies get a little sun. It was just the sun showing through the bars above the sheet they still had hanging. After we were out there for about two minutes, they brought us three mugs of Donald Duck orange juice. Anyway, the weather really felt good. Too bad we couldn't stay out longer than the five minutes we were out.

When we were brought back to the room Dick and Bill were still sleeping, but the student had come and got them to go outside while I was sleeping. I woke at lunch, which consisted of chili and cucumbers. Al said that Santa had come in while I was sleeping, asking about me. He came again after lunch, asking if I would go with him to fix the video machine, but Al went instead, because he knew more about them than I did. When Al came back, he said that we weren't going to be watching any T.V. because of electricity reasons, not enough cycles or something. Apparently Santa wouldn't take that as an answer, I guess because he didn't want to let us down. Santa's supposed to go back to the Embassy and try to find a different one that would work. So much for the video machine. Wonder what else they'll try to get?

Once again today everyone just sat around on their own, reading

186

and sleeping just like we had done yesterday. Santa came in last night unexpectedly, asking us what was up and then probably waiting for us to ask him the same—but we didn't! Asked him about why the doctor hadn't come yet. He replied that he "couldn't bring one here." Didn't really say why. Otherwise the conversation was just a joking around one. He finally left after about five minutes. I guess because no one asked him what was up!

Right before I started to write tonight, I was in the head while Santa was in the room here arguing with Bill, something to do with Santa accusing Bill of laughing at him. Bill claimed he wasn't, but was laughing about being here. If I understand it right, Santa had come in to ask what they could bring us for the Fourth to help us celebrate. I had just returned to the room to catch the last part of the lecture. Santa was saying that he and the other students who were held in Shah's prison had agreed to help us celebrate our revolution. Even though we were people from the country that took military actions against Iran (like we were really to blame), even though all these things had happened they were still going to help us celebrate. The five of us rather prefer not to have them do anything for us except let us go. Also he mentioned that if we decide to do something stupid, they could put us in a worse cell, dark and all those other awful things he described, I guess showing us that he could do it if he really wanted to. He really makes us wonder about going on our fast.

Not really too much more to talk about. The food's been adequate. Tonight we had soup again, vegetable soup with a couple pieces of a chicken heart, etc. Bill doesn't care for it. He says you never know what it comes from. I'm not even worried about that. My stomach's already messed up to the max. Maybe something exciting will happen tomorrow. *End of entry.*

Thursday, July 3, 1980 (01:30)   Day 243

Not really tired this morning so I thought I'd write a little. The only exciting thing that really happened was that we received mail, all of us except Jerry. It had to be the first time I have ever received 27 letters all at once. But then again, mail's not really exciting me like it used to, although it is good to hear that everyone is doing well. Jerry was really feeling down when he heard he didn't have any. Wonder what the reason is? I sure hope he receives something from his wife pretty soon!

Not too much news in the letters. My Mom and Dad were saying that the students have accused them of being spies. Now I wonder where they ever got that idea?

187

Received four letters from Jill, telling me she was going to be a queen contestant at the fair this year. It was really great to hear that, but I wish I could at least talk to her one time and tell her not to wait for me. At this point it really seems that it would be for the best for both of us. I don't know when I'll get out of here, and I want her to be free from all commitments to wait for me. I know she's got a good chance for that queen contest and I know she could probably have a lot better time not thinking and worrying about me. I want that girl to have the best, and I know she ain't going to have it sitting around waiting for something that might not happen. Anything she would do now I wouldn't take against her. She's done so much for me, and I don't want her to be hurt.

Maybe one of these days I'll get out of here and everything will work out. Really starting to get disgusted though. I wish something would happen. This undetermined sentence is really getting to us. Tomorrow's the Fourth of July, another holiday we'll miss. Wonder what the students will have planned for us?

Found an interesting pastime today—walking 500 times back and forth across the room for exercise. Really passed the time, considering our room's about 20' or 25' long. I believe it took me a little more than an hour, but it was better than sitting on my ass.

We didn't have much conversation with the students today. I believe Santa is still kind of pissed off from night before last. Food wasn't too bad. Lunch was spaghetti, and dinner was two chicken legs and mashed potatoes. Seconds on potatoes, too. Heard a little music this afternoon out in the hallway. The students kept turning it off and on; then after a while it was off all together. A little while after that they were out there messing around on an intercom set, talking back and forth to each other. I guess they've found a new way to keep themselves entertained. Still can't understand what they hope to gain from keeping us here. They must surely know that they aren't going to get the Shah back, but what else do they want? Oh, how I pray to God that this comes to an end very soon. Wonder how all the other hostages are holding out? God please help us! *End of entry.*

Friday, July 4, 1980 (15:10)   Day 244

Fourth of July, the anniversary celebrating 204 years of independence, but to us here being held captive it's just another day in our cell blocks, although we still remember this day in the U.S. as being one of the most important days in our lives. God bless America and its people!

Didn't write last night because I couldn't really think of too much to write about. Yesterday about the only exciting thing that happened was that they brought a tape player and tape of Nat King Cole in to let us listen to. At first they had it on out in the hallway, and I think a few of the hostages didn't really care for it so they turned it down. We went to the door to ask them to turn it up, and instead of turning it up they brought it in, but told us not to listen to it too loud. We kept it for about an hour or maybe a little less, and then gave it back to them to give to the other hostages.

Jerry's really been having some bad times lately. First he doesn't receive any mail from his wife, and now last night he comes up with a loose tooth that might have to come out. It seems to be giving him a lot of pain. I guess now that we can't get any doctors in to see us, we'll have to do the best we can without them. Last night and this morning he's been putting crushed aspirin on it to relieve the pain. We got Santa to come in last night, too. He still seemed to be kind of uptight about the other night, but we asked him to go over to the store on the compound and pick up some Listerine mouthwash. He said he was going to bring it today. Sure hope Jerry's gum doesn't get infected.

Bill traded our Monopoly game for a different one last night, called "Kingmaker". Really seems to be a fucked up game just by looking at it, although we haven't played it yet and I doubt if we ever will. Otherwise yesterday was just like any other day. Wake up, eat breakfast, crash back out, wake up for lunch, wash up, read, maybe sleep/doze off a little, eat dinner, read and then wait for lights to turn off.

Food hasn't been anything special. Yesterday for lunch we had rice and meat sauce (curry), and for dinner we had hard boiled egg, salad, and five slices of Kraft yellow cheese. We were thinking maybe the students would have something special today, but when Sunshine Man came in to serve lunch (hamburgers, fried potatoes and onions), he told us they would've had something special for us but their cook went away.

Not much is happening now, like always. Bill, Al and Jerry are reading while Dick's sitting at the table working on crossword puzzles. No one's really in a good mood today. I guess you can say we're getting fed up with this shit, but we're trying to hold our sanity as best as possible. How much longer will we have to though?

Maybe for a special treat today they'll bring us some mail. Maybe I'll change the monotony a little today and take a shower. I guess I should see if I can get someone to cut my hair. Lately it's really been getting dirty awful fast. Maybe I'll be a hippie once I get out of here.

The weather must really be getting hot outside. It's really been stuffy lately. I feel sorry for this fan we have here in the room. Ever since we've had it, it's been on continuously. Surprised it hasn't burned out yet. Surprised I haven't burned out yet!! *End of entry.*

Saturday, July 5, 1980 (02:30)   Day 245

Like the saying goes, the party's over so it's back to work again. Right after I had finished writing yesterday, the students came around passing out ice cream, chocolate mint cookies, nuts (cashews and pistah) and a piece of cake. That I take as our celebration of the Fourth, which really they didn't have to do, but they did! Why did they do it? Unless of course they know that we'll eventually get out of here and then go back and tell everyone that yes, we were able to celebrate our revolution with the help of the students. Then again, we could've been let loose. But considering we weren't, we were still able to celebrate a little, even if just by eating the goodies we were given. Our morale wasn't high enough to do much of anything else.

We got talking about President Carter tonight, and I asked Santa if he had said anything about the hostages over the Fourth. Santa said no, and then got talking about how the Iranians were trying to prevent President Carter from getting in office again, and how by keeping us here they were trying to get most of the things they've demanded. Other than wanting the Shah and his money, which I know the U.S. isn't going to give up, what else are these people demanding? Are they just waiting to see what becomes of the elections? Surely the new Parliament is going to see that President Carter is going to be reelected, so what then are they going to do? At times I really get pissed sitting around talking about our situation. It seems so out of reach that we can't seem to make anything out of it. The only thing we have to do is sit back and wait.

I keep telling myself that I shouldn't complain, that it could be a lot worse than it is now. Another thing that keeps me going is thinking about all the good times I'm going to have once I get home, especially with Jill. That's if she's still there. If the love is still there when I return home to Jill, we won't have anything to worry about, because love conquers all.

Not too much more to write about. Really wish we had an idea of the month we might get out of here, but the way it looks now, we could be here another one, two, or three years. Let me tell you, that's a sad feeling. *End of entry.*

Sunday, July 6, 1980 (02:50)   Day 246

Our 246th day of captivity and here we still sit. I picked up a little news from Santa. Don't really know if it's true, but from the way he told me he really seemed sincere. I was in the head earlier doing some dishes when Santa and a few of the other students came in. At the time I didn't know what they were going to do with the ladder and drill they had, but what they did was put up a T.V. monitor above the door. Now they're able to watch us as we go to the toilet, probably so we don't try to escape.

Anyway, the news that Santa was telling me while the other students were working was that in seven weeks at the most, the Parliament would finally come to a decision on the hostages. How he said it and the way he looked seemed to tell me that he was telling me the truth. He even asked me when Jill was going to be in the queen contest, like he was wondering if I would make it or not. Even if he was lying (but I really feel he wasn't, at least this time) what's going to happen, except that we'll call him a liar? There's really nothing else we can do except for hoping and picking a day out of each month and shoot for it.

That's also what Al was saying tonight when we were sitting down talking, that one of these days we're going to finally come to a point where we won't be able to go any further, and we're going to do something stupid taking one of the students with us. It's the truth too, because so many times already have I thought about it and a couple of times stopping right at the peak and then getting myself back together. Again, what do they have to lose by lying to us? They've done it so many times before. But this time something inside told me that he wasn't lying, so now the only thing we have to do is sit back and wait to see what happens between now and the 22nd of August. Pray to God he was telling the truth. He said it was up to the Parliament to decide the fate of the hostages; hopefully it will be a good outcome for all of us!

As I said before, they've got a T.V. monitor set up in the head and supposedly one in the hallway too, which I really haven't seen, but they said they do. I asked them if it's really true about us leaving within the next seven weeks, why were they going to all this trouble of putting all these in? They replied that all the things they were doing had nothing to do with how long we were going to be here. It was just for their own security purposes. That's one thing they've always told us. The things they do have nothing to do with the length of time we have here. I pray to God that this thing is resolved soon, and I mean really soon.

Nothing much of anything else happened yesterday. Al and I played a little pitch and catch with the tennis ball, occasionally knocking down a few cups here and there, even a couple bodies too,

191

but of course that's expected. Otherwise we all just read books, or occasionally someone played solitaire. Haven't been into playing too many card games lately, getting tired of it.

Forgot to mention that when I woke for lunch the electricity was off, making the room hot and stuffy. To top it off we had hot chili with lettuce and tomato. Right around the time I finished eating, the electricity came back on. Lucky of that. It was getting pretty hot. Haven't taken a shower for a while. Neither have any of us, hopefully tomorrow though. Well, I guess I'll be off to bed again to wake for another day. *End of entry.*

Monday, July 7, 1980 (02:20)   Day 247

Al, Dick, Jerry and I just got finished playing Hearts. Bill crashed out, but now everyone is just lying around reading, I guess waiting for me to finish and then to turn the light out.

Yesterday wasn't too bad of a day. Started the morning off when Al and I finished breakfast and went down to the head to wash dishes and brush our teeth. The students have been having trouble with the camera (T.V. monitor) in the American head just like they were having yesterday morning, so we went to the Iranian side. Sunshine Man was in talking to us, telling us that everyone who had been involved in spying and so forth would be known to the world and then let free. He was saying that the Parliament was still having problems regarding the new people in office, but said that he thought that they would get all those problems solved pretty soon and then start discussing the hostage situation around the week of "Ramason". He also said he thought it should have been over already (meaning us being released), but that the Parliament had their problems.

Last night Santa came in a little after dinner and said that Imam had been on the radio that afternoon. He said that Imam was telling the people how disgusted he was at the new Parliament for not acting like a revolutionary government. Don't really know if that's for the worst or best of our behalf. Hopefully Imam has set a date for the Parliament by when they have to decide the fate of the hostages. Maybe that seven week thing Santa was telling me about was really a cutoff date. Pray to God it was! Things are starting to look a little brighter. Cross our fingers and hope they're not lying to us. Hanging on patiently.

Finally got a shower yesterday, and boy does it ever feel good to feel clean. They must've had all the hostages taking them. Jerry and Al took theirs right after lunch, and Dick, Bill and myself had to wait till around dinner time to take one. Kept having to wait for the hot water

192

heater to heat the water back up. Anyway it really feels good to be clean. Can't wait to get out of here and start back on my shower every morning and every night. Back to the normal life.

Forgot to mention that when Santa was in talking to us, he was saying that all the hostages would be coming here within a couple days. Making a roundup of all the hostages. Maybe something is about to happen, hopefully for the good of all of us. What a birthday gift that would be if we were freed July 26! Wow! Praying and hoping is the only thing we can do.

Jerry's tooth seems to be coming along pretty well now. It's still hurting him, but not as much. Otherwise everyone else hasn't been feeling too bad, except for our stomachs. Food wasn't too bad yesterday. For lunch we had chicken, fried potatoes and tomatoes. Dinner was a little small, but adequate. Cheese, cucumbers, a hard boiled egg and tomatoes. They brought seconds, too, but one helping was enough. Getting too fat!

Not too much more to say except that things are starting to look pretty good again. Now the only question is how long it's going to take for Parliament to decide. These cells are getting awfully boring! *End of entry.*

Tuesday, July 8, 1980 (15:40)   Day 248

Just got finished cleaning our room, and now everybody's just sitting/lying around staying busy. Jerry's playing solitaire, Dick's trying to make a backgammon board from the chess board, and Al and Bill are reading. At the same time, we are all listening to ELO on the cassette box Santa brought in last night and we've had it ever since. The only problem is the batteries keep going dead on us. The box has a cord attached, but we need a transformer to meet the right cycles that this building has. The first six have gone dead so now we're on our second six.

Not too much happened yesterday. We asked Santa last night about when we might be receiving mail next, and he replied that the next time might not be until we get back to the U.S., whatever he meant by that. The things he's been saying lately, except for that seven week thing, you can't really tell if he's joking or not.

Went to bed feeling pretty bad last night. I've had really bad headaches that might be coming from reading too much without my glasses, although I've been doing it for the last nine months. I sure hope it hasn't affected my eyes any. Anyway, I woke this morning feeling the same as I did when I went to bed last night. I took two more Tylenol before breakfast and then two more again before lunch,

193

which consisted of a noodles, cheese, and meat casserole dish—not too bad. I'm still getting little minor headaches. I guess I have to cut down on reading a little.

Sunshine Man came in this morning to collect sheets to be washed. At first I didn't know what was going on, because I had just finished breakfast and I had crashed back out when all of a sudden Al started pulling my sheet from underneath me. I jumped up not knowing what was going on. Al was saying come on get up; they're doing a raid on this place. I didn't know what to think, until I saw that he was just collecting the sheets. Then I just went back to sleep. Someone's always playing jokes on someone around here, but then again what else is there to do?

They've really been having problems with the electricity lately. Once again this morning right before lunch the electricity was off, making it really hot/stuffy in here. I know if we didn't have that fan in here like we do, it would be burning up. It really seems to be getting hot outside lately. I'd sure like to be hitting a swimming pool right around now. I still might have a chance yet this year!

English Student just came to get the cassette player, so now we're just sitting around in quietness. The students seem to be playing the news in the background, but of course none of us understand Farsi anyway. They moved some more people in across the hall, but we still haven't been able to find out who they are. We all think they might have everyone here now. It seems like whenever we ask Santa about someone, he says that they're doing fine, but he makes us feel that we're taking the situation too hard and that we worry too much. He was saying that we're the only ones who worry.

The students have been treating us pretty good lately, bringing gum in every other night. Last night they brought us some after-shave lotion. It seems as though that they're moving the Embassy store over here. We're not that far from the Embassy anyway. Hopefully all the things they're doing for us are leading up to something good. I'd really like to get the fuck out of here. *End of entry.*

Thursday, July 10, 1980 (02:30)   **Day 250**

Our 250th day of captivity, and still we seem to be hanging on. Although we could last a long time the way the students have been treating us lately. Being kept in this cell block is about the worst of it all.

Yesterday wasn't too bad. We woke (Jerry, Al, Dick and myself) at breakfast (09:30), ate and then decided to have Dick teach us how to play bridge. We hadn't gone to bed that morning till very late so I was still pretty tired, but they convinced me to stay up till lunch which was around (14:30) like always.

After we had our roast beef and baked potatoes, I decided to get a couple more snoozes. Meanwhile Bill was saying that he wasn't going to eat until he got his shirt back, which Al had hidden in return for Bill hiding Jerry's pants last night when we wanted to go to the head. Bill's been walking around all day without one on, but just a few minutes ago Al gave it back to him. Of course Bill thought I had it all along. I guess it's little things like that that keep us laughing.

Anyway, back to yesterday's schedule. I finally woke around (17:00), debating if I should wash my hair or not. Then I found out that they had fixed our water heater in our head, so I decided to wait till tomorrow morning and take a shower. Everyone was sitting around the two bags of cookies that Santa brought in to us, and Jerry and Al were ready to continue to have Dick teach us bridge. So we played till dinner, stopping only to eat, and then continued again and didn't stop till just a while ago. Really a great pastime game. Still learning yet. Maybe by the time we leave here I'll have it down pat. Cross my fingers on that one.

Found out it was Kevin Hermening's birthday yesterday, so Bill wrote a short note wishing him happy birthday (only allowed to give his name), and then gave it to Santa. All five of us have been thinking nothing but good thoughts about the treatment we've been having lately. Anything we need, if it's possible that the students can get it, we'll have it. I sure wish our freedom was like that! It really seems that our time is nearing towards freedom. I pray to God I'm right! *End of entry.*

Friday, July 11, 1980 (11:55)   Day 251

Just finished eating dinner, which once again consisted of soup. We had that last night, too. Tomorrow starts their "Ramadan", so maybe they're trying to get us ready to fast with them during it. I guess we'll find out tomorrow.

Imam was on the radio once again today. Nothing was said about the hostages, the students said. He just talked about Ramadan. Well, the seven weeks that Santa said we have left are getting short, and to-day one of the students was telling me that Imam said that we don't go home until the Shah returns. Just don't know what to think anymore. This shit's really getting old, let me tell you.

The reason I'm writing is that I doubt if I'll have time later on tonight to write, because once we start playing bridge we'll play all night into the morning just like we did last night and this morning.

We started right after dinner last night, and didn't stop playing till (04:00) this morning. Dick was the only one who woke for breakfast. Everyone else woke around lunch. Otherwise nothing else has been happening these past two days, other than sleeping, eating, reading and trying to play bridge.

I wasn't feeling too well yesterday morning, but finally got over it in the afternoon. Today I guess it was Bill's turn, because he wasn't feeling too well. Still isn't, either. We didn't get our fifteen minutes of fresh air this week. Wonder what the problem was there? Wish to God this situation would be resolved soon. This little room's starting to get to me. I also seem to be getting a lot of headaches lately. Maybe it's a sign of going crazy. What's the reason for keeping us here any longer? *End of entry.*

Sunday, July 13, 1980 (20:00)   Day 253

Well, our 253rd day today and still here we sit, waiting it out. Lately things haven't been looking too good, especially for Bill. Yesterday we finally convinced Santa to call for a doctor to look at Bill. He hadn't eaten too much for a couple of days, and then yesterday he started to get cold and hot chills, vomiting, etc. We finally convinced Santa to bring a student doctor to look at him last night, of course escorted along with two other supposed big shots. He also did a small check on Al and me. We hadn't been feeling too good either, but not as bad as Bill.

Doctor really didn't tell us last night what he thought might be wrong with us, but this morning "Beaver" (one of the students) was saying that the doctor thought it might be a bacteria spreading around from the use of the toilet. We were even thinking it might be from not washing our dishes thoroughly, because of the cold water. Anyway, the doctor prescribed some medication for Bill last night, and the students have been coming in all day monitoring his progress. He's really looking better, and claims to be feeling a lot better. We were really worried about him yesterday. Hopefully it doesn't turn into anything serious.

It's really starting to get hard/boring writing about the things that have been happening. It seems as though that they're having a hard time keeping the electricity on around here. Matter of fact, last night when doc came the lights were off, so they had to gather some flashlights up to examine Bill. I think last night was the record breaking length of time for having them off. We were playing bridge when the lights went off, about the same time the doctor and two other people came in. I bet they were awful scared when all of a sudden the lights

196

went off and it was pitch dark. I'd say the lights were off about an hour and a half.

After the doctor had left (we're pretty sure he was checking up on some other hostages, too) we tried playing bridge under candlelight, but the candle that Al had produced burnt down in less than about half an hour. After the candle went out, the only thing we had to do was sit around in the dark and listen to Cat Stevens' Greatest Hits which Santa had brought in earlier with a battery operated tape player. Once again our conversation was based upon what we were going to do once we got home, whenever that day arrives. Finally the lights came back on, and Bill continued to sleep while we continued our bridge game till the early hours of this morning.

This has been happening every night lately. Right after dinner we start playing bridge. Sometimes we start in the middle of the day, like they wanted to do today, but I said no, that if we play so much I'll continue to have the bad dreams I've been having—hearts, diamonds, clubs, etc., keep flashing through my head when we go to bed. Really that's why I'm writing now, because I know right after we eat dinner they're going to want to start once again. It really does pass the time away, though.

The students were saying that the weather's really been getting hot, and even more so when the electricity goes off and our fan stops. The best thing to do then is just sit back on your mattress and try to listen to some of the other hostages' comments throughout the hall. Everything's usually a dead silence, except for the students walking outside in the hallway and the other hostages talking. Once in a while you're able to hear some funny comments from others.

Lately there hasn't been much we've been thinking about, except for the thought of going home, but that's constantly on our minds. Of course the students tell us not to worry about that. We did hear an interesting thing this morning, which came directly from Sunshine Man's mouth (pretty straight). Anyway, he was saying that the students weren't even allowed to leave here. A couple students told me this a couple weeks ago, but I didn't believe them then. I guess I do now. One of the students just brought Al a puzzle with a letter attached, so maybe that means we got some mail in. We deserve something good to happen, and mail would be about the best thing right now! *End of entry.*

Wednesday, July 16, 1980 (15:00)   Day 256

Al just told me that he wanted me to put down that today, July 16, 1980, is one year from the day he first arrived here in Iran. The way I
197

guess we'll celebrate this occasion is tonight at dinner, when we're eating the cookies that Sunshine Man brought us earlier, we'll give Al a couple extra cookies and let him pick which videotape he'd want to watch tonight. Last night was the first night we watched video. Al had to go in earlier to fix the color. He doesn't really know where they got the video machine. Anyway, it was nice watching it once again. We saw M*A*S*H and Bob Newhart, and Santa said this morning that we would watch a couple more tonight. Looking forward to it.

They also handed out mail when we returned. Everyone received something, but Jerry and Bill didn't receive anything from their families, and Al didn't receive anything from his fiancee. I received two from my parents and two from Jill. It sounds as though they're all right, Jill still sitting there waiting for me. I sure wish I could say that she wouldn't have to wait much longer, but who really knows? I received thirteen letters in all, and I do have to say that without them it would just make the day that much worse; they are truly appreciated.

Al received an oil painting from his sister, which he's working on now with Bill looking over his shoulder. The last painting Al did Bill rubbed his hand over, and another time Jerry's cigarette ashes from his ashtray were sprinkled all over the painting by the fan. We're all waiting to see who's going to be the first sabotager of this painting.

Bill's really been feeling a lot better. You can tell that by the mood he's in (sarcastic). Anyway I guess the medication the doctor prescribed worked. Luckily it wasn't anything too serious.

Al and I started a small workout last night, which we hope to continue every day. It's really starting to be noticeable, the fat we are gaining. Starting to cut down on my meals. Not eating breakfast, and trying to cut down on eating bread, too. I guess you can say that all this sleeping and eating is catching up with me. Everybody criticizes me for sleeping too much, but what else is new. They're even joking around about how I'm going to get married once I get out of here. If Jill's still back there waiting like she is now, and if everything else works out, I guess I will get married.

Well, nothing else has been happening. Still playing a lot of bridge. This morning we didn't get finished till about (06:00). The sun was rising. Once you get these guys started on playing, you can't get them to stop. The food hasn't been too bad. Like I said earlier, it seems like they're trying to fatten us up. Doing a good job of it too. There really isn't too much more to talk about. That's why I guess I've passed the last two days without writing. We're just waiting patiently to go home. *End of entry.*

Everyone's just sitting around trying to make themselves busy. Al's working on his painting, with Bill looking on to make sure he's doing it right. Dick's walking his daily three miles back and forth across the room, and Jerry's lying in his mattress reading. About a half hour ago we were in watching videotape (Dallas). They must've skipped us last night, but the night before, Al's one year anniversary, we watched "Three's Company" and M*A*S*H. Trying to update everything that has happened since then.

After we returned from the movies the night of the 16th, we once again started our usual bridge game which lasted till early morning (05:00). It really hasn't been too bad though, because once I crash out I don't wake till lunch, which is served around (14:00).

Yesterday was really a strange day. I'd say it wasn't till about (21:00) last night that we really started to have strong conversations. Before then I'd say forty words, no more, were passed between any of us. I guess you would say it was a depressing day. I remember when we were first together, none of us hardly stopped talking. Now we've really run out of things to say. Occasionally we sit around and try to analyze our situation, but that gets depressing at times. Can't really make anything out of it.

They used to have newspaper articles in the video room right next door, but the other night, the 16th, Santa noticed Bill reading a news article which had to do with us. It was written a couple weeks before the evacuation attempt, talking about the Red Cross visit. Bill got halfway through it when Santa came up behind him, grabbed that paper and the rest that were on the floor too and gave them to Sunshine Man to get rid of them. Ever since then there haven't been any newspaper articles in there. There were only supposed to be sports pages, but I guess that one page with a few of the others got through without being noticed. Of course they might've been planted there also, just to let us know what's going on. All the news we've been reading hasn't been too good, though. Like always, nothing to do except sit and wait.

My mother has been calling the Embassy. That's surprising, because all the other times they've tried, they couldn't get through. But now they are. Santa said they couldn't record them. The tape player over there isn't in working order, but I could make a one minute tape if I wanted to, so the next time they called they would play it for them. I've decided not to do it. Since no one else in the room has had a chance to, neither will I. I think my family would understand this.

Eight more days till my birthday (23), and so for I've received about four birthday wishes from the previous times that we have gotten mail. My first birthday wish is that we would be released, but I know that won't happen, so my second wish is that we receive mail. If neither of those things happen I guess I'll have to do without, just like we've been doing the last nine months. When are we ever going to get out of here?

I wonder what has happened to our once a week of fifteen minutes of fresh air. Been about three weeks now since we've had any. I'd at least like to get some sun on my face, to maybe cure the scars. Wonder how the summer is back home? *End of entry.*

Sunday, July 20, 1980 (18:00)   Day 260

Just finished a strenuous exercise—walking back and forth across the room 500 times. I feel like I've just finished running three miles instead of the six miles I just walked. It will no doubt take me a while to get back in shape when we get home. Really embarrassed at times to even take my shirt off. The fat really seems to be setting in around my waist. Al and I were supposed to start a workout but neither of us has had enough energy to get up and start it. I guess that just shows how lazy we've gotten.

Not too much happening around here once again. Dick's reading here at the table, Al's reading in his mattress, Jerry and Bill are both sleeping. I guess you can say we're just sitting around waiting for dinner, because after that we're going to watch a Clint Eastwood movie. That will be the main excitement of today, besides watching Al work on his painting earlier today. Everything's been cool so far; no one's sabotaged it yet!

Yesterday Sunshine Man was saying that some of the hostages had gotten Red Cross messages, but I guess none of us got any. We haven't received anything. Santa was also saying last night that they were expecting mail sometime this week, so we're looking forward to that.

Our late bridge games have been pretty successful. We even have it now to where the students bring cookies for us to eat while playing. Each night Al and I joke about what we're going to serve during the game, and every night just about we seem to get something.

The lights are continuing to go out just about every day or night. Last night we had to eat our dinner in candlelight, how romantic! We tried to play cards but the candles burned down too fast, so we had to sit and wait until they came back on to do anything. Once the lights did come on Santa came in to take us to watch video ("Three's Company" and "WKRP in Cincinnati"). It seems like our scheduled time to go is at night, because every morning we can hear the video machine. They must have a schedule to show everyone a tape at a certain hour. Going to break for now. Al and I are going to try to do a workout to lose a little of this fat. *End of entry.*

Wednesday, July 23, 1980 (00:15) Day 263

Two hundred sixty-third day we've been held hostage and still here we sit. Excuse my sloppiness, I'm lying on my mattress, leaning over the front and writing off the floor. Jerry and Dick are up at the table discussing how to play solitaire, and Bill and Al are sleeping. Al hardly got any sleep yesterday. We didn't end our previous night of bridge till early hours of yesterday morning, but Al didn't hit the mattress till a couple hours before dinner last night (July 22), so it looks like we might not be getting our bridge game in, our exercise either. We've been working out since I wrote last (July 20) doing sit-ups and push-ups. Since then I've been starting to feel my muscles hurt once again.

The 21st there wasn't too much happening. Just the usual, watching Al work on his painting, reading, eating (really been putting the food on us lately); then after dinner that night we went into the T.V. room to see a Clint Eastwood movie ("Fistful of Dollars"). For the occasion, Bill dressed up in his Clint Eastwood outfit. He cut a hole in his one dirty sheet, big enough to put over his head to make a poncho. We got a laugh out of it, even the students. He does some of the craziest things sometimes.

After the movie was over, we came back and continued our bridge game (24:00-05:30). After that, everyone was ready to hit the rack. Al thought he was, too, but he didn't. I went to bed having some wild dreams. Don't really remember much about them except that they were a little crazy. The next time I woke was right before lunch was being served (spaghetti), and believe it or not we played two more rubbers before hitting the mattress again, this time not sleeping long before being wakened for dinner (beans, huge hunks of tuna and slices of tomato). Plates were piled to the top; barely got mine down before being stuffed. After dinner everyone went back to their mattresses to lay down, but Al was the only one to crash out. I've been thinking about doing it too. Nothing much else to do. Sounds like they've got a few of the hostages in the T.V. room showing them "Fistful of Dollars".

Sunshine Man was telling us some news the other day; could take it either good or bad. It seems that the Parliament has gotten all straightened out, and now the President has to name a Prime Minister. After that position is filled, which we're hoping is done by the end of the month, the government should be in full structure and ready to decide about the hostages' fate. That's what we're hoping for. Of course Sunshine Man was also saying that their new Parliament is plagued with every day problems that need to be solved, but it is also plagued with the hostage problem, so hopefully they'll work on our case first.

When he was telling us all this, it sounded as though our government is going to be expected to make a trade. What the trade is going to be is unknown to us. We're kind of thinking money, though. He did say that everyone would be going home. Hopefully the Parliament thinks the same! Maybe Santa's seven week estimation might make it yet.

From looking out the bathroom windows, the weather seems to be pretty humid/hot. Nevertheless, I'd love to be out getting some solar energy. Maybe one of these days.

Forgot to mention that the night of the 20th, Al was taken to a room to listen to his fiancee (on tape). He said that the tape wasn't more than two minutes long, and mostly crying was all he heard. That same night mail was brought in by Four Eyes. He must have just gotten here. Not too much news from home. Everyone is doing well, which is good to hear. Received a couple more birthday cards. Three more days until the big day of 23 years old. Wow! What a way to spend a birthday.

Well everyone's up now, and we're listening to some more adventures of Billy Gallegos. He's also trying to get them to play spades, but I think they want to play bridge instead. *End of entry.*

Friday, July 25, 1980 (02:30)   Day 265

Our 265th day of captivity. Tomorrow's my 23rd birthday. As late as it is, we (Al, Bill and myself) just got finished doing a small workout of sit-ups, and now Al's finishing it up by walking a little while. Everyone else is lying in their mattresses reading. I do have to give credit to Al this morning for being in the shape he's in, especially for the age he is. He really surprised me by doing those 200 sit-ups all at once, Bill and him both. I don't know what was wrong with me, but of course I did 220 the night before while they both did less. Anyway, my stomach just wasn't feeling the same, really sore. Jerry's really kind of disappointed. His back's been hurting a little, so we've made him lay off. He really doesn't like that.

Can hear the students out in the hallway getting ready to eat their first meal of the day. That's their custom during Ramadan fasting, eating one meal in the morning, usually around sunrise, and another one at sunset. Sunshine Man was saying yesterday that people aren't forced to fast and pray, only if they're capable, do they have to do these things. Ramadan is supposed to stop at the next full moon, which is also when they started it (July 13). The next full moon is August 10, at least by the calendar we have. That's when they'll stop. Hopefully around then we'll be starting on our way home.

I asked Taco Kid yesterday about when he thought we might be going home, and he said that the Parliament had started talking about the hostage situation. Then said he thought maybe in about three more weeks. I hope he was referring to going home. He might have meant to say that that was when the Parliament would start talking about us. Once again we'll just have to wait and see. He told me, which I really believe, that the students don't really know when we're leaving. They're just here to take us to the toilet, bring us our meals, and get us anything else we want that they can get. Talking about going to the toilet, the night before last when we came back from watching TV ("Barney Miller", "Carter Country"), Bill and I asked to go to the head. Four Eyes was the one who answered the door. I was the first one out of the room, and I had to wait with my towel over my head for Bill to put his hand on my shoulder, and for Four Eyes to close and lock our door behind us. While Four Eyes was doing that, Bill reached around and grabbed me by the throat, just messing around, and then I threw a punch with my elbow to his rib cage. When he took his arm from around my neck, he pulled my towel with him, leaving my face wide open. I thought we were overdoing it a little, and so we wouldn't get in trouble, I covered my eyes. Luckily Four Eyes is a pretty good guy. He knew we were only messing around, so didn't say anything. Some of the craziest things we do around here!

Last night Santa came running into the room and told Al to go with him because he had something for him. When Al came back, he told us that he had made a tape recording for his fiancee who is supposed to call back tomorrow, and they will play it for her then. One of the strange things that's been puzzling us is that Santa told Al that he couldn't mention anything about the food. Usually all the other times they want us to tell everyone how we've been fed, and tonight Santa told him not to say anything about it. He said the tape wasn't very long, only about one minute. He told her how he was, and said he hoped that soon the situation would be solved. Wonder why all of a sudden they want tape recordings? We're looking at it as being a good sign. Hopefully it is! *End of entry.*

Well, here we are resting up from the big day we had yesterday (my birthday). Really my birthday started at (00:01) July 26, while we were sitting here playing bridge. The students had brought in a bag of cookies the night of the 25th, so at (00:01) we took the bag of cookies, placed a candle in the middle, and then sang Happy Birthday. Even a couple of the students came in. While we were sitting around eating my birthday cookies, I told Santa jokingly that I would like to have a pasta for lunch. When I was at home for my birthday, I usually told my Mom what I wanted for my birthday dinner and she made it. So I told Santa that I wanted pasta, and he said he'd see what he could do. I also asked him if we could watch a movie, too, so he asked how "Annie Hall" would be? We said great!

Just about forgot to mention the birthday card (Christmas card) the guys gave me. I even had Santa sign it, saying he wishes me to go home soon. Boy how great that would be. Matter of fact, that's the wish I made when I blew my candle out.

After the birthday cookies were finished, we continued our bridge game till about (03:30) in the morning before hitting the mattress. Since that day (July 26) was such a special day I woke for breakfast along with Jerry, Al, Dick for the first time in a long time. After breakfast, after some more kidding about how old I'm getting, etc., we crashed back out again, and I had a crazy/nice dream about Jill.

Right before lunch I woke to go to the head, and when I returned Santa was right behind me with a platter of pastries which we could eat for lunch, for my birthday. He then asked if we wanted to go see the movie "Annie Hall", but everyone was still sleeping so I asked him if we could see it later on that night. He started speaking Farsi to Sunshine Man, then came back with an answer to me saying yes. Just thinking about that, probably the reason Santa wanted to show the movie and have the party in the afternoon was because he wasn't here last night.

Anyway, lunch came and I didn't get my wish for pasta. Instead we had roast beef. It was my turn to do dishes, but instead Al and I had switched the day before; I did his the 25th and he did mine the 26th. When I went down to the head, Al to do the dishes and I to go to the toilet, Sunshine Man told me they had a surprise for me later on that night. Al and I figured it was going to be a tape from my family or Jill, but we were wrong.

The rest of the afternoon went as usual. Read a little, slept a little, walked a couple miles, then dragged Al and Bill out of their mattresses to work out. I didn't really have to drag Bill, just Al. We did about a two hour workout right before dinner. I guess it was about a half hour before they brought dinner that I thought I smelled pasta. I bet Bill that they made it for my birthday. Right when Bill was telling me that they wouldn't do that for me, the students came to the door and asked for plates. While I was giving them the plates I motioned for Bill to come see what they had, and sure enough it was pasta. I guess the word was already out that it was my birthday, 'cause the students serving the food even wished me happy birthday. I guess the students got suspicious when they went to pick up the food and saw that it was pasta. Usually the night meal is Iranian food. Even the cook (Ali) came to wish me happy birthday and said that the meal was fixed especially for me. I knew if it wasn't for Santa I would've never gotten it. I bet all the other hostages were wondering what was going on, too. Anyway it was really good. To tell you the truth, I thought that was the special surprise they had in store for me, along with the movie we were going to see, but boy was I every wrong!

Before dinner we got the idea of dressing Bill up as a dog, and when we went to see the movie we were going to walk him in like a dog. I guess you can say we've been doing some weird things lately, like giving horsey back rides down the hallway, of course with our towels still on our heads, etc. So this little thing of Bill dressing/acting like a dog we can just add to our collection of crazy things we did when we were hostage.

Right after dinner Al and I started fixing Bill up, putting three sections of his hair in rubber bands and getting Jerry's belt to use as a leash. Bill put a little black water paint on his nose to make it look even better. When they came to get us, Bill put his blanket on and got down on all fours with my towel on and held onto the leash. Al was going to bring a water bowl, so once we got in the T.V. room he would put it down right in front of the T.V. and Bill would drink right out of it just like a dog. Which he did, too, and the students loved it. Anyway, before we even got out of the room, Bill hit the table near the door with his head, and that's when he started barking. While we were out in the hall and Bill was barking, I thought I could hear some of the other hostages in the other rooms laugh too. It was really funny. The students were running all over. They didn't know what to think. Of course Taco Kid calls Bill Psycho Kid.

When we got into the T.V. room, it seemed like all the students came to see my dog Togo. After Bill sniffed everyone, we finally got situated to watch the movie "Annie Hall", which I thought was great. That Woody Allen is something else. Even the students liked it. There were about six of them in there watching it with us. Once in a while one of the students that hadn't wished me happy birthday earlier that day came in and did Also a couple of the students from the hallway had to come in and tell us to keep the noise down because other hostages were sleeping, which they probably were. It was closing on around midnight.

The movie finally finished around (00:30) the 27th, and while the students were taking Bill, Al, Jerry, and Dick back to the room I had to wait in the television room. I then started thinking that the dinner really wasn't the special surprise after all, and that they were going to bring a tape recording for me from home. Once again I was wrong.

Sunshine Man finally came in and said that I could go back now, smiling real big. I really couldn't believe this was happening. I got in my room, they sat me in a chair facing the table, and then they took my towel off. In front of me, sitting on a white table cloth, was a huge box with three candles on top. Sitting around the box were five bowls with our cups inside filled with orange juice, and right in front of me is a platter of cashews and chocolate chip cookies. Besides that, standing in front of me are about 10-12 students along with Bill, Al, Jerry and Dick singing Happy Birthday. It was unbelievable, and I know it's one birthday party I'll never forget. It was, like Al said, one of the longest birthdays he had ever seen, starting from (00:01) July 26, ending at (01:00) July 27. We cut up the watermelon and offered some to the students, along with the cookies. It was really thoughtful of them. I know there's never been a hostage situation like this ever, and I mean ever...

After all the excitement was over and the dishes cleared away, we started our normal bridge game which lasted till about (05:00) this morning. While we were still playing, Sunshine Man came in with a *Time* magazine talking about Reagan running for the Presidency. Nothing about the hostages though. Al kind of thinks it's a good sign that they're at least letting us look at magazines, especially of the elections, but it's like what Santa said this morning about how they don't really care who makes President. He thinks Carter will, anyway. But he says it doesn't have anything to do with the hostages' fate, which I hope is right.

Beaver was telling Al and me this morning that their new Prime Minister has already been picked, and that they're working on internal affairs and also picking the Prime Minister's cabinet. So when they'll start talking about us it seems like no one knows.

Something else Santa was telling Al this morning was that he should hurry up and get his painting done before he goes home. In fact, he said that a couple times. Really curious to know where he was last night. Couldn't really tell if Santa was hinting or just teasing about that painting, how Al should hurry up and finish it before he leaves. I just hope they're not messing with our heads, but that little party they gave me, like Dick was saying, shows that they know we're going to get out of here, and they want us to go back and tell everyone what they did for us. But when we go is a question I don't think the students even know the answer to.

Well, the workouts we've been doing are starting to finally catch up with me. I'm really sore today. Al and I are the only ones up. Everybody else is crashed out, and I'll probably join them after I finish here. Makes the time fly by. Hopefully get some mail soon— like to see how everyone is doing. *End of entry.*

Wednesday, July 30, 1980 (00:20)   Day 270

Not too many exciting things have happened since the last time I've written, except that we saw about four hours of video yesterday. The first tape we saw was called "Kaleidoscope". It interviewed Father Darrell Rupiper, one of the priests who was here at Easter time. Can't really say too much about the things he mentioned, although some of the things he said I agreed with full heartedly. But when the question was asked if he thought there were spies being held now, he answered it kind of like we were all spies. He probably didn't mean to say it like that, but that's how we interpreted it. Just by the way the students sat around to listen/watch the tape, it reminded us of how much time they'd had to get the Shah back since that tape was made, and it's just that much longer we sit here. I know Father Rupiper was trying his best for us. I just hope the people of the U.S. rise up to the truth about the Shah and his puppet, and have him sent back to Iran.

The other tape we saw was a movie, "The Message", which had to do with the Islamic religion. Both tapes took up most of the afternoon, so that was great on our part, but the tape of Father Rupiper was a little depressing.

When we returned it was about time for dinner, which consisted of hamburgers and potatoes. After that everyone went to bed, pretty much still thinking about the tape we saw and wondering if we'll every get out of here this year yet?

Woke up this afternoon like usual just around lunch time, which this time consisted of turkey, carrots and rice. Once again the turkey wasn't done, so we ended up throwing it away just like all the other times. It's really a shame to see all that meat go to waste, but I wish they'd find someone who can cook it right. This afternoon we spent pretty much to ourselves, reading, sleeping, and Dick walking back and forth across the room. Dinner consisted of shrimp soup and of course, like every night when we're still hungry, cheese. Bill didn't like his so I ate it, while Al ate Dick's, because Dick didn't like it either. Two hours before dinner, we had had another workout, which we hadn't done for the last two days. Too "busy" I guess. It's really hard getting started, but once we get going it turns out to be a pretty good workout. Three hundred and fifty sit-ups and about four hundred push-ups. Have to keep our figures.

Just got finished taking a shower, and now everyone's just sitting/lying around reading while someone's talking over a radio. It sounds as though someone's giving a talk in Farsi. Well, tomorrow's the last day in this month and then we start on August. God, how I dread to go through another month while being kept here, but then again, what choice do we have? We're really staying optimistic on something happening in August, just hope we're right. In two to three more weeks they should have their Prime Ministry cabinet complete and ready to talk about us. That would be putting us around Santa's seven week deadline he was telling me about earlier this month.

Looking forward to getting some mail pretty soon. If I'm not wrong the Fair back home starts today, the 30th, or is it next week the 6th? Jill's in the queen contest, and she and I both were hoping I'd be home by then, but I guess somebody upstairs sees this to be even more important. If she doesn't get queen I know she'll at least get runner-up; that's how confident I am of her.

Hope everyone's doing well back on the ranch. I know they haven't heard from me for a while, but they should know not to worry. Well that's all for now. I guess I'll sit around with Bill here at the table and watch Al play solitaire. That is until Al starts asking who wants to play bridge. *End of entry.*

Friday, August 1, 1980 (15:00)   Day 272

Santa was just in with a tape recorder and said that I was able to make a recording asking if Jill made queen at the Fair this year. I was only given one question to ask, so I hope the family won't be offended. At first I really didn't feel like making it. I know there are a couple other hostages that are being treated worse than me, so why should I get this special privilege. I know since we haven't been writing, our families are worried about us, so by doing this tape and my family hearing it they'll know I'm doing all right.

It was really strange when Santa first came in. I wasn't talking much, so I guess Santa thought the only way to get me talking was to ask about going home. He knows I'm still keeping track of how many more days he has left to his deadline he promised. So he asked how many more days we had. I told him 22. Then he told Al he wished he'd hurry with that painting, and have it done before we leave. Then he came back to me and asked if I would write him when I got home. It seemed like he was trying to make it sound like we were going to be freed soon.

From the conversation I had with Sunshine Man last night, it sounded like we might have a chance of getting out of here next month, September. He was saying that the people of Iran have been saying that they would never change their demands, although he did say that the Parliament will decide. He also said, sounding really serious, that he thinks Kennedy will get put into office, and once he does, they will get the things they want. But this morning Santa was saying that he thinks Reagan will get put into office and that Carter has no chance whatsoever. Could it really be possible that the Iranians are waiting to see who gets put into office before deciding the fate of the hostages?

One interesting thing I read last night from one of Jill's letters said that she heard that maybe they might start talking about releasing of the hostages in September. That goes back to what Sunshine Man was telling me last night, but from what Santa's been saying it sounds that it might be this month, which has 30 more days in it. *What a drag!* We received mail last night, and everyone received one from their families. Jerry even got one from his wife. It had been a while. Once again I received 12 letters, but everyone else received less. It's really starting to get me down, even to the point where I want to tell them not to give me anymore mail since they're not giving everyone else's out. That's one thing I don't want is having special privileges when I know there are other poeple not even getting the things we're getting. Santa did say we had more but didn't say when we were going to get it.

Things are really starting to get to me. I guess it's all the lying, etc. When will this thing ever be solved? It's been about four days now since we've watched T.V., so hopefully soon it will be our turn again.

Forgot to mention the boxes we received the day before yesterday, the same day all the rest of the mail came in, but it takes them that long to read over it. I received a small box of goodies (can of peaches/pears and a can of mixed nuts) from a person named Mr. Frank, and also a package from my godparents, a drawing book on how to draw. Al received a package with books, deck of cards and a couple other things. Dick received a backgammon set from his wife, which we've been playing with since last night. Santa was even in this morning playing a couple games. Really a good game to pass the time Wonder if I'll be getting any more birthday presents.

The food hasn't been too bad lately, really filling, at least for me it is. Not too much happening now. Bill's sitting here watching Al paint, Jerry's walking the floors, and Dick just came back from the head. Haven't worked out for a couple days now. Really haven't felt up to it, but I guess we'll probably start back up again today. *End of entry.*

Sunday, August 3, 1980 (23:10)   Day 274

Two hundred seventy-fourth day today, and in 50 more minutes we'll be going on our tenth month—unbelievable. But here we still sit. We just finished having dinner which consisted of soup, bread, goat cheese and American cheese. Al and I really didn't feel like having soup (too hot) so instead I ate the goat cheese with sugar while Al ate the American cheese. Right now Jerry and Al are playing backgammon while Bill is looking on. Dick just returned from the head doing the dishes, and now he's also watching over the backgammon game. I don't really care to play it very often, so I let everyone else play it.

Really been doing a lot of reading lately, *Sports Afield*, *Sports Illustrated* and even *Time*. First the students take out all parts about Iran. What is it that they don't want us to see/read? Santa was saying tonight that the Parliament might start talks about the hostages sometime this coming week. That doesn't really mean they'll talk about releasing us. Anyway, Santa was saying that once they do start talking about us, that it would take a couple of days. It seems like when he said that it would take days, he probably means it would take months. Al doesn't think so, and I've still got my eyes set on August 22, Santa's seven week cutoff day. It is good to hear, that is if it's true, that the Parliament is going to start discussing us. Tomorrow we'll be going on our tenth month. It's about time they do something.

Maybe the boycott that Carter imposed on this country is hurting them and the Parliament knows the only way around it is the release of the hostages. Really curious to know the demands the Iranian government is asking from the American government, since they know they aren't getting the Shah back. Although the Iranian people are still asking for him, their new Parliament is hopefully telling the Iranians that they aren't ever getting him back and that other demands should be asked for. I hope their demands won't be too far-fetched. August might be our month yet! How I pray to God it is!

M*A*S*H and "Rhoda" were the last T.V. shows we saw the other night, August 1. We were hoping we'd go tonight, but I think tomorrow night's our night to watch. Been hearing music coming from the T.V. room all day so they must've been showing movies to all the other hostages.

Sunshine Man just came in and said that if we wanted to write letters we should, because someone is going to hand carry them back to the United States. So everyone wrote a letter to their families. Al wrote one to his fiancee, and I wrote another to Jill. Hopefully she receives this one. Al was thinking that this might be a good sign, having us write to let people back home know that we're well so that maybe they can start negotiating. Really what else could it mean. This is the first time since we've been here (June 15) that they've asked us to write home. Why all of a sudden now?

Haven't played bridge for the last couple of nights. Had an argument the other night. Of course that's been happening a lot lately, playing bridge and backgammon. I guess our nerves are starting to get shot, but still we continue to struggle on. Other than the small arguments we've been having, I think we've been coming along nicely. The name of the game is to stay cool and keep yourself busy. This might be our month. I pray to God it is. We have one thing, one thing only to give us the spark of joy, hope! *End of entry.*

Tuesday, August 5, 1980 (22:50)   Day 276

Well, in a way today was a good day, and then again it wasn't. We received mail today. As usual I came up with the most letters (25), while no one else exceeded ten or even five. What they're trying to prove I don't know, but this shit's really got me pissed. How can anyone not think anything about a person who receives 25 letters when he only receives maybe three or four. I know it kind of makes a person wonder, but maybe that's what the students want them to do. I've talked it over with everyone here in the room, and they all seem to understand that it's not my fault in any way. I really hope they see it that way! Most of the mail wasn't too old, July 3, but then we've still been receiving mail from way back till January 30. Wonder what the hold up was there?

The recent letter I received had a lot of pictures which I really have enjoyed looking at, along with showing them to everyone else. they really make you wish you were at home, though. The birthday cards are still arriving. I found out through Lorrie's letters that my Mother had called the students and had told them to give me a nice birthday party. The letter also said that they had been making tapes for me, but not one have I received from the students. Sounds as though that everyone is doing well, including Jill. She's still saying that she's waiting, praying and hoping that we'll be together soon. What a beautiful day it's going to be when we get out of here.

Well not much has happened since the last time I've written. Yesterday and today were like any other boring day, except that last night Bill and I were offered a chance to go in the T.V./Library room and sort some new books that had been brought from the Embassy. We both went, and when we were finished we asked if we were going to see video since we helped sort books. What could he do except to say yes, so we watched "Kaz". Really good show.

Once we returned to our room (cell), we all went to our own mattresses and started to read the new books we just picked up. That went on into the early morning hours till we all decided to crash out. Bill and I woke right before lunch and started the reading right back up. Breakfast has just been a waste lately. Jerry, Al and Dick are the only ones who wake for that anymore. On special occasions I might take a bite, but lately I've just decided to lose a little weight.

Right before lunch was brought in is when they brought the mail in. I already went over that, so I don't think I'll do it again. After everyone picked on their lunch consisting of roast beef and eggplant, and decided they all had enough, I was escorted down to the head to do the dishes. Once I returned everyone had started back on their reading, and I finished reading my letters. I do have to say once you get yourself a good book and really get involved, the time passes by quickly.

Here we are again just about ready to wrap up another day. Bill and Al are playing backgammon while Jerry's walking his three miles and Dick is reading. I do have to say that it's really been lonesome without our late bridge games. We're going to have to start them up pretty soon.

Really don't know what to say about our situation. Some students say the Parliament has started talking about us, and some say they haven't. Still looking for something to happen this month yet. Once again cross my fingers, like always. The only thing that seems to be standing in the way now is the negotiating with the U.S. and deciding what the demands are going to be. But then again, they might have some representatives in the Parliament that might not want us to leave. Always a thing to think about. *End of entry.*

Friday, August 8, 1980 (16:20)   Day 279

Decided it was time that I continued writing. Been about three days now. Just returned from the head after having a long talk with English Student. He's such a strong believer that if the Shah doesn't return, we don't return to the U.S.A. I sure hope the Parliament isn't thinking like that. English Student said whatever the Parliament decides, the people will abide by. Supposedly the Parliament is working on internal affairs, economic and political problems, but after they are finished talking about those, we're supposed to be next on the agenda. Realistically the only way it seems they can get around their economic problems is to give the hostages back and then the blockade will be pulled away. What fewer problems they would have over here if only they released the hostages.

Right after lunch Santa came in and took me to the T.V. room to make a tape for my family. Really didn't have much to say, except that I was glad to hear from all their letters that they were all doing well, and to keep up the good work. Told them I was looking forward to hearing how Jill did in the queen contest, and told them how we've been watching T.V. every fourth night, and how I've learned how to play bridge. Supposedly my family's to make a reply, and I'm to hear it later. The tape was only for about two minutes. At the time I was making it, I really didn't know what I wanted to say. Hopefully I get a reply!

Last night before we went to bed, we went and saw the movie "What's Up Doc?" in the T.V. room. Pretzels were even served for refreshments. The night before, August 6, we asked Sunshine Man if they would go out and buy us some pastries. They were really delicious deep fried pastries. Besides the movie last night and Bill losing his title to Al in backgammon yesterday, nothing much of anything else happened.

(18:40) Bill and I received our first haircuts today from (Ali) the cook. He really didn't do too bad of a job, and already I can feel the difference. Maybe my face will have a chance to clear up now that I won't be having hair fly into it. I think Bill's haircut has already affected him in some way or other. He's been jumping around a little more than usual, running into the wall, etc. I think he's a little disappointed that Ali didn't leave a little hair over his ears.

Right before we left the T.V. room after vacuuming it, Beaver came in to say that he was going home for a couple days. We told him to make sure to bring some pastries back with him. They don't have it as bad as I thought they did. They all must have their individual days they have off, and here we still sit. It really must be nice to be free! Anyway, I hope he brings some pastries back with him.

Like I said before, not much of anything else happened yesterday. Just another long boring day spent reading. I really wish we'd start our bridge games back up. There's really not any difference between bridge games and backgammon games. Both games we do the same

213

amount of arguing, but I guess it's true if you can't get around the arguing you just have to give the game up. Anyway, I've been keeping myself pretty occupied just by reading, which really doesn't bother me any. Sleeping's usually my second alternative, but I haven't been doing much of that lately until the early mornings, then waking around lunch time with half the day just about gone.

Day before yesterday a little after lunch, Ali the cook came in with a pot of potatoes he wanted us to peel. Bill and Al accepted the job, just like we accepted peeling the onions and shrimp. Nothing else to do, so why not? It's really surprising all the stuff we've been peeling. We really don't see too much of it after we're finished with it. It makes us wonder if we've been cleaning their food, too.

Still been hearing the yelling/moaning which seems to be coming from the basement. It doesn't seem to be an American, at least it doesn't sound like it, and I hope it's not. It sounds like the guy is out of his head crazy, or even from the yelling/moaning he does, you'd think he was being tortured. At times I wonder if they don't just put this guy right down in front of our window just so we'll be able to hear him. Al was talking to Sunshine Man the other day about the guy, but Sunshine replied that it doesn't concern us so we shouldn't worry about it. That's just like English Student saying that I worry too much about going home. I should just be patient and not worry about it. But then again, they've been saying that for the last ten months.

Some of the students were out in the hallway sorting mail last night after we got finished watching T.V. I was just returning from the head when they put three magazines in my hand to take back to the room. A little while after that, Sunshine came in with two cans of pistachios to give us. Lately it seems like anything we ask for we get, if it's reasonable. I sure wish releasing us was reasonable in their eyes. Getting ready to work out in a few more minutes. We haven't worked out for the past four days. I want to see if my short hair has any effect!

(23:50) Just returned from the head where I had a short meeting with John McKeel, and I mean short! The students must've forgotten that I was still in the shitter when they came to get Al. I knew they did right off when they left the door wide open. So I just sat there and continued to take my shit. A little while later I heard someone running down the hallway, and knew right off they were coming to my head. Sure enough, McKeel came running into the head, threw open the shitter door where I was looking up at him. He was holding his mouth closed with one of his hands. Right as he saw that I was occupying the shitter, he turned around all of a sudden, ran to the door, knocked and ran across the hallway, where then I heard him relieve himself—hopefully in the shitter.

It was the first time since Christmas that I had seen him, and seeing him like that I really felt sorry for him. But after he had gone across the hall to the other head, I couldn't do anything but laugh at the expression he had on his face when he opened the shitter door and saw me sitting there on the shitter. I guess I was kind of lucky that he didn't relieve himself right on me. Anyway I just hope it wasn't anything serious. Really would've like to have talked to him for a while if he hadn't been in such a hurry. *End of entry.*

Sunday, August 10, 1980 (23:50)   Day 281

Just came from watching T.V., "Dallas" and "How the West Was Won". Sunshine came in right after dinner and took us in to watch them. While we were in there, Beaver, who must've just returned from home, came in to say hello to us. The first question I asked him was if he brought any pastries. He replied that at (02:00) we'd get them. Why ever at (02:00) I'll never know.

Al and I had a little discussion with Taco Kid tonight right before dinner. He had come to the toilet to take us back to our room when I asked him if we'd be going home soon. His reply was somewhat happy and then a little sad, it seemed like. He said "yes" and I said that he was joking, but he replied back "no", that something has happened. We asked if it was for the good, and he said "yes". Then I asked him if it was for the good of them, and he said no, for us, and then he added that we would understand soon! Maybe something did happen today.

Their attitudes today were a whole lot different than they were last night, when Santa, Sunshine and another student came in to talk to us. They really seemed happy last night, but today the students really seemed sad, and we noticed the day was a lot quieter than other days. Really a strange day.

They must've been sorting out mail last night. A little while after Santa had left with the other students, he came back with a picture of Dick's wife and a picture (newspaper clipping) of my sister, mother, and a man holding up a book with my name on it. Then followed one of my little cousin Carol, whose birthday was the same day as mine. The picture might've had something to do with my birthday. There was one more of my little brother and a gentleman I didn't recognize. The heading of the picture was cut off, so I asked Santa if he knew what the picture meant and he said they were campaigning for Carter and me. It seems like Santa still has grudges against my family for taking sides with the President of the United States. My family is doing what they believe and have been taught to do, so I hold nothing

215

against them. My family is very patriotic, and they know the way they're standing up against this situation is the way I'd want them to. They can say anything they want to say about my family, but nothing can ever be said to change the love that I have for them. Hopefully Taco Kid was telling the truth tonight. Maybe something's up! Oh, God, please help us.

Nothing much has happened since I've written last. Days seem to be going by, not too fast and not too slow, although I wish this would hurry up and end. From looking out the toilet window, the weather seems to be gradually changing. It looks like we're going to miss summer after all. What a drag! At times I get the feeling that we're never going to get out of here, but then, like today, you hear one of the students say these encouraging words, and you think freedom is right around the bend. Once again, the only thing we have is hope, and hoping is what we're doing. *End of entry.*

Tuesday, August 12, 1980 (23:00)   Day 283

Here we are on our 283rd day today, and the only good news (if you really want to call it good news) is that Sunshine said that things were looking a quarter inch better this week than they were last week. Usually whatever Sunshine says we take as being the truth.

A little after Sunshine left, Santa came in to talk to us for awhile. I think his real reason for coming in was to check up on Al. He hadn't been feeling too well this afternoon, so he asked for some medication from one of the students, and I guess the student told Santa that Al wasn't feeling good. It was just last night that the doc came around (along with a couple other students) to check up on us. Everyone was feeling well, but I did ask him for some medication for my acne. He wrote the prescription on a piece of paper and then gave it to Santa. Well, that was last night and I still haven't received it yet. Anyway, we were kind of curious about why the doc came by. Maybe one of the hostages was sick, and while he was here he decided to check everyone.

Last night mail was passed out, and like always, I received the most, 27 cards and letters, while everyone else received less. That's not really what I want to talk about. What I do want to talk about is the tapes Jill and my family made to give to me but I never received. In the letters from Jill and my Mom, they said that the students on the phone had told them I'd already received the tapes, which is a damn lie. No one's given me a tape since I've been here, and here they are lying—why? And then they expect people to believe them when they're doing the same thing they're criticizing our government for

216

doing. That goes back to the time when one of the students told me that Moslem students didn't lie. There's not a person alive who hasn't lied in one way or another. It's really fucked that they don't give us the tapes. I guess they get a big kick out of holding them from us.

Santa was telling us this afternoon that Carter won the Democratic Convention, so now I guess it's against Carter and Reagan. Santa still says the presidential election has nothing to do with the hostages' fate, but I'll tell you one thing, they've sure been keeping tabs on those conventions. Just before he left, he gave us the impression that this situation would come to an end soon, and that at least for some people it would be a happy ending. Like to know what he meant by that. If and when we ever get out of here, I hope it's just not some of us, *but all of us!* Some of the students have been saying that the Parliament has begun to talk about the hostage situation. Yesterday while I was talking to Beaver in the head, he was saying that last week sometime the chief Parliament official had said that this situation should be solved soon. Wish I knew what "soon" means. At least it's good to hear that they've started talking about us.

Getting back to mail, I still haven't heard how Jill did at the queen contest. Although I do know that Tim Siebert, my best friend and one of Jill's high school crushes, escorted her to the ceremonies involved. It seems like everyone's taking care of her back home. Anyway, I hope she had a good time (Tim too!). I guess I'm a little jealous. Nothing much I can say while I'm over here. She did pick the only one person I'd trust with her. Anyway, I can't wait till I get home. It sure sounds as though I'll be awful busy.

My family told me about the big day they had on the Fourth of July. I'm so grateful for all the things that people are doing for them. I know it helps them keep their minds off this situation. How great it's going to be to be home once again. It sounds so good it's hard to believe it's going to come true!

Not much more happening around here. It was thundering and raining last night. Kind of early to be doing that. We've been reading and playing a lot of backgammon lately. Still haven't started our bridge game back up yet.

Food hasn't been too bad. In fact we just finished eating our late dessert of pudding (banana cream). They brought it at dinner, but it was a little watery. We told them it needed beating, so they took it away and brought it back a little better. Al had a bag of coconut in the room here, and we decided to add a little of that to the pudding. It tasted pretty good.

We were supposed to go in and see "Hee-Haw" tonight, but it seems like some of the other hostages beat us to the T.V. room. Maybe
217

tomorrow. Sure wish this situation would come to an end. Really getting bored sitting in this cell day after day, looking outside and watching all those beautiful days pass by without us. *Oh God, please help us!! End of entry.*

Thursday, August 14, 1980 (23:55) Day 285

Well here we still sit getting ready to wrap up another day. Another five more minutes and we'll be going on our 286th day, with the outside world still rolling on without us. What the Iranian people plan to gain from holding us is a question I can't begin to answer.

Ali, our cook, has been on leave the last couple days. Sunshine's been taking his place, and really not doing too bad of a job. The soup was pretty good tonight, not as much water as usual. Yesterday's pasta and today's boiled chicken were a little undercooked, though. After we told him about it, he said we wouldn't need to worry after tomorrow because Ali was coming back.

I haven't seen/heard too much of Santa, Taco Kid, or English Student since the day before yesterday. English Student did bring in some medication this morning while I was still asleep (Bristol Tetrex 250 mg) for my acne. I've been taking it, and hopefully it'll do some good. Seems like the Embassy must've ran out of toothpaste. Yesterday we had to wait around until they went out and bought some Iranian paste. Seems like the supplies at the Embassy are running low. According to Al, though, there's enough food there to last for years. I hope we're not going to have to stay here to eat it all.

Bill and I finally got Sunshine to bring us music yesterday, in trade for peeling cucumbers. In fact we even have it again tonight. Right now we're listening to *Electric Light Orchestra*, with additional tapes of Pheobe Snow, "Never Letting Go" and "The Wizard of Oz" original sound track. I know the music really puts some life into the room. I can think of a lot of other things that could help, too. Last night we saw "Hee-Haw" on T.V. One half hour and that was it. I guess they don't want to show us all the tapes at once. Boy, how I can't wait to get out of here and live another normal life again.

Santa just came in to get Al to take him to listen to a tape he must've just received. They must've just came from the Embassy with mail. We just heard them pushing boxes down the hallway. Maybe there were dates in the boxes, since one of the students just came in to ask if we wanted any. I guess their supply room here is running low, so they need to stock it up.

I wish these people would decide something about us instead of just letting us sit here in a daze. Passed a little of my time away today working on my math. Anything to kill the monotony of each day.

Al just returned from listening to his tape, which was from his sisters. He was saying that they didn't sound too enthused about us coming home. They told him to keep his hopes up. His sister also said something about Al's mother being in California with some other families. Didn't really say what for though. At least he heard his tape. Wonder why they lied to my family about giving me theirs? The lying the students have been doing gets me so aggravated and pissed off I feel like ringing one of their necks. When are we ever getting out of here?

Al wanted me to jot down a little note for him about his tape from his sisters. While he was listening to the tape, music of the *Carpenters* was fading in. A couple times the music overrode his sister so he couldn't hear her, but otherwise he said it reminded him of a movie to hear his sister talking with music playing in the background. Al also said they had some new games in the T.V. room. It seems like they're expecting us to be here a while. *This shit sucks!* Bill and Dick are reading. Al and Jerry are playing cards. *End of entry.*

Monday, August 18, 1980 (00:05)   Day 289

Well, here we are on our 289th day. In just 74 more days we'll have been here one year exactly. When I think about it, it's a surprise we've made it mentally this far. How much longer do we have? Tonight when "Butler" was bringing me back from the head I asked him if we'll be going home soon. He told me that until the Shah returns this is our home. Why can't these people get it through their heads that the Shah's never coming back? But then again, I think some of the students just say that to get us pissed off because they can't face reality. Anyway I sure hope it's not the Shah that's still keeping us here.

Butler just brought us our night snack of pudding. It's the second time they've done that. I guess it gives Ali a little time after supper to fix it. After adding coconut to it, it tasted pretty good. Dick's teaching Jerry and Al a new game at the table, with Bill looking on.

(01:30) Just returned from the T.V. room, where we were able to see half of the Rose Bowl (Washington vs. Michigan). They couldn't find the other half, but before it went off, Washington was leading 10-0. Sure would've liked to have seen the other half. I forgot who really won, but I believe it was Michigan. Anyway here we are once again back in our cage. It's always a drag leaving the T.V. room to come back here. The main lights just went off, so we had to turn on our small night lamp. Whenever the main lights go off we usually know it's about time to hit the mattress.

219

Some of the students think football is a game for crazy people and the people who watch it are even crazier, at least that's what "Smart Ass" said. No matter what they say about the game, we did enjoy watching it. In fact, I was really surprised that we got to see it at all. Last night (Aug. 16) we saw "Charlie's Angels", so I wasn't expecting to see anymore T.V. for another two days at least. But I guess the painting Bill did today got us the ticket for watching it tonight.

The past two days Santa's been pretty pissed off at me, and the only reason is because I don't talk to him. In fact last night before we went in to watch T.V., he brought mail in for Bill, Al, and Dick. Jerry and I received nothing. I don't know what to say about Jerry's case, but before I got Santa mad at me I was receiving 20-25 letters. He keeps trying to say (in different ways) that I'm taking this situation badly, worrying about our situation too damn much, etc. I guess his only way to get back at me was just to hold my mail. Doing what he did last night makes it more obvious than before that our mail is being held back by these people. I know he's going to expect me to ask about mail, but there ain't no way I am. If he thinks he's hurting me by doing that, he'd better think again. All the lying and cheating these people are doing is really getting to me. I try my best to hold back all my frustrations, but one of these days it's all going to blow out.

This afternoon the students did a job of cleaning out the hallway. I cleaned the western head while another hostage cleaned the eastern. I asked English Student if someone was coming to see us. He replied that they just did it for our good health. Isn't that nice! We still believe someone's coming to see us. Hopefully it's for the good.

Dick received a letter from a friend last night giving information about Rich Queen having multiple sclerosis. He was one of the people that worked in the Consulate with Dick. From reading the letter over several times, we analyzed that Rich had been released because of his illness. At least that's what we think from the information. Dick's friend mentioned Rich's press conference she had seen the morning of July 20th, (but didn't say where) and how the doctors (but not which doctors, Iranian or American) predict/assume multiple sclerosis. Another thing that led us to believe he was released is why would the Iranian government tell the U.S. that one of the hostages had multiple sclerosis when there's no cure, and keeping him in this situation would only make it worse.

Dick was pretty close to Rich, and last night when he read the news it kind of put him pretty low. He asked Santa if there was a way to see him. Santa said no, but said that he was at the Embassy and doing well. Santa did tell Dick that he could write a note that he would give to Rich, so today Dick wrote a note and gave it to "Mr. Fix-It", explaining what Santa had told him last night he could do. "Mr. Fix-It" got kind of curious, and wanted to see the letter that had the information about Rich. I guess someone's going to get in trouble for letting that news in. Anyway, I hope Rich has been released because of his illness. If these people still have him here, they're really desperate for something. Pray to God he's all right!!

There's really not that much more to write about. How much longer are our nerves going to hold out? I know our tempers are really getting weak. How much longer are they going to hold out?

This afternoon Sunshine came in with some canned clams, asking what could we serve with them. We told him they were best served with crackers and a martini before dinner. How nice that would be. Boy, how I can't wait to get out of here and live normally. Not too much more to say. Trying to stay busy as much as possible. *End of entry.*

Tuesday, August 19, 1980 (23:50)   Day 290

Just returned from watching T.V. ("All in the Family", M*A*S*H and "Bob Newhart"). That Billy's been getting us a lot of programs with his paintings. In fact he's working on another painting right now. We're hoping this one will get us to see "Kaz".

Well, from talking to Taco Kid last night and this morning, we understand that the Parliament started once again today to talk about the hostages. Supposedly they were on recess or something. Sure wish we knew how far along they are with this situation. After today, it's just two more days until Santa's seven week deadline. Maybe something will happen yet. Hearing anything will be good news.

Al and Bill were working on the tape box today. There wasn't much room for another one helping, so I just decided to watch. The little rubber belt that was used to run the tape broke, so now we're waiting for Sunshine to bring us another one so we can fix it. Hope we won't have to wait too long.

Worked out a little yesterday afternoon and then afterwards went in and took a nice hot shower. That hot shower is really something nice to us to draw all the frustration out of you. Otherwise, everybody else is up to their usual activities, Jerry and Al playing cards, Bill painting and Dick reading. Everybody's not feeling too well tonight. All had eggplant for dinner. It didn't seem too bad then, but now it's getting to us. They brought around the yogurt once again tonight and Bill was the only one who took it, but like always he didn't eat it. I know not too many people eat it but still they make it.

Santa's been gone for the past three days—wonder where he's at? Tonight was the first time in two days I've seen English Student. Tonight when he took us to watch T.V. he told us that when we go home we can tell everyone we watched T.V. It kind of gets you pissed off when they say these things. It's like they're teasing us. They might not know they're doing it, but they are. Still, not too often does English Student say anything at all about going home. He's one of these guys that says when Shah comes back, you go home. Sunshine said tonight that we might be receiving mail sometime tomorrow or the day after. Wonder if I'll get mine kept from me like the last time?

It really seems obvious that the Church is communicating between the Iranians and our government. It goes along with what some of the students have been saying about how their government doesn't have to speak with our government, but with other people. The only other people I can think of is the Church. Hopefully these people aren't pressing Reagan if he's elected President. The United States showed they weren't bluffing about military action the first time, so I hope they aren't going to press the next President. What these people are waiting for besides the Shah I'll never know until the day comes that we are freed. My hopes are still pretty strong for this month. Eleven more days, so there's still a chance. *End of entry.*

Friday, August 22, 1980 (01:00)   Day 293

Today is our 293rd day, and also Santa's seven week cutoff date he promised back in July. Really curious to know what he's going to say towards his promise. He really doesn't have anything to lose. It's us that are suffering. It just shows that you can't believe anything these people say until you see it actually happening.

We did have a little action yesterday morning. The students were out in the hall rearranging the rooms, bringing new people in and taking old ones out. Really thought we were going to be moved, but no orders were passed so we're still here with our new neighbors, whoever they are. Santa finally returned yesterday morning, probably with the rest of the new group. Three days he was gone, wonder how far he had to go to pick up the new recruits? He really hasn't said too much to us, just gives us the big grin. He came in for a little while last night while we were watching "Kaz," didn't say too much, just looked at Bill's new paintings, said a few more words and then left.

We're back in our cell once again. Jerry's walking his three miles, Dick and Al are reading, and Bill's painting another picture off a post card. Bill and I just got finished peeling potatoes for our potato salad tomorrow, at least that's what Taco Kid said. After we were finished doing that, we had him bring us some crackers and cheese. What else is there to do besides eat?

Bill and I started to play backgammon last night, but we didn't get too far before we started to argue and then decided it was time to quit before we got out of hand. Nerves are just about getting shot. At least Taco Kid said yesterday that things are being worked on, and that we would be going home way before Christmas. A little earlier Four Eyes said just about the same thing, but mentioned that we would be going home some time in the Fall. (Fall begins September 27th.) Although they kept saying that those were their own predictions, and that the final decision is up to the Parliament. What is taking the Parliament so long to decide anyway? Today I asked Beaver that, and he asked me why should it be up to our Parliament? He really makes me wonder if the Parliament is even talking about the hostages' release. Some students say that the Parliament hasn't started talking about us, then others say they've started, but it's going to be another one or two months before they make the final decision. All news is kept from us, but it really seems like we're going to be here for another couple months. Oh God, please help me make it through these days.

Day before last was mail day. It was the second time in a row that Jerry didn't receive a letter, not one! Al had a talk with Sunshine, but Sunshine swore they weren't holding his mail from him and said he'd see what he could do about a Red Cross message. I really hope nothing is wrong back home for Jerry. This situation is bad enough for a person's mind.

I finally received mail again last night, I guess because Santa wasn't here to hold it back like the last time. Received a lot of birthday cards, and four letters from Jill and one from her sister-in-law and brother. Still wondering about her queen contest. Her letters were kind of mixed up. One envelope had nothing but a check list; another one had part of one letter with another letter. Who's to blame for that? Anyway, it was good to hear from her, and so good to know she's still there waiting. Everyone else received letters, except for Jerry, and from their letters we finally realized that Queen was released, so maybe there's still hope for us. Pray to God! Maybe next time we get mail I'll hear about Jill's queen contest. Not too much more to write. We're still keeping our hopes up high. What else can we do?

Just returned from the head, where I asked Santa about his seven week promise. He told me he's not a man that makes predictions, and left. Wonder what lies he's going to use next! *End of entry.*

Saturday, August 23, 1980 (23:50)   **Day 294**

Two hundred ninety-fourth day, how many more? Santa came in

a little after lunch and took me into the T.V. room to listen to a tape from my mom. It was really so good to hear her voice and to hear that they were all doing well. She had said that they received my letter and heard the tape I had made, which brought relief to them, too. Her tape had to have been made around the second or third week in August, because we sent our letters out around the 4th or 5th of August. They were supposed to be hand carried. She mentioned that Jill was fine, but nothing about how she did at the queen contest. I don't know what was at the end of the tape. Maybe she said something the students didn't want me to hear, because I didn't get to hear the end of it. I guess I was lucky just to hear it.

When Santa first took me in there he said he wasn't going to play it for me, but at the last minute he decided he would. It was the first tape I've ever heard from all the other ones that must be lying around, or ones they just played something else over. Anyway, it was just so good to hear, but most of all it really made me homesick. After I came back, Bill went in and heard one from his family. He was also happy to hear from them but didn't think they sounded too good. We've been here so long, why is it they keep torturing our families like this?

A little while after Bill returned, Santa came back in with a picture of Jill and the other queen candidates. It was taken at the Diamond Inn the night of the dance/dinner, the night she had a date with Tim. She really looked beautiful in the picture. I guess I was jealous of the fact that Tim was escorting her that night. Anyway, that picture shows me that we have mail—looking forward to that. How I can't wait to get my arms around Jill. I love her dearly! I'm really glad she got to do this. I know I didn't want her just sitting around at home all the time. If she does find someone else, there isn't much I could say about it, except that I really did love her. Get off that subject.

Last night Sunshine came in with another picture of Bill and me reading Christmas cards at Christmas time in the ambassador's house. During the time he was in talking to us (two hours) he was saying that we might be getting a scrapbook, with pictures marking different events, when we leave here. I'd love to have one, *if we ever get out of here*. Something you can always remember!

He was also saying last night that the Iranian people would never change their demands for the hostages' release, but if the Parliament decides on something else, the people will abide by their decision. So far, I guess the Parliament agrees with the people, because we're still here. He claims that they have a duel going on with the U.S., but I know if they plan to continue to wait for Reagan to become President, they're going to wake up some morning with a war on their hands. Of course we're going to be in the middle of it, but as each day passes here, I start to feel that I don't really give a damn anymore. That's the I-don't-give-a-fuck attitude. Analyzing all the things he said last night, it shows that we're going to be here a lot longer! This shit is getting old. Really getting tired of staying in this fucking room and then going to the head and looking out the window watching each beautiful day go by without us—why? Because we're American, and I'll tell you one thing, I'm awful proud of it too!

Forgot to mention that last night Santa and a couple of the other students came in with a picture that was a drawing by Jim Lopez; it was great! The picture showed one of the hostages going to the head and walking into the door. The hostage said "ouch" and the student replied "no speak." We all really got a good laugh out of it. That was the first picture we've seen drawn by Jim, so he must have been one of the new people that came in the other day. Anyway that guy is a fantastic artist.

I started a new thing today—oil painting! It's really hard, you have to match the number on the board with the number assigned to the paint. Really made the time pass by well. Trying to take my time on it so it will last. Al's just about finished with his. Ali the Cook said he would like to have it by next Friday, so Al worked a long time on it today to get it finished for him. That Ali's a good guy though!

It's another quiet night/morning once again. Bill just crashed out, Al and Jerry are reading, and Dick's walking his three miles—it might even be six. Jerry worked out by himself last night. I've been meaning to, but just haven't had enough get-up-and-go in me. This fucking place is boring! If the other hostages don't agree, they're crazy. Sure wish we could go outside one of these days. I remember on my mom's tape she was hoping that we were getting to go outside, but if we weren't, we were to ask the students to let us. I wish it was that easy!

Four Eyes brought me some lemon juice the other day for my acne. He was saying that when he had it bad, he moistened his face with lemon juice, and it went away. I think what my face needs now is some sun, but I doubt if we'll get that. Not really too much more to talk about, except that this shit is getting old. How much more of this can we take? Dear God, please help us! *End of entry.*

Monday, August 25, 1980 (23:40)   **Day 296**

Two hundred ninety-sixth day and still here we sit. Bill and I just got finished playing backgammon, and now Jerry and Al are playing Scribbage. Dick just went to the head with his escort and Bill's over on his rack saying a rosary. Nothing much of anything else happening.

Last night we went in and saw the Carol Burnett Show, so it will probably be another four days before we see T.V. again. Received a couple letters from home today, dated around July 28. One of the letters said that one of my best friends was killed July 27 (suicide). My friend that wrote the letter was saying that the family hasn't been doing too well. But I would expect since he's dead that everything will be back to normal soon. We figure it will take a while before they adjust to it, though. May he rest in peace.

Everybody else's mail was about the same, wishing we were home, etc... Why this situation hasn't been solved by now I'll never know! We've just given up on asking the students about the situation. I guess we'll just have to sit here and continue to wait. What a fucking bore! Last night before we went in to watch T.V., about six students came in to sing us a revolutionary song. It was supposedly made up after November 4th of last year (new song on the top 40's). After their recital, we were escorted into the T.V. room where we found a can of cigars. A little later they brought us some pretzels and potato chips, just like at the movies. They still continue to treat us well, but nothing is said about going home.

Ali the Cook must really like the way we've been peeling the potatoes and carrots. Yesterday and today he brought in more stuff to be peeled. At times I don't really mind doing it. It gives us something to do, but other times I feel that they're just using us for things they don't want to do. Really getting good at peeling potatoes, though!

Managed to get myself to do a small workout yesterday, 300 sit-ups and 200 push-ups. To tell you the truth, I sweat my ass off. I took care of that when I went down to take a nice hot/cold shower. Someone must have fixed the pressure of the shower, because now we have no more of that sitting around waiting for the water to come out. Now it comes out with strong force.

The days seem to be continuing on without us outside these walls. The weather really seems to be pretty nice, also. Sure wish we could get some of that sun on us. Hasn't been any problem getting enough to eat, but I do have to say I sure miss the home cooking my mom/Jill always made. Yesterday when Ali the Cook was in talking to us, Al asked him if he could help with the Christmas dinner. But Ali replied that we would be free then, he hoped! I sure in the fuck hope so too! It does seem that some of the students are getting tired of this shit also. I wish the Parliament was. What are these people waiting for? God—Please help us. *End of entry.*

Ending our 298th day. Two more and we've been here 300 days; what a fucking drag! We just came in from the T.V. room where we saw "How the West Was Won." Really enjoyed that, although we enjoy anything that breaks the routine. We were expecting mail to be handed out today, but I guess they didn't have enough time to read it all, so they said it would be a couple more days. I guess that's all right; then we wouldn't be having everything happening in one day, movie, mail, etc. Now we still have mail to look forward to.

It was kind of strange tonight while we were watching television. Santa came in with a letter from my parents saying that I wouldn't be able to read it, because he wasn't able to censor it (read it). A little while after he left, he came back and asked me why my parents would write such a thing. I knew the reason I wasn't going to get it wasn't due to his not being able to read it; it's just because he doesn't want me to read whatever she wrote. Wish I knew what it was though! It's really strange that Santa even came in and told me about not getting it. Why doesn't he do that to everyone else when they can't receive theirs? Looking forward to mail though! While we were in the T.V. room, we picked up some new books plus a new *Sporting News* which was pretty recent (August 9). Hopefully our mail will be up to date.

Not too many exciting things been happening around here. They came in once again this morning to collect sheets for washing. They've been doing that every week now. Before that it wasn't so frequent, so maybe this is a good sign. Food's been coming around pretty well. Today for breakfast we had blueberry jam, or maybe it was just pie filling, plus butter, bread and tea—not too bad for being a hostage. For lunch we had hamburgers, french fries, brussel sprouts and onions. I didn't find it too bad, but Al got stomach aches from it. He asked the students to get him something for a stomach ache, and a little while later they came back with a box of Pepto-Bismol tablets. He hasn't said anything more about it so I guess the tablets worked. Then tonight at dinner we had tuna fish, eggs, cheese and bread. The food's been adequate, keeping us healthy. In fact we just asked them for something to eat and they brought us Ritz Crackers—a whole box!

Been keeping to my small workout lately. Yesterday I didn't do too much, just 200 push-ups and then did the same again today. Tomorrow I guess I'll start back up on my sit-ups. My gut's still a little sore from the last 300 I did. I'd sure like to be outside doing these exercises where it's really nice. It has been pretty nice out lately. We've been getting a lot of flies in our room, so this morning Al asked for a fly swatter, and the flies haven't been around since.

Santa was just in for a little while and mentioned something Jack Anderson said about the United States trying another military intervention over here (supposedly his own thoughts on what he thinks the U.S. ought to do). Santa's only comment was that Iran really isn't looking forward to a war, but at times I wonder.

Well, three more days in this month and then comes September. Jill said in her last letter that something regarding the hostage release was supposed to be talked about in September, and told me to just hold on till then. Well, I'm holding on, so I hope something happens. It's (02:05) in the morning and the main lights just went off. Dick and Jerry are sitting at the table talking, Al's working on another of his hard puzzles and Bill's taking a shower. I'm going to close for now, read a little and then hit the mattress. Really looking forward to that mail. *End of entry.*

Friday, August 29, 1980 (22:30)   Day 300

Three hundred days today that we've been in this unbelievable situation. Sixty-five more days and it will have been a year. Unfucking real! When will it ever end? What do these people want? We still haven't received any mail yet this week. Three days ago we asked if they had any and they replied yes. So once again today I asked Santa if we had any mail, and he said yes! They know mail means a lot to us, but still just to fuck with us they hold it back. That's what I call cheap shit! I hope the sonofabitch that's holding it rots in hell!

Santa came in this afternoon accusing us of communicating with some of the other hostages. He didn't say who. He said that we've been using a card with letters, but the only one I know of that we have is the eye chart. All these things they accuse us of, no doubt that's probably why we haven't gotten any mail. It seems like something is up though. Yesterday and today it's been pretty quiet. I saw Sunshine once yesterday morning. I asked him if we were going to get mail, and he said yes. Haven't seen him since. This morning once again Santa came into the room and just looked around while we were sleeping. Why they all keep doing that I'll never know.

I worked on my painting once again today. It should be finished pretty soon. Last night I worked out a little, 200 sit-ups and 100 push-ups, then took a nice hot shower to take out the rest of my frustration. This shit's really been getting me pissed off. The only times I'm not aggravated are when I'm painting, sleeping, or taking a nice hot shower. Those are my relaxers. How much longer they're going to hold out I don't know. I do know that the paint is running out, so I guess I'll lose that one.

228

Here I am again, sitting on my mattress with another headache (been having a lot of those). Jerry and Al are playing Scribbage, Dick's walking his laps and Bill's reading. Everything seems to be going pretty well in our room. Hopefully it's the same in the other rooms. Forgot to mention that when I went to the head early this morning (02:00), one of the guards we call Plow Boy took me down there, and when he left he must've gone back to the couch and fallen asleep. I wasn't down there more than five minutes, and then I had to wait for Plow Boy to wake up. I waved into the T.V. camera and motioned to the door, and I think the person watching must've understood what I was trying to say and sent someone to wake Plow Boy. I don't know what would have happened to Plow Boy if I had been really determined to get out of here.

Santa just came in with mail. Everyone, even Jerry, received something. I still haven't heard anything of Jill making Fair Queen. The four letters I received from Jill were all from June, Xerox copies of ones I've already received. Received one from my parents dated July 16, but nothing earlier. Wish I could've read the letter Santa was holding the other night. Well, maybe next week I'll hear what happened with the Queen Contest. Anyway, the mail was great. I even received a couple from Jill's sister-in-law and her brother, Jerry and Judy Ditch. Everyone's been saying that they're looking forward to the day I reach home. Big times when I get back—party hardy!

It looks like the little talk that Al gave Sunshine the other day about Jerry not receiving any mail helped out. Jerry received two letters, up-to-date ones, too. All is well around here so far; now we're looking forward to the next mail call. Even more than that, we're looking forward to getting the fuck out of here! *End of entry.*

Monday, September 1, 1980 (00:30)   Day 303

Well, here we are, our 303rd day (Labor Day), and still no signs of this situation letting up. I myself can see no reason for us still being here, whereas I guess the Iranians can. What they're planning to get I'll never know until we're released. The only thing I know now is that I'm getting filled to the top with all this "be patient" shit. All I can do is say that I'm getting tired of all this, because there is nothing I can do to change the situation. Just keep sitting and hoping that something happens soon.

Well, Jill's month of September is here. This is when she believes they might start talking about our release. Wonder if her source of information was telling the truth. The days really seem to be dragging lately. This cell's starting to get to me, I guess.

We just returned from the T.V. room where we saw "Hee-Haw". Bill had already seen it, so returned to the room to continue reading. I'll tell you, once you start listening to the love songs they sing, you really start to get depressed, really depressed and homesick. It seems like it was getting to Jerry, Al and Dick, too. Each time someone would come on to sing a song, they would draw their attention to something else. Go over to search for a book or start reading the one they had picked up previously, taking all their attention away from the T.V. It might've been that they didn't like the singing, but I really doubted that. Once we got back into the room, someone mentioned something about being depressed. But who wouldn't be depressed, knowing that you weren't going to see T.V. for another three or four days, and returning to a cell where you have to continue to keep your sanity. Little do these people know how they're hurting us. But someday, someone will pay for this, and when that day comes I wish them a lot of mercy!

Once again tonight the electricity went out, and we had to eat dinner (soup, olives and cheese) by candlelight. Really romantic. The only thing we were missing was the wine and the women. Send up the harlots! When the electricity goes out, you can usually hear the other hostages. When they finally turn the lights back on, there's applauding up and down the hallway, and the students run up and down trying to get everything quiet again. That was about the only exciting thing that's happened within the last two days.

Ali the Cook came in yesterday and found Dick walking his laps. He asked him if he was exercising, but if he wasn't, would he please exercise by cutting carrots. It was really funny how he said it. We all got a good laugh. Anyway, Dick cut the carrots for Ali. Later in the afternoon we did a small workout, and then right before dinner took a nice hot shower. One of my few pleasures.

Everyone's in good health, just getting a little depressed. It's been getting a little cool at night lately. If we're going to be here too much longer I'll have to ask them for a blanket for the winter. That will really be a drag if we're still here till then. *Oh God, please help us! End of entry.*

Wednesday, September 3, 1980 (00:05)   Day 305

Last night Al had a close call after working out. We had done a pretty strenuous but short workout. Al did about 400 push-ups and 100 sit-ups, and I did 200 push-ups and 400 sit-ups. Afterwards we were down in the head, and I was taking a shower while Al was shaving. He had been complaining about feeling sick and having a hard time catching his breath. I was talking to him from the shower, telling him to let me know if it got any worse. Not long after I said that, he called me out of the shower. He was sitting in the chair with his head between his legs, said he was having a hard time catching his breath, and needed fresh air. I immediately started knocking on the door continuously until someone came. I thought maybe he was going to have a heart attack.

The student who came to the door, Butler, was kind of angry with me for rushing him, but when I told him Al was sick and we needed to talk to Sunshine or Santa, he became a little curious. Whenever the students are out in the hall serving meals (which they were doing at the time) they don't like to be disturbed with anything else until everyone is served. But Santa and Mr. Fix-It came immediately.

At first they thought we were only joking around. I was standing there naked, telling them that Al needed fresh air immediately, that he was having a hard time breathing. I told them that it might be his heart and that they better get him to fresh air fast. I pointed to the window that had a nice breeze coming through, but I guess they thought we only wanted to look out the window. Santa just told me to mind my own business and to get dressed. Somebody was sitting there sick and they were worrying about me getting dressed! I told them to fuck the getting dressed, and to get this guy some fresh air. Finally after a few words of Farsi were passed between the two of them, they reached for Al to stand him up. Al's face was as white as this sheet of paper. I think when they saw that, they got kind of worried, but still they had to find something to put over his head, because he had his towel around his waist. So they put his pants over his head, and took him out on the terrace.

Al said he didn't remember walking down the hall, but I guess when the fresh air hit him, he recovered to find about five students surrounding him. He said that Mr. Fix-It brought him out an ice cold drink of grape juice. Meanwhile, I had returned to the room. Santa came in and asked if we knew the cause of Al's illness. We told him that he hadn't been feeling well lately, and that maybe his kidney was acting up. I also told him I thought maybe Al was on a verge of a heart attack, especially after that strenuous workout. I could see that Santa was concerned, so I asked him if it was possible for Al to see a doctor and he replied, "Yes, probably tomorrow."

The students have been coming in and out today asking Al how he's been feeling. Sunshine says there is a doctor coming tomorrow to see him, so it's obvious that they still care a lot for our health. Tonight Beaver even brought me some medicated face conditioner for my

231

acne. Little by little it does seem to be going away, but I still have the scars. Hopefully when I get some sun they'll go away also. Sun! What's that, something to eat?

A lot of book reading being done. Al's just about finished with his painting. The students have been saying that Ali the Cook is really looking forward to getting it. Mine's also just about finished, and Hollywood is looking forward to it, too. Bill made a carving of an Indian out of wax this afternoon. It turned out pretty good, considering all the wax he left all over the floor when he had finished. We all sat around, watching to make sure he picked it all up with the vacuum cleaner, teasing him at the same time about what his next invention/masterpiece is going to be. Earlier in the morning he ripped his sheet up, but I think decided not to do what he was going to do. Every day he comes up with some unbelievable thing.

This morning Santa came in with another picture that Lopez drew. The guy is unbelievable. He's really good. He won't have any problem finding a job once he gets out of here. That guy was born to draw.

The meals really haven't been too bad lately. Tonight for dinner instead of just having soup (beef noodle), we had eggplant and cold roast beef also. That was a change to the menu. This morning one of the students came in and put a bag of coconut on my rack. I guess it was one of the students I'd been asking to get it for us.

This afternoon Al found a recipe for German chocolate cake. Tonight when they were serving dinner, we attached it to the outside of our door with a note telling Ali we wanted a cake like the one that was in the picture. Tonight when Santa came in he brought our recipe. I told him Dick and Bill's birthdays were coming up and that they should cook a cake like the one on the recipe for them. He said that we would celebrate the occasion, but I know we're not going to have German chocolate cake. We've still got the recipe. Maybe we can hit them up for some pastry, though. It's sure nice being in a cell with all these guys having their birthdays soon!

Jerry and Al are playing cards now, Bill's reading and Dick's checking over his moves in backgammon. Al saved me from playing Billy in backgammon tonight. He played instead. Bill said that was the last time he was ever going to ask me. It does seem like every time he asks me I turn him down. There are really two reasons why I don't always like to play. First, I don't really care for the game that much, and second, everytime we play we usually end up in a fight. So instead of getting in an argument, I just don't play.

Signing off for now. This is Rocky Sickmann from the Tehran Hilton saying good night, reminding you to never believe a group of students when they come to *your* embassy saying they only want a sit-

232

in. The only people that would be doing the sitting-in would be the hostages they hold. GOD BLESS AMERICA! *End of entry.*

Thursday, September 4, 1980 (23:00)   Day 306

Our 306th day and our ten month anniversary. The students just finished serving us angel food cake, raisin spice cake, and nuts. That was the students' surprise for our celebration. I really forgot all about it until tonight when they started bringing all the stuff in. Wonder what we're going to have for our one year anniversary? Ali came in and asked us if we like the cake, and we said, "Yes, very much—do you have any more?" He told us if they had any left over after serving everyone else he would bring it back. Well, he hasn't returned. Anyway, it was all delicious, but I think the students got even a bigger kick out of just serving it to us. They love to see us smile.

Al and I just finished beating Billy in backgammon, with everyone around the table watching. I guess the spectators bothered Bill, or maybe it was the dirty table. Anyway, he didn't do as well as he usually does. Now since that's all over Jerry and Al are playing Scribbage, Bill's reading and Dick's practicing his backgammon game. That's about all the excitement around here for tonight.

We all kind of thought that since it was such a big day today we might get some mail. We were wrong about that, and I doubt if we'll even get it tomorrow. Tomorrow would be the day that we were scheduled to get it, but there hasn't been any sound of them going through mail this week, so I guess it'll be a couple more days yet. Santa hasn't been here today, so maybe he's over at the embassy picking up mail and some other things. I wish it was our plane tickets he was getting instead.

Ali just stepped in to see if we liked the cake again, and he was telling us that his birthday is the 20th of September. Al told him that his painting would be finished by then. You can really tell that Ali wants that painting. Everytime he goes over and picks it up it just seems that he gets a big smile on his face. Really good guy that Ali is.

Yesterday morning I was so mad at Beaver I could've knocked him out. It started before breakfast when they brought us some bad butter, so Beaver took that back and brought a different kind. Well, after breakfast I piled all the empty containers of jelly and butter wrappers on the plate and took it to the head to dump away. In the first place, I was really in a pissed-off mood already. I was wishing I would've never woke up, but I did. While I was in the head I dropped Dick's glass mug and broke it on the floor. After I had gotten the glass cleaned up (throwing the glass in the same place I throw the morning
233

trash) I had been in the head for about ten minutes, pissed-off and all. After I had got back to the room, Beaver came in asking how the breakfast was. We said it was good after we had gotten the fresh butter. Then he held up the piece of butter that must've been on the bottom of the plate under the garbage, and asked what it was. I replied, "Butter." Then he asked me why I had thrown it away and gave me a little sermon about wasting food, something I didn't need, especially after waking up and still finding myself here. I was pissed-off to the max, so much I just wanted to get up and knock the shit out of him.

They really have room to talk, after all the things they've thrown away over at the embassy. I remember the first couple months when we were still at the embassy they wouldn't let us have pork because they couldn't have it, and they threw away whole packs of lunch meat just because they couldn't eat it. He's got a lot of nerve to come in and give me a sermon about throwing food away.

After his sermon was finished I told him about the glass I had broken and thrown in the same basket, and not to save that butter because glass might've gotten in it. He said it didn't matter, that they would eat it anyway, and then left. When lunch time came around, they were serving hamburgers so I asked them if we could have some cheese. Butler said no, because I had thrown a piece of cheese away earlier that morning. That really got me pissed-off. For one thing, I didn't mean to throw it away, and for another, it wasn't a piece of cheese but a piece of butter. So I told him to forget it and just get the fuck out.

I guess Beaver changed the whole story around telling all his brothers, making it sound like a federal crime. A little after lunch Sunshine came in, and Al told him about the butter being thrown away accidentally. Sunshine knows we hardly ever throw food away. Anyway, usually whenever we have something left over and want to give it back, the students won't take it. All these small things are starting to get on my nerves. I guess it just goes to show that my patience is running out. This shit's growing old!

Not much of anything else happened yesterday. Last night we went to the T.V. room and saw "Police Woman", a tape that Jerry, Bill and I had already seen but Al and Dick hadn't. So Bill went back to the room, while Jerry and I stayed with Dick and Al. For me it was just to get out of that cell, plus I really didn't mind watching it over anyway.

Today was another one of those depressing days. Read a little and then wanted to work out, but there wasn't any fuel for the hot water heater so I cancelled that until tomorrow. The doctor that was supposed to come see Al hasn't come yet. Sunshine said that he was going to come and do an EKG. Probably forgot about us, just like their Parliament has. I wonder how long it would take for a doctor to get here if someone really needed one? *End of entry.*

Saturday, September 6, 1980 (23:50)   Day 308

Just returned from watching T.V. We saw "Three's Company," "Carter Country," and a few shorts of a car race and baseball. Sunshine said that someone had recently sent them to us. They did seem to be pretty new. The programs were really good, plus Sunshine brought in a box of new books, not brand new, just ones we haven't read yet. So everyone's sitting around reading, except for Jerry. He's playing solitaire.

The rest of the day was pretty much miserable, just like yesterday, up until the time I worked out. That took out all my frustrations, but I still have plenty in me yet! Wanted to take another shower after I was finished, but I guess Bill used up all the fuel when he went in and took his. I took one yesterday, so I guess I really didn't need another one. The fuel runs out pretty quickly, and when it does you have to keep reminding them to get more. You'd think since they have so much over here, they'd never run out. One of the students said that they'd have more tomorrow, though.

Mail was finally passed out tonight. Last week we got it on a Friday; this week we got it on a Saturday, so now probably next week we'll get it on Sunday, except for Jerry. He didn't receive a single letter once again. Why they are doing this to him I'll never understand. At first he was taking it pretty good. (I'm not saying he isn't still.) It's just that you can only go for a certain amount of time, and then after that you start thinking things and your morale drops all of a sudden, and you become really depressed. I know it would be the same with me if everyone I was rooming with was getting mail from their families and I wasn't receiving anything from anyone. What do you do when everyone is sitting around reading mail, and you don't have any? I really feel sorry for Jerry because I know mail means so much to us now. At times I just wish I could trade all my letters and cards in exchange for Jerry having that many.

Anyway, I received about thirteen letters and cards. I'm still receiving birthday cards from July. I was glad to hear that Jill made second runner-up in the Queen Contest, but disappointed I wasn't there. I knew she could do it! Sure wish I could've seen it though. I am so happy for her, and I miss/love that girl so much—Oh God, please take us home. The letter I received from my parents dated August 6 mentioned that they were going to San Francisco to meet

235

with all the other families. Then later on in the letter, written while in San Francisco, they said that Rich Queen was doing time, and after the meeting with the families he was going fishing—something I wish I was going to be doing instead of sitting in this cell. Lucky dog! At least these people did let him go because of his illness. Wonder how much longer it's going to take for the rest of us to be released? Nothing much of anything else in the mail, just wishing we were home, etc.

We've just given up asking the students about the situation. Before, whenever we used to ask about it they'd lie to us anyway, so what's the use? I think they are kind of wondering why we haven't asked, and why we've cut down the chit chat with them. Santa's been playing a little game with us lately. He's been walking up and down the hall to let us know he's there, I guess expecting us (like we used to) to go running to the door and ask for him. Well, that's changed. We don't even ask for him when we need something. Instead we ask Sunshine.

Tonight while we were watching T.V., Santa came in. Everyone maybe nodded to him, but that was about all. I don't think he liked that, so he left. After he had brought us back from the T.V. room, Al asked Santa if he could start to work out once again, but Santa said that the doctor had told him to tell Al not to continue until he'd checked him out. Santa reassured once again that the doctor was still coming, but didn't say when. They're continuing to make sure that we stay in good health. I don't think they care too much about our mental health, so maybe we'll be getting out of here anyway. Cross my fingers on that one.

The weather seems to be getting a little chilly at nights lately. Fall starts this month (Sept. 22), and then soon after that will be winter. Walking back from the head today, being tugged by Bill, I was thinking about how long now we've been doing this shit—walking back and forth from the head with a towel over our heads and a nanny leading us. A whole fucking year it's just about been, and still it continues to drag on.

I read in a magazine tonight that some top White House officials believe Carter will try another raid attempt before election to obtain the Presidency. Like I've said before, I don't really give a fuck. I'm tired of just sitting on my ass and having nothing done. If what it takes is a raid to end this thing, then a raid it is! I know if I go someone goes with me! There's got to be a solution out of this mess somewhere. God, please help us! *End of entry.*

Monday, September 8, 1980 (23:30)   **Day 310**

Just finished playing one of my daily four games of backgammon with Billy. We tied 2-2. Al's playing him now and he isn't doing too well. Jerry's reading while Dick's walking his laps with his orange socks on. When I first saw him put them on this afternoon, I asked him if he was going trick or treating. Ever since then I've been joking him about his socks.

In another hour and a half it's going to be Dick's 51st birthday. I reminded Ali the Cook today about it and he said maybe he'd fix brownies for him. We ran out of chocolate chip cookies, so it looks as though we're not going to have anything to celebrate tonight. Maybe we could still get one of the students to go out and get us some pastries. It seems as though all the hostages are going to have to spend a birthday here, a birthday I doubt any of us will ever forget.

Well, things have been going pretty slow around here lately. Just about all afternoon their president was speaking on the radio. The students played it loud enough for us to hear, plus whoever escorted us to the head was usually carrying a small radio. None of us asked anything other than who was speaking, and the students never said what the speech was about. I guess if they don't want to tell us, we won't ask them. Besides the speaking over the radio this afternoon, the sounds of airplanes (C-130s) and helicopters (Hueys) filled our ears earlier this morning, and then continued on till later this afternoon. Nothing was mentioned by the students about that either. I got this odd feeling that something's up, and hopefully it's for a worthy cause of getting us home.

Tonight I happened to have a small talk with Santa while I was in the head cleaning my clothes. Nothing was mentioned about when he thought this situation would be over. Once again, he didn't mention it so I wasn't going to ask him. Yesterday morning Al was saying that he had a little discussion with Sunshine. Sunshine had supposedly asked why we weren't talking to the students. Al told him that it really wasn't worth talking about when the students tell us one thing and something else happens, or they just lie to us so we'll stop talking about it. Al did ask him what he thought about this situation ending soon, and he replied that he really didn't know, but said that Santa thought it would end before the election (Nov. 4). I ain't going to believe anyone until it is actually done. Just like tonight Santa told me that we might be getting some sunshine tomorrow. Once again, I won't believe it until it is proven to me.

They finally got the toilet fixed today so we all did a small workout on our own. I did 300 sit-ups, 200 push-ups and 100 jumping jacks, then took a nice hot shower and soaked my face in hot water. My face really doesn't seem to be clearing up. Maybe if I get some sun on it, it might help. Sure hope so!

237

Well, Billy lost to Al in backgammon, so now he's up at the table wearing a mask. I guess it's for Dick's birthday, or maybe even for Halloween next month. Bill's mask, Dick's orange socks and a garbage bag and we'll be all set. I'm really hoping we'll be home by then, but if we're not, at least we'll be ready for our own Halloween. I'm really hoping to be home by Thanksgiving. If not, I'm going to be one mad Marine.

Been trying to cut down on the sweets again lately, because it's bad for my face and it's been bothering my teeth. Think of the cavities I'm going to have when I get out of here.

We just finished singing Happy Birthday to Dick and received nuts and Charm Pops from Beaver to celebrate with. One of the highlights of tonight was the birthday card Jim Lopez drew up for Dick, and then attached it to a bag of coconut with a rag tied around it as a ribbon. The card said, "Happy Birthday to a fellow political prisoner." It's a picture of one Iranian presenting Dick a cake, and Dick's standing there shaking with a cane holding him up, trying to blow the candles out. Another Iranian is standing on the other side of him with a fire extinguisher waiting to put the fire out. Then inside the card it says, "Do not give up hope; you are not forgotten (just written off!). Love and kisses XXXO." That Jimmy's got one hell of a sense of humor. Oh yes, besides having the nuts and candy we also had Canada Dry soda. Here's a birthday Dick won't forget for the rest of his life. *End of entry.*

Wednesday, September 10, 1980 (23:10)   Day 312

Our 312th day today. Only two more days till Bill's birthday. We've got it nice this week, with two birthdays in a row. That means more goodies!

The students had me kind of curious yesterday. Instead of watching T.V. after dinner, we went at (17:00) and saw "Lou Grant." It seems like they've got us on a schedule to the point that whenever they don't go by that schedule we start thinking something is up.

Really it's to that point whenever they do anything, and I mean *anything*, I start trying to analyze their actions to see if it's any sign of us getting closer to being released. For example, this morning when I woke for breakfast there were a couple of students outside in the hallway working on the air conditioner/heater, I guess trying to convert it from an air conditioner to a heater. At least that's what I was thinking. They kept turning it off and on. Just thinking, not really knowing, that they were out there switching it to a heater made me think they were getting it ready for winter, meaning we're going to be here that much longer. Well, that spoiled my whole morning, making me even more aggravated with the students. Lately it seems like each morning I just want to knock one of these guys out, and it's getting harder to hold it back.

For dinner last night Ali the Cook had peach pie for Dick's birthday, along with the soup. The pie really tasted good. We're back to the old schedule of soup every other night now. Tonight for dinner we had fried chicken, barbecued potato chips and cheese. It was pretty good, especially after the nice workout I had today, 300 sit-ups, 350 push-ups, and a nice hot shower. I'll sleep good tonight. I guess I really shouldn't be doing so many, though. I keep burning my ass from the rubbing of my underpants. But I doubt if I'll ever quit. It's like I've said before; it takes so much frustration out of me and I need to take it out on something.

Once again today, the radios were on and everyone was listening to them. Hopefully they're talking about us. This shit's really getting old. Al's been coming down with a small cold. I guess we're going to have to pay a little more attention to our health since fall's coming on. Really don't know what to think of this situation. Supposedly the Parliament is working on us. I wish we knew what they're saying. Hope is all we've got left.

There are a bunch of students down the hall making a lot of commotion. Sounds as though they're having a good old time. Boy, how I can't wait to get out of here! Everyone's just about at their usual tonight. Al and Jerry are playing Scribbage, Dick's practicing his backgammon game and Bill's just lying on his mattress, daydreaming, I guess. I'll close for now, go down to the head, then come back and read a little more. Signing off from another two days here at the Tehran Hilton! *End of entry.*

Friday, September 12, 1980 (23:15)   Day 314

Today is Bill's birthday; now he's 22 years old. He didn't have as big a birthday party as I did, although the food Ali cooked today was pretty tasty. For lunch we had little round roast steaks with corn, and then for dinner we had shrimp (which Jerry and Bill cleaned yesterday), onion rings and fried potatoes. Boy, did that shrimp ever taste good—we had about eleven shrimp apiece. Then about (15:00) Beaver and Taco Kid brought Bill a plate with cashews and pistachio nuts, two containers of Faladay, a candle on top the pistachio can and a birthday card signed, "The students following Imam." Then right before dinner, Beaver, who's in charge of the music, brought us a tape recorder with some run down batteries, so we've been switching the

239

batteries we've had in the room here with the ones inside. Getting by like that.

Just awhile ago Four Eyes brought in our mail, and everyone received letters from home, even Jerry. Not much was really said, except for the fact that some of them confirmed that they had received our letters we had written August 4. So they were happy to hear from us. Received nothing from my family, but did receive a letter from Jill's parents and family. They all assured me that Jill was still waiting, and they were hoping I still had the same feeling. If only I could show them how much I cared! That letter was worthwhile. I still haven't heard anything from Jill since July 23. Wonder if she still has the same feelings now, after the Fair and all? I truly miss and love that girl, but if things must change there is a reason for it. There isn't much I could say being over here anyway. Otherwise it seems like everything's going well back home. Can't wait till next Friday when they give us more.

Last night was T.V. night, and we got to see two parts of "Salvage One" while eating dates for refreshments. I guess it's starting to be the season for them. The ones we had last night weren't too bad.

Not too many exciting things have been happening around here. We were supposed to go outside the other day, Santa had said. But nothing came of it. It all goes back to what I've said before; you can't believe anything these people say until you actually see it. When some of the students talk about this situation they try to lead us on by telling us that we will be going home soon, like Taco Kid was telling Jerry the other night. He actually came out and told Jerry that we'd be going home soon. How many times have they said that in the previous months? Then again it might be true, but I won't believe it until I see it. I really can't picture us walking out of here. The next date I'm shooting for is September 30. If not that one, like all the other times, I'll just continue shooting for another day. Closing for now! *End of entry.*

Monday, September 15, 1980 (23:50)   Day 317

Just about ready to wrap up another miserable day, and I do have to say this one was miserable. I woke this morning at breakfast with a runny nose, and here I am closing the day with a sore throat and hot and cold chills, in addition to the runny nose I started with. I guess the walking-around-without-a-shirt weather has come to an end. In fact this morning Al had to give me his blanket since I was feeling so cold. They finally brought him another one tonight, so now I guess we're all ready for winter. It seems like my cold's getting worse. I guess I should start wearing my socks, too, like Dick does when he walks.

I wasn't the only one who felt miserable today. Hardly anyone had a conversation with anyone else. The only words that were spoken were phrases like, "Pass the salt," "How are you feeling?", "Not bad!", "May I go to the toilet?", etc. Just little things like that. We've all been pretty much to ourselves these past three days, reading once in a while, Jerry and Al playing Scribbage or Bill and I playing backgammon, but otherwise we've all been in our own little dreamland, sitting on our mattresses. I know I don't have to mention what we were sitting there dreaming of.

Wonder what the problem is with the video? The last time we saw it was last Thursday night, and it seems like ever since then the students haven't been taking anyone in there to watch programs. When we were in there Thursday night they had taken down the pictures some hostages had drawn, criticizing various things like mail service, etc. I guess they can't accept the truth. They really haven't said why we weren't watching T.V., but I would guess it's because of all the criticizing pictures. So here we sit in our cells, trying to find things just to keep us busy. The students have really been acting strange lately. I guess they were feeling that we were getting a little out of hand, so they had to start showing who was still boss.

I haven't worked out for the last three days because of my sore shoulder and sore ass, so my frustration is really starting to boil inside of me. Maybe they're finally starting to realize that they're doing no good by keeping us here any longer so they're going to start taking it out on us. Surely they should know that they're not getting the Shah back. But maybe they can't accept that. I don't know what I'm going to do if the days continue to drag on like today did, especially feeling as miserable as I felt.

Well, I just took my socks out of summer storage, patched up a couple holes in one pair, and took the other pair down to wash. Boy, were they ever dirty. I guess you can say I'm all ready for winter, so let it come. *End of entry.*

Thursday, September 18, 1980 (01:00)   Day 320

Just wrapped up another day. Here we are going on our 320th day and still no word. Just got finished wasting a couple hours with Bill by playing backgammon, and now he's eating the leftover Spam we had from dinner last night. Al's playing solitaire, and Dick and Jerry are reading. Everyone's kept pretty much to themselves these past couple days again.

Al's kidney has been bothering him this last week pretty badly. He's asked Santa if he could get some pain killers from the doctor, but hasn't received them yet. In fact, it was at the same time that I asked Santa for some Vicks, too. Tonight shortly after dinner he came in without speaking to anyone, put the bottle of Vicks on the table and left. He did about the same thing yesterday, when he opened the door and threw a *Sporting News* on the table and left, also without saying a word.

We've been wondering if the way the students have been acting has anything to do with the other night when we heard Santa having an argument with another hostage. . Really couldn't understand what they were arguing about, but it did sound like it got out of hand. Although we haven't heard anything since, Sunshine hasn't been around this week either. I'm thinking maybe that's why we haven't seen T.V., because Sunshine hasn't been around. There's really been a change of attitude on the students' part. They've been acting really tough. I guess they thought we were getting out of hand and they had to show us who was still running the show. They're probably starting to get tired of all this, too, and beginning to realize they aren't gaining anything from keeping us here.

I wonder if the way they're acting has anything to do with something they might have heard, like Parliament telling the people they have no chance of getting their demands and that the hostages must be released. Just by the way they're acting, it really seems as if they have been let down and are starting to take their frustration out on us. Some of us still have our hopes of getting out of here by November 4th, still thinking that the election might have some effect towards our release. Never know what these people are thinking.

The temperature seems to be dropping every once in a while, getting a little chilly. We've finally turned off our fan, but the air conditioner out in the hallway still seems to be running. It keeps the air circulating pretty well. Everyone seems to be coming down with runny noses/colds. Not as bad as mine, though, at least not yet. That Vicks that Santa brought is really doing the job for my nose. Hopefully it will improve.

My face is breaking out again, so this afternoon I had to take a shower. My hair was really getting greasy, and I think that's what starts my face breaking out. I guess I won't ever get the right medication for it until I get out of this hole in the wall. Otherwise there really isn't anything to talk about. Everyone keeps continuing to try to analyze everything out, but it's really no use. It seems like these people don't even know what they want. *End of entry.*

Here we are just sitting around the room shooting the shit. Al's working on Ali's painting which he hopes to give him tomorrow for his birthday. Dick's walking his laps across the room, while Jerry and Bill are lying on their mattresses daydreaming. Lights just went out, so I know in just a couple more hours I'll be turning in also.

Well, yesterday was supposed to be our day for mail, but like we predicted from the way the students have been acting, we didn't get any. I guess they're waiting for us to beg them for it.

It seems the videotape machine was out of order after all. Last night a little bit after dinner Santa came in to ask Al if maybe he could fix it. The problem was that the tape wouldn't eject, so Al told them how it could be fixed. A little while later we heard the machine being played, and we think they got it working. Maybe tomorrow they'll start showing shows again. It's not that we really need it; it's just that it's a change of routine and it's something nice to look at.

Right before dinner last night Porky Pine came in and took us to the T.V. room, where we were able to choose two new books each to take back to the room. After being here for 322 days it's about time we got new books.

The morning of the 18th we were awakened by a thunder of noise coming from the top and lower floors. Whistling, slamming doors, yelling, etc. It was really kind of nerve-racking but that no doubt is what the students had in mind. I guess they didn't have anything else to do at the time and decided to do that. Right after they had finished, some of them hopped into their cars and on their motorcycles and left. Anything they can find to pass the hours of the day with.

Yesterday morning Mr. Fix-It came in and asked if any of us needed blankets. Al told him we didn't need any blankets, but mentioned that he needed some medication for his kidneys and also asked if he could get a water bottle. So last night right after dinner Mr. Fix-It brought in the hot water bottle, all heated up. Al said the bottle really relieved a lot of pain, and just a minute ago he asked Santa if he could refill the bottle with hot water since we haven't had any fuel for the water heater, but Santa said to wait till tomorrow. Service is really dropping around here.

In a way the days seem to be dragging by, and then again they seem to be flying. A week and a half left to this month and then we're off on October, and then the elections (Nov. 4). Then after the elections is Thanksgiving, and so on. I'm really going to hate to see what this place is going to be like if we're still here for those occasions. I pray to God we're not still here.

Well, my cold's improving a little, still have a runny nose along with a couple other hostages down the hallway. Every once in a while you can hear some of them sneezing and blowing their noses. Hopefully everyone's all right. *End of entry.*

Sunday, September 21, 1980 (23:50)   Day 323

Three hundred twenty-third day. I really don't feel like writing tonight, headache and all, but I figured what else is there to do besides read? I just got finished playing Bill in chess (I won), which we haven't played for a while, and then even played backgammon following the chess game. To me that's too much excitement in one day. Anyway, there really wasn't too much more to do, so I just decided to write down a few things (notice how I say few?) from the past two days.

I'll start from the 20th (yesterday) which seemed to be the only day anything exciting happened. It wasn't only exciting, but good physically and mentally, and also worthwhile. We went outside for fifteen minutes of sunshine. As of yesterday, the 20th of September, it had been *three months* since the last time we went out. They even brought us orange juice while we stood out there collecting the rays. We still had our two bodyguards standing watch within ten feet of each side of us. Al and I went out first, and then Dick and Jerry went. Bill said he didn't want to play their stupid games, which is probably true. I know if they were really concerned about our health, shit, we'd be going out every week at least. Three months to wait for sunshine is ridiculous.

It really surprised us that we even got to go outside. It's been ten days since we've received any mail or watched T.V. Yesterday when Bill and I were in there collecting books, the video machine was all set up and the power was on, but we haven't heard anyone being taken in to watch. I wonder what their excuse is about that. We still haven't received oil for the hot water boiler. I don't know how many days it's been since we last had a hot shower. Each day we keep reminding them about it, and they keep replying, "Tomorrow, tomorrow." Well, the next day comes and we still don't have any fuel.

Today I just got tired of waiting, plus my hair was really getting greasy and my face was breaking out really bad. So I went down after lunch and washed my hair in the sink. It seemed like the person who used the head before me had taken a shower. I know just by the sound of a lot of people coughing and sneezing that there are a lot of colds around, and if everyone's going to start taking cold showers just to stay clean they're going to end up with more than just a cold.

244

My cold seems to be breaking apart. Still have the runny nose, though. Jerry didn't sound too good this afternoon. He has about the same symptoms I had at the beginning of my cold. It looks like it's going to hit everyone right on down the line, especially now that it's been getting chilly. Al's continuing to use the water bottle that was given to him the other night. He says it really helps him sleep at night a lot better than before. The doctor still hasn't come to see him, but then Al's been telling them he doesn't really need one, so I guess the students just called it off.

They were taking pictures yesterday afternoon. Took one of Al returning from the head, taking his towel off, walking through the door. A little while later we asked Sunshine (who had supposedly just returned from one of the small villages) what all the pictures were for. He replied that they were taking them of the place we're living in, and then said to keep our room clean because they were going to come in and take some of our room. Well I'd just like to see them try. They can shove that camera up their *uterus. End of entry.*

Wednesday, September 24, 1980 (10:00)   Day 326

Three hundred twenty-sixth day. Thought I'd sit down here at the kitchen table/card table/drawing table/workbench and jot down a few things before they bring me my hot water I asked for to soak my face with. Now if they had oil for the hot water heater, I probably wouldn't have to continue to ask them for hot water to soak my mug, my scarred up mug at that. Beaver is the person in charge of medication, and this morning I was pleading/begging with him to get me either penicillin or any other antibiotic that would work against a virus infection. My face is continuing to swell with small sores, and I've been trying to tell these guys for the past ten months that I think it's more than just acne. Hopefully Beaver will get the penicillin.

(11:15) Just returned from the head, where I was washing the breakfast dishes, brushing my teeth and rinsing my face after using the hot water Beaver brought me. The soaking with hot water seems to help a little. I asked Beaver about the medicine again, and he said maybe by tomorrow or the next day.

Down in the head for the last three or four mornings we can hear them playing football (Iranian soccer), yelling and screaming. I really feel sorry for the guys living on the other side of the hallway where they get all the noise.

Anyway, English Student was on head duty, and when he came down to bring me back to the room we happened to get on the subject of going home. I told him we weren't ever going home, and that

245

home really wasn't important anymore, because this was our new home. He really started to get upset when I said that, and replied that "he didn't want to talk about the matter," but said that I was wrong thinking like that. Then I told him that maybe within two more years we might get out of here. He came back with a look like I was crazy thinking such a thought. From that little encounter with him this morning, I get the impression that they still believe we'll be going home pretty soon.

Yesterday we were sitting around the room talking about the planes (cargo and fighters) flying over. The only thing we came up with was that either they're sending supplies to Afghanistan or that there was strong fighting with the Kurds/Iraq. Whoever they're fighting is really keeping Iran busy. Two days ago was the day we heard the cargo planes and fighters flying over. Quite a few as a matter of fact. The sounds of planes are still heard frequently. Not so much cargo as fighters. Really makes you wonder what's going on out there. It's a bitch being held by the Iranians, but I can imagine having another country come in and take over Tehran and then be held hostage by them, too. That would be our luck. If there is fighting going on it seems like we're right in the middle of it all.

Something else we were thinking of yesterday and that is if Iran is fighting another country and fighting them with the American weapons that were leftover from the Shah's regime, they're going to need parts to keep those things running. The only way to get the parts they need is to buy them from the manufacturer, which is the U.S.A. No doubt the U.S.A. isn't going to make any agreements with this country until we're released. Also if there is a war going and the U.S.A. and Europe still have that boycott in effect, that's really going to hurt them. Maybe we still have a chance of being home before November. That is, of course, if Iran is desperate for parts (war items), and willing to make an agreement with the U.S.A. Supposedly the Parliament is discussing us, and November is still in my dreams.

Something else that started two nights ago (really doubt if it has anything to do with the fighting) is that they've started to turn the electricity off at (20:00) till the next morning. The first night we thought it was only a power failure, but when it happened last night at the same time we asked Beaver about it. He replied that they were working on the power plant the last two nights, and supposedly tonight it isn't going to happen again. We'll wait and see. The funny thing about the whole thing is that we're only allowed to have one candle, which they've been issuing right after the lights go out. Last night we asked Beaver if we could possibly "please" have one more,

246

because we usually didn't go to sleep till (04:00) in the morning and here they are turning lights off at (20:00). The candle they issue us lasts about three hours, and then what are we to do when our bodies aren't used to sleep for another four or five hours?

Luckily we had a couple of small candles still lying around which have been helping keep light for us. Still with just the two (one large, one small) candles they issue, we manage to keep them lit for about eight hours with the help of the remaining wax from the night before. So once the lights go off, everything has to be done by candlelight. There's even enough light for Dick to walk his six miles. Really curious to see if they're going to go off tonight, too.

We were thinking last night that they might just be trying to change our routine. They've taken our mail and video privileges away from us, the oil is gone again so we'll probably have to wait till next week to shower, and so now since they don't have anything else to fuck with, they're going to fuck with our daily routine. The only thing we can do is just play along with the ballgame.

Ali finally received his painting from Al yesterday, along with Bill's painting of a birthday cake. I guess to show his thanks he knew that Jerry had a cold so he asked us what we thought was good for a cold. We told him chicken soup and juices. So a little while later while we were sitting on our mattresses smoking cigars, Ali comes in with a bucket of grapefruit juice. Then about ten minutes before the regular beef noodle soup, olives and cheese were served, Ali brought Jerry a pot of chicken noodle soup. The guy is 100% considerate.

They finally brought oil the 22nd, so the washroom was busy practically the whole day with people taking showers, including the Iranians. By the next morning the oil was all gone, so now once again here we sit without any oil until we don't know when. I guess they got teed off because we were taking showers every second day. Using too much oil I guess. I did a workout the day we took showers, but only did 200 sit-ups and 200 push-ups. It had been seven days since the last time I had worked out, so I'm not that discouraged. I'm not going to work out if there isn't any water to take showers with, that's for damn sure.

The weather's really been getting weird lately. A lot of clouds starting to gather like rain or maybe even snow. *End of entry.*

Friday September 26, 1980 (6:35)   Day 328

Three hundred twenty-eighth day today and we're still sitting on our rear ends. Tehran has been awfully busy this past week. Within the past half an hour Huey's have been flying over with 105's hung from the undercarriage, moving towards the east. Last night around (20:00) we heard, in the far distance, something that sounded like artillery fire. It was well loud enough for everyone in the building to have heard. We think now that the story about the power plant being worked on is a crock of shit. We're starting to think it's really a blackout against air attacks. There's always the sound of fighters flying over during the day, and even early in the mornings. We know they're not just up there for the hell of it, because they really don't have the parts to spare. *This country is under attack from someone!*

This morning when Ali took me to the head I asked him about the explosions, and he replied that we weren't supposed to worry because it didn't involve the hostage situation. Sometimes I really wonder about that. They seem to be turning the lights out each night an hour earlier than the night before, so that's why I'm writing now before the lights go out. They're really starting to get stingy with the candles. Last night and the night before we were only issued one, but luckily we had part of one left over from the previous night to burn before we burned the new one. Last night they came in and asked if we had any candle left from the night before, and we told them no. Probably if we would've said yes, they wouldn't have given us any. We fooled them though and said no, so we got a 6" to 7" candle. From that we have about an inch and a half left to burn, so definitely we'll need another one tonight.

Ali really surprised us yesterday morning when he came in right after breakfast and asked if we would like to watch T.V. Right away we said yes. It had been about sixteen days since the last time we watched, so I guess they figured it was about time. We've been hearing them take a couple of the other rooms down the hallway today, so we're not the only ones getting to watch it. That cancelled Dick's prediction of receiving mail yesterday—hardly ever do we get two treats in one day. But I guess yesterday was an exception. We got T.V. in the morning, orange juice for lunch, and a choice between two different kinds of soup for dinner (beef noodle or shrimp). Starting to spoil us!

We got a little laugh when Ali the Cook was out in the hallway before dinner giving the student that was on duty (Smiley) an English lesson on what to ask us when he came around to pick up the bowls. Ali would say to the student, "Ask them if they want beef noodle or shrimp soup," and the student would repeat what Ali said. Finally we interrupted Ali, because the electricity was off making it impossible for us not to hear them. We just yelled through the door that we would take two shrimp and three beef noodle. We really got a laugh out of that one.

Starting to adapt to our new routine little by little. Instead of going back to sleep after breakfast, we try to stay awake so it will be easier to fall asleep at night. This morning Al and I stayed up till about (03:00) reading by candlelight. Everyone else crashed around (01:30) or so. At least we're improving from our normal bedtime, (04:00). There's really not much you can do for nine hours with a candle except ruin your eyes reading under candlelight. Although I don't think my eyes can get anymore fucked up than they already are. I've given up on asking them for my glasses. I'm tired of asking these people for anything. They'll pay for what they have done.

It's starting to look as though my prediction was right about only receiving oil for the hot water heater once a week. It should be within the next two or three days that they'll bring some, and then after that we'll have to wait until next week. Jerry wasn't too lucky last week and missed out on taking one. No doubt he won't miss this weekend.

The students have really been glued to their radios lately. Wonder what the main discussion is. Neither Sunshine or Santa come in to talk to us anymore—giving us the old silent treatment. Forgot to mention that the other day Plow Boy came in and collected Bill and Dick's glass mugs, and in return gave them two plastic ones. Either someone's tried to commit suicide or they're getting scared that someone's going to take their life. Yet they still let us keep the glass "Listerine" bottle and the two coffee jars.

They have been treating us a little strict lately. No mail, showers once a week, no more talking going down the hall to the head. Wonder what they're so paranoid about. Maybe they're starting to get scared that Carter is going to come over here within the next month to try to rescue us. Maybe all this military action they've been taking is to prepare against that. But then again, maybe they are under attack from another country. Anything is possible over here.

Wonder when we're going to receive mail next. They're all bastards for holding it in the first place, and then telling the priest at Easter it was the United States holding it. Well, the light just went off and then came back on again, so we guess it's a sign to expect the cutoff coming. Signing off for now. Expecting another dark and quiet night. Boy, how I wish I was home!! *End of entry.*

Monday, September 29, 1980 (00:30)   Day 331

Our 331st day, and we don't really know what to think after the last seven of them, especially last night's air raid siren, artillery and anti-air fire which seemed to be going on right over our heads. From the sound of a couple of those artillery guns, I'd say that they were within three to four blocks of us. Just heard a couple more shots of artillery, and then heard the explosions. Pretty far off in the distance now, though. We really don't know what to think anymore, but I guess that's the way these people want it. They enjoy leaving us in terror. You ask some of the students about it and they say not to worry, that it doesn't involve the hostage situation, and then you ask another student and he denies ever even hearing the explosions. Then they wonder why we don't believe them.

Yesterday (the day before yesterday, the 27th) I heard a story from Plow Boy which, like always, we don't really know if we can believe. I asked him if there was any new news and he told me the Parliament had said last week to the people that they have started talking about the hostage situation. Jill wrote to me in July that the Parliament would begin discussing us in September. If what Plow Boy said was the truth, Jill must've gotten her information from a pretty reliable source. That news of Plow Boy's is the only good news we have— that's if you want to believe it. But the way things have been going around here these past seven days, you'll want to believe anything that sounds good. Anything to give us hope and keep us going!

I also had a short talk with Beaver yesterday morning in the head. It seems like they feel freer to talk with only one person. Anyway, he gave me the feeling that someone might be coming here to brief us on our standings, etc. I was telling him how they seem to be treating us like animals, keeping us locked up, feeding us three times a day, but never saying anything of our situation and what was going on out in the streets of Tehran. He came back with a thing about how it wasn't his duty to give us all this information, and then said someone will be coming to explain everything to us. We'll just have to wait and see if that's true or not. I do know there are a lot of curious people here who wish they knew what was becoming of their lives.

Beaver also said that the student doctor was coming to see us within the next two days, and I should ask him about the antibiotic for my acne. If the doctor does come, that'll be a good sign. While the Parliament is working to find a solution to this, they should want to make sure that we're all in good health. The one year mark is approaching, and it's going to make them look bad if they're still holding hostages. Even they've said themselves that there are innocent people here. (I say we're all innocent.) They can't continue to keep us in the dark if they believe so much in human rights, or else they're going to end up just like the Shah.

Speaking of darkness, yesterday was really miserable. Woke for breakfast, which was served at (08:00), and stayed up till about

(11:00) when the lights went off and didn't come back on until (15:00). Well, by then I was too tired to stay awake any longer (we hadn't gone to bed that morning till 03:30) so I crashed out. I finally woke at (18:00). Five minutes later the lights went off. Then, starting at (18:55), the fireworks began. As we looked through screened/barred windows from our dark room (they came in and told us to blow our candles out) we could see the fireworks flying overhead, it seemed like. We could see reflections of explosions on the side of one of the buildings—it seemed to exploding in the southwest of Tehran.

Like always when the fun starts happening, they keep us in our rooms until it's all over, no matter how bad you have to go to the head. I guess they're scared we're going to flip out on them while they're walking us down to the head with all the firing going on outside. We notice whenever someone comes on duty, they close and lock the huge doors that lead to the outside, so I guess they figure they can lose one student while he's inside with us. Lately it seems like they've really been paranoid, really playing it cautious. They've also been keeping their radios plugged into their ears. I hope they get some king of ear disease from having it plugged into each others ears so much. We don't really know if something is happening of if that's just what they want us to think when we see them listening to it. I pray that something is being said about us.

Yesterday morning Sunshine came in and asked if we needed any winter clothing. When things like that are said, you really get discouraged. I really hate to think what my family and Jill are going through. Especially if this country is planning to go to war with another country. What this country plans to gain by keeping us here any longer I'll never know, I guess.

When I was talking to Beaver yesterday we got on the subject of the Shah. It was strange even hearing that name. The students haven't mentioned him at all lately. At the beginning of this situation that's all we heard about, and now you hardly hear the name mentioned. Anyway, something's up about the Shah. Beaver, with his big smile, asked me what I knew about him. Like something has happened that we don't know about. So I asked him what he thought Shah thought about all this and he replied, "He's probably laughing at us."

Still no mail (they've said they haven't received any yet) and the same goes for oil too. With so much oil here in Iran, they can't even go out and get two gallons for a hot water heater! That's what I really call sad! This country really seems to have its problems. The worst of it is though, we're right in the fucking middle of it. *End of entry.*

What a day it was today when we read in *The Sporting News* a comment about CBS interrupting a golf game to run a live coverage (half-hour) on the "Death of the Shah". He supposedly died on July 27, a day after my birthday. What a shocker it was to read that! I really wonder where that leaves us. If he died July 27, it's September now and what are we still doing here?

When Al and I were down in the head this afternoon we made a little comment about it to Sunshine, who denied the Shah's death and then asked where we got the information. So we showed him *The Sporting News* with the article, but still he denied it. It was really funny to see his face when we told him about the Shah being dead. What an expression!

What Plow Boy told me the other day about the Parliament beginning to talk about us last week was probably true, because Sunshine just gave us the same news. We asked Sunshine when he thought they would finish discussing the problem, and he replied that he really didn't know. He said maybe by Christmas or even earlier, because the Parliament has many other problems within the country to discuss. That really makes sense. I just hope we're home before Thanksgiving—how great that would be. To me it was really a morale booster to hear what he said. I just hope it's the truth. We also commented on the fireworks, asking if there were going to be more tonight but he said that he really didn't know.

The lights went off late this morning just as they did yesterday morning. After breakfast, though, they came in and asked us if we wanted to watch television, and of course we said yes. Bill was sleeping, so just Jerry, Dick, Al and I went. We watched "Three's Company" and "WKRP in Cincinnati". I always enjoy watching those two.

After we came back to the room at about (11:00) they turned the lights out. I slept for about an hour and then woke to go down to take a cold shower. The last one we had was last Monday, and I couldn't stand it any longer so I took a freezing cold shower. I do have to say it sure does feel good to be clean.

It would really be nice if the lights didn't go out tonight. The lights just came on, but now everyone is sound asleep except Jerry and me. Jerry's walking his laps to pass the time. Hopefully the longer I stay up now, the earlier I go to bed tonight. Cross my fingers on that. Signing off for now. How I pray to God that this all comes to an end soon. *End of entry.*

Three hundred thirty-fourth day. Here we are starting on another month, hoping it will be our last one. The only thing we can do is hope and pray for our release. The last time I wrote was September 29. Not too much has been happening, and I've spent most of my time daydreaming about all of the things that took place last year at this time (Sept. 29, 30 & Oct. 1, 1979). Those were the three days Jill, my parents and aunt and uncle came to Quantico, Virginia for my graduation ceremonies from MSG school. The last couple of days I've been thinking of those last three days I had with them all, and especially of my time with Jill. A beautiful weekend I spent with her, but still at that time I had a slight feeling that I wasn't ever going to see her again. It wasn't what I wanted, but that was the feeling I had at the time.

We received mail last night, everyone receiving something except for Al. I got one letter from my parents, two from my sister, one from my aunt and uncle, and three Red Cross messages. Still nothing from Jill. The last I heard from her was July 22, before the queen contest. My sister Debbie sent a few pictures, including one of the runners-up and queen of the Fair. Jill definitely looked beautiful. Really makes me wish I was out of here. No doubt she's being well taken care of. Besides the picture of Jill, I received some more of my little niece and two little nephews. Boy, how they're growing. How I can't wait to get out of here. Oh, God, please let it be true!

Sunshine just brought my medicine that was prescribed by the student doctor, who was here yesterday to see Al about his kidneys and me for my acne. Hopefully the medicine I received (Tetrex, 250 mg) will help a little. The stuff is really getting irritating. At least it shows that they're still strongly concerned about our physical and mental well-being. The night before last they even got fuel for the hot water heater so that we were able to take a hot shower, and filled it back up again this morning, too. The night they got fuel it seemed like they wanted to get everyone all in that night. We went in by two at first and three the second time. The head was kept busy all that night by people taking showers, I guess so that we were all clean for when the doc came. Since they filled it up again this morning (for the students, probably), I'm going to do a nice hard workout and then take another shower, making it a total of two showers in two days. Wow!

Yesterday morning right after breakfast Little Ali took us in to watch "Charlie's Angels." Meanwhile the doctor came, so we put the tape on pause until we came back, which took about ten minutes. We went back to finish watching the tape when all of a sudden the electricity went off, and we had to return to our room. Then they served us our lunch, and right after we ate, the power came back on so we went back in to watch T.V. It seems like they're getting back on the schedule of letting us watch it once every week again. Maybe the same will go for the mail, too. All this excitement at once is starting to get to me!

The lights haven't been too much of a problem lately. Every once in a while like yesterday and this morning they flicker off and on, but every night so far they've kept a schedule of turning the lights off around (18:30) or (19:00). You can tell that they're trying to get us back into the normal routine of sleeping at night and staying awake during the day. They still continue to give only one candle a night, but usually we have a little leftover from the previous night so we try to make them last as long as possible. Whenever we ask them for another candle they insist that it's getting too late and that we should go to bed, but they usually give in and let us have another one anyway.

Sunshine just brought in a few pillows that everyone's been asking for. They've been using their blankets for one, but now that the weather's been getting chilly they need the blanket to cover up. last night it was lightning and raining for a short time—typical fall weather. If we're going to be here for the winter I sure hope they start putting windows into the head, and do something about the broken windows in our room also. At times we really get a nice cool breeze coming in, but the weather's been pretty much partly cloudy. It's getting close to winter again. I'm going to really hate it if we're still here during the winter, especially at Thanksgiving and Christmas time. But supposedly the Parliament is working on our situation, and most of the students feel that we'll be home a lot earlier than Christmas. How I pray they're right.

Five days after today it's going to have been one year since I first got here. My one year anniversary! Not much going on now. We're all just sitting around going through our mail (except Al), re-reading everything, making sure we didn't miss anything. They're still taking people in to watch television, so it seems like everyone is getting the run of things.

Talking about changing our routine, they've started to feed us breakfast every morning now at (08:00), consisting of bread, butter, jelly and tea with our daily vitamins. Lunch and dinner are served around the normal hour. Dinner is still soup every other night, but last night we had baked chicken, dates, potato chips and bread. I do have to say, the food really hasn't been that bad. I've gained a kilo since the last time I weighed myself. I'll hate to see what happens when I get out of here and start eating at home once again.

Well, things seem to be looking up for us lately. I know I've been wrong before (a lot of times) but I've got a strong feeling that something might happen within this month yet. How I hope to God I'm right. *End of entry.*

Saturday, October 4, 1980 (8:30)   Day 336

Three hundred thirty-sixth day, 48th week, 11th month. Maybe we'll get some more goodies today like we got on our nine and ten month anniversaries. I'm really looking forward to seeing what we get for our one year anniversary in 31 days. Al reminded Sunshine about today's holiday this morning when he was serving breakfast, so we might have some kind of goodies.

I finally gave Hollywood his painting I made for him this morning. He looked as though he was really happy and privileged to receive it. He's always been a pretty good guy, never giving us any kind of shit so it was just a little something to thank him for his kindness.

Beaver brought us music last night so we're listening to as much as we can. Jerry had a long talk with Beaver last night in the head when he went to wash the dinner dishes. Beaver was saying that the situation could be solved any day now since they've been working on it so long. Most of the things he told Jerry they've been saying for such a long time now, but still nothing happens about our release. They're still claiming it's our government they're mad at, not us. But we're still held here and for what reason? Because we're Americans! That's the price you've got to pay to be one of the best.

While Ali was cutting Al's hair yesterday, he kept bringing up the subject about when you go home you will do this and you will do that. At least they're still hinting that this thing will have a happy ending, but when is it going to happen? Lately when you ask a student that question, it seems like they bring up Christmas every time. "With God's will, before Christmas." So my feelings are really strong that we'll get out of here by then. I sure wish it could be before Thanksgiving though, but then we can't have everything. They've really kept close to their radios, and at times you can hear what sounds like someone giving a speech. It seems like they might be talking about us so maybe we're not forgotten yet.

We started playing cards last night again. Been a long time since we last played, but one game was enough for Dick and me after losing to Al and Bill. After playing our game of cards, we played a little backgammon before crashing out. I think everyone's gotten used to our new routine. Lights out at (19:00), do what you want till (24:00),

255

which is about the time everyone crashes out now. Wake in the morning at (08:00) for breakfast, and then stay up the rest of the day. By midnight I'm pretty tuckered out and fall asleep fast. Sometimes we sleep a little later, until (11:00) or around then. But that's rare.

A little incident happened the other day when Jerry needed to go to the head, knocked on the door and supposedly Santa Claus said to wait, but no one heard him so Jerry knocked again. Well, Santa came down all pissed off and asked who knocked on the door, and Bill said he did, although he had been sitting back in his corner. We tried telling Santa that we didn't hear him, but he said that was no excuse and told Bill that he couldn't go to the toilet for another four hours. Well, when Jerry went down to the toilet he explained to Santa what really happened. When Santa came back to the room Al tried telling him that nothing was ever said about rules for knocking on the door, so how could they punish us when the rule didn't even exist? Santa said that wasn't the problem anymore, but that it was lying (like they've never done it before), so after a few sentences were shot back and forth, Santa laughed at Bill and left. Small things have been getting on people's nerves. Some people have just been letting them fly by, while other people let things like that bother them. The biggest thing I've got to accomplish while I'm here is keeping my cool. If I can keep my cool, I can keep my sanity. I've got that strong feeling an end is going to come soon.

Well, they've really been putting the food on us lately. Don't really know if it's a good sign or bad, but we've really been getting fed. Last night with our soup we had a plate of sliced carrots along with that heavy bread they've been giving us instead of that skinny stuff. It should be about time for some more of Ali's pasta so I'm looking forward to that, along with mail call in another four days.

Just returned from the head and noticed that they filled the fuel container for the hot water heater, so that means I'll be able to work out today and then take a shower. How strange things have been happening around here. Last week we went seven full days without taking a shower, and now this week they've filled the tank up every time it's gone dry. One week things seem to go against us and then the next week things seem to be all for us. I'd say that something was up!! *End of entry.*

Monday, October 6, 1980 (10:00)   Day 338

Three hundred thirty-eighth day, and the news from the students is that they "think" that within 2-4 weeks the Parliament might come to a conclusion. Of course that's what they think, but it's not just been one student that's said that. At least the Parliament must be talking about us a couple hours each week, once again matching each student's story. The two week estimation from the students is just a guess to them, but to me it's a big morale booster. Now I just hope it's true!

There still seem to be a lot of difficulties about our situation. Supposedly the Shah is dead, but some of the students claim that they just made it seem that way and that really he's still alive. And they say Iran is asking four things from the United States. The only one I know of so far is the money. Another one could possibly still be the Shah, but the other demands are unknown to us. What they've been saying most frequently is that the Parliament will decide for all of us and that they think it will be soon. I hope and pray they're right.

Well, yesterday the students passed around some goodies for us for our anniversary. Cookies, a piece of pastry and a pack of Life Savers. All these signs of good treatment could mean nothing more than the fact that they still expect us to go home, and want us to go home with good reports. Just by the way they've been treating us I know there's bound to be an end to this situation. It's really hard to believe sometimes, but my hope is still strong.

The lights are still being kept off at nights with the exception of candles, but last night a couple of times they came in and asked us to please blow our candles out. The only explanation we seem to get for these occurrences is that they're practicing, practicing for what they won't say. This week it will have been two weeks since they started all of this. How much longer is it to go on?

Everyone's pretty much gotten settled in on the new routine, waking at (08:00) and staying up the rest of the day, taking a nap every once in a while. But otherwise everyone's usually crashed out by (01:00), and then we wake for breakfast to start the day out when we have the advantage of the lights being on. Everyone's just sitting around now reading, trying to stay busy while in the background we can hear them playing soccer, laughing and yelling, having a good old time. Boy, how I can't wait to get out of here to become free again. What a change it's going to be.

Santa and Sunshine—not so much Sunshine as Santa—have been staying away from us as much as possible lately, but still everything continues to go well. Still three meals a day, watching video a little more often, and hopefully mail call this Wednesday just like last Wednesday, but this time maybe Al will get some mail. Why they held his the last time I'll never know. Well, the only thing we're riding on is hope and so hopefully our hoping and praying will pay off—for everyone! *End of entry.*

Three hundred fortieth day. One year ago last night (October 7, 1979 - 20:00) was when I first arrived in Tehran. If this wouldn't have happened, I would probably be heading to my new post about this time, but anyway this happened so here I'm still sitting. Only 27 more days till our one year anniversary, and since the talk from Santa last night our hope and morale have really increased. It was the first time in a long time that he's come in to talk to us, but what he said was truly encouraging. Twice he mentioned the fact that one year wasn't up yet, like he was trying to tell us that a solution was going to be found by November 4. Now if he was just coming in to boost our morale by lying, that we don't know, but what he said and how he said it gave us true hope. He also mentioned that a committee was formed last week and it is trying to come to a conclusion.

That's when he started telling us that the year we've been here anything we've asked for that they were able to get, we received. It was like he was trying to sum up the past, the things they did and the things they could've done, but didn't. He also mentioned the fact that they had proof of one of us communicating with other hostages. Well, if that's true why didn't they take action, unless they're just guessing. Anyway, he said he decided against taking action, but hoped that it never happens again. A little was also mentioned about the so-called practice firings they've been having every night along with the black-outs, etc., but said they had no bearing on the hostages and that we weren't supposed to worry. He said that we were just to continue being patient (not to try to cause any more trouble—mentioning Bill's incident. Santa described Bill as trying to be a hero by accepting Jerry's blame for knocking on the door too many times.) Santa brought him (Bill) a little note and cookie from Kevin Hermening for Bill's birthday. I'm not sure, but I think Bill wrote a note back to Kevin thanking him.

We've got a big thing going on now. Dick and Al are at the door trying to explain to English Student that Al wanted mint flavored cigarettes (Salem's), and English Student is bringing ointment and other things, thinking that's what Al wants. English Student is really something else.

Santa said last night that they heard we had mail at the Post Office, so they were going to go down there today and pick it up and then in a couple days we would receive it, after they have checked it. The day before yesterday just before lunch they escorted us out to get fresh air for half an hour. It hadn't been that long since we went out last so it wasn't like waiting three months to go out, but anyway it really felt good.

All these things happening lately really seem to look good for my theory about getting out of here before November 4. Receiving sunshine twice within a sixteen day time period, a doctor coming to check up on us, mail received last week after a lapse of about two weeks, television pretty frequently, oil refilled in the hot water heater whenever it's out, the food really being piled into us, and especially last night when Santa told us that the Parliament has gotten a committee together, and then talked about how we didn't have it that bad "the year we were here"—making it sound like we can be leaving any day now. Anyway it just seems too good to be true. It really does!

Last night (or really this morning) we sat up talking about how we thought they would release us, and it sounded so good I didn't want to stop talking about it. I think Santa went to every room last night to give a little speech, so our morale is really up now and will probably stay up for the rest of this month. I'll hate to see what I'm like if we're still here next month, especially after Santa put all that stuff he said on the line. The main thing now is keeping myself busy, continuing to let the time fly by. Basically that's been everyone's idea, but it really seems to mean something this month. This just might be it!!! *End of entry.*

Friday, October 10, 1980 (09:15)   Day 342

Three hundred forty-second day, and all is well as of today except for being a little impatient. As for the hope Santa gave us the other night, we're staying optimistic, hoping that what he said is really true.

The nights have really been getting miserable. The electricity is turned off around (18:00-19:00), candles lit, air raid sirens, explosions in the background (firing of artillery/anti-air), candles blown out, and total darkness except for the light coming from the candle out in the hallway. Once all that happens there really isn't much we can do except lay on our mattresses and think. That's when we really feel miserable, because there isn't much to think about except for going home. Usually the candles aren't made to stay off for long, but something new they've come up with is having us place the candle in the corner of the room instead of on the table. There's really not much anyone can do when the candle is placed in the corner. I can read right at the back of my mattress, and usually one or two others can walk their laps. Everyone else just has to sit down and wait until they come around and tell us we can put the candle back up.

Next week it will have been one month since they started this blackout. Wonder how much longer they're going to continue? It would seem that the people would get frustrated with the lights being off

259

every night and the air raid siren blowing and the explosions going off. It really seems hard to believe that whatever is going on out there has no bearing on the hostages. I'd really like to believe that, though.

The service from the students has really been pretty good lately. Yesterday morning we watched video ("Saturday Night Live" with Chevy Chase), and they even let us pick the tape. We came back to our room and ate lunch which consisted of spaghetti. The plates were piled high with it, and it was really good, too. Vitamins were given out yesterday. Also Al received a brand new wrap for his kidneys, which he's been wearing ever since. Just awhile ago Beaver brought in some Carnation Instant Breakfast. The way they've been treating us seems to be a hopeful sign. We still haven't received mail, so we're kind of expecting some today.

The weather's really been getting chilly lately, especially in the morning when you go to the head. There are a few windows out there, so a nice chilly breeze flies in while you're sitting on the porcelain taking a shit. You try to get in and out as fast as possible.

Not too much more to talk about. We're trying to stay as busy as possible, especially this month when we're expecting something to happen. God bless American and its wonderful people!!! Oh, God, please help us. *End of entry.*

Sunday, October 12, 1980 (09:20)   Day 344

Three hundred forty-fourth day and we're still here, stranded like ducks at the opening of duck season. Twenty-one more days till our one year anniversary. Really curious to find out if what Santa hinted to us the other night about being out of here within a year is really going to come to be true. He really made it sound as though we were going to be released by then.

The student doctor and Santa came in yesterday morning to see if we were all feeling well. Nothing was prescribed, except that he told Santa that Jerry should see a dentist for his tooth. He was mostly concerned with Al's kidney problem. That's about the second time in a month that he's been around checking up on us. I hope it's a good sign that he came, even though no one was sick. Right after he left, the students got down on their hands and knees to scrub the hallway down. Some of the other hostages cleaned the head. They asked me to do it when I was down there, but at the time we were playing bridge. I guess they just asked someone else.

We've started playing bridge again, which really helps to make the afternoon fly by. We would play later into the night, but the lights have been continuing to go off around (18:00). There's not enough light to continue, so we just stop. Lately, these last couple of nights, they haven't made us blow our candles out so we've been able to read, walk our laps or play Parcheesi. Ever since they put those new games in the T.V. room, it seems as every time we walk down to the head you can hear all the other rooms rolling dice and so on. I guess everybody got a chance to get a game.

Our new routine consists of getting up for breakfast (08:00), and then trying to stay up till lunch reading. Now lately we've even had refreshments, cheese and crackers. Anyway, we play till around (18:00), when the lights go out, and then wait for dinner. Then after dinner we usually play Parcheesi or just sit around and read under candlelight.

Yesterday afternoon they got fuel for the hot water heater, so last night around (22:00) Al and I did a nice little workout before taking our showers. The workout wasn't that bad; it was just the thing about taking a shower in that head with the breeze coming in. We did finally manage though. Boy, how I can't wait to get out of here and hop into a nice tub of hot water. Wow! That's going to feel good. Supposedly they're to come in and put plastic over the broken windows. It's really been getting cold in the mornings. I'm going to have to see what it's going to be like this winter if we're still here. How I pray to God we're not, though.

Mail still hasn't arrived, so we're still looking forward to that. Otherwise nothing else has been happening, just sitting around waiting patiently for a conclusion to all of this. I really have my doubts at times, though. When will this ever end?? *End of entry.*

Tuesday, October 14, 1980 (09:15)   Day 346

Three hundred forty-sixth day. It seems like anything we do lately has an effect on the students. Bill and I just came back from the head (eastern), where there are two toilets, American and Iranian. The students put a sign on the Iranian toilet door a while back that said "for students only." Well, I've been having diarrhea recently, and this morning was just one of those mornings I had it again. Also Bill had to relieve himself awful bad, too, so Bill used the Iranian shitter and I used the American one. Well, when we were finished, English Student came in and started to chew Bill out for using their head. I then asked him how he knew Bill did. I was trying to get him to confess that he was spying on us. It was like he was trying to tell us that our waste was poison or something.

That was only one of the small things that happened today that they made into a capital crime. This morning a little earlier he tried jumping on Al's ass for knocking on the door too loud. Al knocked the same as he does any other time, but this time I guess English Student tried to show who was boss. And yesterday morning I had to listen to a small sermon from Santa for the way I spoke to Beaver. Usually we're able to joke around with Beaver but evidently not anymore. That's the second time he's gone crying to Daddy. It all started when he came in to take us to the head and I smelled an odor, so I asked him what smelled like a French whore. Of course, I should've known better to say something like that to him. I was only joking around with him, but he took it seriously and went crying off to Daddy. About an hour later Santa came in, in a friendly way I guess, and said (pointing at me, knowing it was the incident with Beaver) that one of the students had mentioned to him that I had made a comment about the odor. Right away I told him to tell Beaver I was sorry, and that I was only joking. Santa then mentioned that we knew things like that weren't permitted here in Iran, and that I shouldn't say things like that. Overall he was pretty friendly about the whole thing, but now we know not to even fuck around with Beaver.

Otherwise, not too many lively things been happening around here. Ali the Cook asked us last night to peel potatoes, which he hasn't done for a long time. Of course we had to finish our bridge game first. Boy, how the time flies when we're playing bridge. Same goes for our nightly Parcheesi game after dinner. Trying to stay busy.

Yesterday Mr. Fix-It brought us plastic to put over the windows. Not as much cold air comes in anymore, but we still get a little. The little air we do get sure comes in handy when we're playing bridge, smoking cigars and cigarettes. Gets a little smoggy.

Haven't heard too many air raid sirens lately. Come to think about it, I don't think we've heard any. Still the lights continue to go out every night at (18:00). We really haven't heard any explanation, and I doubt if we ever will. Maybe a bunch of lies, but probably never the truth!

The same goes for our situation, too. We're really starting to believe that Santa's one year bullshit was just a put-on to make us think something is being done. As each day goes on, it gets harder to believe that we're actually going to get out of here. Plus it seems like the students are just trying to find things to blame on us, which makes it that much harder to keep our tempers. Don't know how much longer it's going to be before one of us flattens one of them out.

One good thing I can say is that we're getting fed pretty well, like they're trying to fatten us up or something. Doing a good job of it if they are. Well, we don't have too much longer to go before our one year anniversary. Still kind of hoping that something will happen

262

before then. Oh, God, please help us!! *End of entry.*

Thursday, October 16, 1980 (09:45)   Day 348

Three hundred forty-eighth day, and we're still hoping. The weather has gotten tremendously colder here in this concrete room, and also in the head. This concrete really keeps in the cold air, especially during the morning hours. I think I mentioned the other day that they brought us plastic to nail up around our windows, but still a little cold air was flowing through. So yesterday we asked Sunshine to bring us some tape so we could tape them up. It's still pretty chilly in here, though, and it probably will continue to be so.

I don't know if the students are getting ready for a long winter or what, but yesterday we were asked if we needed underwear, sweaters, shirts, socks and blankets, which we all needed and were given a little while later. Don't know if that could be added on to all the other signs that give us a feeling of getting out of here or not. After Sunshine had given it all out to us, we asked if we were preparing for a long winter. He said no, but then added that he really didn't know. Whatever that means. Well, at least we should have enough clothes to last us through this winter if we need to. They said they've got a heater in the hallway, but doesn't seem to be turned on yet. I guess they'll probably wait till the first snow drops.

Right after I got finished writing the morning of the 14th, we were taken to watch video ("Charlie's Angels"). Since the morning before (the 13th) when I had that misunderstanding with Beaver, he hadn't spoken much to us. But when we were watching video he came in with a platter of nuts for us to eat. He kept coming in, like he wanted to associate with us, but none of us wanted to associate with him. The only thing I'm going to say to him is "please" and "thank you," and that's all.

Other than those small incidents with Beaver and English Student, everything else has been going pretty well. At times we have to wait a while to go to the head. For instance, last night we sat around knocking on the door for fifteen minutes. Then they wonder why we knock so hard on the door. It's just to get their attention while they're sitting back jabbering.

The days really seem to be flying by, especially with the help of our afternoon bridge games, which last from about (15:00-18:00). I guess I can say I'm even getting better at the game. The food's been quite adequate lately, too. Last night we had stew for dinner, and I also had some of Ali's yogurt. The only reason I eat it is that Ali says it's good for my health. Maybe I'll live longer here in prison than anyone

263

else. Anything he serves at dinner which in hot is great, especially since it's been this cold.

The lights are still continuing to go out every night at (18:00). We really wonder if it's because of the blackout, or just because the students want to do it this way. Last night when I went to bed around (22:30) I thought I heard some far off explosions, which Bill said he also heard. It's been some time now since we heard the last air raid siren, so maybe they're finished practicing and now just waiting for the real thing.

Still haven't received any mail lately. I wonder what's going on that's so important they don't want to give us our mail. They continue to tell us that they haven't received any. Lies, lies. I'm getting tired of them, and tired of all this shit. *End of entry.*

Saturday, October 18, 1980 (09:30)   Day 350

Three hundred fiftieth day, and we're still waiting patiently. We finally received mail yesterday, something we needed to get our spirits back up. I believe the last time we received anything was October 1st, so it was really a treat. We were kind of expecting to get some Oct. 16, after they brought us some magazines. Whenever they do that we kind of figure that they got some mail in. The handing out of magazines is something like a teaser. We know that whenever the magazines are handed out, we'll be expecting mail, but when? Anyway, the mail was terrific. Some of the letters sounded as if we'd be getting out of here soon, which I hope is true.

Received another beautiful letter from Jill, this time with a present enclosed. She sent her Fair Queen 2nd runner-up ribbon, which she won just for me. Also enclosed was a beautiful picture of her. She is so beautiful and I miss her so much. This is the first letter I've received from her since the one she wrote July 22nd. I was kind of wondering if I was ever going to hear from her. Anyway, this letter answered all my questions and ended all my worries. But how I can't wait to get out of here.

Also received a letter from my sister Judy, who I haven't heard from since I don't know when. She wrote that everything was well, and that she'd heard my tape which the students played over the phone. A strange thing she kept on saying in her letter was "see you soon!" Hopefully she wasn't just saying that to keep my spirits up, but saying it because it might be true. It does seem that the two governments are talking to each other, but a problem has come up in the negotiations. At least that's what we got out of a letter that was sent to Bill.

If the Shah is really dead, what is our reason for still being held?

Once again, the best thing we can do is try not to even think of the mess we're in, but continue to keep our cool and stay as busy as possible. With Thanksgiving and Christmas right around the corner, it's really been hard trying not to think about home and all our loved ones. How I'm going to dread it if we're still here for those two special occasions.

Everyone received mail. Dick and Al even received some goodies from home. We've got a new game we can play now, which Dick's family sent him. It's called "Master Mind."

Things have been about the same around here. The other day while we were playing bridge, Bill went down to the shower room and put plastic around the windows so it wouldn't be so cold while we were taking showers. You can really tell the difference now. Beaver had BBC on again last night in the hallway, but we heard nothing of interest. What a great day that's going to be when they announce that the hostages have been released. That is if that day ever comes!

We're getting fed pretty well, but the books are getting a little old. Really don't know why they don't give us any new ones. Maybe the next time we go in, there will be more. Cross my fingers on that! I think I'll stop now and take a short nap before lunch. May a solution be found to solve this problem, and may we all return home to our families and loved ones, amen! *End of entry.*

Monday, October 20, 1980 (09:20)   Day 352

Three hundred fifty-second day, and still here we sit. I just got finished washing the breakfast dishes and a few of my own clothes, which I should've done last night when I took my shower, but forgot. Now that I've got that finished, I'll have to find something else to keep me busy. My blanket needs sewing so I guess I'll do that when I'm finished here. Reading gets a little boring at times so I try to find other things to occupy my time.

The students have found something to do right outside our window. It started yesterday, the scraping of metal and loud talking, and has continued into today. Since we don't have any way to avoid the noise, we have to listen to it. We were free of it for about 52 minutes yesterday morning when we were taken to watch video ("50 Years of Rock & Roll"). Once again nuts were served, but most of all it was just great to get out of this room and to be able to see other people on television. Plus it really helps pass the time.

Before we were taken in to watch it, Sunshine came in to try out our new game (Master Mind). A lot of time has been surprisingly taken just playing that game. I don't mean to brag, but I've already gotten it in two tries. So I guess you can say I'm the champion of this room, so far!

Like always, bridge has been taking up the better part of the afternoon. Then after dinner is Parcheesi, which does the same as bridge, takes up a lot of time. Last night after we were finished playing, Jerry, Al and I worked out. We can't let our ugly bodies get too badly out of shape. I did my normal routine, 200 sit-ups and 300 push-ups. After taking that shower and then coming back to read a little, walk my laps and say my rosary, I slept like a rock. Anything's good that keeps your mind off this situation.

We've been trying so much not to even think of our situation, and believe it or not, we've even been having a lot of laughing sessions, which really must be making the people outside our door wonder what is becoming of us. I guess I can say things have been going well these past couple days, except for wondering how everyone is doing back home, etc. We really try to keep things like this to ourselves, but at times you can see that it's really eating up the person to the point where he's got to say what's worrying him. After talking about it you start to feel a little bit better, knowing there isn't much you can do except keep strong and continue hoping and praying for the best.

Well, it doesn't seem as though my prediction is going to come true for this month. But then again, we still have eleven more days (the last day being Halloween), so something might still happen. Fifteen more days is our one year anniversary. I'm really waiting to see what happens then. Once again, like always, the only thing we can do is sit back and wait. That's all we've been doing these past eleven months. It's still hard to believe that a government, especially a newly elected government, is holding hostages. Still, the students say that the Parliament is working on us three hours a week. Well, that's better than nothing.

Maybe we'll receive mail once again this week. Santa's been gone for the past couple of days, and usually when that happens something's up. Hopefully it's our release that's up. *End of entry.*

Wednesday, October 22, 1980 (08:10) Day 354

Three hundred fifty-fourth day. Nine more days till Halloween and thirteen more till our one year anniversary. Still hoping that something happens within either of those times. Something that raised our spirits pretty high last night was Beaver telling Al that something was happening. He didn't say exactly what is was, though. The good thing about it is that at least they are talking about us. We still might have a chance on getting out of here before the end of this year. Haven't seen Santa for about a whole week now, and when he's gone something's always bound to happen.

The blackouts are still continuing, with the regular issue of one candle a night. Lately we've had a little project of making our own candles out of the leftover wax. Last night Beaver was telling us that the guys in another room are boiling their own water for coffee by their candles. Times like these are when your sense of imagination comes in handy.

The atmosphere around the room has been maintaining quite well. We're just sitting here hoping each day that they bring us good news of our release. I know that every time I write in this diary, I write just about the same thing over and over again. But really that's what our lives consist of here, doing things over and over again. Anything we can find to do to pass the time is great.

Well, we just heard Santa's voice in the hallway—sounds pretty happy. Maybe he'll have something good to tell us. Not much is going on around here otherwise. I'm sitting here at the table bothering Al while he's playing Solitaire. Jerry's reading at his mattress, Dick's walking his laps and Bill's sleeping. The next enjoyable thing we're looking forward to is lunch, which is still four and a half hours from now. When I finish this I'm planning to read *The Sporting News* some more and then take a nap from about (11:30-13:00). Then when I wake it should be about time to munch down. Hopefully pasta today.

Al and I can smell pipe tobacco, probably coming from one of the hostages' rooms. We asked Beaver if he'd be able to get us a pipe, and he said he'd see what he could do. Well, Beaver just came back in and said that the pipe tobacco was only for the normal smokers. Well, so much for that idea. Dick just came back from the head and said that they just got finished lighting the water heater, so tonight we'll have hot showers. Signing off for now! *End of entry.*

Thursday, October 23, 1980 (11:50)   Day 355

Three hundred fifty-fifth day. Well, we won't be having anymore bridge games. Last night around (21:00) while we were playing backgammon, we started to hear Santa going to all the different rooms saying a few words and then leaving. Something we've been talking about and hoping wouldn't happen, happened when Santa came in and told Dick and Al to pack all their things. Al had always predicted this to happen, saying that when the time came for only some of us to go home, that they would be coming around to take Dick and himself to a different place to be held while we were being released.

I'm not saying that we are going to be released, but just by the way the students have been acting and the things they've been saying, something's up. Last night when Al asked Santa what was going on, he mentioned that the elections are near, and something is likely to happen. Then Al asked if we would see each other again, and he said yes, soon.

This morning while we were in watching T.V. (part of "Starsky & Hutch" and "Kaz"), Bill asked Sunshine if we were going to see Dick and Al again. Sunshine replied it all depended on the situation. Situation of what, though? Then just awhile ago Jerry was talking to Taco Kid down in the head, where Taco Kid was saying that something is happening and that he thought that we would be home soon. He also mentioned the elections. I just pray to God that Al wasn't right about having the low level people released and holding the high officials. I can't see the United States making a deal for only half of us, that is if they are making deals. It might even be this Parliament making such a decision.

I don't know how I'd feel if I knew that I was being released and those other people weren't. But it does seem that something is up. Once again the only thing we have to do is sit back and wait, hoping for the best. We had our last bridge game with Dick and Al yesterday. They said they took them to a place not too far from here, to one of Shah's places, whatever that means. Maybe house or prison.

Everything seemed to be normal yesterday morning, although we knew that Santa was back. He was in a good mood, too. We were right again, though! Whenever he's gone for a while, that usually means that something is up. Anyway, they came in and got us to go outside. Jerry and Dick first and then Al, Bill and myself. The sun was hot—temperature about 64 degrees. Really felt good. We found out from Sunshine when we were out there that this place was built by the Germans in World War II. We also learned that Santa was held prisoner here for two years, and two years in another place something like this place. This place is really big, probably would hold a lot of people.

Other than the visit outside, everything else was the same routine. Oh yes, and they also brought fuel yesterday, which Al never did use to take a hot shower. Dick took one earlier in the afternoon. Hopefully they'll have the same facilities at their new place. It was really sad to see those guys leave last night, and having that feeling that we were going to be released and them still left behind. How I pray to God that that isn't going to be the way it happens. I gave Al my cross necklace for a small gesture, and told him he can hand it back to me the next time he sees me. I thought since it had seen me through safely, it would do the same for him. I have a feeling they're going to need the prayers more than me.

Now since they're gone, the room seems a little more cold, I guess from the lack of body heat. It also seems a little more empty. This morning seems to have gone by pretty fast. Woke around (08:00) for breakfast, then read a little. I had started to doze off when Quaker came in and asked if we wanted to watch T.V., and of course we said sure. Nuts were served again. We came back to the room and rearranged it a little. It really feels vacant with those guys gone. It's kind of sad. Don't know how many people they took from each room, but it really seems quiet.

They have been taking people to watch T.V., trying to keep us occupied, I guess. It's really going to be hard staying occupied, but we're going to have to do the best we can. Well, lunch is coming so I hope Ali made a lot; I'm really starving. Hopefully something good is up for *everyone!* God please help us! *End of entry.*

Saturday, October 25, 1980 (09:30)   Day 357

Three hundred fifty-seventh day. We've got ourselves a new roommate, Sam Gillette. He arrived the night after Al and Dick left. He had been in the room to the left of us ever since July 11th, with Scott and Sharer. Scott and Sharer were taken the same night as Al and Dick, so Sam had to spend that night and half the next day alone until Santa brought him in with us. It's always nice seeing new faces, especially when it's a person you really get along with. Sam's a really good guy! Before they brought him here he was in Trebrez from April till July. He says that things were going well, just getting a little impatient at times, until the other night when they came in to move Scott and Sharer.

Santa came in last night and talked for a while, telling us it was only a precaution they were using since the elections are coming up. He was saying that Carter is probably willing to do anything to get re-elected and might try another raid, so they separated us, leaving the people they trusted here and taking all the supposedly high officials away. Santa said last night that he had seen Al and Dick earlier that morning in some garden that they must've been walking around in. They must not be too far from here, then. Santa did say that they were coming back here, probably right after the elections.

I then asked him if Iran is really scared/worried about the U.S. coming over here again. If that is true, how could he say that there is progress regarding our release? He reassured us that there is progress, but that they were still taking precautions against another attempted raid. He never gave us any indications of going home soon.

This morning when I went to the head, I asked Plow Boy if our situation was looking good and if it would be soon that we'd be getting out of here. He replied that our situation was looking good, but anything I wanted to ask I had to ask Santa. I guess Santa told them not to give out any information, but to let him do all the talking.

Since Al and Dick are gone we've really been wondering if that's the true reason they've been taken away. Why are they going to all the trouble to move just the high officials when they could have moved us by rooms? Santa also said last night that they might even move some more people. We really think that something is up, and that it might happen within the next ten days.

(11:35) Just returned from watching "Kaz" again. Sam didn't watch it the other day, so he asked if he could watch it this morning. It was the same one we had watched the other day. Hollywood even brought us some potato chips, but I had already brought my Coco Krispies to eat, so Bill, Sam and Jerry ate the chips.

While we're talking about food, last night for dinner we were overfed. First they brought us Spam and cold creamed corn, so we asked for some cheese to put on the Spam. Smiley came back with two packages of Swiss cheese, and we ended up giving one pack back. A little while later, Ali the Cook brought in some more Spam and then asked if we would like some rice, so we said sure. I really started to get filled up then. Then right after Bill had the dishes cleaned off the table, Smiley came in with leftover spaghetti in a pot and asked if we wanted any of that. Jerry, Sam and I couldn't put any more in, but Bill said he'd have some. I guess they think of us as the garbage disposal room. Anything they want to get rid of, just bring it to our room and we'll eat it.

Santa said last night that we'd probably receive mail sometime today. Something we can look forward to. Sam's got us all in the habit of smoking pipes. Yesterday morning Sunshine brought us three extra pipes and some tobacco. I've only been smoking mine after meals. It's not too bad, either. Something different. Our schedule's a little bit the same as when Al and Dick were here. Some card playing during the day, and at night after dinner we play Parcheesi. Last night we played two games just so the time would pass. It's really been hard trying not to think of this situation. How I pray to God that we all get out of here before or sometime near the elections. Oh, God, please help us! *End of entry.*

Three hundred sixtieth day, and Jerry just heard some very encouraging words this morning from Sunshine. Sunshine told him that Parliament was going to state the demands some time this week, and that the demands will be met from the United States before the election. The reason he said that they're so sure the demands will be met is because the United States has offered them all to Iran already. Jerry was saying that Sunshine felt sure something would be done before election, which is in another eight days. I really hate to get my hopes us. It's too hard to believe that we're really going to get out of here. I really can't picture myself as being free. I pray to God it comes true, but I'm not going to believe it until I see it.

We received mail today. Bill and I received some from our parents, while Jerry and Sam received one or two letters from people they didn't know. My letters didn't emphasize anything about our release; that is if they even know anything about it. They just assured me that everyone was doing great, keeping themselves busy. Boy how I can't wait to get back to that lovable family and Jill. Nothing received from Jill this time, but my parents mentioned she was doing well, etc. Boy, how great it's going to be to be home for Thanksgiving—*Oh, God, please make it come true.*

The other day we were given new white underwear, which they went out and bought themselves. At least we never had any of those kind at the Embassy store. I thought that was really thoughtful of them to go out and buy us all a pair of underwear. The week before we got new shirts and sweaters. I wonder when the new trousers come? Maybe they're trying to get us all dressed up for when we go home.

They got fuel in once again today, too. I did a small workout yesterday (300 push-ups, 80 sit-ups, 100 jumping jacks) and then afterwards took a nice hot shower. I'll probably lay off it today and do it again tomorrow.

Well, it seems like they got the old crew back with us once again. They must've been staying with the people they took the other day, dropped them off somewhere and then came back. Wonder where they dropped them off, and with whom? If something is coming down regarding our release, I pray to God it's for everyone.

It must've been cleaning day today. Heard the vacuum in just about all the rooms; nothing better to do I guess. Time's been passing pretty fast lately. We've been keeping ourselves occupied playing the same old games and reading books. I'm continuing to practice with my pipe, seeing how long I can keep it lit. I'll have to enter the pipe smoking contest at the Fair for sure the next time they have it. Not too much more to say around here, so I guess I'll close and reload my mail. See if I missed any information. Pray to God we go home soon! *End of entry.*

Wednesday, October 29, 1980 (11:00)   Day 361

Three hundred sixty-first day. Well, Smiley just came in to collect our sheets to be washed, which hasn't been done for a while. A little earlier Beaver was playing music in the hallway so that all the hostages were able to hear it. Right now it's off, and we can hear some little kids (out in the compound somewhere) moaning and yelling. Bill and I are the only ones up right now. Jerry and Sam went back to sleep after waking to drink the tea/coffee for breakfast. I wasn't doing much of anything else, so I thought I'd jot down a few things.

We didn't find out until later on in the day yesterday, after I had already written in my diary, that Imam had declared yesterday (Oct. 28, 1980) "Happy Day." How can they expect us to be happy when we're sitting in this cell room? I wonder what the occasion was? Hopefully it is something to do with us.

It's really been hard trying not to think about getting out of here, but when you do, the time just drags by. I really feel that if we don't get out of here soon (meaning months), I'm going to bust right open. The things we've been hearing about the situation being solved any day now I just try to throw out of my head, as if I never even heard it. Like I said before, it's too good to be true. Then again, we're bound to get out of here sometime. Well, the kids are still out there screaming and yelling "God is great" (in Farsi, of course). God, please take us home to our family and loved ones safely. *End of entry.*

Friday, October 31, 1980 (12:15)   Day 363

Well, here we sit. Our 363rd day, Halloween. Just another day to us though. Sam's sitting here playing some songs on the ukulele that Santa brought yesterday afternoon. Too bad we don't have a guitar; we could really have a good time. Sam really seems to know how to play it.

Some more people moved in last night. One of the newcomers was giving them a ration of shit last night, and then this morning we heard Mr. Ode asking English Student for some sheets. We don't know how many newcomers we got. They really aren't in a good mood, that's for sure.

Well, yesterday there was a day of a lot of excitement. Earlier in the morning we were taken in to watch T.V. Passed a little of the time away pretty nicely. Then a little before lunch, we were taken outside for a half-hour. Sun really felt good, so while Bill was showing Beaver how to shine boots, I was talking to Taco Kid and Plow Boy about the situation. Really couldn't understand Taco Kid all that well, but I thought for sure he had said, "The Parliament has been talking to the United States government," and then said something about Saturday being the day their Parliament is going to announce their demands to the United States. It's about the same thing Sunshine said to Jerry earlier this week. Taco Kid also said that the United States had already offered the things that the Iranian Parliament would demand. He really didn't give us any kind of date we'd be out of here, but he said the situation was looking good.

Mail was just delivered to us once again, making it the second time this week that we've received it. Jerry, Sam and I received only one letter, and Bill received about four or five. Received my letter from one of my best friends that had just gotten out of the Marine Corps and is now a freshman at the University of Ohio. Besides that, his wife Bernice is going to have a baby in March of next year. Really can't wait to see them all again. Last night Sam, Bill and I were discussing our plans for a motorcycle trip throughout the U.S.A. That's something Bill and I mentioned in February. It's like I told them last night; every time you sit down and start talking about something you want to do in the near future, you never end up doing it. Hopefully we'll make our motorcycle trip, though!

I wonder what got into them about giving us mail again today? Forgot to mention that the doc was around the night before last checking to see if anyone needed to be seen. He wasn't needed in our room, but probably some other room had called on him. All these things happening lately seem to be looking good for us. Hopefully this thing's coming to an end, and we'll all be home for Thanksgiving. Pray to God for that.

I don't really know if it meant anything, but yesterday when Bill and I had just returned from outside and Jerry and Sam went out, Taco Kid came in and said that he hopes we see Mr. Morefield and Al in the United States soon. Don't really know if he was trying to tell us that they had already been released. Well, it really seems that something's going to happen between these next four days, or maybe a little while after. It's really hard to believe that we're going to get out of here soon. I hope I'm right, though. *End of entry.*

Sunday, November 2, 1980 (11:00)   Day 365

If the days are correct on the calendar, today should be our **365th** duy (one fucking year we've been here) and still here we sit. Santa was around yesterday spreading word that the time of our release was so near that it could even be tomorrow (today). He was also making small comments like once I get home I can practice the guitar as much as I like, but not now because the other hostages are complaining.

Anyway, he was saying that our situation was looking great. Bill asked him if Carter had done something, and Santa said no; it was something they were going to do. He really seemed serious when he said that it could be today. It really would be cheap of him to say something like that, knowing that we really get our hopes up and then have nothing happen.

There are a lot of vehicles running out there today, plus the treatment's been super. Yesterday morning we went in to watch T.V. again, plus they brought us fuel for the hot water heater. Then Santa did something he usually doesn't do; he mentioned a person (hostage) who is being held in one of the rooms in this wing (Mr. Ode). Santa said he was one of the people complaining about my practicing, and then someone mentioned that he complains about everything just about (just joking around), and Santa came out and said that he was an old man. I wonder how long they're going to keep that old man along with us in this situation?

We've got the feeling that something's up, but we just can't register in our heads that we're going to get out of here. Today is supposed to be the day that the Iranian government is to give their demands to the U.S. If that's true, then I wonder what Santa was meaning about the Iranian government doing something, and not the U.S.? Last night I was asking one of the other students (Quaker) about the situation, and he was saying that the situation was looking good. I asked if it was looking so good that we'd be going home tomorrow, and he started laughing, saying no, he thought maybe around Christmas we'd be out of here. It seems like every student's got his own story. You don't know who to believe, so I just do as I've been doing—*and that's not to believe something until you see it.* It's bad enough being held, but when they come in and tell us lies about going home—getting our hopes up and nothing happens—that's the pits.

Last night we heard the air raid sirens again, and then they even came in and told us to put our candle under the table. Things like this that happen really make it hard to believe that we're going to get out of here, but still I'm continuing to hope and pray every night.

Beaver brought us music yesterday, and luckily enough we still have it. Like I said before, the treatment's really been pretty good lately. I've still got that small feeling that something's going to happen between now and the election. God, please make it come true. *End of entry.*

Wednesday, November 5, 1980 (09:30)   Day 368

Three hundred sixty-eighth day. Well, we were just told that Reagan was elected President. I wonder if that's going to change our present status of being released soon? I don't know if it was true or not, but we heard a little while back that if Reagan was elected President he would give the Iranian government 48 hours to release us, and if they didn't, he would start bombing this place until we were. Taco Kid really didn't say anything else, just the fact that Reagan was elected and that's all.

Day before yesterday Santa came in and told us just to be patient, because we've already been here a year and a few more days aren't going to hurt us. Then yesterday Taco Kid was in talking to us, telling us that the situation was very, very good. He said that in the elections Carter was winning 43% to Reagan's 41%. It was like he was trying to say that they wanted Carter back in office. Like I said before, now that they have Reagan in as President, I wonder if it's going to change our situation? If they are waiting for Reagan to do something, I guess we're just going to have to sit back and wait to see what happens when he's inaugurated next January. I wonder what's in store for us up ahead?

Yesterday, November 4, 1980, really wasn't as exciting as I'd predicted. The only exciting thing that happened was the food. Earlier in the morning Ali the Cook came in with some shrimp and onions to be cleaned for dinner that night. They really tasted good. Sure wish we had had more, though. Then for lunch we had pasta made out of noodles, which also tasted good. Oh yes! I just about forgot. We also had jello for dessert at dinner. I was really disappointed we didn't have cake. Well, maybe we'll have it next year. (I pray to God I'm not here!)

We really haven't heard too much more from the students this morning, so we're still curious to know how we stand since the election. Some of the students have been saying that their demands have already been turned over to the United States, and the only thing they're waiting for is the U.S. to respond. Well, if that is true, what's taking them so long back in Washington, D.C.? Then, on the other hand, you have to wonder what the Iranian demands were. You really don't know what to believe. One student might say the Parliament is still talking secretly; another student says we might get out here before Christmas, and then other students make it sound like we could
275

be released tomorrow. What are you supposed to think?

For myself, I think the worst, like maybe not getting out of here till next year. And then even worse than that, never getting out of here. I told Sam last night that I got a strong feeling yesterday, while lying in my mattress, that Dick, Al and the other guys they took out of here that night were sent home. He was saying that he had a similar feeling. I also told him that if we are still here at Christmas, there was going to be one mad mother-fucker in this room. He agreed with that, too. Thanksgiving's going to be bad, but missing another Christmas is going to be twice as bad. They're always talking about human rights. I wonder why they don't start practicing what they preach by releasing us!

The weather's been getting a little chilly again, and people are starting to come down with colds. If we are here during the winter, this place is going to turn into an ice box. Still keeping ourselves as busy as possible during the days. Most of the time's taken up thinking of the things we're going to do once we're released, and what's in store for us at home. For myself, I can't picture us getting out of here. I know eventually we're going to get out, but I just can't picture it. Once again, the only thing we have to do is sit back, pray, and hope for the best. Hopefully soon! (They're probably lying about that, too.) *End of entry.*

Saturday, November 8, 1980 (11:15)   Day 371

Three hundred seventy-first day, and the fifth day of a new year here. It's been three days since I've last written, and not too much has happened except that we went and watched T.V. yesterday morning ("The Osmond Show"). The only good that did for us was just make us that much more homesick. Seeing Marie Osmond really made me think of Jill. A whole year it's been. I wonder how much more we'll have.

Ever since the elections they haven't been saying too much more about going home. Even Santa has been doing his best to stay away from us. This morning while breakfast was being served, Santa was standing outside our door like he was observing them, and then when I knocked on the door to go to the toilet, he took me but didn't say a word. Maybe he's waiting for one of us to start a conversation with him. I'm waiting for the next time he comes in to see us and to fill us with some more bullshit. They've been doing this for so long now, feeding us a bunch of bullshit, but never do they show us a newspaper to let us see for ourselves. Lies, lies, that's all we've heard since we've been here, but then there isn't much we can do about it.

Well, they're out there again this morning, scrubbing down the hallway. I guess it's their day for field day. They're still showing T.V. to the other rooms, so that's one good thing we've got going for us. Otherwise we've just been left in our room to get by on our own, like always. Sleeping and reading in the morning. After lunch it's pinochle time, and then a little bit of reading till dinner. After dinner it's Parcheesi time, and then we end the day with a little more reading. Been getting tight with the candles again, too. One candle a day again. It's also been getting very chilly in here, but still we haven't gotten any kind of heater. These concrete walls really put off some cold air. It's really going to get cold here this winter. Two blankets are barely enough now, so either they're going to have to bring more blankets or a heater.

It really seems that the students have been staying away from our room a lot, only coming when necessary to take us to the toilet or to serve us food. Sunshine was just in to ask if we would like to have a hat to wear to keep our heads warm. Bill asked him about mail, and he replied that they've got some, but they're still going through it. So it will probably be another week before we get it, that's if we have any.

Well, two more days until the Marine birthday. It'll be the second one in a row that we've missed. We'll probably be missing another Thanksgiving, too. I hate to say it, but we'll probably be missing Christmas, too. I've been thinking about what the students have been saying about it all being up to our government. If that's all true, and if the demands the Iranians are asking for are reasonable enough, our government would want us out of here before Thanksgiving. Cross my fingers on that.

I guess my family's probably been a little worried about not hearing from me in four months. I hope they understand, though. Well, so much for now! *End of entry.*

Tuesday, November 11, 1980 (12:00) Day 374

We just got finished eating ice cream, which they found at the embassy when they were going through the freezers looking for meat. Although it's a little too cold for ice cream, it was a nice treat. While they were going around serving it, we were in here singing our new song we made up. Before we finished, we had about five students in here listening to it. Now just awhile ago Beaver came in and said that we couldn't sing anymore today.

(14:30) Just got finished eating lunch. We had spaghetti and warm bread. Now that it's cold, everything we've been eating is warmed up, even the bread at times. The food's really been pretty good lately.

Plus the students have really been treating us well. Yesterday Mr. Fix-It brought us new trousers. In fact, he brought me the pair I was wearing the day of the takeover.

Well, they've brought us all nice clothes. Now all we need is our shoes, and we'll be ready to get out of here. Never know, that's what they might be doing, getting us all dressed up and ready to go. They keep saying that the situation is looking good, so what else do we have to believe? Nothing else has been happening except for the things that have been keeping us busy. Signing off once again—time for bridge.

(17:00) Just finished our daily bridge games. Jerry and I won the second one, and Sam and Bill won the first. Today was great, because we played in the morning and in the afternoon. I think we played too much, though; got a headache now. Everyone's just lying around reading till the lights go out, which should be in another hour.

Well, Santa finally came to the door today. First time since he told us about going home soon. Anyway, he said he was coming to talk to us tomorrow night. I guess we'll just have to wait and see what happens then. He sure didn't have too many encouraging words to say today.

Today was Veteran's Day and yesterday was the Marine Corps birthday, and here we had to end up for both occasions, just like last year. We went and watched T.V. yesterday ("Chips"). It was something different to change the routine. *End of entry.*

Friday, November 14, 1980 (11:00)   Day 377

Jerry just came back from the head where he had a talk with Taco Kid. Taco Kid was telling him that Carter has agreed on the conditions and said that we would be home before Christmas, which is in another 41 days. He told Jerry we'd be home way before Christmas. Boy, does that ever sound good.

Four Eyes just brought us in mail. What a treat that was. Jerry was the only one who didn't get anything from his family. Some of the latest ones we got were around September 17, and no later. I even got one from Jill (Angel Face) wondering if I still loved her. It sounds like none of my letters got to her, or else she wouldn't be wondering that. Of course, I love her...more than anything! I've just been wondering if she was still waiting for me? Whatever will be, will be! I pray she's still there if and when I ever get out of here.

Got some more pictures from my parents and sister—it's amazing what pictures do for your morale. With Thanksgiving and Christmas coming up, I'd so much love to be home with them all. If what Taco Kid was saying about Carter accepting the demands is true, we should be home by then.

I just came back from the head a minute ago with Santa and asked him how the situation was. He gave me the okay sign over the top of his head, and then I asked him if we'd be home before Christmas. He said he didn't know, but he hoped. How I pray to God every night that we are. Maybe even before Thanksgiving, too.

Yesterday morning Sunshine Man told Jerry that the demands were given to the United States 20 hours before election day (Nov. 4), and that they were simple and easy, and that they expected this situation to be solved any day. Then this morning Taco Kid told Jerry that Carter has accepted the demands and we'll be home way before Christmas. Yesterday, while thinking about this situation down in the head, I wondered if they released those guys they took out of here that night and sent them back to the United States with their demands. I've got this strong feeling they did release them. How great that would be to be home for Christmas with all my family and loved ones.

If things are as Taco Kid and the other students say they are, the Democratic Party would really gain respect if they could get us out of here before Reagan is put in. Especially before Christmas, so we could turn on the Christmas lights at the White House. The Democratic Party will really have a bad name for themselves if they leave us here. Well, if anything's going to happen, it's going to happen within these next 41 days. I can't picture us getting out of here, but I know it's got to happen eventually. I continue to pray and hope.

The students really seem to be going out of their way to be friendly with us. Just now Sunshine and Santa were in here, listening to our new song we made up. I wouldn't be surprised if they had someone record it outside the door. Santa said he wanted to record it, so we said okay. *End of entry.*

Monday, November 17, 1980 (9:50)   Day 380

Well, ten more days till Thanksgiving, and it seems as though we'll be spending another one over here. If it's true that Carter has agreed on the terms of our release, why aren't we gone yet? The students continue to say that the situation is looking great, and that we must believe that. Just the way they've been acting shows that something is up. Once again the day before yesterday they brought us ice cream with a little dab of strawberry icing. The fuel container for the hot water heater has been continuously filled. The food's been filling and plenty. Ali the Cook just came in a little while ago with a pot of onions to clean and said that we were having pasta for lunch.

Last night we asked Santa how the situation was doing and he said he'd come back tonight to talk to us. He said that the last time, too, but never came back. I guess he probably needed a day to think of something he could tell us. They all still believe we'll be out of here before Christmas, but then again they thought that last Christmas, too.

Four Eyes was just in to see us, telling us that Carter has agreed on some of the demands informally, not publicly. He said there wasn't any chance of us getting out of here in ten days, but it was sure to happen sometime around Christmas or a little before. Just thinking about being home for Christmas brings a big boost to my morale—so great that would be!

There must be something about the demands that our government doesn't like, or else why is it taking so long? Well, if everything Four Eyes was saying is true, we've got 38 days to wait for something to happen. God, please make it come true! Four Eyes told me a little after we had first got here that he thought we'd be out of here around the end of fall, which comes December 22. I hope he was right.

Last night we hit Santa up about some heat, and he said that they don't have any either. I wonder what the problem is there? Have to just continue to sit back, keep ourselves busy, and hope/pray the best happens to us within the next 38 days. After four Christmases away from home, it would sure be nice to celebrate this one there. It's really too hard to believe that we're going to get out of here, but still my hope prevails.

Television was shown to us yesterday ("Hawaii Five-O"). They've been keeping pretty much to their schedule. Now I wonder when we are going to listen to music? Signing off for now. *God, please help guide us home to our family and loved ones safely. Amen! End of entry.*

Wednesday, November 19, 1980 (12:15)   Day 382

Well, here we are another day, and things seem to be looking up. Last night, after two months (60 days) of the lights being turned off each night at six o'clock, they were finally turned back on. It was kind of strange at that, too. The lights had been turned off, and Beaver was walking around to each room passing candles over the top of the door, through the bars. When he got to our door I asked why they had to keep turning the lights off, and he replied, "Because it is dark outside."

It wasn't any longer than a minute later when Santa came in and asked if we would like the lights back on. Of course, we said yes, and then he said that we would have to put blankets over the windows to

280

prevent the light from reaching outside. I had it in my head that they were going to turn on the overhead lights and leave them on all night, just because I had made that remark to Beaver. He then explained that it was only for the small reading lamp, not the overhead ones. Then he left, and we figured he was going to go get some nails for us to use to hang up the blankets. But a little while later he came back and said that we didn't need to put anything over the windows, but just something over the lamp. That was even better! I wonder why they decided to turn on the lights all of a sudden. I know it wasn't just the remark I made to Beaver that changed their minds.

Then this morning for breakfast we had fried potato pancakes, which is really a change from bread, butter, and jelly or cheese. I wonder if all these changes have anything to do with our release coming up. Asked Beaver this morning if the news was good, and he replied that there hasn't been any news to determine if it was good or bad. Still, he thinks it's looking good for us.

They also came in yesterday and asked us to write home since we haven't written lately. Jerry was the only one who did. I didn't feel like writing because the things I wanted to say probably would've never gotten out. I kind of feel bad now that I didn't write, 'cause I know they would've liked to hear from me. But I know that from the things that I would've said, they would've known I was disgusted. Also, if it is true that we're going to be getting out of here soon, I'll be seeing them before long. Sunshine seemed kind of concerned that we didn't write. I hope my parents and family/Jill don't take it as a bad sign that I didn't write. I just thought I'd hold all my frustrations in me a little bit longer.

Yesterday Bill had one of his fits while playing cards, disturbing everyone to the point where we just left him at the table by himself to clean up the mess he made (spilled tea and cigarette ashes all over). He'd fucked up on a play in pinochle, and after denying it several times he just hit the table with his fist, knocking Jerry's tea all over the table and all of us. We asked him why he had done that, and he replied that he had just gotten pissed off at himself.

That finished the card game with everyone upset, maybe not Bill though. He thought it was pretty funny, asking Jerry a little while after it happened if that was wild and crazy enough for him? Jerry replied, not really having much else to say, that it was a little bit too wild. So last night while Jerry and Bill were in the head, Sam and I discussed if we were going to play Parcheesi or not. We finally decided we would pass off yesterday's mishap, hoping it would never happen again. (Not only did it disturb us, but one of the students had to come in and see what was going on.) Besides, if we didn't play games we would have to find something else to do to pass the time.

We finally ended up playing, using the lamp as our light source, which really seemed different from the candle. The game really wasn't long (Sam won), so after that game Sam challenged me to a game of cribbage, which I won. Having the lights on once again really made a difference. Didn't have to strain our eyes as much. Hopefully they'll be left on tonight, too.

We got a set of barbells to work out with the other day. Trying to put a little more muscle back on the old arms, if I can. Treatment's really been good; they're starting to bring us around hot water now for coffee without even asking. Food's been plenty and fattening. I can feel the pounds forming. But like Jerry was saying this morning, if they really want to spoil us, they can bring us some mail. I really do feel bad now that I didn't write yesterday to let them know I was doing fine. Hopefully we'll see them soon anyway.

The weather's really been getting chilly lately. It's lucky we all have two blankets. I know I said it once, but if we're still here during winter it's going to be one helluva cold one. But I'm really starting to feel sure that we'll be out of here before Christmas. When before Christmas I don't know, but I do feel certain it will happen by then. If it doesn't, what else can we do except be pissed at these guys and then shoot for another day?

Been doing a lot of daydreaming lately. Try not to, but it's really hard. So nice ... it would be to be home for Christmas. God, please help us! *End of entry.*

Saturday, November 22, 1980 (11:30)   Day 385

Well, here we still sit, supposedly waiting for word of what our government will decide on the demands of the Iranians. Thanksgiving is only five days away, and I've already given up hope on being out of here by then. I really didn't expect to be anyway. All my hope is still set on Christmas, though. If we're not out of here by then ... I've said that so often, and when the time comes and we're still sitting here I won't have any other choice but to choose another day.

Sunshine told Jerry this morning that they're still waiting for a response from the United States. I had thought that the United States would want to get us home before Thanksgiving, but there must be a problem that's stopping them from doing it.

Took us to watch television this morning ("Hawaii Five-O"). Refreshments were served like always (nuts and pretzels). Now that I've started smoking cigars part time, they've been bringing incense for us to burn. Treatment's been pretty good. Hot water is still brought to us for coffee whenever we ask. They know how cold it gets in these rooms, and anything warm in our body feels great. An example of how cold it is in here is the butter which they gave us yesterday morning for breakfast. It's still sitting on our dish table by the door, just as hard as we got it. I'm walking/sitting around with two pairs of socks on to keep my feet warm.

Sam's been lying on his mattress this morning composing songs. So far he's made three and he's still not finished. Last night I was talking to Beaver about the things that have been sent to me that I never received. I told him about a book that was sent to me, and showed him the letter and a picture of it. He went to ask Santa, and came back a few minutes later saying that they had never received it. What else can you say? So much stuff has been sent, but very little has ever been received. They're still telling us that the letters they receive and can't read, they won't give to us. Scared of the things they might say. What could be so damaging—unless they wrote that we weren't ever going to get out of here.

I asked Beaver last night why they had a candle in the toilet instead of lights like in the other rooms. They've got the hall lights on, but their window is covered with a blanket. I guess using the small lamps in our rooms doesn't put off enough light that we have to cover our windows, too. Anyway, Beaver said that the reason they are doing it is to conserve energy and to practice their blackout drills. I wonder how much of that is the truth?

Bill's growing a potato plant with one of the potatoes the students gave him the other day. He's experimenting on everything he can get his hands on. It's either him tearing up things or running around making noise.

Got to go down and do the dishes before lunch comes. *End of entry.*

Monday, November 24, 1980 (13:10)   Day 387

Well, three more days till Thanksgiving, so it looks like we won't be home for this one either. Jerry claims that he's been hearing the students talking to the other rooms, telling them it would be about another three weeks before something would happen. I told Jerry this morning that if we weren't out of here by Christmas, I would probably be going to solitary. I told him it would either be going crazy in this room with everyone present, or going crazy by myself in solitary, which I would prefer. That's after I told him what I think of this situation. They keep building our hopes up and nothing ever happens. I pray to God that they're not doing the same thing this time, like all the others. If it does turn out to be like that, things are really going to be changing after Christmas.

Something's happened recently that's been a big psychological change for us. To us it's bad, but really we don't know if it means what we think it means. Anyway, a new student has been walking around with Beaver and English Student—it's like they're breaking him in on things to do around here. We asked Beaver if they were going to be breaking in new people and then be leaving afterwards. The only reply he had was that they weren't going to be leaving us, but that they *were* going to continue breaking new people in. (After that's all done they will probably leave, and leave us here for another year. That's my own feeling, which I hope is wrong. *What's this new kid here for anyway?*)

Having the light on at night is really a change; it seems to make the time go by just that much faster. We haven't played pinochle since Billy's little fit. Instead Jerry and I play cribbage or gin to pass the time. Oh yes, we even do a small workout with the weights they've been letting us use. Parcheesi is still played at night after dinner. Each time we play it, though, it seems to get more boring. Need something to pass the time.

Yesterday one of the students brought us a *Sports Illustrated*, dated Oct. 31, 1980. Asked him if we got any mail, but he said he didn't know. The last mail we got was dated the first part of September, and that was about two weeks ago. Since then we've gotten new magazines from October, but still no mail. It's like they're trying to keep something away from us. Some sort of news that happened around September or October. *Why, though?* Well, maybe we'll get some for Thanksgiving. Cross my fingers on that! *End of entry.*

Friday, November 28, 1980 (12:10)   Day 391

Yesterday was Thanksgiving, and to us here it was just another day. The students tried giving us a little Thanksgiving spirit by feeding us turkey, mashed potatoes and cherries. After lunch, when they came around to serve tea, they also passed around angel food cake. A couple pieces tasted pretty good, and a couple didn't (meaning the cake wasn't done all the way). They also brought peach pie filling, butter and bread. Then for dinner last night we had shrimp (which Jerry and I cleaned in the morning) and rice. Really tasted pretty good. I guess it's that I'm just getting used to it, along with everyone else, too. Other than the good meals, nothing else was done.

We started to play pinochle once again—Billy didn't have any of his fits. And then last night after dinner we played Parcheesi, like always. I also wrote a letter to Jill, and I'm planning to write some more letters today. Getting rid of my stubbornness, I guess. Sam's been going right to town with it—I believe he wrote about eight letters yesterday, when I only got out one. Out of all the single girls he's writing, he plans to at least get one!

We did get mail the night before last (Nov. 26). Sam and I got the most, while Jerry got two (none from his family), and Bill got one from his girl friend (old girl friend, I guess it is). My letters didn't sound too encouraging, except that everyone is well and Jill is still holding on. Oh yes! I did find out that my little brother has a broken leg. I would imagine it's from football, but no one really says. Poor little Kurt! My sister Debbie wrote and said that another one of my relatives is getting married next year, and then said, "Maybe you'll be home for that one." I really shouldn't laugh. I'll probably still be sitting here.

Another big psychological event happened to us yesterday, which really made us all feel that we're going to be here till at least next year. They brought a huge heater in and put it in the hallway, so it would circulate to all the other rooms. I told Hollywood yesterday when he took me down to the head that that was a good sign of us being here another year. But he replied that it doesn't have anything to do with how long we'll be here. They just brought it in because it was cold and they needed some heat. If they were sure of us going home soon, they wouldn't have gone to all that work. They must just be saying that to keep our spirits up. I have no doubt in my mind about what they're doing—leading us on!

I just mentioned to the other guys how we haven't seen Taco Kid for a while. Haven't seen him ever since this new guy has gotten here. I wonder if Taco Kid just got fired for spilling too many beans, or if he found out that we were going to be here longer and didn't want to stay around. He was really keen on wanting to get this all solved so that we could go home to our family and loved ones. He probably felt that he couldn't stay around lying to us, so instead he got out. If we don't see him within the next month, I'll know one of my predictions is right.

All the students are on this thing about how it's all up to our government, and where they see that I don't know, because our government doesn't have to do anything. I truly hope that when Reagan gets in office and we're still here, that he gives them 48 hours to release us and if they don't, just write us off and send in the B52s. Then again, they don't even have to do that. Just write us off and let us rot over here, leaving the blame on this country for holding innocent people. I'll bet

285

any money on it that the United States doesn't go along with these people's demands. Lately I've been hoping they will just come in and blow this country sky high to show the rest of the world that they don't fuck around. We've got to set the example somewhere, so why not *here!*

I still say that all night firing they were doing not too long ago was preparation for an attack from the United States. This country can't be stupid enough to think they can take on the United States during a time of war. But then again, we don't know what's going on out in the outside world. Will this thing ever end?

Television is still shown to us once in a while. In fact, it should be our turn sometime soon. The last show we saw was "The Osmonds", Bill's favorite. Well, lunch is going to be coming, so I'll sign off for now. God, please take us home! *(God bless America!) End of entry.*

Sunday, November 30, 1980 (17:00) Day 393

Here we all sit around the room once again. Sam is playing the uke, Bill is reading and Jerry's playing cards. Just a few minutes ago we were disturbed by an explosion which couldn't have been more than a block away. The concussion was so strong it shook the building and rattled the plastic over the windows. What a dangerous life I've been living since I've been here.

After our daily pinochle game, we were met at the door by a new student when we asked to go to the head. My prediction about Taco Kid being gone was wrong, although he was gone for a couple days. He returned yesterday morning, but now instead of one new student we've got two. Now, if that's not a sign of us being here a little longer, I don't know what is!

This morning Taco Kid was telling Jerry that they are really expecting Carter to get us out of here before Christmas or before Reagan is put into office which is January 20, 1981—two months from now. If we're not out of here by Dec. 25, 1980, Carter isn't going to get us out before Reagan is put in. I don't really know if they're just telling us this shit or what, but they're really believing that Carter's going to have to get us out. I wish I could feel like that, but I've already got myself psyched up for being here through another Christmas. Of course, I'll still be pissed if we're still here, but I'll gradually get over it and then set my heart on another day. It's really hard to believe that that's what I've been doing the last year and months. How many more months/years will I have to continue this?

Our sense of humor is really going to the birds. Practically everything we say—whenever we're joking around—we crack up at. Last night was a helluva night for the giggles. Yesterday we finally got some of the new books that were sent to us. It was about time, too. Plus yesterday when we went in to watch television, they had taken all the tapes. Either they were getting pissed at us for changing the tapes they wanted us to watch or else they took them out to get new ones. Hardly ever know what they're up to nowadays.

They brought fuel for the showers last night, but it was too late to take one then so we all took them this morning. One of the enjoyable things that only come around once in a while. I don't believe I mentioned that Sunshine brought us a yo-yo to play around with the other day. (*I wish he would bring something else I could mess around with. Sure has been a long time.*)

The lights still go off once in a while during the day. But ever since the night they turned them back on, they've been turned on every night. Well, I believe I'll play Jerry in some gin or cribbage. He's been down ever since we saw that new student today. So have I. Psychological morale drop. *End of entry.*

Friday, December 5, 1980 (22:20)   Day 398

Back again. Been five days since I've last written, and to tell you the truth, nothing has really happened. I did get my hair cut this morning by Ali the Cook. Jerry had planned it, but he was sleeping at the time Ali came in, so Ali just did me instead. Ali even had the boys (as he calls them) fill up the fuel tank so I was able to take a shower afterwards. Bill wanted his cut, too, but as I got out of the chair and Bill wrapped the sheet around himself to sit down, Ali walked out. Bill never got his hair cut. Long hair gets dirty too fast, so I was glad to get rid of it and get back to the short hairstyle.

Like I said before, not much has happened in the last couple of days. Yesterday Beaver brought in four tubes of toothpaste and told us that they should last us two weeks. Just coming in telling us that four tubes of toothpaste should last us for two weeks was a morale drop. Although they don't know when this situation is going to end, I've got that feeling (big feeling) that it's not going to end this year. Maybe next year. If the demands that this government gave to the United States were so irresistible, why haven't they been answered? I really find it hard to believe the U.S. would answer any kind of demands for a hostage situation, or any kind of situation.

Today Santa came in with a *Time* magazine which supposedly had an article on all the hostages' families. He read a part of Jerry's wife's interview, saying how she wished *Time* magazine and several other organizations wouldn't keep calling her in the wee hours of the morning. Then he gave us a quick glance of a picture taken at my mom and dad's house. It was a picture of them standing in front of their flagpole. He then asked me if everyone flies American flags in their yards, like he was mad because my parents are supporting the U.S. government and not these people. I'm glad my parents are the way they are, but it really seems to be getting to these guys.

I wonder if those articles have anything to do with the demands that were made around November 3? He also showed a quick shot of Dick Morefield's family, but didn't say anything else about the articles. He also mentioned something about a letter that Joe Hall's dad had written. He said Joe Hall's dad understood everything, and he was going to bring it in to let us read it—I guess to learn something from it. We never get anything else from the outside world except for *Sporting News* and some old letters. It would be nice to hear what's going on in real life.

They told us today that they haven't received mail for about two months now. They're planning to go down tomorrow to the post office to check a rumor of some arriving. Asked Beaver once again tonight, and he said sometime this weekend we would probably get some. It would be nice to receive some mail. (That's probably the same thing my family's saying.) *End of entry.*

Saturday, December 6, 1980 (16:15)   Day 399

Just got finished playing our daily pinochle game and we're still sitting around waiting for tea. It seems as though they're a little behind schedule. Bill and Sam aren't too happy with the game today. I guess you can say that Jerry and I smeared their asses. Of course, Jerry and I feel the same when our days go bad, too.

I just returned from the head, where I lit the hot water for anyone who wishes to take a shower. Bill was saying this morning that he tried to get it lit, but couldn't. I think his problem was he forgot to turn the fuel valve on. Talking about hot water, the students got themselves a coffee maker out in the hallway, but instead of making coffee they just make hot water, and from there we do the rest. So now it's not too big of a thing when we ask for hot water.

Well, nineteen more days till Christmas, and we already know we're still going to be here then. It would take a miracle to get us out of here for Christmas. Then again, I'm really starting to think it's going to take a miracle to get us out of here, period. It just seems too unreal for us to ever walk out of this place. Still I'm continuing to pray and hope for the best. What should we do, treat Christmas with the regular good spirit *(and meanwhile get homesick for all the things you're missing at home)* or treat it just like any other day?

It's really hard to believe that we're still being held by a country with a newly formed government, but still the students assure us that a solution to this problem is being worked on. They've been telling us that for the past year, but what else do we have to believe in? We don't get to read any kind of newspapers. The only news we hear is from the students.

Yesterday ice cream was passed around for a midday treat, and for the last three nights we haven't had soup (but I guess I'd better knock on wood because tonight we'll probably have it). I heard someone say that Ali was gone. I guess everyone is getting to go home to see their families for a while. Anyway, I've got that feeling we're going to have soup tonight. They've really been loading us down with that thick bread of theirs. So far today the only thing I've had to eat is two bread, butter and jelly sandwiches. I'm still not that hungry.

A lot of air traffic has been heard in the far distances at nights. It seems to vary during the week, though. Wonder what the explanation is for that? Anyway, I really hope they got mail in for us. Would really like to hear how the things are in the outside world. Well, going to close for now, go down and wash the dishes for dinner and then come back and play some cribbage with Jerry. Got to stay busy; that's the most important thing. *End of entry.*

Tuesday, December 9, 1980 (16:55)   Day 402

Finished our bridge game early today, and now everyone's just sitting around reading (Bill and Jerry) while Sam's working on writing his book. He decided to start about two nights ago, and has progressed pretty well. All the news we've been hearing lately makes it seem like we're going to be here quite a while, so Sam's decided to start on his book.

About three nights ago Santa came in with the letter that was sent by Joe Hall's dad, addressed to Joe. I guess Joe approved of having Santa take it to all the rooms to let us read. The letter, dated Oct. ?, was talking about the demands that the Iranian government had given to the United States. The letter mentioned that the demands were approved by the Senate and Congress, but not by President Carter. The letter also stated that it didn't look any better if Reagan was going to be elected. He was saying that the only hope we would have is if the Iranians released us on humanitarian reasons. The demands, if I remember right, were the money, the stop of the intervention, and an apology from the President. He had stated that the Senate and Congress had approved of the demands, but Carter wouldn't. Why would Carter refuse when the Senate and Congress

289

approved it? Seems as if Carter has some personal reason not to approve, but really don't know the full story, so I can't make any assumptions.

Then we also read a four line letter from Steve Kirtly's sister, which said that they hadn't heard from him for a while and were worried about him. Why they showed us that letter I'll never know, but Joe Hall's dad's was pretty interesting. Santa told us that he was going to come back the next day and tell us more of what was happening, but he never came back the next day.

The only person who came to see us the next night was Beaver. He said that he had just finished doing the dishes. I guess each night a different student is assigned for doing dishes, and that night was his. It was kind of strange how he just opened the door, asked us how we were doing and so forth. We told him to take a seat for a while and talk to us, and he did. Sam and I were playing gin, so we explained to him how the game went. He brought up the subject about seeing my family in the *Time* magazine articles, and said something about my family not having any complaints about the mass media; whereas a lot of other families did. The question was asked again about mail, and he replied that we would probably get some sometime this week. I'm expecting it tomorrow or maybe Friday. Cross the fingers on that one.

Some of the students are still going around telling us that it will be soon; whereas others are saying not before Christmas. I've got my doubts if we'll ever get out of here. It seems as though the U.S. is giving in to no demands, which I always suspected. Our only way out is the Iranians releasing us.

They got fuel for the hot water heater, so the toilet's been filled ever since. Our turn doesn't come till tonight sometime, like always. Last night the lights went out for about fifteen minutes, and at the same time explosions were heard outside, like another practice air attack along with artillery fire. After it was all over the lights came back on, and no more explosions were heard after that. If it was a practice or not we don't know. Nothing was ever mentioned from the students. We don't ever know what's going on outside, which I guess is better. So much for now. I'm waiting to take my shower, which will probably be a while, so I guess I'll do a little reading. *End of entry.*

Saturday, December 13, 1980 (16:50)   Day 406

Well, only twelve more days till Christmas, and here we still sit waiting. Some of the students just come out and say that we'll still be here for Christmas, while other ones try to make us believe we'll be home. I've already prepared myself for being here, like I said before. You just don't know what to think.

Last night Jerry accidentally met Gary Lee in the head, and they were able to get a few words in to each other before taken back to the room. Gary kind of thinks that there was/is a small war going on between Iraq and Iran. We're caught in the middle of it. He also said that they've already stopped asking about what was going on and when we were going to be free. That was about all they talked about before they were separated. The students accidentally do that at times. Someone will be in on the shitter and all of a sudden a student brings another person in to use the toilet, and bingo, you're able to see who else is here. They really can't say anything against us, because they're the ones that brought the other person in.

I just returned from the washroom a little while ago, where I was down lighting the hot water heater. When I went down to light the pilot light I didn't notice the fuel on the floor around the tank until it was too late. Other times I used to see it, but today I didn't, and it was too late to withdraw the flame because the fuel was at its max, overflowing. Once it was lit the only thing I could do was sit back and let it burn its excess oil off the top, hoping it wouldn't catch what was on the floor. Luckily it didn't, but the heater made such a fuss, with puffs of fire shooting out the bottom, that Plow Boy came down to take me out of there, I guess because he thought it was going to blow. At one time I really thought it was, too. It was making such a fuss that I turned off the fuel valves so it wouldn't receive any fuel. That must've worked. It died down after a while, giving relief to both of us. He was worried about the guards on the roof getting too much smoke. Finally it came under control, and we were able to leave. Plow Boy looked awfully relieved. Myself, I thought it was quite funny.

Just returned from taking my shower, and everyone in the room here is all doing his own little thing. Sam's working on his book, Bill's reading and Jerry's working out. Everyone's trying to stay busy.

Forgot to mention that we got our mail the other day. Jerry received one from his mother and a few others from people he doesn't know. Bill received one from one of his friends at home. Sam and I were the only ones who received quite a bit from people we knew. Jill is still writing, which means she hasn't given up hope. Really makes me feel good to know she's still there. Can only hope for the best, though, and if she's not there whenever I get home, there isn't going to be much I'll be able to do about it. She's one helluva loyal soldier. That's my angel.

Also received one from my sister Debbie, telling me that the family is doing fine, staying busy, etc. It was good to hear that everyone is still holding out. Hopefully they'll continue to do so. I've started to receive letters from all my friends back home. Not many, though. I received one from Judy Feltmenn (a good friend) which stated that she had been writing, and hopefully I was receiving her letters. That was the first I had received from her. She said that millions of people have been writing, but whenever we receive mail (which is at the most four times a month—at times not even that), we only receive a couple of letters. What's happening to all the millions? Oh well, a few are better (a lot better) than none at all. Hopefully we'll receive a bundle at Christmas time.

Some of the students that we haven't been seeing for quite a while have been popping up again. I guess they were able to go home on vacation or something. Anyway, they're back. Ali the Cook has really been concerned about whether we're eating or not. Not that it matters any. He's always been concerned. Lately, whenever we have soup at night he brings us rice instead. I've even gotten to the point where I ask for rice instead of American lunch.

The other day Beaver was handing out lunch consisting of mashed potatoes, chicken and cranberry sauce. Once it was all served, I said out loud that I didn't want that, but wanted rice instead. So they came back to our room and asked me if I really did want rice? I told them sure, and they looked at me like I was crazy or something for not eating the American food. So the next day we had a plate of rice with a beef sauce. It was delicious to my taste buds, and I believe it was the same for everyone else in the room, too.

Well, we just got finished with dinner, and good old Ali came through for us once again. Rice and chopped beef. Once again it was delicious. Everyone else in the hallway got chili or soup, I believe. I think he said that the other hostages don't care for rice as much as we do. So much for now. Sam's got the uke out, and I'm going to stop for now so we can sing some songs. See how many people we can get to bark at us tonight. *End of entry.*

Sunday, December 14, 1980 (17:55)   Day 407

Strange things have been happening around here lately. Last night we were sitting around singing songs, and I guess we were singing a little bit too loud. Santa came in and was going to take the uke away, but he changed his mind. He said we were singing too loud, but that we should wait for another couple of days and the place they would take us we could sing as loud as we wanted. Right after he said that I told him I wished he wouldn't lead us on like that, but he had no reply. Bill then said that he didn't have to tell us that we were going to be here for Christmas, because we already knew that. His reply was that he never said that, and then he left the room.

That was last night, and just a little while ago we were talking to Porky Pine. Someone had asked him if we were going to be going home tonight. He replied, "No, not tonight, *but soon!*" It was just how he said it that made it sound as though he knew what he was saying. Anyway, this morning they were out in the hallway moving things around, and Bill said he heard Santa outside directing traffic. Something does seem to be up, but it's too hard to believe that they're getting ready to release us. Then again, I could see a slight chance of being released on humanitarian reasons. Maybe their government's demands were even met.

Once again, it's too hard to believe that we're going to get out of here. It just doesn't fit with all the things that have been happening. Some of the students have been gone, and they've taken the video machine away to somewhere. Since yesterday the students have been showing back up, even English Student, who we saw once again this morning. I've got a feeling that they've been at the place that Santa was talking about last night, where we're going to be going. They must've been assigned there to get all the things set up, like the video room, etc. Haven't seen Sunshine for a few days either. He must be assigned there also. If those guys weren't released (Al, Dick and all) I wouldn't be surprised if we see them again.

Why would they want to be taking us from a secured spot like this, unless of course they want to show us to the public at Christmas time, which is in ten more days. I'd think they would be foolish to do that. No doubt so many people are bitter from being here so long that you'd never know what we would say on T.V. Then again, you never know what these people have up their sleeves. I guess we'll just have to wait and see. Expecting a movement any day now.

Well, the lights went off out in the hallway, and they're out there trying to get them to come back on. The lights on our side are on, but the hallway and other side are off. I hope ours don't go off; the atmosphere really gets bad. I guess I'll work out and then go down and take a shower. It's really surprising that they had fuel yesterday and then filled it back up this morning. Take advantage of it while we have it.

Only ten more days till Christmas, and no doubt the Christmas spirit has started back in the States. So nice it would've been to have been home. Oh well, maybe next year. Cross my fingers on that one. *End of entry.*

Last night I was telling Sam my thoughts of what might be happening. Although they're probably not right, I've got this feeling that something is on the verge of happening. If it is true that the Iranian government gave their demands in September, everything seems to fit into place. Sitting here thinking about all this, I really wouldn't be surprised if the people they took out of here October 22nd weren't released, but were just taken to another place.

My feelings are that when the Iranian government gave the demands to the U.S. in September, they had it planned ahead of time that if the U.S. didn't answer the demands by Oct. 22, 1980, they would separate people once again, moving the high officials to another place. Then if the U.S. had not answered the demands by Christmas, they (the Iranian government) would release the innocent people and keep the high officials until the demands are met.

It's been about two months since they took those guys away, and since then they've been fattening us up, issued us new pants, new underwear, and yesterday brought us in a *Time* magazine dated November 24, 1980. They've been telling us that soon we will be going home, and Santa has been emphasizing that we are going to be moved to another place where we'll be able to sing as loud as we want. The only thing that I can't figure out is all the moving of equipment, especially the video machine. Maybe they took it to the place where the other guys are. Maybe they are just fixing up a new place to show us off at Christmas time.

Anyway, all the things that have been happening over the past two months really seem to show sure signs of us being released. Santa says it would be soon that we'd be moved, so once again we'll just have to wait and find out. I really pray to God that if we are released, *everyone is released.* Something is definitely up. Oh, God, please make it be that we're going home! *End of entry.*

Here I am writing from our new location which seems to be an apartment. Beaver claims it is just a house. For this just being a house, the room we're in is really fixed up nice. A huge room about the size of 25' x 20', cabinets and bookshelves off to the side, a huge patio door which is barred off from the inside, and a toilet with tub. Sam and Bill were the only ones to take showers before the hot water pipe was supposedly broken outside somewhere. They said tomorrow they'll have it fixed, and we'll be able to take a shower.

How strange it was this morning, after finally getting arranged around (04:30) and then getting some shuteye, to be awakened by Sunshine at (08:30) and having our attention directed to the patio door to look outside and see the ground covered with snow. I could've sworn that it wasn't snowing when we first got here early in the morning (02:00). What a beautiful sight it was to see. To tell you the truth, I sat by that window all day watching it snow with everyone else. The rules are that we can have the curtains opened during the day, but at night they have to be closed with the main light turned off. The small little studio lights are good enough, though. Anyway, just being able to see the scenery we're seeing now is five times better than the scenery we had seen in the last seven months. To tell you the truth, we hadn't seen trees and grass since June. Now we're able to look outside as much as we want, and no more towels over our heads to go to the toilet, because now it's right here in the room. What a change from the prison/jail to this place.

Yesterday was kind of a strange day with different things happening, which should've told us that something was up. The morning and part of the afternoon went by like usual, until after lunch when they served us ice cream. Then right before dinner was served, Santa came into our wing and turned on the tape player for everyone to hear classical music. Then it came time for the lights to go off, but no lights went off. Still the music was playing. Dinner was served and still the lights weren't off, so we just figured the war between Iraq and Iran ended.

I guess Ali the Cook wanted to treat us special since he knew it was our last night there, so for dinner we had chili, rice and Spam or cheese, and then for dessert, pudding. That was really a filling meal. Our regular Parcheesi game was played, and after it was over Sam and I started to play gin. That's when Santa came in. Meanwhile, Jerry had just found out that he'd lost his wedding ring. What a fix he was in at the time. Right when Santa came in I kind of thought something was up by the way the students were walking around in the hallway. A couple of them we didn't even recognize. After shooting around the bush a little, Santa finally came out and said that we should start packing our stuff, because we were going to be moved. Then Little Ali came in and started to take pictures. Pictures for what, he never said. Santa was saying that we were going to a place that was "the best". Just by taking another look around this room, I would say it's pretty nice indeed. I'd say they really fucked over the room when they put those bars over the patio door, though.

Right before we left, Santa told us that we were going to get another roommate.

295

(00:55) Let's see, I was talking about our new roommate when I had to quit all of a sudden for dinner, which Ali is still going around serving. Tonight we had soup.

Our new roommate is Regis Ragan, who used to be in the cell across from us at the prison. Anyway, he had been in solitary for 40 days until this morning. All day he's been saying how glad he is to be with someone again. I wouldn't doubt it, either. We're all sitting around tonight playing pinochle, and now Sam's playing some music for us. A little something of everything, Christmas songs and etc.

Getting back to our move last night, it seems like they took two van fulls. Bill and Jerry were in the first van, and Sam and I were in the last. There was an obstacle they had trouble going through at the prison. It must've been a small exit that led out to the main road. We could hear the van in front of us scraping its fenders and everything else, and then our van got stuck and had to be shimmied off the wall with a jack. Although we couldn't speak to the other seven or eight guys, we all got our laughs.

Of course, everyone was handcuffed together, but fortunately the ride wasn't that long. We did get stopped once along the way by a sirened vehicle. They spoke to the first van, and must've got it solved right away 'cause we were off really quick after we stopped. Then we stopped once again before getting here. I guess they had to wait for an escort or something, but it wasn't that long.

Right as we got out of the truck I could smell sawdust, like they were doing some kind of construction work on the bottom floor. We were taken to the second floor, where we were made to wait until a couple students came in to search us. We were still blindfolded. It only took about five to ten minutes, and then they took the blindfolds off. I found some interesting items in my pocket after we were searched. For one, I found a joker card with a friend's name on it. I had thought they had taken it away, but it was still there. A nice souvenir I'll like to keep.

Jerry was saying that he saw them carrying some more bags through the hallway tonight (different people's items). They must've moved the other wing tonight, so maybe now they have everybody here. Why are they doing this? Santa said last night that this movement was a definite improvement in our situation. He said that both countries are negotiating (except Carter). Sunshine was saying the other day that the Republicans want Carter to solve this situation before he left office. He also said that there was a good chance of us not being in Iran for Christmas. Now if he was just saying that for morale purposes, we don't know. Maybe he just said it so we'd write something nice in our Christmas cards home, which he had given out right before he said it.

Really think this move was just so they could film us at Christmas. They'd really be fools if they did, though. So many people are bitter for being here so long that they're risking a lot if they're going to put us on T.V. I just can't see walking out of here, so I've got that feeling that the move wasn't because our situation is looking good. Maybe it's so they can show us at Christmas, or maybe it's even the reason they gave last night—people were complaining about it being too cold so they were taking us here to this warm spot. To tell you the truth, you don't know who or what to believe anymore. So many times they have told us that the situation was looking good, but nothing has happened. Just leading us on! *(I wish I could think that this move was because we were going home. So nice that would be, to be free at Christmas. God, please help us!) End of entry.*

Monday, December 22, 1980 (??:15)   Day 415

Well, here we are two days before Christmas Eve, and still here we sit. Being in our new room (apartment room) really makes a difference. Mornings are more pleasant and the days are passed much more easily with all the things we've been doing. Today, for instance, we woke around (11:00), and then everyone except Bill did a long workout, which I'm still feeling tonight. Then at the end Bill joined us, and we ran around the room for about 40 minutes. About a half hour after we were finished, lunch was served, which consisted of turkey, mashed potatoes, and cherries. Not too bad, considering the first couple days we were here they were feeding us Iranian food.

I guess when they first moved us, they didn't have any American food over here. They also said that they had to replace pipes in the kitchen so that it would be in working order. They knew we were going to be moved from the prison, so why didn't they come ahead of us and fix all these things? The only thing it seems like they did was put the bars over the patio door. Anyway, getting back to today's routine, we finished our lunch and then sat around a little shooting the shit before Sam got up and started to clear the table off. We still take turns doing the dishes, but everyone helps clear the table off. The sooner we get the dishes done, the sooner we can start on our daily pinochle game.

Right as we sat down to play, Ali the Cook came in and said he would cut Bill's and Jerry's hair. Well, after Jerry saw what Ali did to Bill's hair, he asked me if I would trim his tomorrow. Ali was a little disappointed that he couldn't cut Jerry's hair, too. Meanwhile Jerry and I beat Regis and Sam in gin.

297

The funniest thing happened, though. We were sitting there and all of a sudden we felt the floor and our chairs vibrate. We looked up, and the light fixture was swinging back and forth. Iran is known for their earthquakes, so we just figured that's all it was. It was a weird feeling, though. The last time I witnessed something like that was when I was in Mount Fugi, Japan, in '79. What an exciting life I live!

After Ali was finished cutting Bill's hair, I went in and took a shower, followed by Regis. Now Jerry's lying on his mattress with his feet propped up on a chair reading, while Sam's playing Regis in chess, and Bill is looking on. Got to stop now, Ali just came in with dinner.

... Dinner is over, which consisted of mushroom soup or Iranian. Bill picked Iranian, while everyone else except Sam took mushroom. Sam didn't have any. The dishes are over and Sam and Regis are still playing chess. Our pinochle game will probably be late tonight.

It really seems as though the students are avoiding communication with us as much as possible. Whenever we need more soap, or anything like that, we fill out a note and give it to them between the hours of (12:00-13:00) in the afternoon and (18:00-19:00) at night. We all think it's great that they leave us alone. Hopefully they won't take us right back to prison after Christmas.

Yesterday Little Four Eyes came in and said he had a job for us. The job ended up being separating five huge bags (couple thousand in each bag) of Christmas mail. We separated individual mail from mail that just said "Hostages", "Prisoners", "Our Heroes", etc. One card we happened to read was from a guy who said that he thought we should stay over here 10, 20, 30, or 40 years of our lives. He said it wasn't any better back in the U.S. Really a bitter mother-fucker. Pissed me off seeing that.

It took us the whole day to search through it all, but it gave us an idea of who was here. Right as we were finishing, Little Ali came in with a camera and wanted to take some pictures. It was too late, but I know they'll come again. Really looking forward to seeing what they have planned for us. Ali came around today to cut hair, so I guess they want everyone looking nice. *End of entry.*

Friday, December 26, 1980 (8:00)   Day 419

Well, here we are the day after Christmas, and so much has happened since we left our first hotel/motel the night of the 23rd. I have to bring everything up to date since the last time I wrote. I'll start from the night of December 23, when they moved us from the place where we had been for just five days. It really surprised us when

Beaver came in (around 21:00) and asked us if we were ready to go.

Regis had just gotten out of the bathtub and we were sitting around playing pinochle. We asked Beaver what he was talking about, because no one else had come to tell us to pack our things. He then told us that we were going to be moved. Regis asked if we were going to be staying together, and just by the way Beaver answered we knew we were going to be divided up. Regis had the feeling that he was going to be the one, and sure enough, he was.

He wanted to stay with us so much. At times we were begging the students to leave Regis with us. It was probably the first time in fourteen months that he's ever had a good time. His Christmas present to all of us before he left was a container of jam for each of us. It was something he was saving just to eat for Christmas, but instead he gave them to us. We really didn't have much to give him, except for a few items that we had gotten a few days before, like shampoo, etc. He really hated to leave us. As I was the last one out the door, I wished him a Merry Christmas. His reply was that he hoped they'd put us all back together again. Really a good guy, Regis was. I hope the students put him in with a good bunch.

The only thing the students said was that we were going to a fancier place. As Sunshine was directing me out to the van with my blindfold on, he mentioned that we were going to see Al again, which really took me by surprise. They didn't even handcuff our hands on the fifteen minute ride over here. I had two apples in my pockets so I ate them. When I was finished with them I just handed them back to the student who was sitting in the rear. I wonder what he did with them?

I was the first one out of the truck, and as I led the way the smell of the place didn't remind me of anything nice. As they led me through one of the doors, with everyone behind holding on to each other, I felt some bars on the door as I passed and it gave me the feeling that they had taken us back to prison. After going up three flights of stairs they took us into a room and placed us on a couch. As we came through the door, the lights we saw seemed like movie lights, but when we were told to take off our blindfolds, we found they were just small table lamps.

The room itself was something else to talk about. Hanging from the ceiling were two chandeliers, which were not lit; the only electricity was from the wall fixture. But the furnishings around the room— marble tables, gold-framed mirrors, cloth-covered walls, and in the toilet, which was about half the size of the room, mirrors on the walls, a nice bathtub with a shower—all gave me the impression of a very, very rich place. After we had the tour of the place, Sunshine Man told us that he'd be bringing decorations the next day to put up around the room. Right when he said that, I knew they were going to use this room for the big propaganda pitch.

We then asked Sunshine Man when Al was going to be coming, and he said probably later that night. He came around (04:30) in the morning of the 24th. Dick wasn't with him, although he had been with him when they left the prison they were staying at. He said he figured there were about twelve other guys here in other rooms. I couldn't believe the big change from the place we were staying at. We just figured they were getting ready to show us at Christmas time, and wanted to have us all at two different places, the place we had just left and this place.

Al and those guys had been in a different prison ever since they left on October 22. He'd confirmed that the two countries were negotiating, with Algeria being the middle country for the negotiations. Supposedly the government has taken control of us, and things are looking good.

The day of the 24th was spent mostly talking and playing cards, and then around (07:00) the students came in with a pine tree and a box of decorations to decorate the room. We were also asked to clean the room, and one of the students hung up some drapes for the window. We finally got everything set up, but as the night progressed, the ornaments kept falling down. The students were really concerned about the decoration of the room.

It wasn't until about (21:00) that all the movie cameras arrived. Santa came in while we were singing and asked if we could be recorded. We were singing "Let It Be", "Jingle Bells", and "En Sha La". No one had any objections, so we agreed. Supposedly it's to be heard in the States around the same time that we're all televised. I believe the Algerian Ambassador is supposed to have taken the tapes back with him last night. I'll get around to the Algerian Ambassador later.

I guess it wasn't until about (23:00) that the services started. No priest from the States, just two brothers from the Protestant congregations here in Tehran. Before the services, we sat around talking a little, asking about what was happening. The only reply was that the two governments were negotiating, and that progress was being made.

Once the services started, the five of us just sat and listened to the sermon, sang a couple of songs, and Bill read a short passage from the Bible. Communion was served, which ended the services. They then asked if we had any announcements we wanted to give on the air. Everyone gave a brief speech, thanking everyone, giving our love to our families and so on.

Next our attention was directed to the goodies on the table, where they had cherry pie, pastry, oranges, apples and a couple other things. While Sam and I were trying to stuff our pockets with goodies without being observed by the T.V. cameras, the students brought in some mail and even some Christmas presents. We all received sweatsuits with names of different colleges—mine is Penn State. The mail was a little disgusting for Jerry, Al and Bill. Sam and I received quite a few from our families.

When all this was over, we were taken to another room to wait while the other hostages heard the sermon. We passed the time with reading our mail and checking out our new sweatsuits. We also talked about how the students have been working day and night trying to get everything ready. You really have to give them credit for things they do. We also had a little discussion about the situation, and what we had read in our mail. From my parents, I heard that the two governments have been talking back and forth, and that things are looking good.

So much for now, going to close so I can work out and take a nice bath again. *End of entry.*

Saturday, December 27, 1980 (09:30)   Day 420

Hopefully I'll finish updating everything tonight. I ended last night with when they took us down to another room to wait until everyone had finished with the services. I guess we waited down there about an hour before one of the students came down to take us back to our room. When we returned, we found that everyone was gone, and so were the goodies. Since we hadn't gotten much the first time, we asked Beaver if they had any left over. He said yes, then stepped into the hallway for a few seconds and came back with a plate of pastry and cherry pie. After that was eaten and all our gifts were opened, Sam, Jerry, Al and I played some pinochle for a little while. Before long, we could hardly keep our eyes open, so we decided to hit the rack. Christmas Eve was over, so we were looking forward to what they had planned for us Christmas Day.

Everyone slept on Christmas morning, waking a little before noon to have lunch, which was chicken and potatoes. The night before Ali the Cook had made pasta for us, knowing it was our favorite. If they are keeping hostages over at the other place, I wonder who was cooking for them?

After lunch on Christmas Day a couple of the students brought in a huge box of goodies—chocolate, jelly candy, marshmallows, and many other things. Strangely enough, we all received separate boxes

301

and bags with books, etc. The students said that all the embassies here in Tehran had given these items to them to give to us, which I thought was really nice. We also got soap, shampoo and many, many other things. By the end of the day we already had most of the chocolate eaten. It really flipped us out when they brought that box, though. So many wonderful people we have in this world.

After the students left, Santa came in to fill us in on things happening. After he finished, we got another shock when he said that the Algerian Ambassador was going to come that night and answer any questions regarding our situation, and that we would be able to write a letter to our families for them to hand carry back to the States. Fifteen minutes later (after we had gotten the room looking reasonable) they came in—the Algerian Ambassador and another gentleman, along with a T.V. crew and the students). It was kind of weird when they first came in. They introduced themselves, and after that we just stood there until finally Al said something. It seemed like their main purpose was to get a head count and to encourage us that things were happening. They had said (in French to Al) that negotiations have been going on, and that they were going back to the U.S.A. with new demands for the United States to look at. Supposedly they're in the States now. They had told us that they didn't want to get our hopes up, but that profitable negotiations have been occurring. They really encouraged us that the end was near, and that by the end of the week they would probably have an answer.

I wonder what made them so sure that the end was near? If it's true, the Iranian government must've really cut down their demands to the point where the American government will accept. The body count was really a good encouragement. It shows that the American government wanted to make sure everyone was here before they agreed to anything. Another surprising thing was that we were allowed to write a letter to our families without being censored by the students.

Those two gentlemen from Algeria gave us the most encouraging news we've had in the last fourteen months. I still can't picture this thing coming to an end, but with the encouragement they gave us, it's really hard not to think of it. It really seems like the Iranian government is trying to get this solved before Carter gets out of office. I really can't see Carter doing anything before he gets out, but just by the way the students have been acting, it seems like it's coming to an end. The less we think about it, though, the better off we are. We really hate to get our hopes up and then watch them fall apart. Trying to stay busy as much as possible, but still the thought of going home is on everyone's mind. *End of entry.*

The day after Christmas, December 26, Santa came in with two models. One he gave to Bill, and the other was addressed to Sam from Rich Queen. Bill's model was of a boat, and Sam's of a car. Weird enough though, Sam received a note from the American Alliance for Health, Physical Education, Recreation and Dance, which stated that the equipment AMF and MacGregor donated (the chest bands we received Christmas night) were the only things they were encouraged to send. They said they wanted to send more, but couldn't. The Scandinavian Airlines volunteered to fly it over, so it shows that there are many people who are concerned and still thinking about us.

Well, the routine around here lately has been pretty much the same each day. Yesterday we woke and started out the day by exercising. We worked out all the way to lunch, and then after that we started our normal pinochle game. That was continued till dinner, and after that we played another game of pinochle, worked out a little more, and then ended the day by taking a shower. That's something to look forward to every day, either a shower or a nice hot bath after a workout.

Today, since it was Sunday, we didn't work out in the morning, but I'll do a little before I take my bath. We have a nice size room to work out in, even run, so there's no reason why we can't work out. Plus, now we even have hot water to take a shower with.

We also received mail again today. A lot of old mail, but old mail is better than no mail. Jerry was the only one who didn't get anything from his family. I also got an interesting letter from my brother, saying that the jackasses over there don't want to give the jackasses over here the money. This was written December 5, so hopefully with negotiations they've been having they've been able to come up with a solution. It seems like the money is the big hold up. Never thought I was worth that much. Otherwise, all the other mail was sounding good on being home soon. Really don't know what to think anymore.

The other four guys are playing pinochle, so I guess I'll go over and watch to see who's going to win. Things are looking good, so maybe we'll be out of here before the end of January, 1981. *End of entry.*

Friday, January 2, 1981 (22:30)   Day 426

Happy New Year! Our New Year wasn't as happy as we wanted it to be, but still it was happier than the one Bill, Jerry and I had last year when we were living in the basement of the embassy. I can definitely say we've come a long way from last year. This year we celebrated New Year's by playing pinochle (like always), and then at midnight we had Santa come in to tell us it was time. We all shook hands, and then ate my two chocolate bars I had saved from Christmas Day. We didn't have too big of a celebration, although we did get Bill to stay up past his bed time.

New Year's Day we were expecting some more goodies like we got Christmas Day, but hardly anything was given out. Come to think of it, nothing was given out. All the mail we sorted out at the last hotel/motel before coming here, we haven't even received. Tonight I asked Beaver about it, and he said they didn't think we wanted it. So he said he'd tell them to bring it to us. I know our families have written, but still we haven't received any Christmas mail from them.

The other day we asked Santa if our families had seen the Christmas films, and he replied that they had. He also said that the American people said they were pleased to see us, but they wanted us home instead. Other than that one question, nothing else has been mentioned to the students regarding our situation since the Algerian President left. It seems like it's really eating them up that we're not asking anything about it. The last we heard about the Algerian Ambassador (which was last week) was that they were headed to the States with new demands from the Iranians. It's been just about a week now and still nothing has been said to us. The students really seem to think that this situation is going to be solved before Carter leaves office. This they were telling us when we were still back at the prison. I wonder what their feelings are now?

Forgot to mention that on New Year's Eve morning when we woke and looked outside, we were surprised to see that it had started to snow the night before and had covered the ground with a good 14" of snow. Really looked beautiful. I guess they decided we were seeing too much of outside, or maybe someone was seeing us from out there, so they've put up more tarp blocking off the scenery just about completely. We still have a spot where we can see the schoolyard with the children playing. Since it's been snowing, though, they haven't been out there. We've been wondering if we aren't right across from the other place we stayed before coming here. At the other place we heard children playing, but couldn't ever see them.

We've been having a different routine just about every day. Since yesterday was New Year's Eve, we just sat around all day. Then today, since we didn't wake till about (13:00), we just pushed our exercise off till tonight before dinner. We're still playing our pinochle games, and we've taught Sam how to play bridge, so now we're playing that again, too. We all did a workout tonight, which consisted of an hour run around the room, 100 jumping jacks, and 100 windmills.

By the time we finished, it was close to dinner time, so we started a game of pinochle. Just then Plow Boy brought us a pitcher, and I said I wanted to go down to the toilet and wash it out. Well, while I was gone they all fixed my hand so that I had a double round in diamonds (150 points) and aces all around. We never did start the game until after dinner. Anyway, here I am with a good 160 point hand and we're just about finished with the game, when suddenly Al's partner Sam pops up and says he's only got five cards left to our six. Not knowing they were playing a joke on me again, I said "No way, this game counts!" Then they all started laughing and told me what they did. Anything for a laugh nowadays.

Nothing else is happening. The food is getting really low. Tonight for dinner we had cheese, bread, pickles, eggs and potatoes. Although for New Year's Eve day Ali the Cook made us pasta, just like he did on Christmas Eve. Maybe they're moving him back and forth between places so he can cook for everyone.

I probably mentioned it once already, but Santa comes in once in a while, really in a good mood, doesn't say much of anything and then goes back out. Tonight he came in, and as he walked over to the table I thought he was going to tell us to pack our things 'cause we were going back to prison. I asked him if we were going back to prison and he replied, "No!" He asked if I wanted to be moved, and I told him yes, I wanted to go home. No answer to that. Then he just walked around the room and played with the uke. Right before he left, I asked him about the mail we had sorted out but never received. He told us that we would receive more mail, but he didn't say when.

Well, maybe we'll hear some news this week sometime. We're still hearing artillery. I forgot to mention that we also heard it Christmas Eve night. Really close, too. I guess they're still having the war with Iraq and here we are right in the middle. *End of entry.*

Wednesday, January 7, 1981 (21:00)   Day 431

Jerry just finished clearing away the dinner dishes (his turn today), so I decided to grab the table before anyone else does. Everyone else is reading, so I doubt if there will be much card playing tonight. Getting a little run down on cards anyway.

Dinner wasn't worth shit tonight. If it wasn't for the cheese and crackers, I don't know what I would've been eating. Tonight we had some kind of Iranian soup (green shit) which Sam, Bill and myself didn't eat, so we asked Porky Pine if we could have some cheese and butter instead.

The doctor came the other night and told me I should be watching my diet, not eating too many oily foods, starchy foods, potatoes, and bread. I then asked him what I was supposed to eat. For breakfast we have bread, butter, jelly and tea. For lunch we sometimes get a good meal of American food, but lately it's been cold by the time we get it. We've been wondering if they haven't been fixing the meals at the other place and just driving it over.

It doesn't seem like Ali the Cook is cooking. At dinner time they've been bringing us Iranian food, rice with topping or soup. Ever since the doc said to lay off the good things I like and all the things they feed us, I've just been eating lunch. Then at dinner I have cheese with crackers plus the fruit they've been giving us. Now since we've been running every other day for an hour, and on the off days doing 300 sit-ups, I've gotten my weight down to 77 kilos, about 171 pounds. The only bad thing is the bottom of my feet. It's turning to blisters. That doesn't bother me though; anything to lose the weight hanging around my belly.

Our routine's set up now so that we don't go to bed till around (02:00) in the morning, waking right before lunch. We wake for breakfast, but I only have tea and then go right back to bed. After lunch it's card time, so we play till about (17:30) on running days, and then run from about (18:00) till (19:00). That's about the time they come for dinner dishes. We're just able to get a shower in before we're fed, so we spot our time pretty closely.

Between (18:00 and 19:00) is the time we write the list of things we need, too. It's supposed to be received by then, but we don't give it to them until about (19:30). Lately we've been asking for everything. Out of a list of about fifteen things we're usually lucky if we get five items. Some of the things we ask for are pretty crazy, but they've always told us to ask for anything we want, and they'll see if they can get it. One of these days we might get lucky.

The 4th of January, three days ago, we celebrated Jerry's birthday. All day long I kept telling the students that it was Jerry's birthday, and that it would be nice to make him a cake or something. The whole day went by like this until we received a visitor about (19:00). An Iranian doctor came around taking blood pressures and checking to see if anything else was wrong with us. He told Jerry that he had high blood pressure and that he shouldn't do hard workouts anymore. Filled out a prescription for him, and then one for Al and one for me. The one for Al was for a rash, and the one for me was for my acne. Both Jerry and Al have received their medication, but I'm still waiting.

The doctor was kind of nice. He asked me where I was from, and then said that he had spent five years in the States working. That was about all, except for the students running around the room. Little Four Eyes was taking notes on our ages and health. I guess someone's curious to know how we're doing.

Right after the doctor left, Sunshine and Plow Boy brought in some pastry which they had bought for Jerry's birthday. To get a little of the birthday spirit, Bill put some candles on top of the lid for Jerry to blow out. So for Jerry's birthday we had pastry. Better than just a brownie, which is what Al got last year for his birthday. *End of entry.*

Thursday, January 8, 1981 (18:00)   Day 432

Back again tonight. Last night after Little Four Eyes brought us our mail he sat around to discuss a few things, so I never got a chance to finish writing. Well, Jerry didn't receive any mail last night once again. We gave Four Eyes a little shit about it, asking him what happened to all the mail that we had sorted out at the other place. After we had asked him that, he left and came back a few minutes later with some Christmas cards for Jerry, and then began to explain that a lot of the hostages had thrown it back in their faces because it wasn't from their families. We told him that we'd take it, 'cause it's not too often that we receive it. So this morning Beaver came in with some Christmas cards from people we didn't know. We haven't received any cards from our families yet, but it was nice to read the ones we got. It helps to know that we're not forgotten.

Some more little news Four Eyes gave us last night was that they are expecting the Algerian Ambassador any day now. Supposedly they were to be in Washington, D.C., for ten days before returning here. We asked him what his thoughts were about all this ending, and he replied maybe within a month, which we think is a lot of bullshit. If something doesn't happen between now and the 20th, it's going to be another 100 days before Reagan does anything, and that's *if* he does anything.

Our prayers and hopes rest on what the Algerian Ambassador brings back with him from the States—hopefully good news. This shit's really been getting bad, sitting in the same old fucking room each day. It still seems too good to be true that we'll be getting out of here. Then again, I can't see myself staying here for the rest of my life. God, please help us. *End of entry.*

Tuesday, January 13, 1981 (17:30)   Day 437

Well, here we are another day, just waiting patiently for something to happen. I really can't say we've been all that patient today, though, because this afternoon during lunch we were so wound up we just about did something.

It all started when they brought the uncooked chicken in. Al then knocked on the door to ask Plow Boy if they could cook the meat some more. It was so bad that there was blood dripping off it. Well, Plow Boy's answer to Al was that they didn't have any more chicken. Al told him that he didn't want any more; he just wanted it cooked. Plow Boy just waved his hand at Al and walked out. Well, that really pissed Al off, so he commenced to beat on the door until it was opened by Smiley. Of course by then they had gotten some students together in the hallway where we couldn't see them. No doubt they were all standing out there armed with pistols and rifles.

We started to explain to Smiley that we wanted the meat cooked, so we handed him the plate. Either he couldn't cook the meat or he didn't want to. So we stood there handing the plate back and forth, arguing at the same time that it wasn't right to just throw it away because they couldn't cook it. Meanwhile, he kept saying that they were going to come back later. He doesn't speak or understand English very well, but when he made that little comment about them coming back later, we started to get ready for a fight.

A little while after Smiley left, Al knocked on the door again and asked to speak to Sunshine or Mr. Fix-It. A few minutes later they both appeared, along with some unknown students standing outside in the hallway with jackets on. No doubt security personnel. They came in, leaving the door ajar, and spoke with us for about ten minutes. We explained to them that the only thing we wanted was to have the meat recooked. So they started telling us how hard it is to cook because it's been frozen. We told them if they couldn't fix it right, they should just start feeding us Iranian food. Then they tried to tell us how it's the Islamic way that we should be treated better, etc. Anyway, apologies were made, and before they left they asked if there was anything else we wanted. We were still a little angry, so we just said no. Jerry and Al ate their potatoes and cherries. Bill ate his potatoes, leaving his cherries and Sam's cherries for me. Really a big meal.

I had stopped eating bread and butter, but since last night there hasn't been much else to eat. I guess my face will start breaking out again. Sunshine finally brought my medicine today, after our morning skirmish. Hopefully it'll help me out a little.

Other than the thing this morning, things have been about the same. Playing a lot of pinochle and reading a lot. The other day we rigged up a basketball hoop made out of cardboard and a ball made out of a sock, so once in a while we stand around and shoot baskets with a sock. Anything to make the time pass. It seems like we're going to be here another year, too. Nothing has been said about the Algerian Ambassador returning. Four Eyes said that when he does return, he'll probably be bringing some recent mail from our families. That's the best news I've heard for a while.

So many of the students were so sure that Carter would give in to the demands, but here we still are. It's something we've tried telling them ever since the beginning. My own outlook—and it might be a little extreme, but it's what I've always said—is that I can't see myself walking out of here. It's too good to be true. Well, one of these years their people will get tired of holding us, and then we might make it out of here. It's really hard waking each morning to find yourself still in this mess. The only thing we can do is keep praying and hoping. *End of entry.*

Coming Home

Although I hadn't written in my diary for a few days before we were released, it wasn't because I knew what was coming. During those last days, we had several indications that things were looking good. But we'd thought that many times before and nothing ever came of it. We were trying, as usual, not to get our hopes up in case we were going to be disappointed once again.

January 19th was the first exciting, unbelievable day that we first began to believe we might be going home. It started out, however, just about like any other. I do have to say that right down to the last minute, the students kept it from us pretty well. The morning of the 19th, they had come in to take urine samples. That in itself was out of the ordinary and a good sign, but it still didn't seem possible for us to believe that we were going home. One of the students told us at that time that things were "looking very good."

The rest of the day passed as usual. Between 6:00 and 7:00 that evening, I made out a list of things we wanted to give to the guard. When I went to the door to give it to him, I saw one of the big wheels—one of the main characters among the student organizers— passing in the hallway. He was looking in and smiling at me. I went right back into the room and told Al and Sam about seeing this guy, and that it might mean something was up. We almost never saw this person. I think his name was Josane. The last time we had seen him was April of the year before, at Easter. And I had never, ever before seen him so much as crack a smile.

We just sat around that evening talking about how great it would be to go home, and all the things we wanted to do and places we wanted to go when we got there. That conversation didn't mean anything special—we'd had it so many times before. We were playing basketball at the same time, with our cardboard hoop and rolled-up sock. All of a sudden the door opened, and Ali came in and started hugging us and wrapping his arm around us. I think it was because he knew we were going home. Some of those guys really liked us, and some other ones really hated us.

A little while later, after it was dark outside, they came in and told us we were going to have a physical. We said, "O.K. Are they coming here?" They answered, "No, you are going to another building, so put your slippers on and put something warm on." Then they came in with new towels to put over the top of our heads. They took the old towels and just threw them in the corner. Right then we knew something was up. So many times we had asked them for new towels, and we'd had to wait a month to get them. Now here they were bringing us all clean ones, when we hadn't even asked, and just throwing the old ones in the corner.

They took us down the stairs from the third floor of the building we were in, which was supposedly a foreign ministry guest house. Then they walked us outside, and into the bulding right next door. We recognized this building as the one we had been living in just before our last move. It was just 50 or 100 yards away, but they had put us in a car and driven us around on the highway just to mess up our heads and make us wonder where we were.

They led us into a kitchen. We opened some cabinets and saw cigars, cigarettes, shaving cream, crackers, candy and everything else you could think of. These were things we had asked for repeatedly and often never received. Now they started giving us this stuff and letting us open doors and take whatever we wanted. Four Eyes was one of the students with us, so I pulled him off to the side to try to get some information. I asked him how the situation was, and he gave me a great big smile. "The situation is very good," he said. I asked him how long he thought it would be, and he answered, "A week. Within a week's time." I told him I didn't believe him, and right then I noticed the headlines on a newspaper they had lying there. In big, bold print it said something about the hostages being freed, negotiations complete, assets transfered, etc. I only caught a glimpse of it before someone grabbed it up and took it away.

Sam had already gone in to take his physical, and five minutes later they came and got me. They put the towel over my head and took me through a room where there was a whole lot of noise and commotion. Then they put me in a room by myself, and a minute later Santa Claus walked in. He sat down and asked me if I knew why I was there. I said, "Yes, to get a physical." Santa said, "That's right. You are going home tonight." Right then and there my heart practically stopped. This was something we had waited for for 444 days, but I just couldn't

313

believe it was really going to happen. I told him he was lying, and he said, "No, you are going to be free tonight." Then I asked him if everyone was going to be free. At first he said that was not important, but I insisted on knowing. I told him that after this long, I just couldn't face it, wouldn't be able to take leaving someone behind. Finally he told me that everyone would be freed.

Next, they took me to a room with a television camera set up for an interview. There were about ten students in there, and Mary the Kidnapper was sitting there wearing her chador. She was the interviewer. The first thing she asked me was if I'd heard the good news. I told her yes, but I wouldn't believe it until I saw it. She started smiling and everyone else started smiling, too. The interview lasted about five minutes. They asked the same old usual questions; how the treatment had been, what we thought of the situation, where we had been staying, etc. When it was over, all the students came over to me and started patting me on the back, being real nice. I asked if it was true we were going home, and they said yes, but maybe in a week; they didn't know for sure. They were starting to play their games again to keep us guessing.

After that, I finally did have a physical. Some Iranian nurses had me lie down on a table while they did an EKG on me. Then I went across the hall and talked with an Algerian doctor who was interviewing all the hostages. I asked him the same thing I'd asked everyone else—if it was true we were going home. Right away, he said yes. It wasn't that I didn't believe him; it was just so hard to get it through my head. I think I was in a daze. By the time Sam, Jerry, Bill, Al and I finally got back together and returned to our room, we were all in a daze.

Back in our room dinner was waiting for us on the table. Ali, the cook/haircutter, had cooked us a special dinner—roast beef, corn, pickles and jello. Usually we just got soup or Iranian food for dinner. We were so excited, though, that we didn't even feel like eating. We kept asking the students if they would bring us a newspaper so we could read about our release. They all said, "Sure, we will bring you one," but none of them ever did.

Sam played the ukelele for a while and we all sang songs, with the students listening. One of them asked for Bill's autograph before they left. He really didn't want to do it, but they were standing there smiling and asking so politely. If it was true that we were going to be released, we wanted to be as friendly as possible. Yet at the same time, we were getting really pissed off because one student would say we were going home that night; another would say tomorrow; still

314

another would say maybe next week. And they hadn't brought us our newspaper. We were starting to think it might all be a fake.

After they left, we all started packing our things, because heck, waiting 444 days we wanted to get everything packed right away and be ready to go. That's when Ali the Cook came in. He was one guy who always tried his best to do good things for us. He didn't cut hair very well, but we encouraged him anyway because he was doing it just for us. He got really upset when he saw that we hadn't eaten the food he'd fixed. Ali was really a sensitive person, and we had to be careful how we treated him. If we didn't eat his food, he just automatically assumed it was because we didn't like it. We told him we were going to eat; that his food was very good but we had just been too excited to eat. He said, "O.K. sir, I cook special for you." We told him thank you and promised him we'd eat. Then he shook our hands and said good-bye. That was the last time we ever saw Ali.

We eventually did eat a little—in fact, I had dish duty that night. Then we played cards until about midnight, when Santa came into our room. We asked him why we hadn't been released yet. He said, "Well, it's your own government's fault. We are waiting for the money to reach the banks in Algeria, and it hasn't arrived yet." We thought maybe he was lying and just messing around with us. We asked him if we could see a newspaper, and he said sure, just like all the others we'd asked. Then he left and never came back with the paper.

We played cards until about 3:30 a.m. and then tried to crash out. We really didn't sleep very well. The next morning we woke up to the sound of kids screaming on the playground nearby. We were all really upset, because we were supposed to go home the night before, and there we still sat. Al got really aggravated and went to the door and knocked. When a student came to the door, Al asked him if we could have a newspaper stating that we were supposed to go home. The student said, "No, we don't have to give you anything." Al got totally pissed off and slammed the door right in the student's face. We were half expecting the students to come back in with a small army and just take us away. All the things they had said the night before about going home didn't really touch us, because they had lied to us so much before.

But then about a half-hour later Four Eyes came in, bringing an Iranian newspaper with him. He told us he thought we owed his brother an apology for the way we'd mistreated him. We told him we were the ones who had been mistreated, and a small argument followed. Then he left, leaving the newspaper with us. We spent most of the morning reading that paper. It was written in English, but it
315

was an Iranian paper. We weren't sure if we could believe it or not, but it was the best thing we'd seen so far. It stated that we would be freed no later than the afternoon of the 20th.

They brought us our lunch as usual, though, and we started to get really discouraged. We almost started unpacking our bags, figuring we'd be going nowhere for a while, but a sort of inertia had come over us. We didn't want to believe we were going to be released, and we didn't want to believe we weren't going to be released. One of the only things we could think of that might explain the delay, was that the Iranians were trying to humiliate President Carter by not releasing us until Reagan was inaugurated.

After lunch, Al did the dishes and we started playing cards again. We tried not to talk much about going home. Finally, at about 4:00 or 5:00, Santa and Mr. Fix-It came in and started messing around with us. They asked us if we wanted to go home, and then said maybe we'd go home next week. Then just before they left, they turned around and said, "Pack your things and we'll be back to get you in half an hour." We sat there and actually begged them to tell us the truth. They swore they weren't lying; that we would be leaving in half an hour.

So we all jumped up and started gathering the rest of our things together. We brushed our teeth, combed our hair, and I even took a shower while the other guys were getting dressed. Half an hour later, we were still there. Half an hour after that, they came back into our room and told us we were taking too much stuff. We didn't care about that, and just started throwing things out of the bags. That's when Santa came over to me and told me he knew I had a diary, and not to worry about it because I was going to be allowed to take it out. He said this really quick—that I would be the only hostage allowed to take a diary out. I remember I told him thank-you.

After he left, as I was finishing my re-packing and getting ready to tape up the bag, I started wondering why Santa had made such a point of mentioning my diary unless he just wanted to reassure me so I'd put it in my luggage. I knew they'd check our luggage to see if we were ripping anything off, but I didn't think they'd check our bodies. I decided not to believe him, so I finished taping up my bag and then taped my diary to the inside of my leg.

As soon as I finished dressing again, they came in, grabbed our bags and put them in the hall. Then they blindfolded us and started walking us down the stairs. When we left the room, it was really a mess. Not that we really cared; if they wanted to clean it up, let them.

When we got outside, it was dark. We could hear the sound of a big bus. I thought to myself that the bus would take us to the airport, and just hearing that sound really excited me. Santa was guiding us in, yelling, "No one will escape; No one will escape!" I can't understand why he said that, because who would want to escape now that we were finally going home. They pushed me against a wall and told me to sit down. What I found myself sitting on was a hot radiator, and I happened to have a hole right in the seat of my pants. Needless to say, I burned my ass all the way to the airport. There was no place else to sit, though. Everybody was all cramped up, kneeling on their legs and rear end. They had taken all the seats out of the bus.

We didn't stop one time for a stop sign. It seemed like a long ride, and everybody was really quiet. We were still blindfolded, and I know a lot of thoughts must have been running through everyone's head. I was thinking about the things we had gone through for the past fourteen months, where we had been, all the nights I had sat on my mattress wondering if we were ever going to go home. Now, supposedly, we were on our way to the airport, but none of us really knew for sure what was happening.

We finally did get to the airport. We stopped several times; people were yelling and shouting but we didn't really care. What we were listening to was the sound of the jet engine from the Algerian plane that was going to take us out of there. It was one of the most beautiful sounds I have ever heard.

All of a sudden the bus stopped, the lights flicked on, and we were all told to take off our blindfolds. Seeing everyone for the first time in 444 days was also another beautiful experience I'll never forget. Some guys had real long hair. Some had lost a lot of weight. At first we just stared at each other, then all of a sudden everybody was hugging everybody. We were having one big huge reunion inside that bus. Outside, there were groups of students chanting, but we were too busy to pay them any attention. Some of the students, though, had been on the bus ride with us, and were sitting at the front of the bus. When we started hugging each other, one of the students on the bus started to cry. It was really a surprise to me, because here was this student sitting there crying as he watched us. He even had to turn around to try to hide his emotion.

Four Eyes grabbed me from behind and pulled me toward the door. He told me I was going next. As they pulled me out the door, one of my sandals started to fall off. I managed to get it back on, and then looked up past the rows of students and saw the Algerian airplane. Boy, was that ever a beautiful sight, especially the ramp leading up to it. The students sort of pulled me along. When I got on board that plane and saw the beautiful faces of the stewardesses, my heart really started to choke up. I was the first one on the plane. The
317

stewardesses were just standing there smiling at me, and so much I wanted to go up and hug them, but for some reason I didn't do it. I couldn't believe this was really happening.

It took about half an hour to load everyone on the plane. We spent that time greeting each other all over again. It was so great to see everyone. We had all been close before this had happened, but now we felt even closer to each other in a way I can't even describe.

For some reason, they wanted to keep everything dark. The shades were drawn inside the plane, and there were no airstrip lights on at all. The only lights showing were the lights from the plane and occasional camera lights flashing. The captain spoke to us before we took off. He was Algerian, but he spoke really good English. He said we were going to take off even if there was two feet of snow on the runway. That was a statement I just loved. Finally we did take off, and as we lifted off the ground there was a huge cheer inside the plane.

The stewardesses brought us bottles of champagne, cigars, cologne and perfume, cookies, sandwiches—the treatment was so wonderful. We were so grateful to these people for what they had done for us. All the times we said thank you was nowhere near the number of times we felt it. We even got a little tipsy from the champagne.

We stopped in Athens, Greece, just for refuelling. None of us got off the plane, although they changed the pilots and stewardesses there. Then we took off once again and headed across the Mediterranean. The new pilot had told us we could come up and ask him questions, so I went up for about five minutes and saw the instruments. The pilot showed me where we were going, then asked where I was from, what I was planning to do when I got home, etc. He asked me for my autograph. I really got a kick out of that. My first autograph was to the pilots of the Algerian plane. Those guys were so fantastic.

The landing in Algeria was perfect. When we taxied up to the terminal, most of us still had our shades pulled. We weren't really aware of all the people that were out there waiting for us. There were also four United States Air Force DC-9 Nightengales. I didn't see any of this until I walked off the plane. It was an unbelievable sight. It was raining as we walked toward the building, but none of us cared. We were splashing each other with the sandals we had worn from Tehran. As we got closer to the building, the crowds really started to get loud. That's when I started to get a big lump in my throat; my heart started pounding and my eyes got all watery. It was just so hard to hold back all the emotions. All these people were standing out in the rain waiting for us, and we'd had no idea that anyone would be there.

We went inside, and people were clapping their hands and shaking ours. When we sat down, they brought around tea and soft drinks. Just seeing all these smiling faces made me feel so good. I realized I was back in civilization—no more rifles pointed at me, no more going to the toilet blindfolded, no more asking to have a piece of bread or a piece of cheese, no more asking to go outside, no more asking for anything! *I was free*, and I just sat there in a chair feeling dazed at what had happened, and that it was all over, really and truly all over.

We were divided alphabetically into four groups to board the DC-9's for our flight to Germany. That was another very enjoyable trip. We got our first American meal on that plane. It was turkey with gravy, pudding, milk, asparagus and potatoes. It was so good we all had a second tray. One of the flight attendants talked to us for a while. He told us about John Lennon being dead and filled us in on other changes in the music world. I guess you could say we were starting to be prepared for things ahead. A psychiatrist, Dr. Ray, was on board evaluating everyone. He said he was going to be my doctor, and I would see him again at the hospital in Weisbaden.

We arrived at the airport at about 6:00 in the morning. The reception there was unbelievable. There were people all over the towers, movie cameras, people lined up with signs, people yelling, screaming, crying. It just made me cry, too. Those people were there for us so much. We had no idea people were so involved in our situation. As we got off the plane, we were told to board busses they had waiting to take us to the hospital. We each had our own double seat on the bus, with a blanket and a newspaper on the seat beside. I started reading my newspaper after we got on the autobahn, but the people at the airport were unbelievable—I thought they'd never stop screaming and waving the flags.

The bus ride took about half an hour, and all along the way there were people waiting for us, getting out of their cars in the cold, waving and hugging each other. Mothers with babies, guys with their girlfriends, everybody. The people there in Germany were so beautiful. It was just like a big dream.

When we got to the hospital, people were hanging all over the patios outside waving flags, calling our names. I just started kissing these ladies, little girls and babies. I was so happy to be home with all these wonderful people. It was a feeling I'll never encounter again for the rest of my life. I dropped my emotions there, too. I just couldn't hold it in anymore. They kept congratulating me, but I felt like I wasn't the one to be congratulated. If it wasn't for their support, we would never have gotten out of there.

They took us to our rooms. I was in a room with four other marines, and there were fruit baskets on our beds and folders of mail waiting for us. Some was dated from January, 1980, so they had been expecting us for a long time. They had 28 telephones on our wing, and we were allowed to make all the phone calls we wanted. I called my family. When my dad answers the telephone at home, he always answers "Krakow Store" or "Droege's Supermarket." I wanted to reverse the trick on him, so when I called, I said, "Hello, is this Krakow Store?" "No, this is the Sickmanns," he said. So I said, "Oh, hi Dad, how ya doin'?" I guess I stayed on the phone for about an hour and a half. I also called Jill about three times that day and was on the phone over an hour each time.

President Carter came to Weisbaden that night to welcome us home. I really felt sorry for that man. He had done so much in his efforts to get us released, and the Iranians would have to wait until he was out of office to finally come through with it. I always felt they did it just to make him look bad. We were all in our pajamas and housecoats when he came. I never thought I would meet a president, and I especially never thought I'd meet one in my pajamas! He had some really nice things to say, and once again I became very emotional. He really made me feel good to be an American—anybody that's not an American I just feel sorry for, because there's nobody better than us.

We had a lot of medical tests performed on us while we were there, and I was really pleased that I came out with a clean bill of health on everything. I also had a couple of sessions with my psychiatrist, Dr. Ray, who told me that my family was well, and talked to me about coping with stress in different situations I was likely to encounter.

Meanwhile, we were getting fitted for uniforms, flowers arrived for us every day, and everyone was always asking for our autographs. Kids came to sing us Christmas carols, even though it was after Christmas. Levi-Strauss had sent blue jeans and sweatshirts for us. Someone even flew us in lobster from Boston, which we had the second night we were there. Some of the nurses took us out to see a little of the city the last night we were there. I don't think we were really supposed to leave. They took us to a discoteque, and we really had a great time. That helped us get our heads back on straight as much as anything else. Those people were really wonderful to us. It was really sad when we had to leave the next day, even though we were excited to see our families. Everyone there had done so much for us, and we didn't know how to thank them.

As we boarded Freedom One planes to fly back to the States, we waved goodbye to everyone one last time. That was another very emotional day. We just loved them all so much and hated to leave, but they understood what was happening. We took off in the rain and fog and were on our way home at last. After one stop in Ireland, where still more wonderful people were waiting to greet us, we flew on to the U.S.

We landed at Stewart Air Force Base at West Point. There I met my parents, and it was the happiest moment I'd had in more than 444 days. Since Jill and I weren't married yet, she had to wait with my brothers and sisters to see me the next day. When I was finally together with all of them I felt like I was the happiest man alive. There had been so many moments when I thought I was never going to see any of them again. Then all of a sudden I was *free*, and everyone I love just appeared in front of me like magic. I can never explain the way it felt to be reunited like that!

Our welcome home was such a thrilling experience for me. After being cut off from the news for so long, I never dreamed we meant so much to all the millions of people back at home—people we didn't even know. So many letters I received spoke of the sense of unity, the drawing together that our experience had provided for the United States, and I was really glad to hear that. It was such a wonderful, wonderful surprise, and something I'll never forget for the rest of my life. God Bless America!

-- Rocky Sickmann

Rocky and Jill — together
again. Photo by Jim
McTaggart, Kansas City
Star.

Sergeant Rocky Sickmann
and Jill Ditch, August, 1979.
This is the photograph
Rocky received from Jill
soon after he began keeping
his diary.

Virgil and Toni Sickmann pray
for their son's safe return.
Photo by Jim McTaggart, Kansas City Star.

Virgil Sickmann pops the cork on a champagne bottle
to celebrate news of Rocky's release.
Photo by Rick Stankoven, St. Louis Globe.

Virgil Sickmann strides across campus at West Point,
on his way to meet Rocky. Photo by St. Louis Globe.

Rocky prays in church, soon after his arrival home.
Jill is seated in the background, beside him.
Photo by T.V. Vessell, St. Louis Globe.

Rolling hills and country road near Krakow, Missouri.
Photo by John Dengler, St. Louis Globe.